A Phoenician-Punic Grammar

Handbook of Oriental Studies
Handbuch der Orientalistik

SECTION ONE
The Near and Middle East

Edited by
H. Altenmüller
B. Hrouda
B.A. Levine
R. S. O'Fahey
K. R. Veenhof
C. H. M. Versteegh

VOLUME 54

A Phoenician-Punic Grammar

Charles R. Krahmalkov

SBL Press
Atlanta

Copyright © 2001 by Koninklijke Brill NV, Leiden,
The Netherlands

This edition published under license from Koninklijke Brill NV,
Leiden, The Netherlands by SBL Press

All rights reserved. No part of this work may be reproduced or transmitted in any form or by any means, electronic or mechanical, including photocopying and recording, or by any means of any information storage or retrieval system, except as may be expressly permitted by the 1976 Copyright Act or in writing from the Publisher. Requests for permission should be addressed in writing to the Rights and Permissions Department, Koninklijke Brill NV, Leiden, The Netherlands.

Authorization to photocopy items for internal or personal use is granted by Brill provided that the appropriate fees are paid directly to The Copyright Clearance Center, 222 Rosewood Drive, Suite 910, Danvers, MA 01923, USA. Fees are subject to change.

Library of Congress Cataloging-in-Publication Data

Krahmalkov, Charles R. (Charles Richard)

A Phoenician-Punic grammar / by Charles R. Krahmalkov.

pages cm. — (Handbook of Oriental studies; Volume 54)

English and romanized Phoenician and Punic.

Previous edition: 2001.

Includes bibliographical references and index.

ISBN 978-1-62837-031-7 (paper binding : alk. paper)

1. Phoenician language—Grammar. 2. Punic language—Grammar. I. Title.

PJ4175.K73 2014

492′.6—dc23

2014036333

For Laura and Jeff, Michelle, Ken and Joshua.
With love and respect.

CONTENTS

Acknowledgments XI

Foreword XIII

Grammars XIV
Dictionaries, Lexicons and Glossaries XV
Reference Sources XVI
Abbreviations XVI

Chapter One: The Phoenician Language 1

Chapter Two: The Alphabet, Orthography and Phonology 16

The Alphabet and Orthography 16
Phoenician 16
Punic 18
Neo-Punic 18
Phonology 19
The Consonants 20
The Vowels 27

Chapter Three: The Independent Personal Pronouns ... 38

Chapter Four: The Suffixal Pronouns 50

Possessive 50
Direct and Indirect Object Forms 68

Chapter Five: The Demonstrative Pronouns and the Definite Article 75

The Demonstrative Pronouns 75
The Definite Article 85

Chapter Six: The Relative and Determinative Pronouns 93

The Relative Pronouns 93

The Determinative Pronoun 103

Chapter Seven: THE INTERROGATIVE PRONOUNS, INDEPENDENT POSSESSIVE PRONOUNS, INDEPENDENT OBJECT PRONOUNS AND OTHER PRONOUNS 108
The Personal Interrogative Pronoun 108
The Neuter Interrogative Pronoun 109
The Independent Possessive Pronouns 112
The Independent Object Pronouns 114
Other Pronouns 115

Chapter Eight: THE NOUN AND ADJECTIVE 120
The Noun 120
The Adjectives 143
The *Nisbe* Noun and Adjective 148

Chapter Nine: THE VERB: INTRODUCTION AND THE SUFFIXING FORM 151
Introduction 151
The Forms, Tense, Aspect 151
The Verbal Stems 154
Voice 157
Person, Number and Gender 158
The Suffixing Form 159

Chapter Ten: THE VERB: THE PREFIXING FORMS 180
Prefixing Form A 180
Prefixing Form B 185
Prefixing Form C 192

Chapter Eleven: THE VERB: THE IMPERATIVE, PARTICIPLES AND INFINITIVES 195
The Imperative 195
The Active Participle 197
The Passive Participle 201
The Infinitive Construct 202
The Infinitive Absolute 209

Chapter Twelve: THE NUMERALS 215
The Cardinal Numbers 215

The Ordinal Numbers 223
Other Numeric Designations 224

Chapter Thirteen: THE PREPOSITIONS 227

Chapter Fourteen: THE ADVERBS AND CONJUNCTIONS 259
The Adverbs 259
Adverbs of Degree and Manner 259
Locative Adverbs and Adverbial Expressions 260
Adverbs and Adverbial Expressions of Time 263
The Conjunctions 266
Subordinating 266
Conjunctions and Disjunctions 269
W- As Clause Marker 273

Chapter Fifteen: THE PARTICLES 276
Particles of Anticipation 276
The Particles of Existence 276
Negative Particles 277
The Accusative Particles 281
The Presentative Particles 285
The Particle of Citation and Quotation 287
The Verbal Proclitic and Enclitic Particles 287
Directional Ending *-a* 289
Accusative Ending *-am* 289

Chapter Sixteen: CLOSING OBSERVATIONS ON SYNTAX 290
The Equational Sentence 290
The Syntax of the Verb in the Clause or Sentence 290
The Syntax of the Complex Sentence 295

Selective General Index 299
1. Subject Index 299
2. Index of Key Morphemes and Words 301

ACKNOWLEDGMENTS

To Professor Baruch Levine of New York University for his good offices in recommending this scholar to Brill Academic Publishers for the preparation of a grammar of the Phoenician language I extend special thanks. To Patricia Radder, Desk Editor for the Ancient Near East and Asian Studies at Brill, sincerest thanks for her professionalism and patience in seeing this work through to publication. To my wife Karen, profoundly heartfelt acknowledgments: she was ever my support and active partner in bringing this book to fruition.

FOREWORD

The present grammar of the Phoenician-Punic has its origin in a systematic investigation and study of the language which I first undertook more than twenty years ago and have since then pursued in numerous specialized studies. From the start my purpose was to attempt a description of Phoenician and Punic based on an independent analysis of the language and its literature. Motivating my work was the perception that the description of Phoenician in existing grammars of the language was so exceedingly reliant upon the traditional descriptions of Classical Hebrew that the true character and genius of Phoenician had been seriously misrepresented and distorted. My work was also fed by the desire to seek out details of Phoenician grammar and lexicon not recorded in existing Phoenician grammars in order to "fill out the paradigm" with new, fuller and more precise information about all aspects of the language. Presented in this grammar is a comprehensive statement of the results of my work.

It will be immediately apparent to those who consult this grammar that it is fundamentally informed by my personal understanding of the individual texts of the Phoenician and Punic literary corpus and of the rich lexical treasure they contain. My understanding and translations of these texts are registered in my recent work *Phoenician and Punic Dictionary*, to be published in 2000 by Peeters in Leuven (Louvain). The reader may also wish to consult my preliminary sketches of the grammar of Phoenician presented in my reference encyclopedia articles *Phoenician*, pages 222-223 in the *Anchor Bible Dictionary*, vol. 4 K-N (Doubleday: New York, 1992), and in *Phoenician/Punic* in the forthcoming book *The Encyclopedia of the World's Languages: Past and Present* to be published in May, 2000, by the H.W. Wilson Press in New York.

The topics discussed in this work are necessarily selective. It is, needless to say, impossible within the confines of any modest work to cover in detail every feature of morphophonology and syntax. My object has been to provide good general coverage but, perhaps more important, (i) to present data and discussion not contained in other works and (ii) to present new and existing data accurately, based on my own researches in Phoenician and Punic grammar. Much of the new information presented in this work, invaluable for an understanding of the morphophonology of Phoenician and Punic, is drawn from the fully vocalized Latin-letter Punic and Neo-Punic preserved by Plautus in his play *Poenulus,* and from the late Neo-Punic in Latin-letters of the inscriptions of the hinterland of Roman Tripolitania. Although I have published studies in both, my larger monographs on this most important literature have not yet appeared. The reader will, however, find the substance of this work in the *Phoenician and Punic Dictionary* and in the pages of this grammar.

In one important respect this grammar differs from others. Rather than adhering to the traditional discrete bifurcation of Morphology and Syntax, this work includes the two within the same chapter, each chapter consisting of Part A Morphology and Part B Syntax and Usage. This in my considered opinion is a rather more "user-friendly" presentation of forms and usage, designed to achieve convenience of reference.

This grammar of Phoenician-Punic, as all scholarly works, has a long and noble ancestry in the rich scholarship of the past and present. For the convenience of the reader, I provide here a comprehensive bibliography of the existing major grammars and lexicons-glossaries of Phoenician-Punic.

1. GRAMMARS

Cunchillos, Jesús-Luis and Zamora, José-Ángel
1997 *Gramatica Fenicia Elemental.* Madrid.

Friedrich, Johannes
1951 *Phönizisch-punische Grammatik.* Analecta Orientalia 32. Rome: Pontificium Institutum Biblicum.

Friedrich, Johannes and Röllig, Wolfgang
1970 *Phönizisch-Punische Grammatik.* 2nd Edition. Analecta Orientalia 46. Rome: Pontificium Institutum Biblicum.

Friedrich, Johannes and Röllig, Wolfgang
1999 *Phönizisch-Punische Grammatik.* 3rd Edition. Revised by Maria Giulia Amadasi Guzzo, and Werner R. Mayer. Analecta Orientalia 55. Rome: Pontificio Istituto Biblico.

Harris, Zellig Shabbetai
1936 *A Grammar of the Phoenician Language.* American Oriental Series Volume 8. New Haven: American Oriental Society.

Rosenberg, Josef
1907 *Phoenizische Grammatik.* Wien und Leipzig: Hartleben Verlag.
Schröder, Paul
1869 *Die Phönizische Sprache. Entwurf einer Grammatik nebst Sprach-und Schriftproben mit einem Anhang, enthaltend eine Erklärung der punischen Stellen im Pönulus des Plautus.* Halle: Verlag der Buchhandlung des Waisenhauses.
Segert, Stanislav
1976 *A Grammar of Phoenician and Punic.* Munich: C.H. Beck.
Shifman, Il'ya Sh.
1963 *Finikiyskiy Yazyk.* Akademiya Nauk SSSR. Institut Narodov Azii. Yazyki Zarubezhnogo Vostoka i Afriki. Moscow: Izdatel'stvo Vostochnoi Literatury.
van den Branden, Albert
196 *Grammaire Phénicienne.* Beyrouth: Librairie du Liban.

2. Dictionaries, Lexicons, Glossaries

Bloch, Armand
1890 *Phoenicisches Glossar.* Berlin: Mayer und Mueller.
Donner, Herbert. and Röllig, Wolfgang.
1964 Kanaanäische Glossar. Pp. 1-26 in *Kanaanäische und aramäische Inschriften.* Band III: Glossare. Indizes. Tafeln. Wiesbaden Harrassowitz.
Fuentes Estañol, Maria-José
1980 *Vocabulario Fenicio.* Biblioteca Fenicia. Volumen 1. Barcelona: Consejo Superior de Investigaciones Cientificas.
Harris, Zellig Shabbetai
1936 Glossary of Phoenician. Pp. 71-156 in *A Grammar of the Phoenician Language.* New Haven: American Oriental Society.
Hoftijzer, Jean. and Jongeling K.
1995 *Dictionary of the North-West Semitic Inscriptions.* Two volumes. Leiden, New York, Koeln: E.J. Brill.
Jean, Charles.-F. and Hoftijzer, Jean
1965 *Dictionnaire des inscriptions semitiques de l'Ouest.* Leiden: E.J. Brill.
Krahmalkov, Charles R.
2000 *Phoenician-Punic Dictionary.* Orientalia Lovanensia Analecta 90. Studia Phoenicia XV. Leuven: Peeters.

Levy, Mauritz Abraham
1864 *Phoenizisches Woerterbuch.*
Lidzbarski, Max
1898 (1962) Glossary. Pp. 204-388 in *Handbuch der nordsemitischen Epigraphik,* I-II. Wiesbaden. (Hildesheim).
Tomback, Richard S.
1978 *A Comparative Lexicon of the Phoenician and Punic Language.* Missoula: Scholars Press (Society of Biblical Literature).

Reference Sources

The epigraphic passages cited in this grammar are, for the purpose of convenient reference, assigned the number of their source texts given in the standard collection *Kanaanäische und aramäische Inschriften* (abbreviated as *KAI*) by Herbert Donner and Wolfgang Röllig (Harrassowitz: Wiesbaden, 1964). A numbered citation not preceded by a specified source reference is drawn from *KAI.* Other well known collections of texts are also used for convenience of reference, among them P. Magnanini's *Le iscrizioni fenicie dell'Oriente* (Rome, 1973), M.G. Guzzo Amadasi's *Le iscrizioni fenicie e puniche delle Colonie in Occidente* (Rome, 1967), G. Levi Della Vida and M.G. Amadasi Guzzo's *Iscrizioni puniche della Tripolitania* 19271967 (Rome, 1987) and J.M. Reynolds and J.B. Ward Perkins, *The Inscriptions of Roman Tripolitania* (Rome and London, 1952). Citations from other collections are preceded by the full or abbreviated name of that source. The reader need be alerted however that my readings and translations of passages drawn from these collections are not necessarily the same as those proposed by their authors or compilers. The specific linguistic origin or character of a given citation is indicated by the *sigla* preceding: Byb for Byblian Phoenician, Pu for Punic and NPu for Neo-Punic; a citation without specific designation is Phoenician.

Abbreviations

AI	*Africa Italiana*
Aistleitner	J. Aistleitner, *Wörterbuch der ugaritischen Sprache.* Berlin, 1967.
Akko	M. Dothan, "A Phoenician Inscription from Akko," *IEJ* 35 (1985), 81-94.
Asarh.	R. Borger, *Die Inschriften Asarhaddons, Königs von Assyrien.* Archiv für Orientforschung Beiheft 9. Graz, 1956.
Assurb.	Assurbanipal Annals: R. Borger, *Beiträge zum Inschriftwerk*

	Assurbanipals. Wiesbaden, 1996.
Aug.	Augustine of Hippo: *Opera Omnia; Patrologiae Cursus Completus,* vol. 32-47. Paris, 1845-9; Pp. 532-34 in Vattioni, *infra*.
BAC	*Bulletin archéologique du Comité des travaux historiques et scientifiques*
BASOR	*Bulletin of the American Schools of Oriental Research*
Benz	F.L. Benz, *Personal Names in the Phoenician and Punic Inscriptions*. Pontifical Biblical Institute: Rome, 1972.
Betlyon	J.W. Betlyon, *The Coinage and Mints of Phoenicia*. Harvard Semitic Monographs 26. Scholars Press: Chico, 1982.
BMQ	*British Museum Quarterly*
Byb	Byblian Phoenician
Byb 13	W. Röllig, "Eine neue phönizische Inschrift aus Byblos," *Neue Ephemeris für semitische Epigraphik* II (1974), 1-15.
CID	P.G. Mosca and J. Russell, "A Phoenician Inscription from Cebel Ires Dagi in Rough Cilicia," *Epigraphica Anatolica* 9 (1987), 1-28.
CIL	*Corpus Inscriptionum Latinarum*
CIS	*Corpus Inscriptionum Semiticarum*
CRAI	*Comptes rendus des séances de l'Académie des Inscriptions et Belles-Lettres*. Paris.
D	R.G. Goodchild, "La necropoli romano-libica di Bir ed-Dréder," *Quaderni di archeologia della Libia* 3 (1954), 91-107.
Diosc(urides)	Dioscurides, *De materia medica*. Pp. 516-28 in Vattioni, *infra*.
EA	El-Amarna Letters: J.A. Knudtzon, *Die El-Amarna Tafeln*. Leipzig, 1915.
Esar.	Esarhaddon Prisms. See R.C. Thompson, *The Prisms of Esarhaddon and of Ashurbanipal*.
EH	A. Berthier and R. Charlier, *Le sanctuaire punique d'El-Hofra à Constantine*. Arts et Métiers Graphiques: Paris, 1953-1955.
FK	M. Guzzo Amadasi and V. Karageorghis, *Fouilles de Kition*. III. Inscriptions phéniciennes. Department of Antiquities: Nicosia, 1977.
GEG	A. Gardiner, *Egyptian Grammar*. 3rd ed. Oxford, 1957.
Hassan-Beyli	*KAI* 23: A. Lemaire, "L'inscription phénicienne de Hassan Beyli reconsidérée," *RSF* 11 (1983), 9-19.
Head	B.V. Head, *Historia Nummorum*. London, 1963.
Hill	G.F. Hill, *Phoenicia* in *Catalogue of Greek Coins in the British Museum*. London, 1910.
IEJ	*Israel Exploration Journal*
IFO	P. Magnanini, *Le Iscrizioni fenicie dell'Oriente*. Istituto di Studi del Vicino Oriente, Universita degli Studi: Rome, 1973.
IFPCO	M.G. Guzzo Amadasi, *Le iscrizioni fenicie e puniche della colonie in Occidente*. Rome, 1967.
IG	G. Kaibel, ed., *Inscriptiones Gracae* 14: Italy and Sicily. Berlin, 1890
IRT	J.M. Reynolds and J.B. Ward Perkins, *Inscriptions of Roman Tripolitania*. Rome and London, 1952.
JA	*Journal Asiatique*

JAOS	*Journal of the American Oriental Society*
JKAF	*Jahrbuch für kleinasiatische Forschung*
Jos. Ap.	Flavius Josephus, *Contra Apionem.* B. Niese, ed. Berlin, 1889.
KAI	H. Donner and W. Röllig, *Kanaanäische und aramäische Inschriften.* Harrassowitz: Wiesbaden, 1964.
Karthago	*Karthago. Revue d'archéologie africaine*
KI	M. Lidzbarski, *Kanaanäische Inschriften.* Giessen, 1907.
Kition	M. Yon and M. Sznycer, "Une inscription phénicienne royale de Kition (Chypre)," *Comptes rendus des séances de l'Académie des Inscriptions et Belles-Lettres* 1991. Pp. 791-823. *Paris.*
JAOS	*Journal of the American Oriental Society*
LA	*Libya Antiqua*
Lapethos	Inscriptions of Lapethos, Cyprus: pp. 123-127 in *IFO, supra.*
Mactar B	J.G. Février and M. Fantar, *Karthago* 12 (1965), 45-59.
Manfredi, *Monete*	L.I. Manfredi, *Monete puniche: Repertorio epigrafico e numismatico delle leggende puniche.* Bolletino di Numismatica, Monografia 6. Rome, 1995 [1997].
Marathus	*RES* 234=1601; P. 40 in *IFO.*
Moran	W.L. Moran, *A Styntactical Study of the Dialect of Byblos as Reflected in the Amarna Tablets.* Unpublished Johns Hopkins doctoral dissertation, 1950.
Müller	L. Müller, *Numismatique de l'ancienne Afrique.* Copenhagen, 1860-1874.
Nabuna'id	J.N. Strassmaier, *Inschriften von Nabonidus, Koenig von Bybylon.* 1889.
NP	Neo-Punic inscriptions: See nos. 1-117, p. 63f., in P. Schröder, *Die phönizische Sprache.* Halle, 1869. See also pp. 160-161 in Z.S. Harris, *Grammar of the Phoenician Language.* New Haven, 1936.
NPu	Neo-Punic
NESE	*Neue Ephemeris für semitische Epigraphik.*
NSI	G.A. Cooke, *A Text-Book of North-Semitic Inscriptions.* Oxford, 1903.
PBSR	*Publications of the British Schools at Rome*
Pliny	Pliny, *Naturalis Historia.* D. Detlefsen, ed. Berlin, 1866-82.
Poen.	T. Maccius Plautus, *Poenulus*: Edition A. Ernout, *Plaute.* Tome V. Pp. 162-257. Paris, 1938.
Pu	Punic
Punica	J.-B. Chabot, *Punica.* Paris, 1918.
Pyrgi	The Punic inscription from Pyrgi (Caere): PP. 158-169 in *IFPCO.*
RB	*Revue Biblique*
RCL	*Atti della Accademia nazionale dei Lincei. Rendiconti. Classe di scienze morali, storiche e filologiche.*
REPPAL	*Revue des études phéniciennes-puniques ete des antiquités libyques.* Tunis.
RES	*Répertoire d'Épigraphie Sémitique*
RPC	O. Masson and M. Sznycer, *Recherches sur les Phéniciens à Chypre.* Geneva and Paris, 1972.

RSF	*Rivista di Studi Fenici*
S	J.M. Reynolds, "Inscriptions of Roman Tripolitania: a Supplement," *PBSR* 23 (1955), 124 ff.
Sanch.	Sanchuniathon, as cited by Eusebius in *Praeparatio Evangelica,* Book I, Chapter IX. Edition: E.H. Gifford, Oxford, 1903.
Sarepta	J.B. Pritchard, *Recovering Sarepta, a Phoenician City*. Princeton, 1978.
Segert	S. Segert, *Altaramäische Grammatik.* Leipzig, 1975.
Senn.	Sennacherib Annals: D.D. Luckenbill, *The Annals of Sennacherib.*
Téboursouk	F. Fantar, *Téboursouk. Stèles anégraphiques et stèles à inscriptions néopuniques.* PP. 375-431 in *Mémoires présentés par divers savants à l'Académie des Inscriiptions et Belles-Lettres,* XVI. Paris, 1974.
Tigl. III	Annals of Tiglathpileser III: H. Tadmor, *The Inscriptions of Tiglath-Pileser* III, *King of Assyria.* Jerusalem, 1994.
Trip.	G. Levi Della Vida and M.G. Amadasi Guzzo, *Iscrizioni puniche della Tripolitania* (1927-1967). Monografie di Archeologia Libica XXII. Bretschneider: Rome, 1987).
Tsevat	M. Tsevat, *A Study of the Languge of the Biblical Psalms.* Journal of Biblical Literture Monograph Series, Volume IX.
Umm el-Awamid	Inscriptions pp. 18-23 in *IFO, supra.*
Ungnad-Matouš	A. Ungnad, *Grammatik des Akkadischen.* Fully revised by Lubor Matouš. München, 1964.
Vattioni	F. Vattioni, "Glosse puniche," *Augustinianum* 16 (1976), 505-555.
Waltke-O'Connor	B.K. Waltke and M. O'Connor, *An Introduction to Biblical Hebrew Syntax.* Eisebrauns: Winona Lake, Indiana, 1990.

CHAPTER ONE

THE PHOENICIAN LANGUAGE

Phoenicia (Φοινικια), the Greek name of Canaan (***KN'N,*** Hebrew *Kᵉnáʿan*), was the region in antiquity that encompassed southern Syria, Lebanon and Israel (west of the Jordan), extending roughly from Arad in the North to the Negev and Sinai in the South. In the Late Bronze and Iron Ages, the region was home to numerous peoples of common origin, sharing a common culture and possessing a common language, which they called ***ŚPT KN'N*** ("the language of Canaan" [Isaiah 19:18]), or Canaanite. At an early period, the peoples of Canaan had differentiated into distinct regional subgroups, part of which development was the emergence of regional dialects, some of which in turn became national languages. Phoenician was one such regional Canaanite dialect: in the strictest meaning, Phoenician was the language spoken along the coast of Lebanon roughly from Sidon in the North to Acco in the South. The indigenous name of this subregion of Canaan was *Pūt* (***PT***), and the name of the Canaanite subgroup inhabiting it, the *Pōnnīm* (Phoenicians), the gentilic deriving from the place-name. *Pōnnīm* was also the name of the Canaanite dialect of the region. It is this toponym and gentilic that are the origin of Greek Φοινικες and Latin **Poenus** and **punicus,** the terms by which Greeks and Romans first came to know and call the Phoenicians; and is the term by which they are still called.

The main cities of Put were Tyre and Sidon, and so the term Phoenicians (*Pōnnīm)* came early to be synonymous with Tyrians and Sidonians and Phoenician (*Pōnnīm*) synonymous with Tyro-Sidonian Canaanite. Accordingly, the Phoenicians came to call themselves freely and interchangeably Phoenicians (*Pōnnīm*), Canaanites and Tyrians. Thus, in the third century of the Common (Christian) Era, Augustine of Hippo informs us, an African identified himself as a *Chanani,* Canaanite, while the Phoenician (Punic) inscriptions of Roman Tripolitania tell us that his contemporaries in Libya called themselves *Sorim,* Tyrians.

With the extension of Tyro-Sidonian influence to northern and southern coastal Canaan in the course of the Late Bronze and early Iron Ages, Phoenician took on a broader meaning, coming to denote the Canaanite peoples and languages of all coastal Lebanon, Palestine and Egypt, from Arvad in the north to Ascalon and Daphnae in the south. For this reason, Byblos on the northern coast of Canaan is properly called a Phoenician city, and the language of Byblos properly called Byblian Phoenician although it is quite different from the language of Tyre and Sidon.

The terms *Pūt* and *Pōnnīm* first appear in the written record at the same time, the early ninth century B.C., at the zenith of Tyro-Sidonian power, marked by extensive commercial and colonial activity in the West culminating in the founding of the city of Carthage in Libya in the year 825 (or 814) B.C. The toponym *Pūt* is recorded in an archaic inscription from Cyprus (*KAI* 30=Cyprus Museum Ph. Insc. No. 6), erected as a memorial at the tomb of the leader of the Tyrian military expeditionary force that had invaded and conquered that island: lines 2/3 ("This warrior came up to Alasiya, and this [. . .] devastated the island."). Of the invaders it is said: (line 1) ("They came to the island from *Pūt.*"), contextually, Phoenicia, the region of Tyre and Sidon. It is possible that this text alludes to the invasion and conquest of Alasiya (Cyprus) recorded in a ostracon-inscription of *ca.* 1200 B.C. from Qubur al-Wulayda near Ghaza (F.M. Cross, *BASOR* 238 [1980] 2-3): ***[Y]ŠM [B]'L 'Y 'LŠ*** ("Baal has devasted the island of Elisha."). Virgil perhaps refers to this same event, which he places in the time of the Trojan War, in *Aeneid* I 619-24: ("Belus, my [Dido's] father [?ancestor], ravaged opulent Cyprus and conquered it.").

Tyrian activity abroad was accompanied in this same period, the ninth century B.C., by political and commercial activity in their own region through the cementing of alliances with powerful neighboring states, Israel in particular. Interdynastic marriage was the means to this end, and it is in this context that the ethnic term *Pōnnīm* appears in a Hebrew poem (Psalm 45) composed to celebrate the marriage of a "daughter of Tyre" to a king of Israel. Although their names are not given in the work, Jezebel, the daughter of Ittobaal of Tyre (887-856 B.C.) and Ahab of Israel (874-853 B.C.) are likely. In verses 12b-14a (reconstructed), the Tyrian princess is adjured. ***HŠTḤWY LW BT ṢR, // KBDH BT MLK PNYMH*** ("Show him respect, O daughter of Tyre, // Honor him, O daughter of the King of the Phoenicians [*Pōnnīma*]!"). Here, the title ***MLK PNYMH*** *melek Pōnnīma*, ("King of the Phoenicians") is synonymous with King of Tyre, and *Pōnnīm* ("Phoenicians") with the Tyrians.

It is the great Roman playwright T. Maccius Plautus (*ca.* 254-184 B.C.) who provides us the rare and exceptional datum that the Phoenicians called their language *Pōnnīm*. Sometime early in his career, Plautus, whose first plays were produced *ca.* 200 B.C., undertook to translate for the Roman stage the Athenian comedy *Karkehdonios* ("Carthaginian"), perhaps the play of this name by the poet Alexis (*ca.* 375-275 B.C.). If Plautus's translation is true to the plot of the original, the *Karkhedonios* told the story of the tireless quest of the noble Hanno of Carthage for his daughters and nephew, who had been abducted from Carthage as children, and his joyous discovery and reunion with them in the city of Calydon. Plautus called his version of the play *Patruus* ("The Uncle"), but the work acquired a second name, *Poenulus* ("Little Phoenician"), by which it is today better known.

At the time Plautus was translating the *Karkhedonios* into Latin, he learned of the existence of a Punic translation of the play. Consistent with his unique sense of the comic, Plautus conceived the highly original idea to incorporate lines of the Punic version of the Greek play into his own Latin version: in his play, Plautus would have the Carthaginians speak authentic Punic, not Greek as in the sedate Attic original of Alexis. Plautus's intent was twofold, to amuse the Roman audience with the sound of outlandish Punic, and to use the Punic as grist for puns and mistranslations. Plautus never meant the Punic to function as real dialogue, for no one in the Roman audience understood Punic. However, in using actual lines and dialogue from the Punic *Karkhedonios*, Plautus was the instrument of preservation of the sole extant specimens of Punic dramatic literature, indeed, of the knowledge of the existence of Greek theatre in Punic and, finally, of the significant datum that the Phoenician (Punic) name of the Phoenician (Punic) language was *Pōnnīm.*

In Act V, Scene II, of the *Poenulus,* Plautus included several fragments of a Punic dialogue from the Punic translation of the *Karkhedonios*. This same dialogue appears in Latin translation in *Poenulus* Act V, Scene II, 985-991. It is in these lines that reference is made to the Phoenician language. The dialogue is an exchange between the young gentleman Agorastocles (*Acharistocles* in the Punic play) and his slave Milphio. The scene is set in the harbor of Calydon, where Hanno the Carthaginian and his entourage have only just arrived. Agorastocles and Milphio, observing their arrival, are eager to learn who the exotic alien leading them is and why he has come. They propose to engage him in conversation; but language is an obstacle. Although Agorastocles, as we learn, is himself a Carthaginian by birth, he knows not a word of Punic since he was kidnapped when a boy of six more than a decade earlier. Since Agorastocles understands no Punic, his slave Milphio, feigning expertise in the language, offers to act as interpreter. Hesitantly, Agorastocles accedes. In the course of the botched exchange between Hanno and Milphio, Hanno will learn that Agorastocles is, in fact, his lost nephew and, somewhat later in the play, that Agorastocles's lover and her sister, both held in bondage by a notorious pimp, are his own daughters. The following are the corresponding Latin and Punic versions of the immediate relevant portion of the dialogue in which Milphio refers to the Phoenician language:

Milphio: Quid ais tu? Ecquid commeministi Punice?
Agorastocles: Nil edepol; nam qui scire potui, dic mihi
  Qui illim sexennis perierim Carthagine?
Hanno: Pro di immortales, plurumi ad illum modum
  Periere pueri liberi Carthagine.
Milphio: Quid ais tu?
Agorastocles: Quid uis?
Milphio: Vin appellem hunc Punce?
Agorastocles: An scis?
Milphio: Nullus me est hodie Poenus Poenior.

Milphio: Say, do you remember any Punic?
Agorastocles: Nothing, by Hercules. How could I, tell me,
  Since I disappeared from Carthage at the age of six?
Hanno: (*aside*) You immortal gods, so many freeborn boys
  Disappeared from Carthage in just this way.
Milphio: Say.
Agorastocles: What?
Milphio: Do you want me to talk to him in Punic?
Agorastocles: You know it?
Milphio: There's no Punic alive today Punicker than I!

The Punic version of this dialogue, reused by Plautus in verses 1023 + 1017a of the *Poenulus*, reads as follows in its original form:

Acharistocles: Mu?
Milphio: Pominim sycartim?
Acharistocles: Bal umer! Iadata?

Acharistocles: What?
Milphio: Do you remember any Punic?

ACHARISTOCLES: Not a word! *You* know it?

The Latin and Punic versions of this dialogue provide and establish the equation *Pōnnīm* = *Punice.* In turn, *Pōnnīm,* the name of the Punic (Phoenician) language, is patently identical to ***PNYMH*** (*Pōnnīma*) in Psalm 45, the name of the Phoenicians. As for the use of the masculine plural gentilic *Pōnnīm* for the name of the language: this is known, attested Phoenician usage, clearly an abbreviation of the fuller, underlying designation *dabarīm Pōnnīm* ("Phoenician language," *lit.,* "Phoenician words"). Evidence of the Phoenician usage is the linguistic designation ***KRSYM*** *Korsīm* ("Corsic"), appearing in the inscriptions of the Phoenician city of Kition in Cyprus, to designate the language of the ethnic ***KRSYM*** *Korsīm,* the Classical *Corsi,* a people of Northern Sardinia, many of whom resided in Kition. Kition, we know from the ninth-century B.C. Phoenician inscription from Nora in Sardinia (*KAI* 46), was the mother-city of Nora (lines 5/6 ***'M L KTN,*** "Its mother-city is Kition."). From Nora and Sardinia, Sardinian *Corsi* emigrated to Kition, in sufficiently large number that the city established the office of ***MLṢ (H-)KRSYM,*** *melīṣ hek-Korsīm,* ("Interpreter of Corsic"). See inscriptions A 9A/B; B 40.2; F 1.3, 5, 6 in M.G. Guzzo Amadasi and V. Karageorghis, *Fouilles de Kition.* III. Inscriptions phéniciennes (Nicosia, 1977). Indeed, the Sardinian origin of the Corsic population of Kition is further indicated by the fact that one "Interpreter of Corsic," Esmunadonay bin Abdmilqart bin Rasapyaton (B 40.1), used the non-Semitic ethnic nickname ***ŠRDL*** ("the Sardinian").

Phoenician (*Pōnnīm*) flourished as a written language for more than a thousand years, the oldest known inscriptions in the language dating from 1200 B.C., the last, written in the Roman alphabet, from *ca.* A.D. 350-400. Although in origin the dialect of a small region of Canaan, Phoenician (Tyro-Sidonian Canaanite) had by the beginning of the first millennium B.C. emerged the prestige language of all coastal Canaan because of the commercial and political hegemony of Tyre and Sidon. From the Levantine motherland, the language was brought in the last years of the second millennium to Sardinia in the West (*CIS* i 145, *ca.* 1200 B.C.) and in the early years of the first millennium to the island of Cyprus (*KAI* 30.2/3 9th century B.C.), which became the seat of numerous Phoenician petty kingdoms, most prominent among them the city-state of Kition. And for a brief moment, in the 9th-8th centuries B.C., Phoenician even achieved and enjoyed the status of *lingua franca* in the Near East (*KAI* 24, 9th century B.C.; *KAI* 26, 8th century B.C.). Although Phoenician gave way to Aramaic in the East, in the West it became the mother tongue of a powerful and brilliant colonial culture that extended from Cyrenaica to Morocco, from Sicily and Sardinia to southwestern Spain. And with the rise of Carthage in the early fifth century B.C., Phoenician emerged a world-class language, rivalling in prestige Greek and Latin and sharing with Latin the unique claim to being the only language into which Greek literature was translated. The specimen of Greek drama in Punic translation cited earlier is an illustration in point.

Although Tyro-Sidonian Canaanite (*Pōnnīm*) was early adopted by all Canaanite-speakers along the Lebanon and Palestine coast as a standard literary language, non Tyro-Sidonian Phoenician dialects survived. Unfortunately, little is known of these languages but for elements of them occasionally found in sporadic regional inscriptions and preserved in the western dialect of Phoenician, Punic. Thus, within "Greater Phoenician" there existed and persisted in all periods and regions a certain degree of linguistic diversity. It is interesting to observe in this regard that classical Tyro-Sidonian Canaanite, that ideal form of the language exhibiting the full range of its morphophonology and syntactic usages, is sparsely evidenced in the epigraphic record; in fact, the classical language is not even evidenced in texts from Tyre and Sidon themselves but only in two inscriptions from outside Canaan, the earlier (9th century B.C.) from Zinjirli (*KAI* 24), the later (8th century B.C.) from Karatepe (*KAI* 26).

Characteristic of Tyro-Sidonian in its classic form was the complementary expression of past perfective action by sentence-initial *qatōl hū'* (the infintive absolute + subject) and non sentence-initial *qatol* (*qatal*, the suffixing form of the verb). The Zinjirli and Karatepe inscriptions (*KAI* 24 and 26) evidence this usage. These same verb forms in the same pattern of complementation were also characteristic of the northern dialect of the city of Byblos (Byblian Canaanite texts *KAI* 9 and 10). In Western Phoenician (Punic), these complementary forms are attested in a specimen of classic Tyro-Sidonian literary prose in *Poenulus* 940-946 drawn from the Punic version of the *Karkhedonios*. But in Punic, this same usage reflected the influence of Tyro-Sidonian; the author of the Punic *Karkhedonios* sought to effect high literary style, which meant imitating Tyro-Sidonian. Western Phoenician (Punic) itself did not employ sentence-initial infintive absolute to express past perfective action, using instead the sentence-initial prefixing form (in this book called Prefixing Form B) *yiqtol*, the reflex of Canaanite *yaqtul* (Hebrew sentence-initial *wayyiqtol*).

As earlier observed, within Phoenician there was linguistic diversity, nowhere made clearer than by the use in some dialects of Phoenician of the prefixing verb *yiqtol* to express past perfective action, as in Judaean Canaanite (Hebrew); this form, as in Hebrew, was restricted to sentence-initial position; in complementation with it expressing past perfective action, the suffixing form of the verb *qatol* was used in non sentence-initial position. This expression of the Past Perfective in Phoenician is early, found in the archaic, early ninth-century inscription from Cyprus (*KAI* 30), in a sixth-century letter from Daphnae in Egypt (*KAI* 50) and in a specimen of Carthaginian historiographic prose from the year 406 B.C. (*CIS* i 5510.9/11). It is possible that in the dialects of Cyprus, Egypt and Carthage, elements of non Tyro-Sidonian Phoenician had been retained. This significant divergence within Phoenician is but one instance of a yet larger inner linguistic complexity and diversity.

The Southern Coastal Dialects

Only fragmentary information survives about the dialects of the coastal region south of Tyre and Sidon; it is nevertheless clear that these were closely related to Tyro-Sidonian while, at the same time, exhibiting minor differences from it with regard to certain aspects of morphophonology. It is most significant, however, that these divergences from Tyro-Sidonian were also characteristic of Western Phoenician (Punic). For instance, in Tyro-Sidonian the consonant *n* is always assimilated to a following consonant, with resultant gemination (doubling) of that consonant. Thus, normative of Phoenician are forms like *titten* < *tinten* ("you give") and *mittit* < *mittitt* < *mantint* ("gift"). Also normative of Tyro-Sidonian is the sound-change *a* > *e*/*i* in a closed unstressed syllable, as in the previous cited noun *mittit*, evidenced in the Assyrian transcription *Mettén* (*Me-e-te-en-na*: Tiglath. III 67.66) of the name of the eighth-seventh century king of Tyre (cf. Μεττηνος: Josephus., *Contra Apion.* 1.125). However, in the sixth-century Phoenician letter from Daphnae in Egypt (*KAI* 50), one finds the form *tintenī* ("you gave"), which differs not in one but two ways from standard Tyro-Sidonian: first, on the phonological level, the assimilation *-nt-* > *-tt-* does not occur; second, on the morphological level, the prefixing form of the verb is used to express the Past

Perfective, a usage unknown in standard Tyro-Sidonian. Then there is the royal name *Mittint* (*Mi-ti-in-ti*: Senn. ii 54; *Me-ti-in-ti*: Esar. v 57) of a late eighth-early seventh century king of Ascalon: although it evidences the sound-change *a* > *i* in the initial closed unstressed syllable that is typical of Tyro-Sidonian, the non-assimilation *-nt* > *-tt* in the final syllable is at variance from Tyro-Sidonian but consistent with the phonology of Daphnae Phoenician. Moreover, forms like *tintenī* (Daphnae) and *mittint* (Ascalon) are characteristic or "diagnostic" of Western Phoenician (Punic), raising the question, whether Punic descended directly from Tyro-Sidonian Phoenician or from another or other forms of Phoenician brought to the West by colonists from coastal Palestine and Egypt.

The Northern Coastal Dialects

Arvad

Morphophonological divergencies from standard Tyro-Sidonian evidenced in the southern dialects, such as those of Ascalon and Daphnae, are also seen in the meager and sporadic specimens of northern Canaanite. For example, the contemporary of *Mittint* of Ascalon and *Metten* of Tyre was *Mattan-Baʿal* (*Ma-ta-an-Ba-'-al*: Esar. v 60) of the northern city of Arvad (Aradus). In the noun *mattan* ("gift"), the typical Tyro-Sidonian sound-change *a* > *e/i* is not present in the initial syllable nor is the no less common Tyro-Sidonian sound-change *a* > *o/u* (under stress) in the second syllable. Compare related Punic names, all of which exhibit these phonological changes: *Mytthumbal, Mitthunbal, Mythunbal, Mytunbalis, Mytthumbalis*; so, too, compare those Punic personal names without the divine name, such as *Myttun, Mytthun, Mythun,* etc. For these names, see Benz, pp. 356-57.

Byblos

Byblian Phoenician is the only non Tyro-Sidonian dialect well attested in the epigraphic record; the Byblian Phoenician inscriptions, now numbering thirteen, span the first millennium. Byblian is sufficiently different from Tyro-Sidonian to require classification as a distinct language of the Canaanite family. It shares however a range of features with Tyro-Sidonian that require its placement in the Phoenician subfamily: Byblian and Tyro-Sidonian share in common the relative pronoun *ʾīs* (Hebrew *ʾašer*), the feminine singular noun afformative *-at* (Judeaean *-a*), the expression of sentence-initial Past Perfective by the infinitive absolute (unknown in Hebrew), the use of the verb *p-ʿ-l* (Judaean *ʿ-ś-y)* for "do, make," the verb *k-w-n* (Judaean *h-y-y*) in the Qal for "be, become" and numerous other features of morphology and vocabulary. Yet, although similar to Tyro-Sidonian in most aspects of morphology, syntax and lexicon, it differed from it significantly with regard to the pronominal system, especially the suffixal pronouns of the third person and the demonstrative pronouns. Indeed, in some regards, the suffixal possessive pronouns of Byblian resemble those of Hebrew more closely than they do the Tyro-Sidonian. The differences between Byblian and Tyro-Sidonian are clearly seen, for example, in the complementary forms for "his horse": Tyro-Sidonian had *sūso* for the nominative and accusative cases but *sūsi* for the genitive case; Byblian, on the other hand, had three forms, *sūso* for the nominative, *sūsiw* (earlier *sūsihu*) for the genitive and *sūsahu* for the accusative. Byblian also possessed grammatical forms not at all present in Tyro-Sidonian, among them a system of dual deictic pronouns, complementary in usage, the one set (masc. *ZN,* fem. *Zʾ*) for near/far deixis ("this, that"), the other (masc. *Z,* fem. *Z*) for nearer (the location of the speaker or immediate object of reference). Tyro-Sidonian has but one set, used for general near and far deixis.

In phonology, too, Byblian diverged fromTyro-Sidonian, exhibiting for instance the retention of the vowel *a* under stress, without the characteristic Tyro-Sidonian sound-change *a* > *o* under stress. Thus, the Assyrians record the name of the king of Byblos in the time of Esarhaddon as *Milk-yasáp* or *Milk-ʾasáp* (*Mil-ki-a-sha-pa*: Esar. v 59); in marked contrast, cuneiform sources record Tyro-Sidonian names with the sound change: *Baʿal-malók* of Arvad (*Ba-'-al-ma-lu-ku:* Asb. ii 84), *Baʿal-yatón* (*Bel-ia-a-tu-nu*: Nabuna'id 282.4).

Remarkably, Byblian maintained itself as a distinct literary language throughout the period of Tyro-Sidonian supremacy in Phoenicia although it played no role in the Phoenician West, there being no single inscription in this dialect found outside Phoenicia proper. To what extent Byblian continued to be the spoken language of the city of Byblos, as distinct from its historic classical language, is unknown.

Western Phoenician (Punic)

The Tyrians and Sidonians began colonization of the West about 1200 B.C.; it is from this time that the first inscriptions in Phoenician appear in the West. Already its earliest manifestation, Western Phoenician (called Punic to differentiate it from the language of the Levantine homeland) showed divergences from standard Tyro-Sidonian. For example, in the earliest western inscription (*CIS* i 145), the tombstone of a Phoenician miller and wheat merchant (*sallāṭ ḥiṭṭīm*) erected *ca.* 1200 B.C. at Nora in Sardinia, the independent personal pronoun of the first singular is *ʾanī*, a form rarely if ever attested in Phoenician, which used *ʾanīki* exclusively. Other features of morphology and phonology, as earlier alluded to, suggest strongly that Punic may not have been the direct descendant of Tyro-Sidonian but of a dialect or dialects of Phoenician from a part or parts of Greater Phoenicia other than the region of Tyre and Sidon.

The distinctiveness of Punic, apparent in the earliest western texts, is yet more apparent in texts of the fifth century B.C onward. For example, the Phoenician definite article was *ha-*, with aspiration; the Punic definite article was *ʾa-*, without aspiration. In Carthaginian inscription *CIS* i 5510, dated to 406 B.C., the definite article is ***H-*** *ha-* as in Phoenician, but there are also two examples of **ʾ-** *ʾa-*, the actual, non-aspirated Punic form. As this text illustrates, dialectical differences are often disguised by the retention in Punic of traditional spellings that reflect Phoenician, not Punic morphophonology. Another related instance in point is the form ***LYRḤ*** ("to make welcome") in this same inscription of 406 B.C.: the spelling reflects the Phoenician pronunciation *liyarīḥ* of the infinitive construct in the causative stem Yip'il; in Punic however the causative stem was Ip'il, as evidenced by the 4th century form ***LSR*** *lasīr* ("to remove"). Punic scribes were hesitant to abandon Phoenician spellings. So, for example, it is not until the Neo-Punic period that the Phoenician spelling ***YQDŠ*** for Punic *iqdēs* ("he dedicated") was abandoned and the phonetic spelling ***ʾYQDŠ*** adopted. Punic also differed from Phoenician in the retention of *-nt-*: in the 406 B.C. Carthaginian inscription, one finds for instance ***MTNT*** *mittint* ("gift"), not Phoenician ***MTT*** *mittit*. Throughout Punic the common word for "stele" is always ***MNṢBT***, found in Latin-letter Punic inscription spelled **myntsyfth** *mintsivt*, never ***MṢBT*** as in Phoenician. As earlier observed, the non-assimilation *-nt-* was characteristic of forms of non Tyro-Sidonian Phoenician, such as the dialects of Ascalon and Daphnae.

Phonology was not the only area in which Punic was demonstrably different from Phoenician. In morphology, typical of Punic was the third singular possessive pronoun *-im* ("his, her"), the Phoenician pronoun *-i* but with excrescent *-m*, appearing early in formal written language alongside the free variant *-i*. This form and the phonological development behind it were unknown in Phoenician. Also present in Punic were grammatical forms not known in Phoenician, notable among them the determinative pronoun ***Š-*** *si-*, used so commonly in Punic to express the indirect genitive but also used to form the independent possessive pronoun ***ŠLY*** *sillī* ("my"), not known in Phoenician.

Among the most salient differences between Punic and Phoenician is the use in Punic of the prefixing verb *yiqtol* (Hebrew *wayyiqtol*) in the sentence-initial position to express the Past Perfective. Tyro-Sidonian literary prose, reflected in the Zinjirli and Karatepe inscriptions (*KAI* 24 and 26), employed the infinite absolute, never the prefixing form. In other words, Punic usage coincided with that of Old Cyprus (*KAI* 30), Daphnae (*KAI* 50), Carthage (*CIS* i 5510) and Hebrew against that of Tyre-Sidon. Sentence-initial *yiqtol* Past Perfective occurs in the description of the Carthaginian attack (in winter of 406 B.C.) on the Siceliote Greek city of Agrigentum: *CIS* I 5510.9/10 ***WYLK*** (*weyelekū*) ***RBM 'DNB'L BN GRSKN HRB WḤMLKT BN ḤN' HRB 'LŠ***, ("Generals Idnibal son of Gisco the Great and Himilco son of Hanno the Great marched at dawn."). Tyro-Sidonian Phoenician did, however, impact Punic literary usage; for in *Poen.* 943-944, a fragment from the Punic translation of the *Karkhedonios*, written *ca.* 300-200 B.C., the Past Perfective, as earlier alluded to, is expressed in the Phoenician manner by the infinitive absolute + subject: **Iulec anec cona, alonim balim, ban[e] becor Bals[illem],** ("I brought hither, O proprietary gods, my firstborn son Baals[illem].").

In the period of Carthaginian supremacy in the West, Carthage and her sister republics became centers of a unique culture that was a blend of the Greek and the Canaanite. Carthaginians warmly embraced Greek literature, long before the Hellenistic Age, and translated its many genres into the Punic vernacular. The conceit propagated by the Romans and disseminated even today by some Classicists that the Romans were the only people in antiquity sufficiently competent intellectually to adopt and use Greek literature and to reproduce it in their own language is belied by ample evidence to the contrary. Ironically, it was a Roman, T. Maccius Plautus, who transmitted this knowledge to us in preserving passages of Greek drama in Punic, some doubtless composed and performed in his time and others perhaps of even earlier date. One specimen of this literature, Milphio's conversation with Agorastocles from the Punic *Karkhedonios,* has been discussed earlierin this chapter. But the Punic *Karkhedonios* was but one Greek play in Punic. Plautus preserved specimens of other Greek comedies in Punic in his *Poenulus*, among them a fragment of Menander's comedy that was the model for Plautus's *Aulularia* ("Pot of Gold"), specifically, the dialogue of Megadorus and Euclio in which Megadorus invites the miser to drink wine but Euclio vehemently refuses for fear of revealing, under the influence, the hiding-place of his pot of gold. Plautus's Latin version of this dialogue appears is *Aulularia* 569-572; the Punic version is preserved (as foreign gobbledygook) in *Poenulus* 1142. First, the Plautine Latin.

MEGADORUS: Potare ego hodie, Euclio, tecum volo.
EUCLIO: Non potem ego quidem hercle.
MEGADORUS: At ego iussero
Cadum unum vini veteris a ame adferrier.
EUCLIO: Nolo hercle, nam mihi bibere decretum est aquam.

MEGADORUS: I want to drink with you today, Euclio.
EUCLIO: No, by Hercules, I won't drink.
MEGADORUS: But I shall order
A jar of old wine sent over from my place.
EUCLIO: I will not drink it, by Hercules. I'll stick to drinking water!

The Punic version, concise and perhaps truer to the original, reads:

MEGADORUS: Neste ien. Neste dum et.
EUCLIO: Al. Anec este mem.

MEGADORUS: We shall drink wine. We shall drink the blood of the vine.
EUCLIO: No, I will not. *I* shall drink water!

No less interesting than the specimens of translations of Greek literature is an example of an original play in Punic preserved in the *Poenulus.* It is a fragment of an entrance monologue of Greco-Roman type (*Poen.* 940-946) from a comedy set in a Punic city, the *dramatis personae* all Phoenicians and the subject purely Punic. The play told the story of a father who had years earlier brought his firstborn son to the city to which he now (about ten years later) returns. To the audience, the newcomer declares that in the past he had brought his son to this city to be adopted and raised by his guest-friend; the latter, he acknowledges, "has done everything for that son of his, as he was to do for him." In the Neo-Punic version of the monologue (*Poen.* 930-936), which preserves passages not in the extant Punic, the father goes on to inform the audience that the purpose of his coming is "that I might get back my only son." This is all of the play that survives; but one may conjecture, with good reason, that the background of the story was the removal to safety in another city of a firstborn son by his father in order to circumvent the rite of infant sacrifice. The play itself was likely a conventional Greek-style comedy in which identity was in question but ultimate recognition achieved. What is positively unique however about this play is that it was not the translation of a Greek model but an original work. Roman parallels, to the best of my knowledge, are wanting.

Traditional Punic literature was also cultivated in the West but save for a few extant specimens preserved in stone, little has survived. One genre represented in the surviving corpus is historical prose, in the form of a brief description of the close of the six-month campaign against the Siceliote city of Agrigentum and the taking of the city in winter of 406 B.C. The work survives because of its inclusion in a Carthaginian inscription (*CIS* i 5510) as a synchronism, to provide an historical reference to establish the date of the suffetship of Esmunamos son of Idnibal the Great and Hanno son of Bostar son of Hanno the Great. The extant Punic text appears to be the closing portion of a full account of the Agrigentine campaign; and it was surely this Punic historical source that was consulted by the Greek historian Diodorus Siculus (wrote *ca.* 60-30 B.C.) in his own account of the taking of Agrigentum by Carthage. The background of the Punic account is the abandonment of Agrigentum by its inhabitants and defenders, fled to safety the night before the city fell to the neighboring city of Gela, the Carthaginian historian describing the capture of Agrigentum the following morning as follows: lines 9/11 ***WYLK RBM ʾDNBʿL BN GRSKN HRB WḤMLKT BN ḤNʾ HRB ʿLŠ WTMK HMT ʾYT ʾGRGNT WŠT H[M]T ŠLM DL BʿL NWS,*** ("General Idnibal son of Gisco the Great and Himilco son of Hanno the Great marched at dawn, and they seized Agrigentum; and they [the Agrigentines] made peace [surrendered], including those who had fled <the city the night previous>."). The fate of this composition is especially interesting. In the course of transmission over a period of more than three hundred years in the hands of the Greeks, the Punic was distorted to portray the Carthaginians as brutal savages. Diodorus (xiii , 90.1) received the following version of the Punic: ("Imilkas [Himilco], leading his army at dawn within the walls <of Agrigentum>, put to death almost all who had been left behind inside."). Diodorus continued his account of the fall of Agrigentum with a detailed description of the looting of the city. Thanks to the discovery of the Punic oiginal, we now know that his account of Carthaginian looting and savagery is based on the misreading and mistranslation of the Punic text as follows: ***WTMK HMT 'YT 'GRGNT WŠT H[MT] ŠLM DL B'L NKS*** ("They [the Carthaginians] seized Agrigentum, and they [the Carthaginians] set loose looters [reading *šōllīm*] and murderers [reading ***B'L NKS*** *ba'lê neks*] <in the city>."). We have here a rare instance of the process of historical revisionism in antiquity, a tendency that Diodorus himself strongly condemned.

In the Roman period, Punic remained the spoken language of a majority of the population of Africa and other regions in the West. This phase of the language, called Neo-Punic (New Punic), differed from Punic largely in one regard: the loss of pharyngeal and laryngeal consonants and the coalescence of the sibilants (*z s ṣ ś*). Neo-Punic was the native tongue of the emperor Septimius Severus (A.D. 193-211, born in ad 145/6 in Leptis Magna), of the poet Apuleius (born *ca.* ad in Madaurus) and of the Church Father Augustine (A.D. 354-430). Even in this late period, Punic remained the vehicle of a signficant literary culture, one that preserved traditional forms and cultivated new ones. Some genres, clearly of great antiquity, are attested in writing for the first time, among them rhetorical rhyming prose, for which Arabic provides the closest analogy. A sample of this genre is a three-line hymn to the god *Ḥṭr*-Mescar (a binomial) from the city of Mactar in North Africa; the hymn exhibits the end-rhyme *-im:*

L'LM HQYDŠ LŠ'T 'ḤT ŠMM	*Lilīm iqqiddīs laset ot semim*
BSWB MLK ḤṬR, MYSKR RZN YMM	*Biswb mūlek Ḥṭr, Meskar rūzen yammīm*
B'L ḤRDT 'L GBRTM	*Bal aradot al gubūratim*

Exalt the name of the holy god!
Ḥṭr, ruler of the *land;* Mescar, sovereign of the seas,
He who commands fear because of his might.

In the late Roman period, the Punic script had fallen into desuetude and was replaced by the Roman alphabet; but Punic literary forms were maintained. Indeed, as late as *ca.* A.D. 350 traditional Canaanite poetry, reflecting form and style going back to the Bronze Age, continued to be written in Roman Tripolitania. One such work has come down to us, a three-verse poem in iambic trimeter by Iulius Nasif, the commander (*tribunus*) of the militia of the hinterland colony of Adnim, in which the poet commemorates and celebrates the capture of his enemy from the colony of Mycne (Mycnim). The poem owes its survival to the friends of Iulius Nasif who inscribed it on his tombstone at Bir ed-Dreder, the site of the necropolis of the the colony of Cleruchia Adnim:

Badnim garasth is on,	From Adnim I drove out the wicked fellow,
MySyrthim, bal sem ra;	From the Syrthis, him of ill repute;
Sab siben Mycne,	(When) our militia surrounded Mycne,
Is ab syth sath syby;	Then did I make that enemy <my> captive;
In aab sa[l]e(m) lo sal:	The enemy asked mercy for himself:
"Un ath ab[dach]a!"	"Spare thou thy servant!"

CHAPTER TWO

THE ALPHABET, ORTHOGRAPHY AND PHONOLOGY

I. The Alphabet and Orthography

A. *Phoenician*

Phoenician was written in a twenty-two letter alphabet, called by the Greeks *ta Phoinikeia grammata* ("the Phoenician letters," Herodotus, v. 58). In spite of its name, this alphabet had not been invented by the Phoenicians but, rather, had been devised in the Late Bronze Age and later, adapted by the Phoenicians to the needs of their language which, in the early Iron Age, possessed a repertory of twenty-two consonantal phonemes. The twenty-two letter alphabet was retained throughout the history of the Phoenician language, well into the Late Roman period, even though many of the original phoneme graphemes no longer existed.

In the matter of orthography, Phoenician scribes of the Iron Age employed the purely consonantal system of spelling used in Late Bronze Age II literary Ugaritic although they were acquainted with the system of *matres lectionis* (vowel-letters) used for the writing of contemporary Aramaean, Judaean and Moabite. Occasionally and selectively, however, they did use *waw* and , principally in the spelling of foreign words but also for some frequent inflectional morphemes. The letter *he* was not however used by them.

Instances of the use of the letters *waw* and *yod* , even in the spelling of foreign names, are exceedingly few: (i) ***W*** is found for *o* in the spelling of Cypriote Greek royal names ***DMWNKS*** (Greek Δαμονικος) and ***'NDRWNKŠ*** (Greek Ανδρονικος) on coins of Lapethos (see *RPC* p. 97-100); (ii) ***W*** is found for *u* in the spelling of the ethnicon ***LWKY*** *Lūkī* ("Lycian," *CIS i* 45). It is used exceptionally in the spelling of the Phoenician noun ***SWT*** *sūt* ("garment," Byblos *KAI* 11). The letter ***Y*** is found for *i* in the spelling of the Cypriote Phoenician city-name ***'DYL*** *'edīl* (Egyptian: Ramesses III Simons XXXV, 11 *'-d_2-l*; Assyrian: Esar. V 64 **E-di-'-il.**) In native Phoenician words, ***Y*** is most commonly found as a word-final vowel-letter for *i* in (i) the occasional *plene* spelling of the pronoun ***'NKY*** *'anīki* ("I," for standard spelling ***'NK***); (ii) in the *plene* spelling of the first singular possessive pronoun -*ī* ("my") although not in Byblian Phoenician or early Tyro-Sidonian Phoenician (*KAI* 24, the Kilamuwa inscription) nor in Cypriote Phoenician; the latter scribal schools preferred the archaic spelling **-Ø** of the pronoun; (iii) in the *plene* spelling of the third person singular (masculine and feminine) possessive pronoun *ī* ("his/her"), of which examples of the original defective spelling are very rare. Rare and restricted in Phoenician orthography, the use of ***W*** and ***Y*** became common in Punic and in Neo-Punic.

Also used in Phoenician, if rarely, is final *ʾaleph* to indicate the presence of a vowel, especially in personal and place-names. This device may have originated in the spelling of hypocoristic personal names like ***ʾDʾ*** *ʾIddo* (*KAI* 20). It is found in the spelling of the Greek personal name ***HRNʾ*** Ηρηνη (*KAI* 56) and the Greek place-name ***LʾDKʾ*** Λαοδικεια (Hill 1, 52). This orthographic device, rare in Phoenician, became very common in Punic orthography, serving to indicate the presence of any vowel.

Phoenician orthography was always a mixture of historical spellings, reflecting the pronunciation of an earlier period, and phonetic spellings, reflecting contemporary pronunciation. Historical spelling is represented by a word like ***MY*** ("who?"), pronounced *mī* but its standard spelling reflecting the earlier form *miya,* the *yod* being the consonant *yod*, not a *matres lectionis*. In contrast, the word for "fruit," *p*ᵉ*rī*, was spelled ***PR*** (14.12), as pronounced, not ***PRY***, reflecting the historical form *piry(u);* so, too, in Punic, in which the word-final vowel was indicated by the vowel-letter (*mater lectionis*) *aleph:* ***GDʾ*** *g*ᵉ*dī* < *gidy(u),* ("goat," 69.9). Sometimes, historic spellings and phonetic spellings existed side by side; for instance, the standard spelling of the third person masculine singular possessive pronoun used with a noun in the genitive case was **-*Y*** -*i*, the *yod* being a vowel-letter (*mater lectionis)*; but still found occasionally is the earlier spelling **-Ø.** The use of a historical spelling or phonetic spelling is also determined by scribal preference and usage.

Inner Phoenician Orthographic Differences

Within Phoenician itself different scribal practices prevailed. For instance, Cypriote Phoenician orthography was distinct from that of Levantine Phoenician: the scribes of Cyprus occasionally used the "phonetic" spelling ***ʾZ*** for standard Phoenician ***Z*** in writing the singular demonstrative pronouns ᵉ*zdé* (masculine) and ᵉ*zdō* (feminine), employing the *ʾaleph* to indicate the presence in pronunciation of the prothetic vowel. The Cypriote spelling was used at Marathus on the coast of Phoenicia and once in Punic, in the inscription from Pyrgoi in Etruria (*ca.* 500 B.C.).

Cypriote scribes also adhered to the older (original) spelling **-Ø** of the nominative/accusative form *-ī* of the first singular possessive pronoun; this spelling is elsewhere found only in the early Tyro-Sidonian inscription of Kilamuwa (*KAI* 24) and in Byblian Phoenician, in which one finds ***QL*** *qōlī* ("my voice") in the nominative and accusative cases but ***QLY*** *qōlī* < *qōliya*. In Tyro-Sidonian Phoenician and in Punic, the normative spelling of the possessive pronoun, from the eighth century B.C., was always *plene* ***-Y***, regardless of the case of the noun.

B. *Punic*

Conservative Punic orthography was essentially identical to that of Phoenician. Punic differed however from Phoenician in the common use of word-final *ʾaleph* to indicate the presence of a word-final vowel. Instances of typical Punic spellings are 68.5 ***QLʾ*** *qūlo* ("his voice") = Phoenician ***QL***; 69.15 ***MQNʾ*** *miqne* ("property, money"); 66.2 ***RPYʾ*** *rafoyo* ("he cured him"); 101.1 ***BNʾ*** *banô* ("they built"), *et passim.* Less frequently, Punic used *ʾaleph* also to indicate the presence of a word-internal vowel: Pyrgi line 9 ***MʾŠ*** *mes* ("statue") = Phoenician ***MŠ***. This extended use of *aleph* would become an important feature of Neo-Punic orthography.

Punic also departed from Phoenician in its willingness to indicate in spelling the actual pronunciation of a morpheme or word rather than always use the historical Phoenician spelling; for instance, the definite article in Phoenician was *ha-*, with aspiration; in Punic it was *a-*, without aspiration. Punic allowed the phonetic spelling ʾ-, indicating no aspiration, while retaining the historical spelling ***H-*** as well. Both spellings co-occur in Carthaginian inscription 5510, written in the year 406 B.C.

C. *Neo-punic*

In its earliest stage, formal Neo-Punic employed conservative Punic orthography although with an increased use of the *matres lectionis* ***W Y*** and *ʾaleph,* always in the manner these were used in Punic. For example, in an otherwise conservatively written text like *KAI* 121 from Leptis Magna, one already finds typical Neo-Punic *plene* spellings such as ***MYŠQL*** *misqil* ("beautifier"), ***'YQDŠ*** *iqdes* ("he dedicated") and ***R'PS*** *Rufus* (the Roman personal name).

In the following stage of the orthography, as a result of the loss of the pharyngeals and laryngeals in the spoken language, the letters ***H Ḥ*** ʿ came to be used as *matres lectionis* alongside the already existing repertory of vowel-letters: the letters ʾ (for any vowel), ***W*** (for *o* and *u*) and ***Y*** (for *e* and *i*). Although the letters ***H Ḥ*** ʾ were used indifferently to express any vowel, the letter *ʿayin* is conspicuous for the frequency with which it was used to express the vowel *a*. No consistent use of vowel- letters ever emerged in Neo-Punic.

In the final period of its existence, the first five centuries of the Common (Christian) Era, the traditional twenty-two letter Phoenician-Punic alphabet fell into desuetude and was replaced by the Roman alphabet. For the Punic of this period a fully developed Latin-letter orthography was devised. A large corpus of inscriptions in this system of writing have been discovered in the erstwhile province of Roman Tripolitania (Western Libya); this corpus comprises texts of all genres: epitaphs, building and tomb dedications, commemoratives and even a specimen of traditional Phoenician poetry (D 6). It is this same Latin-letter orthography that was used in the writing of the Neo-Punic version of the entrance monologue of Hanno the Carthaginian included in the text of the Late Roman period revival of the Plautine comedy *Poenulus* (vss. 930-939). Our knowledge of the Phoenician and Punic morphophonology is based largely on the vocalized Neo-Punic of these texts.

II. Phonology

Phoenician of the Early Iron Age, to judge from the Phoenician alphabet of twenty-two letters (graphemes), possessed a repertory of twenty-two consonantal phonemes; the graphemes-phonemes of this period were ***ʾ B G D H W Z Ḥ Ṭ Y K L M N S ʿ P Ṣ Q R Š T.*** In addition to the twenty-two consonantal phonemes, there were the short vowels *a e i o u*, the long vowels *ī ō ū* and the contracted diphthongs *ê ô*. In the Late Bronze Age (1500-1200 B.C.), the consonantal repertory was larger, as Phoenician words and place-names in Egyptian texts indicate: the language of that period included the phoneme /x/ and no doubt others. In the Roman period, on the other hand, with the loss of pharyngeals and laryngeals and the merging of the several sibilants, Western Phoenician (Punic) possessed as few as seventeen consonantal phonemes. In spite however of the reduction of phonemes, the original twenty-two letter alphabet was retained, together with a highly conservative "historical" orthography, fixed in and reflecting the pronunciation of the first half of the first millennium B.C.; in reality, already by the second half of the first millennium B.C. and increasingly into the first centuries of the Common Era, considerable differences existed between the written word and actual contemporary pronunciation. Because of the highly diverse character of the Phoenician-Punic inscriptions, belonging to diverse periods and regions, and because of the limited, sporadic and often ambiguous character of the evidence they contain, the reconstruction of Phoenician-Punic phonology is an exceedingly difficult undertaking.

The description of Phoenician phonology and morphology in this grammar is based largely on the extant specimens of vocalized Punic and Neo-Punic in Latin letters, the Latin-orthography Punic inscriptions of Roman Tripolitania (*ca.* A.D. 100-500) and the Punic and Neo-Punic passages in the play *Poenulus*; the Plautine Punic passages reflect the pronunciation of *ca.* 300-200 B.C., the Neo-Punic the pronunciation of *ca.* 100 B.C.-A.D. 400. These materials are complemented by specimens of Punic and Neo-Punic in the form of Latin and Greek transcriptions and the few specimens of Phoenician, mostly personal names, in Assyrian and Babylonian sources. In view of the difficult nature of the evidence, the following essay to provide a description of Phoenician-Punic phonology is perforce fragmented, incomplete and always problematic.

A. *The Consonants*

1. *The Articulation of the Consonants*

ʾ (*ʾaleph*): Simple glottal stop /ʾ/ at the beginning of a syllable: ***ʾLP*** *ʾalp* ("ox") but quiescent in syllable-final position, with resultant lengthening and stress-lengthening of the vowel: NPu *Poen.* 930 **carothi** *qarōti* < *qarāti* < *qaráʾti* (***QRʾT*** "I called"). In Neo-Punic, the stop was no longer pronounced.

B: Bilabial plosive /*b*/ in all positions: Punic *Poen.* 1141 **bane** and **bene** ("my son"); NPu *IRT* 873.3 **libinim** ("for his son"). There is no evidence for the fricative realization of the phoneme as in Hebrew although in Neo-Punic /b/ did have the allophone [*v*] (written **f** in Latin-letter orthography) immediately contiguous to a following consonant: *IRT* 877.4/5 **efsem** *evsem* (***'BŠM*** "in the name of"); *AI* 1 p. 233 line 2 **lifnim** *livnim* (***LBNM*** "for his son"); and *IRT* 873.1; 906.1/2 **myntsyfth** *mintsivt* (***MNṢBT*** "stele"). It is possible that this conditioned sound-change was charactersitic of Phoenician as well; for we have an actual example of the grapheme φ in Greek-letter Phoenician where Latin-letter Punic has **f:** 174.8 αφδε (***'BDY*** ("his slave"); however, the manner in which φ in this word is meant to be articulated is uncertain. The sound change may not have been characteristic of Punic: *Poen.* 948 **sibti** (***ŠBTY*** "his residence").

G*:** Velar stop /*g*/: Pu *Poen.* 1033 **migdil** (MGDL*** "magnifier"); NPu *Poen.* 938 **gubulim** (***GBLM*** "district").

D*:** Alveolar stop /*d*/: Pu *Poen.* 944 **duber** (DBR*** "says"); NPu *Poen.* 935 **dobrim** (***DBRM*** "they say"); Pu and NPu *Poen.* 949, 939 **bod** (***BD*** "of, from").

H*:** Glottal fricative /*h*/. The fricative existed in Phoenician and Punic: Pu *Poen.* 946 **hu** (H'*** "he"); *Poen.* 947 **helicot** (***HLKT*** "hospitality"). In Neo-Punic, the phoneme was completely lost: *Poen.* 936 **u** ("he"); *Poen.* 937 **elichoth** ("hospitality"), *et passim.* Deserving special note is the non-fricative pronunciation of the definite article in Punic: in a Carthaginian inscription from 406 B.C. (*CIS* i 5510) the defnite article is twice written **'-**, occurring in free variation with historical spelling ***H*-**; the two spellings are found side by side throughout the history of Punic and Neo-Punic. This spelling may be indicative of an early and wider tendency in Western Phoenician to "drop" the fricative, perhaps in popular pronunciation.

W*-**: Bilabial /*w*/. Represented in Latin-letter orthography by **u:** Pu *Poen.* 1141 **hauo** *ḥawo* (ḤW'*** "may he live long!"); NPu *IRT* 889.1 **uybinim** *wibinim* (***WBNM*** "and his son").

Z*:** Affricate of the shape [*zd*] or [*dz*], represented in Roman orthography by **sd** and **ss** in the spelling of the demonstrative pronoun ***Z ("this"): Punic *Poen.* 947A **esde** and *Poen.* 940P, 944A **esse** (^{e}*zdé* or ^{e}*dzé*). The affricate nature of the phoneme is confirmed by the presence of the prothetic **e**-vowel, which serves to break up the initial consonant cluster; this prothetic vowel is also indicated in the "phonetic" spelling ***'Z*** of the demonstrative, common in the inscriptions of Cyprus as a free variant spelling of ***Z***. See the discussion of the Demonstrative Pronouns.

Elsewhere in Phoenician, word-initial *z* appears to have been early reduced to a simple sibilant, as may be seen in normative spelling ***S-K-R*** ("remember") of the Canaanite verb ***Z-K-R***.: Phoenician 18.6 ***SKR*** ("memorial"); 43.15 ***YSKRN*** ("may he remember me!"); Pu *Poen.* 1023 **sucartim** ("you remember"). Once only in Phoenician is the historical spelling with ***Z*** attested: Umm el-Awamid 14.2 ***ZKRN*** ("remember me!"). Yet, in the spelling of some words, the grapheme ***Z*** was retained: Phoenician 26 A II 19 ***ZBḤ*** ("sacrifice") and Punic 69.15 ***ZBḤ*** ("sacrifice") and ***YZBḤ*** ("he shall sacrifice"). In Latin-letter Neo-Punic, the phoneme is consistently written **s:** *IRT* 893.5 **sebuim** *s*^{e}*bū(ḥ)īm* (***ZBḤM*** "sacrificed ones"), in all probability articulated as a simple *s*; this pronunciation is further indicated by the Punic and Latin-letter spellings of the demonstrative pronouns *S ST* (Latin-letter **sy syth sith su soth**), these all reflexes of the Phoenician ***Z***-demonstrative pronouns. In transcriptions of Punic prepared by non-native speakers, the use of the grapheme **z** ζ is found: Diosc. 2.125 ζερα and Pliny 24.71 **zyra** (***ZR'*** "seed").

Ḥ: Pharyngeal fricative /*ḥ*/ The fricative is represented by the grapheme **h** in Latin-letter Punic: *Poen.* 1141A **hauo** *ḥawo* (***ḤW*** "may he live long!") in the salutations **hauo done silli** ("may my father live long!") and **hauo bene silli** ("May my son live long!"). In Neo-Punic, the fricative had completely disappeared: *IRT* 879.3; 894.4 **auo** *awo* ("he lived") *cf.* Neo-Punic *plene* spellings 134.2 ***'WḤ*** and 158.2 ***'WH*** *awo* ("he lived"); *Poen.*937 **irs** (***ḤRŠ*** "shard"), *et passim.*

Ṭ: Retroflex stop /*ṭ*/. This emphatic dental stop is represented by **t** in Latin-letter Punic: *IRT* 828.1 **Typafi** (***ṬBḤPY*** "Tapapius," family name), the stop perceived as non-aspirated [*t*] (Greek τ); in contrast, Phoenician /t/ was perceived as an aspirated stop [t^{h}] (Greek θ) and represented in Latin-letter orthography as **th:** *Poen.* 930 **yth** (***'T***); *IRT* 827.2 **myntsyfth** *mintsivt* (***MNṢBT*** "stele"), *et passim.*

Y: Palatal glide /*y*/. Represented in Latin-letter orthography by **i:** Pu *Poen.* 942 **iulec** *yûlek* (***YLK*** "bring," Infinitive Absolute); *Poen.* 1117 **iadata** *yada'ta* (***YD'T*** "you know"). In Neo-Punic, *y* as an intervocalic glide appears to have been suppressed in the environment *-eyo-*: *IRT* 865 **baneo** *banêo* < *banêyo* ("his sons"); *IRT* 894.6 **buo** *būo* < *(a)būyo* ("his father"); elsewhere it was retained between vowels: *IRT* 828.3 **ai{a}em** *(ḥ)ayyīm* ("lifetime"); *IRT* 826.3 **auia** *a(ḥ)ūya* ("her brother").

Characteristic of Neo-Punic was the development *yi-* > *ʾi-* in word-initial position, most commonly seen in the suffixing forms of the causative stem, such as 121.1 ***ʾYQDŠ*** *iqdes* ("he dedicated") and *IRT* 873.3 **intseb** *intseb* ("he erected"), reflexes of Phoenician *yiqdes* and *yiṣṣeb* respectively. The suppression of *y* in this environment led, by analogy, to its suppression in other forms of the causative stem: NPu D 5.19 **utseb** *ûtseb* < *yûtseb* ("he erected"). In literary Punic, however, perhaps under Phoenician influence, intervocalic *y* was still pronounced in all forms of the causative stem, as evidenced by the infinitive absolute *Poen.* 942 **iulec** *yûlek* ("brought").

K: Velar stop /*k*/. Represented in Neo-Punic Latin-letter orthography by **ch:** NPu *Poen.* 931 **thymlachun** *timlakūn* (***TMLKN*** "you rule"); *Poen.* 934 **chon** *kon* (***KN*** "he was"); *Poen.* 935 **chy** *kī* (***Kʾ*** "because"), *et passim.* The Neo-Punic stop was perceived as aspirated [k^h] (Greek χ). It is possible that /*k*/, under certain conditions, had the fricative pronunciation [*x*], represented in Latin-letter orthography by the letter **h:** *CIL* viii 27604 **Birihtina** (personal name) and *CIL* viii 4850.2; 16768.2 **Birihut** (personal name; also spelled **[Bi]ricut** in *CIL* 16955.1). These pesonal names are however exceptional; there are no examples of the fricative realization of /k/ in the Latin-letter Neo-Punic inscriptions.

L: Alveolar lateral resonant /*l*/: Pu *Poen. 940* **alonim** *ʾallōnīm* (***ʾLNM*** "gods"); NPu *Poen.* 938 **ily** *íllí* (***ʾL*** "these"), *et passim.*

M: Bilabial nasal resonant /*m*/: Pu *Poen.* 940 **macom** *maqōm* (***MQM*** "city"); NPu *Poen.* 934 **marob** *ma(ʿ)rob* (***MʿRB*** "custody"), e*t passim.*

N: Alveolar nasal resonant /*n*/: Pu *Poen.* 942 **anec** *ʾanīk*(***ʾNK*** "I"); NPu *Poen.* 936 **innochoth** *innōkōt* (***HNKT*** "here"), e*t passim.*

S: Alveolar groove fricative /*s*/: Pu *Poen.* 1023 **sucartim** (***SKRTM*** "you remember"); NPu *Poen.* 937 **sith** (***ST*** "this," masc.); *IRT* 828.2 **soth** (***ST*** "this," fem.), *et passim.* This sibilant had by *ca.* 500 B.C.

merged with the lateral groove fricative /*ś*/ (grapheme ***Š***), as evidenced by the spelling ***ʿSR*** for historical ***ʿŠR*** in Phoenician (14.1) and Punic (112.1).

ʿ (*ʿayin*): Pharyngeal obstruent /*ʿ*/. No orthographic device was used to represent this phoneme in Latin-letter Punic nor is it entirely evident that the phoneme survived in late Punic, as witnessed by its non-representation in *Poen.* 944 **fel** *fel* (***Pʿ L*** "he did") and *Poen.* 945 **liful** *lif'ūl* (***LPʿL*** "to do"). In Neo-Punic, the phoneme had completely disappeared: *IRT* 873.2 **fel** *fel* ("he made"); *IRT* 889.2 **felu** *felū* ("they made"); this is confirmed by the Punic-letter spelling NPu 142.4 ***PHL'*** *felū* ("they made").

P: Bilabial simple stop /*p*/ in Phoenician and Punic. In Punic, the phoneme was still [*p*], as may be ascertained from the word-play between *Poen.* 1023 **ponnim sucartim** ("Do you remember Phoenician?") and the implicit Latin pun **pone eum sub cratim** ("Place him under a basket!") that informs Milphio's translation **Sub cratim uti iubeas se supponi** ("<He asks> that you order him be placed under a basket."), *Poen.* 1025. However, one also finds in Punic the labiodental fricative realization [*f*] in all positions: *Poen.* 944 **fel** ("he did"); *Poen.* 945 **liful** ("to do"). In Neo-Punic, the realization [*f*] is normative: *IRT* 828.1, 877.2 **fel** ("he made"); *IRT* 901.2,4 **fela** ("she made"); *IRT* 889.2 **felu** ("they made"); 178.1 **felioth** ("workmanship").

Ṣ: Alveolar affricate [*ts*]. The articulation of this phoneme is difficult to ascertain, for it appears to have been different from period to period. The evidence is as follows: (i). In the Tripolitanian Neo-Punic Latin-letter inscriptions, reflecting the pronunciation of the late Roman period (*ca.* 1st-5th centuries of the Common Era), *ṣadhe* is commonly represented by the grapheme **$,** a ligature of **st** or **ts:** *IRT* 873.1; 906.1/2 **myntsyfth** and *IRT* 828.3 **my(n)sty(f)th** *mintsivt* (***MṢBT*** "stele"); *IRT* 873.3 **intseb** *intseb* ("he erected"); D 5.18 **utseb** *ūtseb* ("he erected")l (ii). The common Punic name ***ṢDN*** appears in transcription as **Siddin** (*CIL* viii 9106) but also **Stiddin** (*CIL* viii 10686) and **Tziddin** (*CIL* viii 25168); (iii). Greek and Latin transcriptions of the word ***ḤṢR*** ("herb, grass"): Appuleius (Vattioni 529 no. 7) **atzir.** ("herb"); (iv). In Plautine Punic in Roman letters, datable to *ca.* 300 B.C., *ṣade* is transcribed **ss** and **t,** both being graphic devices to convey the affricate *ts*: Pu *Poen.* 949 **iussim** *yūtsīm* (***YṢ'M*** "they who are coming out") and *Poen.*1141 **dum et** *dum ʿets* (***DM ʿṢ*** "blood of the vine" = "wine"). To the use of **t** for *ts*, compare Diod. 2.167, 2.217, 158 ατιρ *(ḥ)atsīr* ("herb").

In late Neo-Punic, the *ts* merged with simple *s*: *Punica* p. 193 ***TST*** ("expenditure") for ***TṢ'T***. The pronunciation as simple *s* is also indicated by late Neo-Punic (*ca.* A.D. 350) D 6 **siben** *sibʾen* (***ṢB'N*** "our militia"), the initial sibilant of which is part of an elaborate alliterative scheme I-SaB-SiT-SaT-SiB-I that depends on the repetition of the the simple sibilant *s*. See C.R. Krahmalkov, *JAOS* 294 (1994), 68-82).

Q: Uvular stop /*q*/. In Punic in Greek and Latin letters, this phoneme is represented by Greek and Latin unaspirated stop κ (Latin **c**) in contrast to Punic /*k*/, which is represented by Greek and Latin aspirated stop χ (Latin **ch**): *EH* Greek 1.4 κουλω *qūló* (***QL*** "his voice"); *Poen.* 930 **carothi** *qarōti* (***QR'T*** "I called"); *Poen.* 931 **macom** *maqōm* (***MQM*** "place"). But **chon** *kon* (***KN*** *kon* "he was").

R: Alveolar median resonant /r/. Unlike its Hebrew counterpart, the *r* may be geminated, as seen in the Greek and Latin transcriptions of the Pi'el active participle ***M'RḤ*** *meʾerreḥ* as Μηρρη and **Merre** respectively, with gemination of /*r*/ (*KAI* 66).

Š: /*ś*/ = [*s*], the reflex of PWS /θ *š ś*/: these phonemes had early merged in Phoenician into a single bilateral fricative, hence the existence in the Phoenician alphabet of a single grapheme. In Classical Phoenician, the fricative merged with simple /s/ (expressed by the grapheme ***S***) but normally continued to be represented in the orthography by the grapheme ***Š***; the merging is exhibited in the 5th century Phoenician spelling ***ʿSR*** for etymological ***ʿŠR*** in the Esmunazor inscription from Sidon (*KAI* 14.1). That Phoenician did not possess [*š*] is confirmed by Augustine (*Epist. ad Rom. inch. Exp.* 13) in a word-play between the Punic numeral **salus** *salūs* (***ŠLŠ*** "three, Trinity") and Latin **salus** ("salvation") that indicates that the numeral was pronounced *salūs*, not *šalūš* (Hebrew *šalōš*). The absence of the sound [*š*] was also characteristic of "Ephraimite," the dialect of the northern kingdom of Israel: Ephraimites were unable to articulate correctly the sibilant in the word *šibbolet*, producing instead a simple sibilant (*sibbolet*). See Judges 12:6. Finally, the coalescence of the phonemes PWS /*z s š*/ as simple *s* is evidenced in a 4th century ad Punic poem that exhibits the alternating alliterative syllable sequence i-SAB-SIT-SAT-SIB-i that is produced by the verse **Is ab syth sath syby** *is ab sit sat sibī* ***'Z 'B ST ŠT ŠBY*** ("Then did I make that enemy <my> captive."). See C.R. Krahmalkov, *JAOS* 294 (1994), 68-82.

Important Obs. In this grammar, ***Š*** is used for the grapheme but *s* for the pronunciation of the phoneme.

T: Simple alveolar stop /*t*/, indicated in Greek orthography by the Greek aspirated stop θ [t^h] and in Latin by **th**: NPu *IRT* 901.3 **byth** *bit* (***BT*** "daughter"); *IRT* 827.1 **myth** *mit* (***MT*** "deceased"), *et passim.*

2. *Noteworthy Phonological Phenomena*

2a. Assimilation -*n*C- > -CC-

In Phoenician (Byblian and Tyro-Sidonian), the consonant *n* contiguous to a following consonant was assimilated to that consonant, with resultant gemination (doubling) of the latter. Examples are numerous: Byb 10.9 ***TTN*** *titten* < *tinten* ("may she give"); 52.1 ***YTN*** *yitten* < *yinten* ("may he give"); 60.5 ***MṢBT*** *miṣṣibt* < *manṣibt* ("stele") *et passim.* In some dialects, this assimilation did not take place: 50.3/4 (from Daphnae) ***TNTN*** *tintenī* ("you gave"). In Punic, the assimilation is often attested in formal language: 69.18 ***NTN*** *nitton* < *nintan* ("it shall be given"); 74.1 ***MŠ'T*** *misse(')t* < *mansi't* ("payment"). However, in Neo-Punic, as distinct from Punic and Phoenician, the assimilation does not take place: 137.6 ***NNTN*** *nintanū* ("they were given"); 119.6 ***MNŠ'*** *minso(')* ("gift, contribution"); 102.2 ***MTNT*** *mittint* < *mantint* ("gift" = Phoenician ***MTT***); *IRT* 873.1 **myntsyfth** *mintsivt* < *manṣibt* ("stele" = Phoenician ***MṢBT*** *miṣṣibt*).

A related phenomenon is the assimilation *-lq-* > *-qq-* that was normative of forms of the verb *l-q-ḥ* in Phoenician and Punic: Punic 69.20 ***YQḤ*** *yiqqaḥ* < *yilqaḥ* ("he shall take"). Again, in Neo-Punic the assimilation did not take place: 122.2 ***NLQḤ'*** *nilqaḥū* ("they were purchased").

2b. Excrescent Consonants

Secondary morpheme-final -*m* appears in Punic with the suffix pronoun -***Y*** -*i* ("his, her") of the third masculine and feminine singular, giving rise to the very common free variant form -***M*** -*im:* Pu 115.2

NDRM *nidrim* ("his vow"). This excrescent consonant arose perhaps (i) in analogy to the final **-*m*** of the third plural suffix pronoun *-om* ("their") and (ii) to differentiate the third singular pronoun from the first singular ***-Y*** *-ī* ("my"): *i.e.*, Pu *Poen.* 1141 **bene** ("my son") but NPu *IRT* 873.3 **binim** ("his son").

Already in Phoenician, one finds secondary word-final *-t* in the preposition ***ʿLT*** *ʿalt*, spelled **alt** in Latin-letter Punic (*Poen.* 946), a free variant of ***ʿL*** *ʿal.* Excrescent *-t* is common in the singular demonstrative pronouns of Neo-Punic ***ST*** (**sith, syth**) *sit* ("this," masculine) and ***ST*** (**soth**) *sōt* ("this," feminine), free variants of ***S*** (**sy**) *si* and ***S*** (**su**) *sō* respectively. See Demonstrative Pronouns.

2c. *Y*-Glide and Euphonic *-n-*

Early in the history of Phoenician, the suffixal pronouns *-o* ("his, him") and *-a* ("her") were extended to use after a vowel, the affixing enabled by the introduction of the intervocalic glide *-y-*: *sūsê-y-o* ("his horses") and *banê-y-a* ("her sons"). Part of this same development was the extension of the suffixal pronoun *-om* ("their, them") to use after vowels; this affixing however was accomplished by means of intervocalic "euphonic" *-n-*: *banê-n-om* ("their son"). In the grammatical description of these pronouns, however, the intervocalic *y*-glide and the euphonic intervocalic *-n-* is always taken as part of these pronouns; thus, the postvocalic forms of the suffixal pronouns of the third singular and third plural are described in this and other works on Phoenician grammar as *-yo, -ya* and *-nom.* In Neo-Punic, the intervocalic *y*-glide with the masculine singular suffixal pronoun was no longer pronounced; thus one finds the Latin-letter spellings *IRT* 865 **baneo** *banêo* ("his sons") and *IRT* 894.6 **buo** *būo* ("his father"); but the glide was retained with the feminine suffixal pronoun: *IRT* 826.3 **auia** *a(ḥ)ūya* ("her brother") and *LA* 1 p. 45 no. 4.8 **chyrymuia** *kirrimūya* ("they honored her").

B. *The Vowels*

1. *The Original Short Vowels*

The short vowels of Phoenician and Punic are the reflexes of the original three short vowels of Semitic: /*a i u*/. As in Hebrew, the short vowels in Phoenician came each to have two phonologically distinct forms: (i) qualitatively short and (ii) qualitatively long. The qualitatively long variety of these vowels fell together to some extent with the original three long vowels and the two contracted diphthongs.

1a. Reflexes of Canaanite *a*

Original short *a* in a closed unstressed syllable had the reflex *i* or *e*; this sound change is normative of Phoenician-Punic phonology and extremely well attested: *CIL* viii 19121-3 **iddir** *ʾiddīr* <*ʾaddīr* ("great," in the divine name **Baliddir**); Pu *Poen.* 940 **imacom** *im-maqōm* < *(h)ammaqōm* ("the city"); Pu *Poen.* 1033 **migdil** *migdíl* < *magdíl* ("magnifier"); NPu *IRT* 906.1/2 **myntsyfth** *mintsívt* < *manṣibt* ("stele"); 145 I 4 ***QYDŠ*** *qiddīs* < *qaddīš* ("holy"); *EH* Gr. 1.2 ρυβαθων *ribbatón* < *rabbatónu* ("our lady"); *Poen.* 934 **thymmoth** *timmót* < *tammát* ("finished, past"). This sound-change is evidenced in Phoenician in the royal personal name *Mettén* (*Me-e-te-en-nu*) (Tigl. iii 67.66).

Original *a* occasionally retained as *a* in a word-initial closed unstressed syllable of the type /*ʾaC-*/: Pu *Poen.* 940 **alonim** *ʾallōnīm* ("gods"); Pu **addir** *ʾaddīr* in the divine name **Abaddir** (*CIL* viii 21481); NPu *IRT* 893.1 **anasib** *an-natsīb* ("the stele"). It is also retained as *a* when the vowel is characteristic of the paradigm, for example in Pu *Poen.* 1023 **sycartim** *s^ikartím* ("you remember") because *-a-* is the paradigmatic thematic vowel of the Qal suffixing form; *cf.* Pu *Poen.* 941 **bate** *bati* ("I have come"); Pu *Poen.* 1017 **iadata** *yadaʿta* ("you know") and Neo-Punic D 6 **garasth** *garast* ("I expelled"). The *a* is also retained in a unstressed syllable closed by a laryngeal or pharyngeal: NPu *Poen.* 933 **marob** *maʿrób* ("custody").

In a doubly closed syllable, the vowel is always *a*: NPu *LA* 1 p. 45 no. 4.2 **sath** *sat* < *šant* ("year"); D 6 **sath** *sat* < *šátt(i)* ("I placed"). However, in nouns of the type *CaCC*, the vowel may appear either in its original form: NPu *IRT* 889.2 **ars** *(ḥ)ars* (***ḤRŠ*** "craftsmanship"), or, as in Hebrew, as *e i y*, *e.g.* NPu D 2.14 **ers** *erṣ* (***ʾRṢ*** "land"; *cf.* Hebrew *ʾéreṣ*); NPu *LA* 1 p. 45 no. 4.1/2, 8 **iyra** *yíra(ḥ)* (***YRḤ*** "month"; *cf.* Hebrew *yéraḥ*).

In an open or closed stressed syllable, the sound-change *a*>*o* was characteristic and distinctive of Tyro-Sidonian among the Canaanite languages: Phoenician *milkót* < *milkát* ("Queen" = Ilat) in the personal name *Ab-di-mi-il-ku-ut-ti* (Esar. ii 65); *malók* < *malák* ("he reigns") in the personal name *Baʾ-al-ma-lu-ku* (Asb. ii 84, Arvad); Pu *Poen.* 947 **helicot** *h^elīkót* < *halīkát* ("hospitality"); NPu *S* 24.5 **aros** *ʾarós* < *ʾaráš* ("he asked"); *EH* Gr 1.3 ναδωρ *nadór* < *nadár* ("he vowed"); *EH* Gr 1.4 σαμω *samóʿ* < *šamáʿ* ("he heard"), *et passim.*

Stress-lengthened *o* < *a* is sometimes found lowered to *u*: Pu *Poen.*1141 **dum** *dum* < PC *dam* ("blood") but also NPu Aug. to Psalm 136:7 **dom.** The interrogative-indefinite pronoun is always found in the shape **mu** *mū* < *mō* < *mā* ("what"). See the discussion of the Interrogative Pronouns.

The sound-change *a* > *o* under stress does not always occur: for reasons of paradigmatic uniformity, certain morphemes are not susceptible to stress-lengthening: (i) The Sg.3. F.of the suffixing form of the verb: NPu *IRT* 901.2 **fela** *felá* ("she made"); (ii) The extending a-vowel of the imperative masculine singular: Pu *Poen.* 1013 **laca** *l^{a}ká* ("go!") and **pursa** *pursá* ("explain!"); (iii) The final *-a* of the subjunctive: Pu *Poen.* 1027P **ierasan** *yer^{ʿa}sán* ("may he shake"); NPu *Poen.* 1027A **iyryla** *yirʿila* ("may he shake") and NPu *Poen.* 939 **lythera** *litīrá* ("let me inquire"). The sound change does not take place in D 6.9, 10 **ab** ("chieftain < father") because the initial a-vowel is characteristic of the full paradigm, which includes forms with different stress, such as *S* 24.2 **abunom** *abūnóm* ("their father").

In an unstressed open syllable, original short *a*, as in Hebrew, was qualitatively long, appearing in Latin-letter and Greek-letter Punic and Neo-Punic always as **a**: NPu *IRT* 879.3 **auo** *awó* [*aawóo*] ("he lived"); *IRT* 879.3 **sanu(th)** *sanūt* [*saanúut*] ("years"); *EH* Greek 1.2 ρυβαθων *ribbatón* [*ribbaatóon*] ("our Lady").

1b. Reflexes of Canaanite *i*

The reflex of original short *i* in a doubly closed unstressed and stressed syllable was qualitatively short *e* or *i:* NPu *IRT* 901.3 **byth** *bit* <*bitt* < *bint* ("daughter"); *IRT* 901.5 **bythi** *bittí* ("her daughter"); *Poen.* 934 **yth** *ʿit* <*ʿint* ("time"); Pu *Poen.* 947P **itt** *ʾitt* ("to/with"), var. 947A **ett** *ʾett.* The sound-change *i* > *a* in a closed and doubly closed syllable, characteristic of Hebrew and Aramaic phonology, is unknown in Phoenician: *IRT* 901.3 **byth** *bit* ("daughter"), not *bat* as in Hebrew; NPu D 6.9 **is** *is* < *ʾiz* ("then"), not *ʾaz* as in Hebrew.

In a closed unstressed syllable, original short *i* was also pronounced *e* or *i* : Pu *Poen.* 1002 **sem** *sem* ("name," unstressed construct form); *Poen.* 948 **sibti** *sibtí* ("his residence"); NPu *Poen.* 934 **ynnochoth** *(h)innokōt* ("here"); *IRT* 877.4 **sem** *sem* ("name," unstressed construct form); *Poen.* 937 **ythem** *ʾittím* ("to/with him").

In a stressed syllable, the vowel was qualitatively longer [*ee*], as suggested by its representation by η in the Pi'el suffixing verb σελημ [*selléem*] in the personal name *CIS* i 119 Εσυμσελημου, and in the Pi'el active participle Μηρρη [*m'erreéḥ*]; perhaps also in Pu *Poen.* 1013 **lec** [*léek*](“go!”). The precise pronunciation of this vowel represented in Latin-letter orthography as **i** or **y** is difficult to determine: NPu *Poen.* 932 **yn** *(h)ín* (presentative particle); *IRT* 827.1 **myth** *mit* (“deceased person”). Unfortunately, in the Latin-letter orthography no means existed to indicate stress-lengthening of this vowel.

1c. Reflexes of Canaanite *u*

In a closed unstressed syllable, the reflex of original short *u* was *o*: *CRAI* 1931 pp. 21-17 **molch** *molk* < *mulk* (“*molk*-sacrifice”). In a closed unstressed syllable the reflex was *u*: Pu *Poen.* 1010 **pursa** *pursá* < *purša* (“explain!”). Original short *u* appears as *u* when stress-lenghthened in an open stressed syllable; the pronunciation was perhaps [*uu*]: Pu *Poen.* 1017A **umir** = 1017P **umer** *'úmer* [*'úumer*]; *cf.* the stress-lengthening in Hebrew. ***'MR*** *'ómer* [*óomer*].

2. The Original Long Vowels and Diphthongs

2a. Reflex of Canaanite *ay*

The Canaanite diphthong *ay* had the reflex *ê:* Pu *Poen.* 940P **bet** *bêt* (“house”); *Poen.* 1142 **mem** *mêm* (“water”); *Poen.* 1027 **samem** *samêm* (“heavens”). Sometimes the contracted diphthong *ê* is found lowered to *ī*: Pu *Poen.* 941A **bit** *bīt* (“house”); Neo-Punic *PBSR* 28 53 no. 6.3 and *Poen.* 931 **byth** *bīt* (“house, building”). The contraction of the diphthong in Phoenician is attested in sources of the 14th century B.C.: EA 144.17 (Beirut) ***ḫe-na-ia*** *'ênayya* < *'aynayya* (“my eyes”); EA 148.12 (Tyre) ***me-ma*** *mêma* (“water”).

2b. Reflex of Canaanite *aw* and *ō*

The diphthong *aw* of Canaanite had the reflex *ô* in Phoenician: D 6.6 **on** *'ōn* < *'awn* (“iniquity”). This vowel fell together with the reflexes of Canaanite *ō*.

In a closed unstressed syllable, the reflex of the Canaanite long vowel *ō* < Semitic *ā* was *ō*: NPu *Poen.* 935 **dobrim** *dōbrīm* (“they say”).

In an open or closed stressed syllable, the vowel was preserved as *ō* or frequently lowered to *ū*: Pu *Poen.* 949, 913 **co** *kō* (“here”) and NPu *Poen.* 934, 936, 939 **choth** *kōt* (“here”) but also Pu *Poen.* 942P **cu** *kū* (“here”). Similarly, Pu *Poen.* 930, 940 **macom** *maqōm* (“city”); *Poen.* 948 **mucom** *m^{u}qōm* (“place, city,” construct form) but also Pu

Poen. 940P **macum** *maqūm*. The lowering of the vowel is very common: Pu *Poen.* 940 **alonut** *ʾallōnūt* < *ʾallōnōt* ("goddesses"); *Poen.* 945 **comu** *kᵒmū* < *kamō* ("like, as"); *Poen.* 940P **macum** *maqūm* < *maqōm* ("city"); NPu*AI* 1 lines 3/4 **arun** *ʾarūn* < *ʾarōn* ("coffin"); *IRT* 828.2 **bur** *būr* < *bōr* ("tomb"); *AI* 2 p. 199 no. 50.2/3 **sanuth** *sanūt* < *šanōt* ("years"); *Poen.* 945 **liful** *lifʿūl* < *lipʿōl* ("to do"), *et passim.*

The vowel is normally *ū* in an open unstressed syllable: Pu *Poen.* 944, 948 **duber** *dūbér* < *dōbér* ("says"); *Poen.* 949 **iussim** *yūtsīm* (***YṢʾM*** "those who are coming out"); NPu. *IRT* 906.4 **buny** *būní* < *bōne* ("builder"); *S* 24.3 **bunem** *būnīm* < *bōnīm* ("builders"); D 5.19 **utseb** *ūtséb* < *yôṣéb* < *hawṣib* ("he erected"), *et passim.* Sometimes, however, the unstressed vowel appears as *ō*, this pronunciation preserved by means of closing the syllable in which the vowel occurs: NPu *Poen.* 999 **donni** *dōn(n)ī* <*ʾadōnī* ("sir"); *cf.* Punic *Poen.* 1141 **done** *dōn(n)ī* ("mein Herr") but also Pu *EH* Gr. 1.1 αδουν *ʾadūn* ("Lord").

2c. Reflex of Canaanite *ī*

Canaanite *ī* was preserved in Phoenician, appearing in Latin-letter orthography as **i e y:** Punic *Poen.* 940 **alonim** *ʾallōnīm* ("gods"); *Poen.* 944 **ce** *kī* ("because"); *Poen.* 940 **is** *ʾīs* ("who") = *Poen.* 943, 949 **es**. Neo-Punic *Poen.* 935 **dobrim** *dōbrīm* ("they say"); *Poen.* 938 **elichoth** *(h)ᵉlīkot* ("hospitality"); *IRT* 828.2 **mythem** *mītīm* ("deceased persons"); *IRT* 879.1 **ys** *ʾīs* ("man"), *et passim.*

2d. Reflex of Canaanite *ū*

Canaanite *ū* was preserved: Punic *Poen.* 1013 **abuca** *ʾabūka* ("your father"); Neo-Punic *Poen.*938 **gubulim** *gᵘbūlīm* ("district, area, region"); *IRT* 893.5 **sebuim** *zᵉbū(ḥ)īm* ("sacrificed ones").

3. *Secondary Vowels*

3a. Anaptyctic *e i a*

In certain nouns of the shape *CVCC*, the final consonant cluster may be opened by means of an unstressed anaptyctic vowel *e i* or, when the final root consonant is one of the series *ʾ h ḥ ʿ r*, by the anaptyctic vowel *a*: Pu *Poen.* 1017 **umir,** var. **umer** *ʾúmir* < *ʾumr* (***ʾMR*** "word"); but *ITH* 4.1/2, 8 **iyra** *yíra(ḥ)* (***YRḤ*** "month"); Diosc. 2.125 ζερα *zéraʿ* and Pliny 24.71 **zyra** *zíraʿ*(***ZRʿ*** "seed"). When the second root letter was a pharyngeal or laryngeal, the anaptyctic vowel was also *a*, although in Neo-Punic the underlying form *CáCaC* of such nouns has been reduced to a monosyllable of the shape *CaC:* **bal** *bal* < *bá'al* in *IRT* 889.2 **bal ars** *bal (ḥ)ars* (***B'L ḤRŠ*** "architect").

Anaptyxis also takes place with the feminine singular noun afformative *-t:* NPu *Poen.* 938 **sibith** *síbit* < *šibt* ("residing"); *ITH* 4.6 **myith** *mí'it* < *mi't* (***M'T*** "one hundred"). Note that in Punic the anaptyctic vowel may be preserved even when suffix pronouns are affixed: Pu *Poen.* 938 **sibithim** *sibitím* ("his residing").

Anaptyxis normally does not take place when the final root letter is the sonorant *l* or *r*: Diosc. 1.128 αλφ *'alp* (***'LP*** "ox"); *IRT* 889.3 **ars** *(ḥ)ars* (***ḤRŠ*** "artisanship"); D 2.14 **ers** *'erṣ* (***'RṢ*** "land"); *Poen.* 937 **irs** *(h)irs* (***ḤRŚ*** "shard"); *CRAI* 1937 **molch** *molk* (***MLK*** "molk-sacrifice").

3b. Furtive *a*

As in Hebrew, a so-called "furtive" a-vowel is heard in a closed syllable with long vowel in which the closing consonant is a laryngeal or pharyngeal: *LA* 1 p. 45 no. 3.2 **lua** *lū^{a}ḥ* < *lūḥ* (***LḤ*** "tablet").

3c. Prothetic Vowels

An initial consonant cluster may be resolved by means of an initial, prothetic vowel: 41.1 ***'Z*** *^{e}zdé* ("this"), a phonetic spelling of ***Z*** in which the prothetic vowel is indicated by *'aleph*; the prothetic vowel appears as **e-** in the Latin-letter spellings Pu *Poen.* 947 **esde** and *Poen.* 940 **esse** of the masculine singular demonstrative pronoun. Compare also the Phoenician phonetic spelling 32.3 ***'ŠNM*** *^{e}snêm* ("two"), with prothetic vowel indicated, and the phonemic spelling 64.1 ***ŠNM.*** As in Hebrew, the initial consonant cluster may be resolved either by means of a prothetic vowel or by the introduction of a short vowel between the two phonemes of the cluster: Phoenician 26 A I 15 ***'GDDM*** *^{e}gdūdīm* ("bands") but Hebrew ***GDWD*** *g^{e}dūd.* The prothetic vowel also appears in foreign words and names beginning with a consonant cluster, *e.g.*, the name Κλεων (Cleon) is found in Punic with prothetic vowel: 66.1 ***'KLYN*** *^{e}Kleon.* In Latin-letter Neo-Punic, the prothetic vowel appears as **i-** or **y-:** *IRT* 855.1 **Ysmun** (***'SMN*** "Esmun") in the personal name **Abd-Ysmun**; *CIL* viii 1562 **Ismun** in the personal name **Abdismunis;** *cf.* Benz p. 279 Υζμουν in the personal name Αβδυζμουνος. Also used are **a-** and **e-**: *CIL* viii 5306 **Asmunis**; Herodt. 2.51 Εσμουνος.

4. *Word-Stress and Vowel Reduction*

Word-stress was, as in Hebrew, on final syllable in most instances. This word-final stress was already characteristic of Phoenician in the Assyrian period, as seen in numerous transcriptions of Phoenician personal and place names in which the word-final stress is indicated by gemination of the final consonant: Tig. Pil. III 67.66 Tyre ***Me-te-en-na*** *Mettén* (personal name); Esar. ii 65 Sidon ***Ma-'-ru-ub-bu*** *Maʿrób* (place-name); Esar. ii 68 ***Ṣi-du-un-ni*** *Ṣīdṓn* ("Sidon"); Tig. Pil. III 9.51 ***Ḫi-ru-um-mu*** *Ḥīróm* ("Hiram"); Esar. iii 16 ***Ab-di--mi-il-ku-ut-ti*** *ʿAbd-milkót* ("Servant of Milkot").

As in other West Semitic languages, vowel reduction in Phoenician was related to word-stress. Word-stress and vowel reduction in Phoenician were essentially identical to Hebrew: full reduction to *zero* or partial reduction, with resultant *shewa.* In Latin-letter Punic and Neo-Punic, simple vocal *shewa* was variously indicated in the orthography by *e i y;* frequently, vocal *shewa* was colored by (assimilated to) a following vowel.

4a. Vowel Reduction in the Verb

4a-1. Propretonic: In the Suffixing Verb
Punic *Poen.* 1023 **sycartim,** var. **sicartim** (***SKRTM*** *sⁱkartím* < *sakartím* "you remember"); *cf.* the same pattern of reduction in Hebrew ***ZKRTM*** */zᵉχartém/*. But, as in Hebrew (as against Aramaic), the pretonic a-vowel of the 1st and 2nd singular forms is not reduced: NPu D 6 **garasth** (***GRŠT*** *garást /gaarást/* "I expelled"); NPu *Poen.* 930 **carothi** (***QR'T*** *qarṓti /qaaróoti/* "I called"); *cf.* Hebrew */qaaráaθii/*; Pu 1017 **iadata** (***YDʿT*** *yadáʿta /yaadáʿtaa/* "you know"); *cf.* Hebrew */yaadáʿtaa/*.

4a-2. Propretonic: In the Passive Participle (Qal-Stem)
Propretonic reductdion is attested in the masculine plural passive participle NPu *IRT* 893.5 **sebuim** s^e*bu(ḥ)īm* < *zabūḥīm* (***ZBḤM*** "sacrificed ones"). Here, the *e*-vowel represents general (non-colored) shewa.

4a-3. Pretonic: In the Suffixing Form (3rd Person) and in the Prefixing Form
Full vowel reduction (to *zero*) occurred in the Sg. 3. F. of the suffixing verb to judge from the Punic and Neo-Punic *IRT* 826.1/2 **fela**

felá < *fe'lá* < *fa'ala* ("she made"). The form *CiCCá* < *CaCaCá*, with full reduction of the vowel, was already characteristic of Tyro-Sidonian Phoenician in 14th century B.C. as indicated by the Tyrian Sg. 3. F. ***ši-iḫ-ta-t*** *šiḥtat* < *šaḥitat* ("it was destroyed") in EA 106.10 ***šiḫtat āl Ṣumur*** ("The city of Sumur has been destroyed"). Contrast the contemporary Jerusalemite form ***a-ba-da-at*** *'abadat* ("it was destroyed") without reduction (EA 288.52). This same reduction explains the Pl. 3. suffixing verb *IRT* 889.2 **felu** *felū* < *fe'lū* < *fa'alū* ("they made").

Pretonic reduction is seen in the Sg. 3. M. Prefixing form Yiph'il Punic **ierasan** *yer'ᵃsán* < *yer'isan* (***YR'ŠN*** "may he shake"), with thematic i-vowel of the Yiph'il reduced to *shewa*, which is colored by the following *a*-vowel. The thematic i-vowel of the causative stem is retained however in the Neo-Punic **iyryla** *yir'ila* (***YR'L*** "may he shake").

4a-4. Propretonic: In the Imperative

Propretonic reduction to vocal *shewa* is evidenced in Pu *Poen.* 1013 **laca** *lᵃká* (***LK*** "go!"), the imperative **lec** with extending a-vowel; the *shewa* is colored by the following *a*-vowel; *cf.* the same reduction in Hebrew *lᵉká (lek + -a)*. Reduction to *zero* occurs in Punic *Poen.* 1010 **pursa** *pursá* (***PRŠ*** "explain!") < *purus + a*; *cf.*.Hebrew ***ŠMRH*** *šomra* < *šᵉmor + a.*

4a-5. Propretonic: In the Active Participle Plural

Full vowel reduction is evidenced in the Neo-Punic Qal active participle masculine plural *Poen.* 935 **dobrim** *dōbrīm* < *dōberīm* (***DBRM*** "they say"). The singular is attested as **duber** *dūbér*in Punic (*Poen.* 944, 946) and **dubyr** *dūbír* in Neo-Punic (*Poen.* 936). It is possible that full reduction of the vowel in the active participle was morphophonemic, for such is the case in the plural active participle of verba IIIgem. in Punic, as seen in *KAI* 37 A 16, B 10) ***GRM*** *gōrrīm* ("sawyers"), the plural of *CIS* I 4873.3 ***GRR*** *gūrér*. Such reduction is characteristic of verba IIIgem. in Aramaic: e.g. ***'LL*** *'ālél* ("enters") but plural ***'LLYN*** *'āllīn.*

4a-6. Propretonic: In the Qal infinitive

Attested in Punic/Neo-Punic *Poen.* 945, 935 **liful** *lif'ūl* < *lifa'ōl* (***LP'L*** "to do") and Punic *Poen.* 948 **limur** *līmūr* < *li'mōr* < *li'amōr* (***L'MR*** "to say"). Compare Hebrew *lif'ōl* (***LP'L***) and *lemōr* (***L'MR***) respectively with the same pattern of vowel reduction.

4a-7. Propretonic: In the Sentence-Name
Attested in the name Benz pp. 401-402 Σοφωνιβα(ς) = **Sophoniba = Suphunibal** (*ṢPNB'L*). The name is the sentence *ṣ°fōni-Bá'l* ("may Baal watch over me!"). The verb *ṣ°fōni* or *ṣ^u^funi* < *ṣafōni* displays reduction of the initial *a*-vowel to *o*-colored shewa. The pattern of reduction does not reflect that of the verb + suffix but that of the name as a whole.

4b. Vowel Reduction In the Noun

4b-1. Pretonic Reduction
Pretonic reduction was characteristic of the construct noun: Pu Diosc. (Vattioni p. 526 no. 51) σιθιλ εσσαδε *s^i^tīl es-sadé* (***ŠTL HŠD*** "shoot of the field," the name of an herb), in which the construct noun *s^i^tīl* < *satīl* displays reduction of the unstressed *a*-vowel to *i*-colored shewa; NPu D 21 **sydy Lybem** *s^i^di Lūbīm* (***ŠD LBM*** "Land of the Libyans," Libya), in which the construct noun *s^i^di* < *sadi* in *s^i^dì-Libīm* displays reduction of the unstressed *a*-vowel to *i*-colored shewa; but also with original vowel retained: D 2.7/8 **sady Lybim**; NPu *EH* Greek 3.2/3 φενη Βαλ *f^e^nè-Bá'l* (***PNB'L*** "Face of Baal," Phanebal, a divine name), in which the construct noun *p^e^nē* < *panē* displays reduction of the unstressed a-vowel; but also with the vowel retained: *EH* Greek 1.2/3 φανε Βαλ *f^a^ne Ba'l*. This same reduction occurs with the noun in construct with the determinative pronoun: Pu *Poen.* 948 **mucom sussibti** *m^u^qōm sissibti* (***MQM ŠŠBTY*** "the place of his residing"), in which the construct noun *m^u^qōm* (=Heb. *m^e^qōm*) < *maqōm* displays reduction of the unstressed *a*-vowel to *u*-colored shewa.

Pretonic reduction is also found in Punic in the preposition *Poen.* 945 **comu** *k^o^mū* and **cumu** *k^u^mū* < *kamū* (***KM*** "like, as" = Hebrew ***KMW*** *k^e^mō*.. The *shewa* is colored by the final *o*/*u*-vowel.

In the noun ***BN*** *bin* ("son") the *i*-vowel may be reduced to *zero* when the noun is preceded and followed by a vowel: **lifnim** *livním* (***LBNM*** "for his son"); *cf.* Hebrew ***LBNW*** /*livnóo*/. This however is exceptional: in all other instances the *i*-vowel of the noun is retained (if perhaps reduced) under these same conditions: *IRT* 828.1/2 **loby[ni]m**; *IRT* 873.3 **libinim.**

4b-2. Propretonic Reduction
Pretonic reduction of an original long vowel is not possible; instead, the vowel of the propretonic syllable is reduced: Pu *Poen.* 937 **heli-**

cot = NPu *Poen.* 937 **elichoth** *h*^{e}*līkót* < *halīkát* ("hospitality"); *cf.* formally Hebrew cognate *h*^{a}*līká*, displaying the same pattern of vowel reduction. Similarly, NPu 178.1 **felioth** *f*^{e}*līót* ("workmanship") and NPu *Poen.* 938 **gubulim** *g*^{u}*būlīm* ("district"), the latter with coloring of the *shewa* by the following *u*-vowel.

4c. *Syncope of Final Unstressed Vowels*

The dropping or suppression of final unstressed short vowels is sporadically attested. For example, the pronoun of the first person, found in *plene* spelling as ***'NKY*** *ʾanīki* (*KAI* 89.2=*CIS* i 6068, Carthage), with the retention of final unstressed *i*-vowel, appears consistently in the contemporary literary Punic of the comedy *Poenulus* (*ca.* 300-200 B.C.) as **anic** or **anec** *ʾanīk,* with syncope of the vowel. The possessive suffix **-*N*** of the first plural is twice attested in Neo-Punic, in both instances without the final *u*-vowel of the etymon *-nu*: *EH* Greek 1.2 ρυβαθων *ribbatón* (***RBTN*** "Our Lady") and D 6.8 **siben** *ṣibʾén* (***ṢB'N*** "our militia").

Syncope was permitted in poetry *metri causa,* for the purpose of maintaining rhythmic flow . For instance, the first person singular of the suffixing verb ended in an unstressed *i*-vowel which, we know, was retained down into the Punic and Neo-Punic periods in literary prose and, indeed, in dramatic speech: Pu *Poen.* 947 **nasote** ("I have brought") = NPu *Poen.* 937 **nasothi**; Pu *Poen.* 940 **caruti** = NPu *Poen.* 930 **carothi** ("I invoke"). However, in a Neo-Punic poem (Dreder 6) composed *ca.* A.D. 350, one finds **garasth** *garast* (***GRŠT*** "I expelled") and **sath** *sat* (***ŠT*** "I made"). In both instances, the verb coincides with an *iamb*; retention of the final unstressed *i*-vowel of -*ti* would have interrupted the perfect iambic rhythm. The verses in which the vowel is suppressed read as follows: D 6.5/6 **Badním garásth is ón** ("From Adnim I expelled the evil fellow.") and D 6.9 **Is áb syth sáth sybý** ("Then did I make that enemy <my> captive."). Also *metri causa,* in the final half verse of the same poem, the final unstressed *a*-vowel independent personal pronoun of the second person masculine singular *ʾatta* is also suppressed: D 6.11 **Ún ath áb[dach]á.**

4d. *Aphetic Vowels*

A well known if infrequently attested feature of Phoenician-Punic in all periods is the loss of the initial unstressed syllable *ʾa-*: Pu *Poen.*

945 **dono** *dōnó* < *ʾadōnó* ("his father"); *Poen.* 999, 1141 **don(n)e** *dōnī* ("my Lord"); NPu *Poen.* 933 **ui** *ūyī* <*ʾa(ḥ)ūyī* ("my brother"); *IRT* 826.2 **uia** *(ḥ)ūya* < *ʾa(ḥ)ūya* ("her brother"); S 24.4 **unom** *(ḥ)ūnóm* <*ʾa(ḥ)ūnóm* ("their brother"). This feature of phonology is well represented also in Phoenician and Punic personal names: ***Ḥ*** *ḥī* < *ʾaḥī* ("my brother") in ***ḤRM*** *Ḥīrom* (31.1); **hi** in the name Himilis (*CIL* v 4919): cf. ι in Ιμυλχ and Ιμιλχωνος (IG 12.279); ***ḫi*** in ***Ḫi-ru-um-mu*** (Hiram, Tiglath. III 9.51), *et passim*. Also **ot** *ōt* <*ʾa(ḥ)ōt* ("sister") in the name ***ʾḤTMLK:*** *CIL* viii 5285 **Otmilc.**. Note however that the initial syllable *ʾa-* is also often preserved: *PBSR* 13 (1957) no. 242 **abunom** *abūnom* ("their father"); *IRT* 826.3 **auia** *a(ḥ)ūya* ("her brother").

CHAPTER THREE

THE INDEPENDENT PERSONAL PRONOUNS

A. *Morphology*

Forms

Sg. 1. C.

FORM A

ʾN *ʾanī*	Ph	*CIS* i 145.1; 49: 29 Ae; *IEJ* 23 p. 120.
[a]ni		NPu D 9.5

FORM B

ʾNK *ʾanīki*	Ph	13.1,5; 14.3; 24.1, 9, 3; 26 A I 1,3,4; 48.1; 4.1, *et passim.*
	Byb	9 A 4; 10.2; 11; 12.2
	Pu	*CIS* i 3785.8; 6000
	NPu	160.3; NP 86.4
ʾNKY	Ph	48.2 alongside ***ʾNK*** in line 1.; 49.6, 13 (graffiti)
	Pu	89.1
anec *ʾanīk*	Pu	*Poen.* 942A, 947, 949, 995, 1142
anech	NPu	*Poen.* 932, 937, 939, 995
anic	Pu	*Poen.* 942P

Sg. 2. M.

ʾT *ʾátta*	Ph	13.3; 14.4, 20
	NPu	Trip. 79.1; Trip. 86.3 (3x)
ath	NPu	D 6.11

Sg. 2. F.

ʾT *ʾatti*	Ph	50.2, 3

Sg. 3. M

FORM A

Hʾ *hū*	Ph	13.6; 14.22, *et passim.*
	Byb	1.2; 10.9
	Pu	*CIS* i 171.7

hu	Pu	*Poen.* 943, 946
u *ū*	Pu	*Poen.* 1010
	NPu	*Poen.* 936

FORM B

H'T	Byb	4.2

Sg. 3. F.

H' *hī*	Ph	40.2, *CIS* i 94.2
	Byb	10.13
	Pu	78.4
HY	NPu	130.3
y *ī*	Pu	*LA* 1 p. 45 no. 4.5; *PBSR* 28 p. 53 no. 5.11

Pl. 1. C

FORM A

NḤN *naḥnu*	Ph	14.12

FORM B

'NḤN *'anaḥnu*	Ph	14.16, 17

Pl. 2. M.

'TM *'attim*	NPu	163.1

Pl. 3. M.

HMT	Ph	14.11, 22; 24.13
	Pu	*CIS* i 5510.10, 11
	NPu	*RES* 669.5

Pl. 3. F.

HMT	Ph	43.5

Comments

Sg. 1. ***'NK*** (*plene:* ***'NKY***): No direct evidence exists for the pronunciation of the Phoenician pronoun, but it is reasonable to think it was *'anīki* (with penultimate stress) as in Punic. The vocalization of the Punic form is readily inferable from the 3rd cent. B.C. Latin-letter spellings **anec** and **anic** and from the Neo-Punic spelling **anech**. All indicate (i) that the *ō*-vowel of the etymon *'anōki* had been replaced by the *ī*-vowel of the short form *'anī*; and (ii) that the stress was on the penultimate syllable, seen in the syncope of the final unstressed *i*-vowel in the Punic and Neo-Punic. The final *i*-vowel was retained however in the Punic-letter spelling of the pronoun into the Neo-Punic period.

The short form *ʾanī* of the pronoun was rare: it is attested *ca.* 1200 B.C. in an archaic inscription from Nora in Sardinia (*CIS* i145) and in the late Roman period in a Neo-Punic tombstone from the Tripolitanian hinterland although the latter example is problematic. It may occur in a graffito from Egypt, but this is perhaps merely a scribal error for ***ʾNK***. Also suspect is the putative example in the Goblet inscription (*IEJ* 23 p. 120) since it is by no means evident that the inscription is Phoenician. However, in spite of the rarity of its epigraphic occurrences, the pronoun must have been current in the language, which fact only can account for its having influenced through analogy the shape of the normative Phoenician-Punic first person singular pronoun *ʾanīki.*

Sg. 2: The only direct evidence for the pronunciation of the singular pronouns of the second person is the Latin-letter spelling **ath** of the masculine, with apparent syncope of the final a-vowel indicating penultimate stress. On the basis of this evidence, the Phoenician was perhaps *ʾátta,* with stress on the initial syllable. However, Neo-Punic **ath** occurs in a poetic verse in iambic trimeter, raising the possibility that the absence of the final *a*-vowel was perhaps *metri causa*; for in this same poem occur other examples of intentional dropping of final vowels for the purpose of achieving perfect rhythm. If so, the vocalization of the Phoenician may well have been *ʾattá,* as in Hebrew.

No evidence exists for the pronunciation of the second feminine singular pronoun. However, in light of the fact that Phoenician and Punic appear to preserve the final unstressed i-vowel of the second feminine singular suffixal pronoun *-ki,* as indicated by the *plene* spelling -***KY***, the second feminine singular independent pronoun may have been pronounced *ʾatti,* although as in the case of the masculine the position of the word-stress is unclear.

Sg. 3: The pronunciation of the masculine and feminine singular pronouns as *hū* and *hī* respectively is based on good evidence: for the masculine, the 3rd cent. B.C. Latin-letter Punic **hu** and later Neo-

Punic **u;** for the feminine, for the Neo-Punic *plene* spelling ***HY*** and Latin-letter **y**.

Archaic Byblian masculine ***H'T*** is difficult to explain. There are two possibilities: (i) it is the oblique form of the third person pronoun, the singular counterpart of Tyro-Sidonian third person plural pronouns (masculine and feminine) ***HMT.*** Archaic Byblian does possess the subject-case third masculine singular pronoun ***H'***; (ii) the form is perhaps to be analyzed as ***H'*** with the archaic enclitic particle *-ti*, attested in the 14th century B.C. several times in the Amarna letters with the Canaanite interrogative pronoun in the expression *miya-ti anāku* ("Who am I?"). On this enclitic particle, see C.R. Krahmalkov, *JSS* 14 (1969), 201-204.

Pl. 1: The pronoun ***'NḤN***, twice attested in the Esmunazor inscription, corresponds to Hebrew *'anaḥnu* and was no doubt pronounced in the same way. In line 12 of the same inscription, in the form of a textual error, the aphetic form ***NḤN*** is also attested: 14.12 ***K 'NK {NḤN} NGZLT BL 'TY*** ("I [we] was snatched away not at my time."); this form corresponds to Hebrew ***NḤNW*** *naḥnu* (Genesis 42:11; Exodus 16:7; Numbers 32:32; Lamentations 3:42; Siloam inscription). The evidence, although meager, suggests that both forms existed in Phoenician, as in Hebrew.

Pl. 2: The masculine ***'TM*** alone is attested. There is no direct evidence for its pronunciation; but the shape can be reconstructed with reasonable confidence: the inflectional morpheme of the second masculine plural of the suffixing verb in Phoenician was vocalized *-tim*, this datum suggesting that the pronunciation of ***'TM*** may have been *'attím*. The second feminine pronoun is not recorded, but it is plausible that it, too, was ***'TM*** *'attím;* this may be inferred perhaps from the fact that in Phoenician the plural pronouns of the third person had fallen together under the masculine form ***HMT.*** One need also observe that in Middle Hebrew the masculine and feminine forms of the pronoun of the second plural had fallen together under the common form ***'TN*** *'attén* (M.H. Segal, *Grammar of Mishnaic Hebrew*, par. 70).

Pl. 3: The masculine and feminine fell together under the common form ***HMT,*** in origin the oblique (dative/accusative) form of the masculine plural. The coalescence of the masculine and feminine independent pronouns is consistent with the coalescence of the third plural masculine and feminine suffixal forms under the masculine form ***-M***. The pronunciation of the pronoun ***HMT*** is not known, and it is therefore not entirely clear if the masculine and feminine had fallen together fully in pronunciation or if there existed a minimal difference in vocalization between the two that marked gender.

B. *Syntax and Usage*

1. *Expressing the Subject of a Non-Verbal Sentence*

1a. Non-Verbal Sentence with Nominal Predicate

1a-1. Word Order: Subject – Predicate in an Independent (non-Subordinate) Clause

As the subject of a non-verbal sentence with nominal predicate, the independent personal pronoun may either precede or follow the nominal predicate.

CIS i 145 ***'N P'L[. . . S]LT ḤṬ[M],*** "I am Pa'ol [-DN, a mi]ller of fine wheaten flour."

17.2 ***'NK 'BD'BST BN BDB'L,*** "I am Abdubast son of Bodbaal."

24.1 ***'NK KLMW BR ḤY',*** "I am Kilamuwa son of Hayya."

26 A I 1/2 ***'NK 'ZTWD HBRK B'L 'BD B'L,*** "I am Aztwadda, he whom Baal has blessed, the servant of Baal."

54.1 ***'NK ŠM BN 'BD'ŠTRT 'ŠQLNY,*** "I am Sem son of Abdastart the Ascalonite."

40.2 ***H' ŠT 57 L'Š KTY,*** "It (year 31 of Ptolemy) is year 57 of the nation of Kition."

43.5 ***HMT L'M LPṬ ŠNT 33,*** "It (*lit.*, they=year 11 of Ptolemy) is year 33 of the nation of Lapethos."

Pu 78.4/5 ***[H]' 'BN 'RKT BKRŠ B'LḤMN,*** "It (the stone) is a tall stele with the figure of Baalhammon."

1a-2. Word-Order: Predicate – Subject in an Independent (non-Subordinate) Clause

14.12 ***YTM BN 'LMT 'NK,*** "I was an orphan, the son of a widow."

Pu *Poen.* 995A **Anno bin Muttumbal leAdrumit anec** = *Poen.* 995P **Anno byn Mytthumbal leAdremeth anech,** "I am Hanno son of Muttumbal of Hadrumetum."

NPu 72 B 4 ***WB'L ḤRŠ H' BTM,*** "He himself was the master architect."

D 9.1/5 **Yriraban byn Isichuar [i]s ys bAbar Timsiuch [a]ni,** "I am Yriraban son of Isichuar, a soldier from the Trans-Timsiuch."

1a-3. Word-Order: Predicate – Subject Obligatory in a Conditional or Causal Clause

RES 922.2 *[']M MLK H' 'M [. . .],* "Whether/if he is a king or whether/if [he is . . .]"

Byb 10.9 ***K MLK ṢDQ H'***, "For he is a good king."

NPu *LA* no. 4.5 **chi ur Sorim y,** "For she is the light of the Tyrians."

1b. The Subject of a Non-Verbal Sentence with adverbial Predicate

With sentence-initial locative adverb *hen*, *hinne* and *hinnokōt* ("here"):

Pu *Poen.* 946 **Hen hu Acharistocle,** "Acharistocles lives here." *Literally,* "He is here, Agorastocles."

NPu *Poen.* 936 **Innochoth u Agorastocles,** "Agorastocles lives here." *Literally,* "He is here, Agorastocles".

Byb 2.2/3 *HNY B'LK TḤT ZN,* "I, your king, am here, at the bottom of this <shaft>."

2. *Expressing the Subject of a Verbal Sentence*

2a. Subject of Prefixing Form A Present/Future

2a-1. Word Order: Pronoun – Verb

The use of the independent personal pronouns with the prefixing forms of the verb (the reflexes of Canaanite *yaqtulu, yaqtula, yaqtul*) is optional. In some instances, the use of the pronoun is clearly for the purpose of placing emphasis on the subject of the sentence, rather than on the predicate. Prefixing Form A is the reflex of Canaanite *yaqtulu.*

Byb 1.2 ***WH' YMḤ SPRH LPP ŠBL,*** "If he shall erase its inscription, his royal robe shall be torn."

48.2/3 ***'NKY LRBTY L'LM 'DRT 'S 'LM 'ŠTRT WL'LNM 'Š'L [TB]RK 'Y[T 'B'T B]NY,*** "I request of my Lady <and> of the great goddess Isis <and of> the goddess Astarte and of the gods: Bless he my four sons!."

Pu *Poen.* 1141 **Al. Anec este mem,** "No!. *I* shall drink water!" *Obs.* This statement is the rejection of the invitation **neste ien neste**

dum et, "Let us drink wine! Let us drink the blood of the vine!" The speaker places emphasis on what *he* will do at the banquet.

2b. Subject of Prefixing Form B and Prefixing Form C Cohortative

2b-1. Word Order: Pronoun-Verb or Verb-Pronoun

Prefixing Form B is the reflex of Canaanite *yaqtul,* Prefixing Form C of Canaanite *yaqtula.* The pronoun as subject of the Prefixing Form may precede or follow the verb.

Pu *Poen.*949 **Anec l-itor bod es iussim limin co,** "Let me inquire of these men who are coming out from here." = NPu *Poen.* 939 **Bod i(ly) a(nech) l-ythera ymu ys lomyn choth iusim.**

NPu *Poen.*932 **L-iphoc anech yth byn ui iaed,** "I would get my brother's only son."

2c. Subject of Suffixing Form Past Perfective

2c-1. Word Order: Pronoun-Verb

In a simple declarative statement that is an independent (non-subordinate) clause, past perfective action is often expressed by the Suffixing Form (*qatalti, qatalta, qatol*). In Classical Phoenician literary usage, this form of the verb, when used to express the Past Perfective, is syntactically restricted to non sentence-initial position. This is to say, the Suffixing Form must be preceded by another part of speech (other than the conjunction *W-*). One part of speech that enables the use of this form with Past Perfective tense-reference is a preceding independent personal pronoun. When the independent pronoun is found with the Suffixing Form, its use is therefore often merely to enable the use of the Suffixing Verb as Past Perfective. However, frequently the pronoun is also used for the purpose of providing emphasis upon the subject of the sentence rather than on the predicate.

Byb 4.2/3 ***H'T ḤWY KL MPLT HBTM 'L,*** "It was *he* who rebuilt all the ruined temples hereabouts." *Obs.* Here, emphasis is placed on the subject of the sentence, hence perhaps the use of the oblique form of the pronoun.

14.12 ***K 'NK {NḤN} NGZLT BL 'TI,*** "I was snatched away not at my time."

24.13 ***W'NK TMKT MŠKBM LYD WHMT ŠT NBŠ KM NBŠ YTM B'M,*** "But *I* took the *mškbm* by the hand, and they felt (about me) as an orphan feels about a mother." *Obs.* In this statement, the speaker (King Kilamuwa) contrasts his attitude and actions towards the *mškbm* (a lower class of society) to that of his predecessors, who "treated the *mškbm* like dogs!"

Pu *Poen.* 943/44 **Hu neso bin us esse,** "He was made the son of (*i.e.*, he was adopted by) this man."

Pu *Poen.* 947 **Itt esde anec nasote hers ahelicot,** "With him I shared a shard of hospitality."

NPu *Poen.* 937 **Ythem anech nasothi li yth irs aelichoth sith,** "With him I shared this shard of hospitality."

2c-2. Obligatory Inverted Word Order: Suffixing Form Consecutive – Pronoun

The so-called "consecutive" of the Suffixing Form is syntactically restricted in a simple independent clause to follow the main (first) verb of the clause; if the consecutive form has an independent pronoun as its subject, the pronoun may not intervene between it and the main verb, but must follow the consecutive form.

Kition 4/5 . . . ***WNṢḤT BKL 'BN WB'ZRNM HPPYM WYṬN'T 'NK . . . 'YT HTRPY 'Z,*** " . . . and I defeated all my enemies and their Paphian allies, and so I did I erect this *tropaion*."

43.12/14 ***KM HDLT HNḤST [Z K]TBT WSMRT BQR. . . WP'LT 'NK 'LT [HMQDŠ} . . . 'PDT BKSP,*** "So, too, did I inscribe this bronze plaque and nail it to the wall, and I made for the sanctuary an ephod of silver."

Pu *CIS* i 5510.10 ***WYLK RBM 'DNB'L BN GRSKN HRB WḤMLKT BN ḤN' HRB 'LŠ WTMK HMT 'YT 'GRGNT WŠT [H]MT ŠLM,*** "Generals Idnibal son of Gisco the Great and Himilco son of Hanno the Great proceeded at dawn, and they seized Agrigentum, and they (the Agrigentines) made peace."

2c-3. Obligatory Inverted Word-Order: Suffixing Form – Pronoun in a Causal Clause

RES 1213.5/6 ***K ŠM' H' QL,*** "<He presented this statue to his Lord Rasap-Alahiota>, because He heard his voice."

2d. Subject of an Active Participle

2d-1. Word-Order: Pronoun – Participle

The independent personal pronoun as subject of an active participle may precede or follow the verb.

Byb 11 ***B'RN ZN 'NK BTN'M. . . ŠKBT,*** "I, Bitnoam, lie in this coffin."

Byb 13.1 ***WKN HN 'NK ŠKB B'RN ZN,*** "And so here do I lie, in this coffin."

13.1/3 ***'NK TBNT . . . ŠKB B'RN Z,*** "I, Tibnit, lie in this coffin."

13.5 ***KL MNM MŠD BLT 'NK ŠKB B'RN Z,*** "Nothing of value but for me lies in this coffin."

2d-2. Word-Order: Participle – Pronoun

14.3 ***WŠKB 'NK BḤLT Z,*** "And I lie in this coffin."

Byb 9 A ***BMŠKB ZN 'Š ŠKB 'NK BN,*** "In this resting-place in which I lie."

2e. Subject of Infinitive Absolute Past Perfective

2e-1. Obligatory Word Order: Infinitive – Pronoun

The Infinitive Absolute with following independent personal pronoun expressed the past perfective action; the infinitive was syntactically restricted to sentence-initial position and personal pronoun, as its subject, restricted to follow the infinitive directly. Examples of this periphrastic tense are many; a few only are cited here.

24.8 ***WŠKR 'NK 'LY MLK 'ŠR,*** "I hired against him the king of Assyria."

26 A I 3/4 ***YḤW 'NK 'YT DNNYM,*** "I kept the Danunians alive."

26 A I 11/12 ***WŠT 'NK ŠLM 'T KL MLK,*** "And I made peace with every king."

26 A 9 ***WBN 'NK HQRT Z,*** "And I built this city."

Byb 10.2/3 ***WQR' 'NK 'T RBTY B'LT GBL WŠM' [H'] QL,*** "I called my Lady Baalt of Byblos, and she heard my voice."

Pu *Poen.* 942/3 **Iulec anec cona, alonim balim, bane becor Bals[. . .],** "I brought here, O proprietary gods, my firstborn son Bals[. . .]."

Obs. In Phoenician, several periphrastic tenses and moods (future tense, subjunctive, jussive/optative) are formed with the Infinite Construct. The pronominal subject of the Infinitive Construct is never the independent personal pronouns but always the suffixal pronouns.

2f. Subject of Imperative Form

2f-1. Word-Order: Pronoun – Verb or Verb – Pronoun
The use of the independent personal pronoun with the Imperative Form is entirely optional. The following are instances of this usage.

50.3 ***'T BṬḤ BDBR[Y]***, "Trust thou in my word!"

NPu Trip. 86.3 ***'T Q'M BB'T 'T HKR S W'T KRY KRY 'T HŠD,*** "You keep to the sale agreement! You heed this! And you buy, buy the field!"

NPu D 6.11 **Un ath ab[dach]a,** "Spare thou thy servant!"

3. *Complementing or Emphasizing a Suffix Pronoun*

The independent personal pronoun often follows a suffixal pronoun, complementing it or sometimes lending emphasis.

Byb 10.12/13 ***ŠM 'NK YḤWMLK MLK GBL [TŠ 'T]K 'L ML'KT H',*** "Place *my* name, Yehawmilk King of Byblos, with your own on that work."

26 A II 5/6 ***WBYMTY 'NK 'ŠT T<L>K LḤDY DL PLKM,*** "<In places that were dangerous in the past, where one used to be afraid to walk the road>, in *my* time a woman walks alone without body-guards."

43.2 ***HSML Z MŠ 'NK YTNB'L,*** "This image is a statue of me, Yatonbaal." *Obs.* In this instance, the independent personal pronouns is required syntactically so that the personal name may stands in apposition to the pronoun *me.* Direct aposition to a suffixal pronoun is not possible.

Pu 79.6/8 ***KL 'Š LSR T-'BN Z BY PY 'NK WBY PY 'DM BŠMY,*** "Anyone who shall remove this stone without *my* expressed personal permission or without the permission of someone expressly authorized by me."

4. *Expressing the Intensive Personal Pronoun (with* ***BT-*** *or* ***BNT-****)*

The intensive independent personal pronoun ("I myself," Latin **ego ipse**) is expressed in Phoenician and Punic by the independent person pronoun followed by the particle ***BT-*** (***BNT-)*** + third person suffix pronoun: NPu 72 B lines 1/4 ***P'L WNDR WḤDŠ 'YT T-GZT ST 'BD'ŠMN BN 'ZRB'L HKHN LRBBTN LTNT 'DRT WHGD WB'L ḤRŠ H' BTM,*** "Abdesmun son of Hasdrubal the Priest made this *gzt* for Our Lady Great Tinnit. He himself was the *gd* (?designer) and architect." *Obs.* The particle ***BT*** *bitt-* and its free variant ***BNT*** *binat-*

were commonly used in Phoenician and Punic after the possessive pronouns to express the reflexive possessives ("my own," "your own," etc.), and with the anaphoric pronoun to express the emphatic anaphoric pronoun ("the same," "the very").

5. *Expressing the Anaphoric Pronoun*

The anaphoric pronoun ("that, the aforementioned") is expressed by the independent personal pronoun of the third person standing in apposition to the noun. The definite article is optional with the noun and normally not used with the pronoun although in Punic one instance is recorded.

5a. The Noun Carries the Definite Article

13.6 ***'L 'L TPTḤ 'LTY W'L TRGZN K T'BT 'ŠTRT HDBR H',*** "Do not, do not open it [my coffin], and do not disturb me; for that act would be an abomination to Astarte."

14.22 ***YQSN HMMLKT H' WH'DMM HMT,*** "They [=the holy gods] shall cut off that king and those persons <who shall violate this tomb>."

5b. The Noun Does Not Carry the Definite Article

14.9/10 ***LQSTNM 'YT MMLKT 'M 'DM H',*** "They (the gods) shall cut off that king or that commoner."

Pu 79.10/11 ***WŠPṬ TNT-PNB'L BRḤ 'DM H',*** "Thinnith-Phanebal shall condemn that person."

NPu *PBSR* 28 53 no. 5.10/11 **Felu tabula y bud bannom,** "That tablet was made (*lit.*, they made) by their son."

5c. The Pronoun Carries the Definite Article

Pu *Poen.* 944/946 **Fel . . . et cil comu con liful alt banim a-u,** "He did everything for that son of his as he was to do <for him>." = NPu *Poen.* 935/36 **Fel yth chyl ys chon ythem liful yth binim,** "He did everything for his son that he was to do for him."

6. *Expressing the Emphatic Anaphoric Pronoun (with* ***BT-*** *or* ***BNT-****)*

The emphatic anaphoric pronoun ("the/that very, the/that same;" *cf.* Latin **isdem**) was expressed by the anaphoric pronoun followed by the particle ***BNT-*** with third singular suffix pronoun ***-Y.*** This same particle is that used with the possessive pronouns to express the reflexive possessive ("his own," Latin **suus**). One example of the emphatic anaphoric pronoun is attested: Kition lines 1/3 ***BMṢ'NM 'BN W'ZRNM HPPYM L'GD LN MLḤMT B[YM]M [x] LYRḤ ZYB ŠT 1 LMLKY . . . WYṢ' 'LN[M MḤ]NT 'Š KTY L'GD LM MLḤMT BMQM 'Z BYM H' BNTY,*** ("When our enemies and their Paphian allies came to do battle with us on day [x] of the month of Zib in year 1 of my reign, the army of the people of Kition went forth against them to do battle with them at this place on that same day [***BYM H' BNTY***].")

7. *Proleptic*

The independent personal pronoun of the third person is used as the grammatical subject of a sentence anticipating the logical subject, normally a personal name, which stands in apposition. The suffixal pronouns of the third person are also use in this manner. An instance of the proleptic independent pronoun occurs in Punic in *Poen.* 946: **Ys duber ci hen hu Acharistocle,** ("I am told that Acharstocles is [lives] here."). = NPu 936 **Ys dubyr ch'innochoth u Agorastocles.** In this sentence, the pronoun **hu** ("he") is the grammatical subject; **Acharistocle/Agorastocles,** which stands in apposition to the pronoun, is however the logical subject of the sentence. Translated literally, the sentence reads: "I am told that he is (lives) here, Acharistocles/Agorastocles."

CHAPTER FOUR

THE SUFFIXAL PRONOUNS

I. Possessive

A. *Morphology*

Forms

Sg. 1. C.

FORM A

-Ø *-ī*	Ph	Old Tyro-Sidonian: 24.3 ***ʾB*** *ʾabī* ("my father," nom.); 24.3 ***ʾḤ*** *ʾaḥī* ("my brother," nom.) Cyprus: 43.2 ***MŠ*** *mesī* ("statue of me"); 43.16 ***ŠRŠ*** *sursī* ("my stock")
	Byb	10.3,8 ***QL*** *qōlī* ("my voice," acc.), ***ŠM*** *semī* ("my name")

FORM B

-Y *-ī* < *-ya*	Ph	Old Tyro-Sidonian: 24. 5 ***ʾBY*** *ʾabī* ("my father"), spelling reflecting earlier *ʾabīya.*
	Byb	Byblian: 10.3,7 ***RBTY*** *rabbatī,* spelling reflecting earlier *rabbatiya* ("my Lady"); 10.5,14 ***PTḤY*** *pittūḥī* ("my engraving"), spelling reflecting earlier *pittūḥiya*

FORM AB

-Y *-ī*	Ph	14.14 ***ʾMY*** *ʾammī* ("my mother") (nom.); 26 C IV 18 ***ŠMY*** *semī* ("my name," acc.) *et passim.*
-e	Pu	*Poen.* 1141 **bene** ("my son," var. **bane**); *Poen.* 1141 **done** ("monsieur")
-i	Pu	*Poen.* 943, 1141 **silli** ("my")

FORM C		
-i *-yī*	NPu	*Poen.* 933 **ui** *(ḥ)ūyī* ("my brother")
FORM D		
-*Y* *-ay*	Ph	EA 144.17 nominative ***ḫe-na-ya*** *ʿênayya* ("my eyes"); 43.11 ***ḤYY*** *ḥayyay* ("my life"); 48.3 ***BNY*** *banay* ("my sons")
Sg. 2. M.		
-*K* *-ka*	Ph	47.2; Umm el-Amed 13.1, 14.2 ***ʿBDK*** ("thy servant")
	Byb	2.2 ***BʿLK*** ("thy lord"); 3.4 ***MGŠTK*** ("your half")
	Pu	82.1 ***ʿBDK*** ("thy servant")
-*Kʾ*	Pu	*cf.* the object pronoun in ***YṢRKʾ*** ("may he protect thee!") in the personal name *CIS* i 598.1 ***PM YṢRKʾ***
-ca	Pu	*Poen.* 1002 **abuca** ("thy father")
-cha	NPu	D 6.11 **ab[dach]a** ("thy servant")
Sg. 2.F.		
-*K* *-kī*	Ph	50.1 ***ʾḤTK*** ("thy sister")
-*KY*	Pu	*CIS* i 3777.1 ***ʿBDKY*** ("thy servant")
Sg. 3. M.		
FORM A		
-Ø *-o*	Ph	24.15, 16 ***RʾŠ*** *rūso* ("his head," acc.); 38.2, 39.3, 41.6 ***QL*** *qūlo* ("his voice," acc.)
	Byb	1.2 ***ŠBL*** *sabīlo* ("his robe," nom.); cf. Byb 12.3 ***L*** *lo* ("for him") and 12.4 ***YBRK*** *yibroko* ("may he bless him!")
-ʾ		Pu 68.5 ***QLʾ*** *qūlo* ("his voice," acc.); 78.6 ***ṢDʾ*** *ṣiddo* ("his back"); *CIS* i 5945.2 ***ʾŠTʾ*** *ʾisto* ("his wife," nom.)
	NPu	119.8 ***QLʾ*** *qūlo* ("his voice," acc.)
-ʿ	NPu	*EH* 4.4 ***QLʿ*** *qūlo*
-ʿʾ	NPu	*CIS* i 3709.6 ***QLʿʾ*** *qūlo*
-ω	Pu	175.4 κουλω ("his voice," acc.); cf. βαραχω ("he blessed him")
-o	Pu	*Poen.* 944 **dono** ("his father," nom.)

	NPu	*PBSR* 28 no. 6.1 **[by]no** ("his son," nom.); ditto no. 7.2 **[XX]utho** ("its . . .s," acc.)

Byblian

-H *-á-hu* (with the accusative) 1.2 ***SPRH*** *siprahu* ("his inscription," acc.);10.14 ***YSDH*** *yasōdáhu* ("its base," acc.)

FORM B

-Ø *-i* < *-ih(u)*	Ph	Umm el-Awamid 6.1/2 ***ʾŠT*** *ʾisti* ("his wife," gen.)
	Pu	61 B 3/4 (Malta 6th cent.) ***ʾDN*** *ʾadūnī* ("his Lord"); *IFPCO* Sard. 35 (Cagliari, 4th cent.) ***ʾŠT*** *ʾisti* ("his wife," gen.); *CIS* i 5522.2/3 ***ʾDN*** *ʾadūni* ("his master," gen.)
-Y	Ph	35.2/3 ***ʾŠTY*** *ʾisti* ("his wife," gen.)
	Pu	111.4 ***MLKY*** *molki* ("his reign," gen.)
	NPu	Trip. 79.4 ***ʾŠTY*** *isti* ("his wife," gen.)
-ʾ	NPu	1x: 119.4 ***MʾKNʾ*** ("its platform," gen.)
-ʾY	NPu	1x: 118.1 ***BTʾI*** *bêtī* ("his temple," gen.)
-η	Ph	174.6 αμαθη ("his female slave," gen.)
-ε	Ph	174.8 αφδε ("his slave," gen.)
-e	NPu	*IRT* 889.1 **byne** ("his son," nom.)
-i	Pu	*Poen.* 948 **sibti** ("his residing," gen.)

Punic, with excrescent ***-m***

-M *-im*	Pu	84.1 ***BNM*** *binim* ("his son," gen.); *EH* 27.2 Pu ***NDRM*** *nidrim* ("his vow," gen.) *et passim*
	NPu	123.3; Trip. 79.3 ***ʾMM*** *ammim* ("his mother," gen.); 124.2, 126.11 ***MLKTM*** ("his property," gen.); 120.3, 121.2 ***TʾRM*** ("his money," gen.); 129.3 ***TṢʾTM*** ("his expense," gen.); 126.8 ***ʾBTM*** *abūtim* ("his ancestors," gen.), *et passim*
-em	NPu	*IRT* 877.5/6, 893.3/4 **banem** ("his son," gen.); *AI* 1 p. 233 line 2; *IRT* 893.2/3 **bythem** ("his daughter," gen.); *cf. Poen.* 935, 937 **ythem** ("to/for him")
-im	NPu	*IRT* 892.4/5 **allonim** ("his god," gen.);

		IRT 873.3 **binim** ("his son," nom.); *Poen.* 936 **binim** ("his son," gen.); *AI* I line **lyfnim** ("for his son"); *Poen.* 938 **sibithim** ("his residing," gen.); *IRT* 828.2 **ysthim** ("his wife," gen.)
Byblian		
-H *-í-hu*		12.2 ***MŠPṬH*** *mispaṭíhu* ("his imperium," gen.) and ***MLKH*** *molkíhu* ("his reign," gen.)
-W *-iw* < *-í-hu*		5.2, 6.2, 7.4 ***ʾDTW*** *ʾadatiw* ("his Lady," gen.); 9 B 4 ***ʾRNW*** *ʾarōniw* ("his coffin," gen.); 10.15 ***ZRʿW*** *zarʿiw* ("his seed," gen.)
FORM C		
-Y *-yo*	Ph	19.3 ***ʿBDY*** *ʿabdêyo* ("his servants"); 34.1 ***ʾBY*** *abūyo* ("his father"); 47.2 ***ʾḤY*** *ʾaḥūyo* ("his brother"); ***ḤYY*** *ḥayyêyo* ("his lifetime")
-Yʾ	NPu	Trip. 79.2 ***ʾBYʾ*** *ʾabūyo* ("his father")
-o	NPu	*IRT* 865 **baneo** *banêyo* ("his sons"); IRT 877.6 **buo** *būyo* ("his father")
Byblian		
-H *-hu*		1.1 ***ʾBH*** *ʾabīhu* ("his father," gen.)
-W *-w*		4.5; 6.3; 7.5; 10.9 ***ŠNTW*** *šanōtêw* ("his years"); 10.9 ***YMW*** *yamêw* ("his days")
Sg. 3.F.		
FORM B		
-Ø *-a*	Ph	26 A II 10 ***ŠM*** *sema* ("its name")
	Byb	Not recorded
-ʾ	Pu	*CIS* i 371.6; 395.5 ***QLʾ*** *qūla* ("her voice")
-ʿ	NPu	*CIS* i 2005.5 ***QLʿ*** *qūla* ("her voice")
-ʿʾ	NPu	*CIS* i 3599.4 ***QLʾʿ*** *qūla* ("her voice")
Byblian:		
-H *-a´h(a)* (with acc.)		Byb 10.6 ***MSPNTH*** *mispantáha* ("its ceiling," acc.)
FORM B		
-Y *-i*	Ph	26 A II 3 ***MBʾY*** *mabōʾi* ("its [the sun's] setting"); 29.2 ***RBTY*** *ribbati* ("her Lady");

		40.4 ***BNY*** *beni* ("her son," gen.)
-i	NPu	*IRT* 901.5 **bythi** ("her daughter," gen.)
Byblian		
-H *-í-ha* (with gen.)		Byb 10.4 ***ḤṢRH*** *haṣerîha* ("her temple," gen.)
FORM C		
-Y *-ya*	Ph	not recorded
***-Y*ʿ**	NPu	*JA* 1917/2, 14.4f **ʿ*ṢMY*ʿ** *ʿaṣmêya* ("her bones")
-ia	NPu	**auia** *a(ḥ)ūya* ("her brother"); **uia** *(ḥ)ūya* ("her brother")
Pl. 1. C.		
FORM A		
-N *-en*	Ph	**ʾ*DNN*** ?*ʾadūnon* ("our Lord": nom.)
-en	NPu	D 6.8 **siben** *ṣibʾen* ("our militia") nom.)
FORM B		
-N *-on*	Ph	47.1 **ʾ*DNN*** ?*adūnen* ("our Lord," gen. case)
	Byb	12.3 **ʾ*DNN*** ("our Lord")
-ων	Pu	*EH* Greek1.2 ρυβαθων *ribbaton* ("our Lady," gen.)
FORM C		
-N *-n*	Ph	After a vowel: **ʾ*BN*** *ʾabūn* ("our father") Kition **ʾ*BN*** *ʾêbên* ("our enemies")
Pl. 2. M.		
-KM *-kom*	Pu	*CIS* i 2632 **ʾ*MTKM*** *ʾamatkom* ("your maidservant"); *CIS* i 5690 **ʿ*BDKM*** *ʿabdᵒkom* ("your slave")
-chom	NPu	*Poen.* 933 **mysyrthochom** *miṣṣirtᵒkom* ("your protection"); *Poen.*933 **syllochom** *sillokom* ("your")
Pl. 3. M.		
FORM A		
-M *-om*	Ph	Umm el-Awamid 6.1/3 ***BNM*** *binom*

		("their son"); Lapethos 3.4 ***MSPRM*** *misparom* ("their number"); Lapethos 3.5 ***MŠQLM*** *misqalom* ("their weight") *et passim*
	NPu	*Karthago* 12 p. 54 IV 2 ***ŠMʾTM*** *semūtom* ("their names," nom.)
-om	NPu	*PBSR* 28 53 no. 5.9 **bynom** *binom* ("their son," nom. case)
FORM B		
-NM *-om*	Ph	26 A I 18 ***LBNM*** *libb^{e}nom* ("their heart"); 34.5 ***NḤTNM*** *naḥt^{e}nom* ("their rest"); 48.3 ***ʾMNM*** *ʾamm^{e}nom* ("their mother")
-nom	NPu	*PBSR* 28 53 no. 5.11 **bannom** *bannom* ("their son," gen. case)
FORM C		
-NM *-nom*	Ph	40.5 ***ʾBNM*** *ʾabūnom* ("their father")
-NʾM	NPu	Trip. 77.2 ***ʿBNʾM*** *ʾabūnom* ("their father")
-NHM	NPu	142.4 ***ʾBʿNHM*** *ʾabūnom* ("their father")
-nom	NPu	S 24.2 **abunom** ("their father"); S 24.4 **unom** ("their brother")
Byblian		
-HM *-hem*		*cf.* 10.6 ***ʿLHM*** *ʿalêhem* ("upon the")

Pl. 3. F.

FORM A		
-M	Pu	*RES* 1543.4/5 ***MSPRM*** *misparam* ("their number," antecedent: ***KTBT***)
FORM B		
-NM	Ph	*cf.*14.20 ***LKNNM*** *lakūn^{e}nam* ("that they might be")
FORM C		
-NM	Ph	*cf.* 14.19 ***YSPNNM*** *yasapnunam* ("we annexed them")

1. *General Comments*

Sg. 1. C.: In early Phoenician orthography, the pronoun of the first singular used with the noun in the nominative and accusative cases

(Form A) was *-ī* (written **-Ø**); its complementary form (Form B) *-ya* (written ***-Y***) was used with the noun in the genitive case, affixed to the case-vowel *-i* of the genitive. Later in the history of the language, the final unstressed *a*-vowel of *-i-ya* was lost, with the result that the suffixal pronoun came to be pronounced *-íy (-ī),* coalescing in pronunciation with Form A. In the Tyro-Sidonian Phoenician of the Kilamuwa Inscription (*ca.* 825 B.C.) and the inscriptions of Cyprus, as well as in Byblian Phoenician, these original (historical) spellings were retained even though Forms A and B were pronounced alike. In Standard Phoenician, however, common form *-ī,* used with all cases of the noun, came to be written *plene* as ***-Y.*** Form D, used with the masculine plural noun, was pronounced *-ay*; the pronoun was the reflex of the etymon *-ayya,* historically, Form B affixed to the inflectional morpheme of the masculine plural noun.

Form C *-yī* was a Neo-Punic innovation in analogy to postvocalic *-yo* ("his") and *-ya* ("her"). It is possible that in Neo-Punic this form may have replaced *-ay* with masculine plural nouns, that is, Neo-Punic may have had *banêyī* ("my sons") rather than *banay*, in analogy to *banêyo* ("his sons") and *banêya* ("her sons"); but there is no written evidence of this development.

Sg. 2. M. and Sg. 2. F.: The masculine was *-ka* and the feminine *-ki*, both retaining their final unstressed vowels, as the Latin-letter spellings and *plene* spellings indicate.

Sg. 3. M.: Form A *-o* is the reflex of earlier *-oh* < *-ú-hu,* the archaic suffixal pronoun *-hu* affixed to the nominative case-vowel. Byblian Phoenician *-o* is of the same origin. However, in Tyro-Sidonian, Form A was early extended to use with the noun in the accusative case; this was not the case in Byblian, which retained a distinctive form ***-H*** (*?-a´-hu*) for the accusative: Byblian nominative case 1.2 ***ŠBL*** *sabīlo* ("his robe," *cf.* 12.3 ***L*** *lo* "for him") but accusative case 1.2 ***SPRH*** *siprahu* ("his inscription") and 10.14 ***YSDH*** *yasōdahu* ("its foundation").

Form B *-i* is the reflex *-ih* < *-í-hu,* the archaic suffixal pronoun *-hu* affixed to the genitive case-vowel; compare Aramaic *-eh* ("his"). The original spelling of Form B was **-Ø;** while this spelling does occur, it is extremely rare, early replaced by the *plene* spelling ***-Y*** *-i*, which was normative of Phoenician orthography. In Punic and Neo-Punic, this pronoun appeared in the free variant ***-M*** *-im*, with excrescent *-m*, perhaps to distinguish the third person *-i* from the first person singular *-ī*, which was identical in pronunciation.

In contrast to Tyro-Sidonian, Byblian Phoenician retained archaic *-íhu* of the Sg. 3. M. suffixal pronoun; the form appears in the archaic Byblian inscriptions as ***-H*** *-íhu:* 1.2 ***MŠPṬH*** *mispaṭíhu* and ***MLKH*** *molkíhu*); and later in Byblian, with elision of intervocalic *h*, as ***-W*** *-iw:* 5.2, 6.2, 7.4 ***'DTW*** *'adatiw* ("his Lady," gen.); 9 B 4 ***'RNW*** *'arōniw* ("his coffin," gen.); 10.15 ***ZR'W*** *zar'iw* ("his seed," gen.). This same pronoun is found in archaizing Hebrew in the genitive form ***MYNHW*** *mīnéhu* ("its species") in Genesis 1:12 (*bis*), which co-occurs with the nominative form ***ZR'W*** *zar'ó* ("its seed") in the same verse.

In late Neo-Punic, Form B, used in Standard Phoenician and Punic exclusively with the noun in the genitive case, came to be used with the noun in the nominative case as well: *IRT* 889 **binim** and *IRT* 906.1 **byne**, both "his son" in the nominative case. Form B also came to be extended to other parts of speech, where Form A had been used, *e.g.*, in the late Neo-Punic preposition *Poen.* 935, 937 **ythem** *ittim* ("for him; with him").

Form C, the form of the pronoun used after a vowel, is historically Form A *-o* extended to postvocalic use, with the *yod* as intervocalic glide. The spelling of Form B is therefore of an entirely different origin from that of Form C ***-Y*** *-yo*, in which the *yod* is purely consonantal. Byblian Phoenician, in contrast to Tyro-Sidonian, retained the earlier forms of the postvocalic pronoun: (i) after a long vowel ***-H*** *-hu* as in archaic 1.1 ***'BH*** *'abīhu* ("his father," gen.) = Tyro-Sidonian ***'BY*** *'abūyo*; but later ***-W*** *-w* as in the object pronoun in 10.9 ***TḤWW*** *ṭeḥawwew* < *teḥawwehu* ("may she give him long life!") and 12.4 ***YḤWW*** *yeḥawwew* < *yeḥawwehu* ("may he give him long life!") = Tyro-Sidonian ***YḤWY*** *yeḥawweyo;* and (ii) with the masculine and feminine plural noun ***-W*** *-êw* < *-êhu*, as in 4.5, 6.3, 7.5, 10.9 ***ŠNTW*** *šanōtêw* ("his years") and 10.9 ***YMW*** *yamêw* = Tyro-Sidonian ***YMY*** *yamêyo.*

Tyro-Sidonian differs from Byblian in the morphology and suffixal pronouns affixed to the feminine plural noun. Byblian, like Hebrew, affixes the pronouns used with the masculine plural noun to the feminine plural afformative *-ōt* (Tyro-Sidonian *-ūt)*: 4.5, 6.3, 7.5, 10.9 ***ŠNTW*** *šanōtêw* ("his years"). Tyro-Sidonian, however, follows the pattern of Aramaic in affixing the simple suffixal pronoun directly to the afformative *-ūt:* Trip. 27.8 ***M'S' 'BTM*** ("the meritorious deeds of his ancestors," *'abūtim*); *S* 7.1/2 **[centen]ari [umiga]lutho** ("the fortified farmhouse and its towers").

Sg. 3.F. Form A *-a* is perhaps from earlier *-ha*, affixed directly the noun stem. It was used, like its masculine singular counterpart *-o*, with the noun in the nominative and accusative cases. Although the Byblian form used with the nominative is not recorded, it was perhaps the same as the Tyro-Sidonian, as indeed was the case with the Sg. 3. M. suffixal pronoun *-o*. The Byblian form used with the accusative case was ***-H*** *-ha*, affixed to the accusative case-vowel a: 10.6 ***MSPNTH*** *mispantáha* ("its ceiling").

Form B *-i* is the reflex of earlier *-ih* < *-í-ha;* the spelling ***-Y*** is like the masculine *plene*. Form B in Byblian was *-ha*, affixed to the genitive case-vowel *i:* 10.4 ***BHṢRH*** *biḥaṣeríha* ("in her temple"); this same form, ***-H*** *-ha*, was used after vowels in Byblian: 10.6 ***ʿMDH*** *ʿammūdȇha* ("its columns").

Form C *-ya* was in origin Form A extended to postvocalic use by means of the intervocalic glid *-y-*. Byblian retained the archaic Phoenician postvocalic pronoun ***-H*** *-ha*, attested in 10.6 ***ʿMDH*** *ʿammūdȇha* ("its columns") = Tyro-Sidonian ***ʿMDY*** *ʿammūdȇya*.

Pl. 1. C.: The precise shape of this suffixal pronoun is uncertain. Two vocalized examples occur: *-en*, affixed to the noun in the nominative case: NPu D 6.8 **siben** *ṣibʾén* ("our militia"), nom. and Pu *EH* Greek 1.1 ρυβαθων *ribbatón* ("our Lady," gen.). Perhaps Phoenician originally used *-on* with the nominative and accusative cases and *-en* for the genitive; but subsequently in the dialects the one or the other came to be specialized for all cases, *-en* in Tripolitanian Punic as in Hebrew, but *-on* in the more westerly dialect of ancient Algeria. Both examples do however attest to the loss of the final short unstressed *u*-vowel of the etymon *-nu*.

Pl. 2. M. The pronoun was *-kom*, the reflex of Canaanite *-kumu* as indicated by NPu *Poen.* 933 **mysyrthochom** *miṣṣirtᵒkóm* ("your protection") and **syllochom** *sillokóm* ("your"). The Pl. 2. F. pronoun is not attested; however, in light of the existence in Phoenician of a common-gender form ***-M*** for the Pl. 3. M. and Pl. 3. F., it is possible that the feminine of the second plural was also ***-KM*** although the feminine may have been vocalized differently from the masculine.

Pl. 3. M. Form A *-om* is the reflex earlier *-am* < *-ámo*, with the typical sound-change *a* > *o* under stress. The pronoun was used with the noun in the nominative and accusative case. The pronoun is early attested in Canaanite, appearing in the 14th century B.C. in EA 252.25/26 *taḥtamo* ("at their feet"). Byblian Form A is not attested but it was probably the same as the Tyro-Sidonian although used only with the noun in the nominative case; the Byblian form used with the noun in the accusative was probably ***-HM*** *-hem*; this form actually occurs in archaizing Hebrew in the genitive form ***MYNHM*** *mīnehem* ("their species") in Genesis 1:21 (*cf.* the genitive form ***MY-NHW*** *mīnéhu* ["its species"] in vs. 12).

Form B *-nom* is in origin Form A extended to use with the noun in the genitive case, affixed to the genitive case-vowel *i* by means of intervening "euphonic" *-n-*; it is the same as Form C, the postvocalic form of the pronoun. Although not recorded, Byblian Form B was probably ***-HM*** *-hem,* affixed to the genitive case-vowel i.

Form C *-nom* is in origin Form A *-om* extended to postvocalic use by means of intervening "euphonic" *-n-*. Byblian retained the archaic pronoun ***-HM*** *-hem* in this use, as attested in the preposition 10.6 ***ʿLHM*** *ʿalêhem* ("upon them"). Thus Tyro-Sidonian had ***SSNM*** *sūsênóm* ("their horses") and ***ʾBNM*** *ʾabūnóm* ("their father") but Byblian ***SSHM*** *sūsêhém* and ***ʾBHM*** *ʾabūhém*. Byblian appears to reflect an earlier stage than the Tyro-Sidonian of the morphology of this and other suffixal pronouns.

Pl. 3. F. Form A is attested as ***-M*** and Form B as ***-NM.*** They are outwardly identical to the corresponding masculine forms although it is possible that masculine and feminine were differentiated by contrastive vocalization, the masculine pronounced *-om* and the feminine *-am,* the *o/a* contrast being that characteristic of the third singular suffixal pronouns *-o* (masculine) and *-a* (feminine). The Byblian forms are not recorded but may be postulated to have been ***-N*** (?) with the nominative case and ***-HN*** with the genitive and accusative case and after vowels.

2. *Comments on the Complementation of Forms of the Third Person*

2a. Form A

Form A is affixed directly to the stem of a singular masculine noun (ending in a consonant) and to the feminine singular noun in ***-T*** in the nominative (subject) case or accusative case. In Tyro-Sidonian Phoenician, it is affixed directly to the plural feminine noun afformative ***-T*** when the noun is in the nominative (subject) case.

2a.-1. Nominative (Subject) Case

Lapethos 3.5 ***[N]R ḤRṢ MŠQL 10,*** "A lamp of gold: its weight (*misqalo*) is 10-weight."

43.14 ***'PDT BKSP MŠQL KR 100 W- 2***, "An ephod of silver: its weight (*misqala*) is 102 *kr.*"

Lapethos 3.4 ***QB'M ŠLKSP MSPRM 6 MŠQLM PRS WḤMŠM WḤMŠT WRB' DR(KMNM),*** "Cups of silver: their number (*misparom*) is 6, their weight (*misqalom*) is one *prs* and fifty-five and one quarter dr(achmas)."

Umm el-Awamid 6.1/3 ***Z MṢBT . . . 'Š ṬN' LM BNM,*** "This is the stele that their son (*binom*) erected to them."

Pu 66:1 ***MZBḤ NḤŠT MŠQL LṬRM M'T 100,*** "An altar of bronze: its weight (*misqalo*) is one hundred 100 liters."

Pu *RES* 1543.4/5 ***KTBT MSPRM 'RB'M WŠLŠ***, "Letters <of the alphabet>: their (3.F.Pl.) number [*misparom*] is forty-three."

Pu *CIS* i 5702.2/5 ***'ZRM 'ŠT 'Š NDR 'ZRB'L . . . WBT',*** "Hasdrubal and his daughter (*bitto*) vowed this female sacrificial victim."

Pu *Poen.* 944/5 **Fel dono . . . et cil comu con liful alt banim au,** "His father did everything for that son of his as he was to do."

NPu 172.4 ***Ṭ'N' T-HM'Š ST BN' ḤMLKT,*** "His son (*bino*) Himilco erected this statue."

NPu *PBSR* 28 p. 53 no. 6.1/3 **Fla(bi) Nahia u[by]no Husudru [b]a[no] byth,** "Flavius Nahia and his son (*bino*) Husudru built <this> house."

Byb 1.2 ***WH' YMḤ SPRH LPP ŠBL,*** "And if he should erase its inscription (*siprahu,* acc.), his royal robe (nominative: *sabīlo)* shall be *rent.*"

NPu **Bynom Mrausyn aurys,** "Their son Mrausyn was the artisan."

2a.-2. Accusative (Direct Object) Case

26 A III 13 ***YMḤ ŠM 'ZTWD BŠ'R Z WŠT ŠM***, "He shall erase the name of Aztwadda from this gate and place his own name (*semo*) <upon it>."

41.6 ***K ŠM' QL***, "For He heard his voice (*qūlo*)."

26 A II 9/10 ***WBN 'NK HQRT Z WŠT 'NK ŠM 'ZTWDY***, "I built this city and named it (*lit.,* made its name [*sema*]) Aztwaddiya."

14.22 ***WYQSN . . . H'DMM HMT WZR'M,*** "And they shall cut off those persons and their seed (*zarʿom*)."

47.3/4 ***K ŠMʿ QLM,*** "For He heard their voice (*qūlom*)."

2b. Form B

Form B is affixed to the noun in the genitive case. A noun is in the genitive case when (i) governed by a preposition or (ii) by the particle ***ʾYT*** or (iii) by a construct noun:

2b.-1. Noun Governed By Prepositions

29.1/2 ***ʾRN [Š]N MGN. . Lʿ ŠTRT ʾDTY,*** "She presented <this> ivory box to Astarte, her Lady (genitive: *ʾadatī*)."

32.2/4 ***MZBḤ ʾZ . . . ʾŠ YTN . . . LʾDNY LRŠP,*** "He presented this altar to his Lord (genitive: *liʾadūni)* Rasap."

33.3 ***LRBTY*** (genitive: *ribbati*) ***LʿŠTRT,*** "To his Lady, to Astarte."

34.1/3 ***MṢBT ʾZ ʾŠ YṬN ʾRŠ . . . LʾMY*** (genitive: li*ʾammi*), "Aris erected this stele for his mother."

40.5 ***HNDR ʾŠ KN NDR ʾBNM . . . LʾDNNM LRŠP,*** "The vow that their father had made to their Lord *(liʾadōninom)*, to Rasep."

174 Αφεθενναυ υιος Αφεσαφουν νεσε οθ αμαθη λεσαθ λαφδε Μα[. . .], "Abdthennau son of Abdsaphoun gave his female slave as wife to his slave (genitive: *lʿabde*) Ma[. . .]."

Byb 7.1/4 ***QR ZBNY . . . LBʿLT GBL ʾDTW,*** "Wall which he built for Baalt of Byblos, his Lady (genitive: *ʾadatiw*)." *Cf.* 5.2, 6.2.

NPu *PBSR* 28 53 no. 5.10/11 **Felu tabula y bud bannom,** "That tablet was made by their son (genitive: *bannom*)."

2b.-2. Noun Governed by ***ʾYT (ʾT)***

Byb 10.15 ***TSRḤ HRBT BʿLT GBL ʾYT HʾDM Hʾ WZRʿW,*** "The Lady Baalt of Byblos shall make stink that person and his seed (genitive: *zarʿiw*)."

48.3 ***[TB]RK ʾY[T ʾRBʿT B]NY . . . WʾT ʾMNM,*** "Bless my four sons and their mother (*ʾamminom*)."

174.1/6 Αφεθεννα υιος Αφεσαφουν νεσε οθ αμαθη λεσαθ λαφδε Μα[. . .], "Abdethenna son of Abdesaphoun gave his female slave (*ʾōt ʾamate)* as wife to his slave Ma[. . .]."

Punic generally does not follow this pattern. However, a few examples do occur, but the accusative particle used is ***ʾYT:***

Pu *EH* 27-PU lines 1/2 ***ŠLM BDʿŠTRT BN BDʾŠMN ʾYT NDRM BT BʿLʾDR,*** "Bostar son of Bodesmun fulfilled his vow (*ʾet nidrīm*) in the temple of Baaladdir." *Obs.* The reading ***NDRʾ*** in *KAI* is erroneous.

Pu *CIS* i 3604 ***TŠMʿʾ ʾYT QLM,*** "Hear ye his voice (*ʾet qūlīm*)!"

2b.-3. Noun Governed by a Noun

40.4 ***BN BNY,*** "The sons of her son *(banê binī).*"

NPu 123.2/3 ***ʾḤT ʾMM,*** "The sister of his mother (*ʾaḥōt ʾammīm*)."

34.5 ***MŠKB NḤTNM,*** "Their resting-place *(miskab naḥtᵉnom).*"

NPu Trip. 27.8 ***LPY MʾSʾ ʾBTM WMʾSM BTM,*** "Because of the meritorious deeds of his ancestors (genitive: *missê(?) ʾabūtim*) and <because of> his own merit (genitive: *missim*)."

2c. B-Suffixes with the Nominative Case in Late Neo-Punic

In late Neo-Punic, the B-pronouns of the third masculine singular was extended to use with nouns in the nominative case:

IRT 906.1/2 **Thanubda ubyne Nasif felu myntsyfth [l]yMasauchan byn Iylul,** "Thanubda and his son (**byne** = ***BNY***) Nasif made <this> stele for Masauchan son of Iylul."

IRT 889.1/2 **Flabi Dasama uybinim Macrine felu centeinari,** "Flavius Dasama and his son (**binim** = ***BNM)*** built <this> fortified farmhouse."

Compare the extension of the suffix pronoun **-em** to the preposition **ythem** ("for him; with him") in *Poen.* 935, 937.

This development did not take place however with the B-pronouns of the third person plural: these continued to exhibit the pattern of complementation characteristic of Standard Phoenician and Punic, *viz.*, *-om* with the nominative and accusative, *-nom* with the genitive: *PBSR* 28 53 no. 5.9/10 **Bynom Mrausyn au[r]ys,** ("Their son [*binom*, nominative] was the engraver."); but lines 10/11 of the same inscription: **Felu tabula y bud bannom,** ("That tablet was made by their son [*bannom*, gen.])."

B. *Syntax and Usage*

1. *Expressing Personal Relationship*

14.15 ***ʾMY ʾMʿŠTRT,*** "My mother, Amastart."

14.22 ***HʾDM HMT WZRʿM,*** "Those persons and their descendants."

Pu *Poen.* 943/44 **Iulec anec cona . . . bane becor Bals[illem],** "I brought here my firstborn son Balsillem." *Et passim.*

IRT 889.1/2 **Flabi Dasama uybinim Macrine felu centeinari,** "Flavius Dasama and his son Macrinus built <this> fortified farmhouse." *Et passim.*

2. *Expressing Possession*

Byb 10.3/6 ***P‘L ’NK . . . H‘RPT Z’ W‘MDH . . . WMSPNTH,*** "I made this portico and its columns and its ceiling."

24.6 ***WKL ŠLḤ YD LL[Ḥ]M,*** "Each one extended his arm to fight <me>."

Pu 78.5/5 ***PNY MB’ HŠMŠ WṢD’ MṢ’ HŠMŠ,*** "His face was to the West and his back to the East." *Et passim.*

3. *Expressing the Reflexive Possessive (with* ***BT-*** *or* ***BNT-****)*

Phoenician possessed a reflexive possessive pronoun (*cf.* Latin **suus** or **ipsius** "his own") expressed by the suffixal possessive pronoun followed by the particle ***BNT*** (or its free variant ***BT***) + Form B of the third person suffixal pronoun. The particle ***BT*** had the shape *bitt-*; and ***BNT*** the shape *binat-*. The etymology of the particle is obscure but in its syntax and use it may be properly compared with the Egyptian particle **d̲s** in the common Middle Egyptian construction **pr.f d̲s.f** "his own house" (GEG §36).

18.3/4 ***’YT HŠ‘R Z WHDLHT ’Š L P‘LT BTKLTY BNTY,*** "I built this gate and its doors at my own expense."

The expression "at one's own expense," employing the reflexive possessive, is common in the Neo-Punic inscriptions. Neo-Punic normally employs the variant form ***BT*** of the particle in this particular expression although it also knows ***BNT***, used in free variation with ***BT***, in other formulaic expressions (see below):

NPu 120.3/4, 121.2 ***BT’RM BTM P‘L W’YQDŠ,*** "He built and dedicated <this> at his own expense." The corresponding Latin of each of these passages has **de sua pecunia faciendum coeravit idemque dedicavit.**

NPu 124.1/2 ***T-‘MDM <YTN> WT-HM‘Q’M YGN WT-HMḤZ RBD LMBMLKTM BTM,*** "He presented the columns and roofed the structure and paved the forum at his own expense." The corresponding Latin has **Columnas cum superficie et forum de sua pecunia dedit.**

NPu 126.10/11 ***MZBḤ WP’DY P‘L LMBMLKTM BTM,*** "He built the altar and the podium at his own expense." The corresponding Latin has **Podium et aram de sua pecunia facienda curavit.**

NPu 118.1/3 ***M'Š 'LM ŠP'R ST WMQDŠ Bt'Y WḤ'RP'T 'Š B'N' W'YQDŠ . . . BTṢ'TM BTM,*** "This beautiful statue of the god and the sanctuary of his temple and the portico that he built at his own expense."

Trip. 67.1/2 ***'YDḤ . . . BTṢ'TM BTM T-HBT ST,*** "He enlarged this building at his own expense."

NPu 129.1/3 ***BN' W'YQDŠ T-'KSNDR' WT-'RPT ST BTṢ'TM BTM,*** "He built and dedicated the excedra and this portico at his own expense."

NPu Trip. 79.5 ***NPL'*** (sic) ***BTṢTY BTY,*** "It (the tomb) was built at his own expense."

Obs. The expression "at his own expense" is also found in the abbreviated form ***BTM***, with ellipsis of the preceding noun:

NPu 132.1/2 = Trip. 68.1/2 ***L'LY'N' P'L' BTM,*** "Laelianus made it at his own <expense>."

Trip. 73.1/2 ***SKST' BN DYDR' P'L' BTM,*** "Sextus son of Diodorus made it at his own expense."

NPu *IRT* 828.2/3 **Bur y-soth . . . fel bai{a}em bithem,** "He built this tomb during <his> lifetime at his own <expense>."

The reflexive possessive is found frequently in Punic and Neo-Punic outside the formula "at his own expense":

NPu Trip. 27.7/9=126.7/9 ***LPNY 'DR' 'LPQY W'M 'LPQY LPY M'S' 'BTY WM'SM BTM YTN' L'BD BṢP'T KL Ḥ'T,*** "The Senate of Lepcis and the people of Lepcis granted him the right to make use of the broad purple stripe always because of the merits of his ancestors and his own merit (***M'SM BTM***)." The corresponding Latin has **cui Primo Ordo et populus ob merita maiorum eius et <merita> ipsius lato clavo semper uti concessunt.**

The most common context in which the reflexive possessive occurs in Punic and Neo-Punic is child sacrifice; in the statement of offering, the pronoun serves to indicate that the child sacrificed was of the parent's own flesh, that is, his natural child, not a child substituted for his own. In this formula, we find both forms ***BNT*** and ***BT*** in free variation:

Pu *CIS* i 5507 ***LRBT LTNT-PNB'L WLB'LḤMN 'Š NDR BDMLQRT BN ḤN' BN MLKYTN BN BŠRY BNTY TBRK',*** "It was to the Lady Thinnith-Phanebal and to Baalhammun that Bomilcar bin Hanno bin Milkiathon vowed <this> son of his own flesh. Bless thou him!"

Pu *CIS* i 5741.1/6 ***LRBT LTNT-PNB'L WL'DN B'LḤMN 'Š NDR ḤN' BN MGNM 'ZRM 'ŠT BŠ<R>M BNTM,*** "It is to the Lady Thinnith-Phanebal and to the Lord Baalhamun that Hanno bin Magonim vow <this> female sacrificial victim of his own flesh."

Pu 105.3 ***MLK 'DM BŠ'RM BTM,*** "A human sacrifice of his own flesh."

Pu 106.1 ***MLK 'DM BŠRM BTM,*** "A human sacrifice of his own flesh."

Pu 107.4 ***MLK 'DM BŠRM BN'TM,*** "A human sacrifice of his own flesh."

Pu *EH* 38.1/3 ***MLK 'DM . . . BŠ'RM BNTM,*** "A human sacrifice of his own flesh"

Pu *EH* 45.1/3 ***NDR . . . BŠRM BNTM,*** "The vow <of a child> of his own flesh."

4. *Expressing the Objective Genitive*

43.2 ***HSML Z MŠ 'NK YTNB'L,*** "This image is a statue of me, Yatonbaal."

43.7 ***MŠ PN 'BY BNḤŠT,*** "The bronze bust of my father."

5. *Expressing the Dative (Indirect Object)*

14.6 ***'P 'M 'DMM YDBRNK,*** "Even if people shall speak to you . . ."

Pu 89.2 ***'T<N>K 'NKY MṢLḤ 'YT 'M'ŠTRT W'YT 'MRT,*** "I, Meslih, commend (give) to you Amastarte and Omrith."

6. *Expressing the Subject of the Infinitive Construct in Periphrastic Tenses and Moods*

In Phoenician and Punic, the Infinitive Construct ***L-P'L*** *lip'ūl* was used to form periphrastic tenses (future) and moods (subjunctive, jussive/optative). If the subject of the infinitive was pronominal, it was the suffixal pronouns that were used to express the pronominal subject of the periphrastic tense or mood, not the independent personal pronouns. Frequently, the suffixal pronominal subject of the infinitive expresses the grammatical subject of the sentence, the logical subject of which follows in apposition.

6a. Subject of the Infinitive Construct Future Indicative

14.9/10 ***LQSTNM 'YT MMLKT 'M 'DM H',*** "They (the holy gods) shall cut off <that> royal person or that commoner." *Obs.* This same sentence is repeated at the end of the inscription (line 22) with the prefixing form 3plural used to express the future indicative: ***YQSN HMMLKT H' WH'DMM HMT,*** "They shall cut off that royal person or those commoners."

6b. Subject of the Infinitive Construct Jussive/Optative

26 A III 4/5 ***LTTY B'L KRNTRYŠ . . . L'ZTWD 'RK ḤYM,*** "May Baal-KRNTRYS give (*lit.,* may he give [*latittī*], Baal-KRNTRYS) long life to Aztwadda!" *Obs.* The pronominal subject of the verb is "proleptic": it is the grammatical subject of the sentence, anticipating the logical subject Baal-KRNTRYS. The proleptic pronominal subject is non-obligatory.

6c. Subject of the Infinitive Construct Subjunctive

14.19/20 ***YSPNNM 'LT GBL 'RṢ LKNNM LṢDNM L'LM,*** "We annexed them (Dor and Joppa) to the territory of <our> land that they might belong (*lakūn^{e}nom*) to the Sidonians forever."

18.3/6 ***'YT HŠ'R Z WHDLHT 'Š L P'LT . . . LKNI LY LSKR,*** "I built this gate and its doors to be (*lit.,* that it might be: *lakūni*) a memorial to me."

19.9/10 ***KM 'Š BN 'YT KL 'ḤRY [HMQDŠ]M 'Š B'RṢ LKNNM L[M LSKR],*** "Just as they built all the other sanctuaries in the land to be (*lit.,* that they might be: *lakūn^{e}nom*) a memorial to themselves."

26 A I 17/18 ***BN 'NK ḤMYT BMQMM HMT LŠBTNM DNNYM BNḤT LBNM,*** "I built protective fortresses in those places that the Danunians might live (*lit.,* that they might live [*lasibt^{e}nom*], the Danunians) with peace of mind." *Obs.* The pronominal subject of the subjunctive is "proleptic."

26 A II 11/15 ***BNY 'NK . . . LKNY MŠMR L'MQ 'DN WLBT MPŠ,*** "I built it (the city) to be (*lit.,* that it might be: *lakūnī*) a place of protection for the Valley of Adana and for the House of Mopsos."

7. *Expressing the Subject of the Infinitive* ***B-P'L*** *bip'ūl in a Temporal Clause*

Kition lines 1/2 ***BMṢ'NM 'BN***, "When our enemies came (*lit.*, when they came, our enemies)."

NPu 159.5/5 ***BŠPṬM MSHB' BN YZRM,*** "When MSHB' son of YZRM was suffes (*lit.*, when he was suffes, MSHB' son of YZRM)."

NPu Trip. 79.5/6 ***NPL' BTṢTY BTY BḤYTNM,*** "It (the tomb) was built at his own expense when they (those laid to rest in the tomb) were <still> living."

NPu D 6 **Byrysth[em] Irirachan,** "When he expelled Irirachan."

8. *Proleptic*

8a. Subject of the Infinitive Construct

The suffix pronoun is often proleptic (anticipates a noun), with the nominal subject in appositon. The proleptic pronoun is the grammatical subect of the verb and the noun the logical subject.

Kition lines 1/2 ***BMṢ'NM 'BN,*** "When our enemies came (*lit.*, when they came, our enemies)."

26 A I 17/18 ***WBN 'NK ḤMYT BMQMM HMT LŠBTNM DNNYM BNḤT LBNM,*** "And I built walled fortresses in those places so that the Danunians might live (*lit.*, that they might live, the Danunians) in peace of mind."

26A III 4/5 ***LTTY B'L KRNTRYŠ . . . L'ZTWD 'RK YMM,*** "May Baal-KRNTRYS give (*lit.*, may he give, Baal-KRNTRYS) a long reign (*lit.*, man days) to Aztwadda!"

8b. With Governing Noun in a Construct Chain (Direct Genitive)

It is exceedingly common that the governing noun (*nomen regens*) in a construct chain carries a proleptic pronoun that anticipates the governed noun (*nomen rectum*). The governed noun is normally a personal name:

14.1 ***ŠNT 'SR W'RB' 14 LMLKY MLK 'ŠMN'ZR,*** "Year fourteen 14 of the reign (*lit.*, of his reign) of King Esmunazor."

Pu 111.3/5 ***ŠŠT 'RB'M ŠT LMLKY MSNSN,*** "The forty-sixth year of the reign (*lit.*, of his reign) of Masinissa."

Pu 112.4/6 ***ŠŠT ḤMŠM ŠT LMLKNM MKWSN WGLSN WMSTN'B',*** "The fifty-sixth year of the reign (*lit.*, of their reign) of Micipsa, Gulussa and Mastanaba."

Pu *Poen.* 948 **<Esse> mucom sussibti A(rist)ocle,** "This is Aristocles's place of residence (*lit.*, this is the place of his residence of Aristocles)."

II. Direct and Indirect Object Forms

The object pronouns, direct and indirect, are expressed by means of (i) suffixal pronouns or (ii) independent object pronouns. The more common of these are the suffixal pronouns.

A. *Morphology*

Forms

Sg. 1. C.		
-N *-ni*	Ph	14. ***Y'MSN*** *ya'mosni* ("he remove me"); 18.8 ***YBRKN*** *yibrokni* ("may he bless me!"); 26.3, 12 ***P'LN*** *pa'ōlni* ("he made me"); 26 A II 11 ***ŠLḤN*** *salḥūni* ("they sent me"); 43.15 ***YSKRN*** *yiskorni* ("may he be mindful of me!")
	Byb	10.2 ***P'LTN*** *pa'latni* ("she made me")
-NY	Ph	Rare *plene* ***ḤNY*** *ḥanni* ("may he favor me") in the personal name *RES* 306 ***MLQRTḤNY*** ("Milqart favor me!")
-νι	Pu	σοφωνι ("may he watch me") in the personal name Benz 401 Σοφωνιβας (= ***ṢPN-B'L***, "Baal watch over me!")
-ni	Pu	**anni, hanni** ("may he favor me!") in the personal name Benz 314 **Annibal, Hannibal** (= ***ḤN-B'L***, "Baal favor me!")); **suphuni** ("may he watch me!") in the personal name Benz 401 **Suphunibal** (=Σοφωνιβας)
Sg. 2. M		
-K *-ka*	Ph	14.6 ***YDBRNK*** *yidborūnka* ("they shall speak to thee")
-K'	Pu	rare *plene* spelling in ***YṢRK'*** *yiṣṣorka* ("may he protect thee!") in the personal name

		Benz 176 ***PMY* <*Y*>*ṢRK*'** ("Pumay protect thee!")
Sg. 2. F		
-***K*** -*ki*	Ph	50.3 ***YP'LK*** *yip'alūki* ("may they make thee")
	Pu	89.2 ***'TK*** *'ettekki* < *'ettenki* ("I give to thee")
Sg. 3. M.		
FORM A		
-Ø -*o*	Ph	26 A III 17 ***YS'*** *yissa'o* ("he will put it out"); 32.4, 38.2; 39.3 ***YBRK*** *yibroko* ("may he bless him!")
	Byb	3.4 ***TNḤL*** *tinḥalo* ("you inherit it"); 12.4 ***YBRK*** *yibroko* ("may he bless him")
	Pu	*CIS* i 4945.4 ***QBT*** *qabbato* ("she shall curse him")
-**'**	Ph	84.1; *CIS* i 196.5 ***TBRK'*** *tibroko* ("bless thou him!"); ***ḤN'*** *ḥanno* ("may he favor him") in the personal name (54.2) ***D'M-ḤN'*** (= Δομανω, "May Do'm favor him!")
	Pu	102.4, 103.4, 104.3 ***BRK'*** *barako* ("may he bless him!")
	NPu	Trip. 68.2, 73.2 ***P'L'*** ("he made it")
-ω	Pu	ανω ("may he favor him!") in the personal name (54.2) Δομανω (= ***D'M-ḤN'***, "May Do'm favor him!") *EH* Greek 1.4/5 βαραχω ("may he bless him!")
-o	**NPu**	*AI* 1 p. 233 line 5 **felo** ("he made it"); **anno** ("may he favor him") in the personal name **Annobal** ("May Baal favor him!")
FORM B		
-***Y*** -*yo*	Ph	14.18 ***YŠBNY*** *yûsibnuyo* ("we caused him to dwell")
	Pu	78.1 ***YBRKY*** *yibrokūyo* ("may they bless him!")
-***Y'***	Pu	66.2 ***RPY'*** *rafôyo* ("he cured him"); *CIS* i

		3784.3 ***YQSY'*** *yiqṣeyo* ("he shall cut him off")
	NPu	146.2 ***BNY'*** *banūyo* ("they built it")
Byblian		
-***H*** *-hu*	Arch	1.1 ***ŠTH*** *šatūhu* ("they placed him")
-***W*** *-w*		12.4 ***YḤWW*** *yeḥawwew* ("may he make him live long!");10.9 ***TḤWW*** *teḥawwew* ("may she make him live long!")

Sg. 3. F.

FORM A

-***'*** *-a*	Pu	*CIS* i 3599.4/5; 4746.6 ***BRK'*** *baraka* ("he blessed her")

FORM B

-***Y*** *-ya*	Ph	60.5 ***YṬN'Y*** *yiṭniʾūya* ("they shall erect it")
	Pu	26 A II 11 ***BNY 'NK*** *banōya ʾanīki* ("I built it")

Pl. 3. M.

FORM A

-***M*** *-om*	Ph	14.21 ***YSGRNM*** *yisgirūn-om* ("they will lock them up"); 26 A I 20 ***YRDM 'NK*** *yôridom ʾanīki* ("I deported them"); 26 A I 20 ***YŠBM 'NK*** *yôsibom ʾanīki* ("I settled them"); 47.4 ***YBRKM*** *yibrokom* ("may he bless them!")
	NPu	Trip. 79.1 ***P'LM*** *felom* ("he made them")

FORM B

-***NM*** *-nom*	Ph	14.19 ***YSPNNM*** *yasapnunom* ("we annexed them"); 26 A I 16 ***ŠTNM*** *sattinom* ("I placed them"); 26 A I 20 ***'NTNM*** *ʿinnītinom* ("I defeated them")

Comments

1. *Affixing of the Object Pronouns*

1a. To the Suffixing Form

In the case of the consonant-final suffixing verb, the object pronoun is affixed directly to the final consonant or to a consonant-final inflectional morpheme. Thus, with the 3.Sg.M. ***BRK*** *barok* ("he blessed") Phoenician always follows the pattern of affixing seen in Hebrew ***ŠMRW*** *šᵉmaró (= šamar + o)*: 102.4 ***BRK'*** = *EH* Gr. 1.4/5 βαραχω ("he blessed him"); Trip. 68.2 ***P'L'*** = *AI* 1 p. 233 line 5 **felo** ("he made it"); ***ḤN(')*** = **anno** = ανω ("may he favor him!"). Unknown in Tyro-Sidonian Phoenician and Punic is affixing to the intervening *a*-vowel of *pa'ala* as in Hebrew ***ŠMRHW*** *šᵉmaráhu (= šamara + hu)*. Similarly, in the case of the 3.Sg.M. inflectional morpheme -***T*** *-at,* affixing is direct: *CIS* i 4945.4 ***QBT*** *qabbato* ("she will curse him"). And this is true as well of the affixing of the so-called "heavy" object pronouns beginning with a vowel, such as -***N*** *-ni* ("me"), which is affixed to the consonantal stem without intervening a-vowel: ***ḤN(Y)*** *ḥanni* ("may he favor me" = *ḥan* + *ni*).

When the verb ends in a vowel or vowel-final inflectional morpheme, the B-forms of the third person suffixal object pronouns *-yo* ("him"), *-ya* ("her"), *-nom* ("them") are used: 146.2 ***BNY'*** *banūyo* ("they built it"); 66.2 ***RPY'*** *rafōyo* ("he cured him"); 26 A I 16 ***ŠTNM*** *sattinom* ("I placed them"); 26 A I 20 ***'NTNM*** *'innītinom* ("I conquered them"); 14.19 ***YSPNNM*** *yasapnunom* ("we annexed them"). In Old Byblian, the 3.Sg.M. postvocalic pronoun is -***H*** *-hu:* 1.1 ***ŠTH*** *šatahu* ("he placed him") or *šatūhu* ("they placed him").

1b. Object Pronouns with the Prefixing Forms of the Verb

When the verb ends in a consonant, e.g., 3.Sg.M. ***YBRK*** *yibrok* ("may he bless!"), the object pronouns pronouns are affixed directly to the stem; in the case of the object pronouns of the third person, the A-form *-o* ("him"), *-a* ("her") and *-om* ("them") are used. Thus, in Phoenician-Punic one finds always 32.4 ***YBRK*** (Pu *plene* ***YBRK'*** *yibroko* ("may he bless him/he blesses him"); 84.1 ***TBRK(')*** *tibroko* ("bless thou him!"); 47.4 ***YBRKM*** *yibrokom* ("may they bless them/they bless them"). Byblian Phoenician follows this same pattern of direct affixing: 12.4 ***YBRK*** *yibroko* ("may he bless him!"). One never finds in Phoenician-Punic affixing of suffixes to the intervening vowel *-e-* as in Hebrew ***YŠMRHW*** *yišm^e^réhu*, ***YŠMRH*** *yišm^e^réha*, ***YŠMRM*** *yišm^e^rem*. Direct affixing to the final consonant of the stem, without intervening e-vowel, is confirmed by the affixing of the "hard" suffix 2.Sg.F. ***-K*** *-ki* directly to the final consonant *-n* of the verb ***'TN*** *'etten* ("I give"), with resultant assimilation, in 89.2 ***'TK*** *'ettekki* < *'ettenki* ("I give to thee").

If however the verb ends in a vowel or vowel-final inflectional morpheme, the B-forms of the third person suffixal object pronouns *-yo* ("him"), *-ya* ("her") and *-nom* ("them") are obligatorily: *CIS* i 3784.3 ***YQṢY'*** *yiqṣeyo* ("he shall cut him off"); 78.1 ***YBRKY*** *yibrokūyo* ("may they bless him"). The Middle Byblian form corresponding to Tyro-Sidonian *-yo,* was *-w* < *-hu*: Byblian 12.4 ***YḤWW*** *yeḥawwew* ("may he make him live long!) = Tyro-Sidonian ***YḤWY**** *yeḥawweyo;* and 10.9 ***TḤWW*** *teḥawwew* ("may she make him live long!").

1c. With the Infinitive Absolute

The direct pronominal object of the Past Perfective expressed by the infinitive absolute + subject is always the suffixal pronoun. The manner of affixing is the same as in the case of the finite verbal forms. In the case of the pronouns of the third person, the A-Forms *-o, -a, -om* are affixed directly to the verb stem: 26 A I 20 ***YRDM 'NK*** *yûridóm 'anīki* ("I deported them"); 26 A I 20 ***YŠBM 'NK*** *yûsibóm 'anīki* ("I settled them"). When the infinitive ends in a vowel, the B-Forms are used: 26 II 11 ***BNY 'NK*** *banōya 'anīki* ("I built it").

1d. With the Infinitive Construct

The infinitive construct governed by a preposition is grammatically a noun in the genitive case; therefore, the B-Form of the direct object pronoun must be used: Pu 5510.3 ***WLŠBTY*** *lisabbeti* ("to destroy it"); Pu 5510.6/7 ***LŠLM WLYRḤY*** *lisellem weliyarīḥi* ("to greet and to make him welcome").

B. *Syntax and Usage*

1. *Expressing the Direct Object*

The principal and most often attested function of the suffixal pronoun with the verb is to express the direct object: Byb 10.9 ***WTḤWW,*** ("And may she make him live long!"); 26 A I 19/20

W'NK 'NTNM, ("But I conquered them!"); 40.5 ***YBRKM,*** ("May he bless them!")

Obs. The suffixal pronoun as direct object is used with all forms of the verb, including the infinitive construct: Pu *CIS* I 5510.3 ***[KL 'DM] 'Š LKP 'YT 'MTNT Z WL'KR WLŠBTY,*** ("As for any person who shall overturn this stele or disturb or destroy it [*lšbt-y*]"). However, when the infinitive construct is used to form the periphrastic future tense, the periphrastic subjunctive or the periphrastic jussive/optative, the suffixal pronoun expresses the subject of the infinitive, not the direct object.

2. *Expressing the Resumptive Direct Object*

2a. In a Resumptive Main Clause

The suffixal direct object pronouns are used in resumptive main clauses of sentences to refer back to the subject of the anticipatory clause:

24.11 ***WMY BL ḤZ PN Š ŠTY B'L 'DR,*** "As for him who had never owned a sheep, I made him owner of a flock!"

Pu *CIS* i 3783.5/7 ***WKL 'DM 'Š GNB T-MTNT Z NKST TNT-[P]NB'L,*** "As for any person who shall steal this stele, Thinnith-Phanebal shall cut him off."

Pu *CIS* I 4945.4/6 ***W'Š YRGZ T-MTNT Z WQBT TNT-PNB'L,*** "As for him who shall disturb this stele, Thinnith-Phanebal shall curse him."

2b. In a Relative Clause

The suffixal pronoun may be used to express the direct object of a verb in a relative clause the subject of which is different from the antecedent; the direct object pronoun refers back to the antecedent. This use of the resumptive pronoun is optional.

Byb10.1/2 ***'NK YḤWMLK . . . 'Š P'LTN HRBT B'LT GBL MMLKT 'L GBL,*** "I am Yehawmilk, whom the Lady Baalt of Byblos made king (*lit.*, who she made me king) of Byblos."

NPu Trip. ***B'RM QN'T 'T M' 'Š P'LM M'ṢWK'N,*** "You have acquired the tomb that Masauchan made (*lit.*, that Masauchan made them=it)."

3. *Excursus:*

The Independent Direct Object Pronouns

The direct object pronoun was sometimes expressed in Phoenician by means of the preposition ***ʿLT*** *ʿalt* + suffix pronoun, and in Punic by means of the particle ***ʾT*** *ʾōt* + suffix pronoun:

Phoenician 13.5/6 ***ʾL TPTḤ ʿLTY*** *ʾal tiptaḥ ʿaltêyo,* "Do not open it!".

Punic *CIS* i 6000.1 ***ʾL TŠʾ <ʾ>Tʾ*** *ʾal tissaʾ ʾōto,* "Do not carry it away!"

4. *Expressing the Proleptic Direct Object*

As in the case of all pronouns used the anticipate a noun, the proleptic direct object pronoun is the grammatical direct object of the verb, with the logical direct object following in apposition:

29.2 ***TBRKY BYMY ʾDNN,*** "Bless thou our master during his lifetime!," *lit.*, "Bless thou him (*tibrokīyo*; verb is Sg. 2. F.), our master, during his lifetime."

5. *Expressing the Dative (Indirect Object)*

The indirect object is normally expressed by means of prepositions, such as ***L-, ʿL, ʿLT, LPN*** + affixed suffix pronoun. However, the suffix pronoun affixed directly to the verb may also express the dative:

14.6 ***ʾP ʾM ʾDMM YDBRNK ʾL TŠMʿ BDNM,*** "Even if people tell you <to do it>, do not be persuaded by them!"

Pu 89.2 ***ʾT<N>K ʾNKY MṢLḤ ʾYT ʾMʿŠTRT WʾYT ʿMRT,*** "I, Meslih, commend (give) to you Amastart and Omrith." The Punic corresponds to the Latin **commendo tibi** in inscriptions of the same genre.

CHAPTER FIVE

THE DEMONSTRATIVE PRONOUNS AND THE DEFINITE ARTICLE

I. The Demonstrative Pronouns

A. *Morphology*

Forms

Sg. M.		
Z ^{e}*zdé*	Ph	13.3,5; 14.3,4; 15.1; 16.1; 18.3; 26 A III 8, 15; 58.1, *et passim* Cyprus: Kition: *FK* B 36, F 1.4; Lapethos: 2.2
	Pu	69.18,19; 80.1; 101.1, *et passim.* NPu 140.1
'*Z*	Ph	Sarepta line 1; Marathus line 1 Cyprus: Kition: *FK* A 29.2, A 30.2, F 1.2; Tamassos: 5.3
	Pu	Pyrgi line 1
Z'	Ph	Archaic Cyprus: 30.2,2,3
esde	Pu	*Poen.* 947A
esse	Pu	*Poen.* 940P, 944A
Neo-Punic ***S***-Series		
S *si*		146.1; Trip. 51.3
sy		*S* 24.5; *IRT* 879.1; D 5.19
With excrescent **-t:**		
ST *sit*		118.1; 172.3; Trip. 52.2
sith		*Poen.* 937P, 937; *PBSR* 28 7.3
syth		*Poen.* 930P, 931; D 6.9
Sg. F.		
Z ^{e}*zdō*	Ph	14.4,11; 24.14; 26 A II 9; 60.4,6, *et passim*; Cyprus: Kition: *FK* B 5.1, B 6.1, B 47.2, E 2.2; Lapethos: 3.5
	Pu	69.10, 79.8

	NPu	137.*5*, 141.1,5
ʾ*Z*	Ph	Kition: *FK* A 1.2, B 2.1, B 40.1, B 45.1

Neo-Punic ***S***-Series

Šʾ *sō, sū*	Trip. 40.1
su	D 2.14
With excrescent **-t:**	
ST *sōt*	151.1, 129.1; *CIS* i 152.1, 4
soth	*IRT* 828.2

Sg. Neuter (Late Neo-Punic)

hoc	NPu	*PBSR* 22 1954 lines 3/4

Pl. *ʾílle*

ʾL	Byb	4.3
	Ph	14.22; 40.3
	Pu	81.2,3,4; 137.2,4,5,6; 139.2
ʾLʾ	NPu	130.1; 139.2
ily	NPu	*Poen.* 938
illi	NPu	*Poen.* 938

Comments

The demonstratives entered in the preceding repertory of forms are the Tyro-Sidonian pronouns. The demonstrative pronouns of Byblian Phoenician will be discussed in a subsequent paragraph.

The shape of the masculine singular demonstrative was *ᵉzdé,* that of the feminine singular *ᵉzdō*. The forms ***Z*** and **ʾ*Z*** were merely orthographic variants of the same pronoun, the former the historical (phonemic) spelling, the latter a phonetic spelling indicating the presence of the prothetic vowel with *ʾaleph*. The prothetic vowel, occasioned by the consonant cluster *zd* or *dz* (as Phoenician ***Z*** was articulated), is evidenced in the Latin-letter spellings **esde** and **esse.** The choice of spelling was that of the individual scribe or scribal school. In the inscriptions of Kition, for example, the two spellings occur about the same number of times; and in one inscription they even co-occur (*FK* F 1). The Old Cypriote form ***Z*ʾ** of the masculine singular is yet a third spelling variant; it is unique however in the scribal tradition, occurring three times but in the same inscription.

In Neo-Punic, the ***Z***-Series singular demonstrative pronouns continued to be normative. However, in Late Neo-Punic, the ***S***-Series singular forms of the vulgar language entered the written language, even the literary language. These pronouns show the phonological development *zd* > *s* of the phoneme /z/ and frequently display the optional excrescent *-t*, known also from the late Neo-Punic locative adverb *kōt* ("here"; Phoenician-Punic *kō*). Excrescent *-t*, it need be stressed, is unrelated to the feminine singular inflectional ending *-t;* thus, Late Neo-Punic feminine singular ***ST*** *sōt* ("this") is entirely different historically from Hebrew *zōt* (***Z'T***).

Neuter (inanimate) was expressed by the masculine singular **sy** in Neo-Punic (D 5.19/20); but in this period, the Latinneuter demonstrative **hoc** was borrowed to express neuter (inanimate) with greater clarity.

The plural demonstrative *'ille* was standard in all periods and in all dialects.

B. *Syntax and Usage*

1. *Pronominal Uses of the Demonstratives*

1a. Subject of a Sentence

Umm el-Awamid 6.1 ***Z MṢBT B'LŠMR,*** "This is the stele of Baalsamor."

Umm el-Awamid 7.1/2 ***Z MṢBT SKR B'LYTN,*** "This is the memorial stele of Baalyaton."

Umm el-Awamid 10.1/2 ***Z MṢBT SKR ŠM 'BD'[NT],*** "This is the memorial stele to the name of Abdanat."

Umm el-Awamid 12.1/2 ***Z MṢBT SKR 'SRBRK,*** "This is the memorial stele of Osiribarok."

Pu *Poen.* 948 **<Esse> mucom sussibti,** "This is the place of his residence."

NPu *Poen.* 938 **Ily gubulim lasibithim,** "These are the environs of his residence."

1b. Direct Object of a Verb

31.1 ***'Z YTN LB'L LBNN 'DNY,*** "He presented this to Baal of Lebanon, his Lord."

NPu Trip. 86.3 ***'T HKR S,*** "You heed this!"

NPu D 5.19/20 **Utseb sy lo Machrus byn Rogate,** "Machrus son of Rogatus erected this/it [the tombstone] to him."

NPu *PBSR* 22 1954 lines 3/4 **Hoc fil lu Thmia,** "Thmia made this/it (the tombstone) for him."

1c. Object of a Preposition

Byb 2.2/3 ***HNY B'LK TḤT ZN,*** "I, your king, am here, at the bottom of this (shaft)."

Pu *Poen.* 947 **Hulec silli balim esse lipane esse Antidamas con. Itt esde anec nasote hers ahelicot,** "Antidamas was my guest-friend in this nation in the past. With him I shared a shard of hospitality."

Obs. In *Poen.* 937, the Neo-Punic version of Punic 947, **esde** is replaced by the suffix pronoun of the third masculine singular: **Ythem anech nasothi li yth irs aelichoth sith,** "With him I shared this shard of hospitality." Plautus renders **itt esde** in Latin **cum illo** ("with him"): *Poen.* 1051 **Haec mihi hospitalis tessera cum illo fuit**, "I shared this shard of hospitality with him."

1d. Expressing the Independent Personal Pronoun

Pu *Poen.* 937 **Ett esde anec nasote hers ahelicot,** "With him I shared a shard of hospitality." *Obs*: For the demonstrative pronoun, the Neo-Punic version of this same statement has the suffix personal pronoun of the third person: *Poen.* 937 **Ythem anech nasothi li yth irs aelichoth isith,** "With him I shared this shard of hospitality."

1e. "To wit, namely (*lit.*, it is)":

Introducing a Complementary, Explanatory Statement

26 C IV 2/6 ***WZBḤ 'Š Y[LKT L]'LM KL HMSKT Z {Z} ZBḤ YMM 'LP WB'T ḤRŠ Š 1 WB'T QṢR Š 1,*** "And I brought to the god (Baal-KRNTRYS) a sacrifice at all the sacrifices, to wit (*lit.*, it being), an ox at the periodic sacrifice, and a sheep at the time of ploughing and a sheep at the time of harvesting." *Obs.* The other version of this same statement in 16 A II 19-III 1 does not have the demonstrative: ***WYLK <'NK> ZBḤ L KL HMSKT ZBḤ YMM 'LP WB['T Ḥ]RŠ Š WB'T QṢR Š,*** "And I brought to him a sacrifice at all the sacrifices: an ox at the periodic sacrifice, and a sheep at the time of ploughing and a sheep at the time of harvesting."

2. *Adjectival Uses of the Demonstratives*

2a. Expressing Deixis

In standard Phoenician and Punic, the demonstrative pronouns, used adjectivally to express near deixis ("this, this here"), followed the noun; in normal usage, the demonstrative did not receive the definite article although two examples of the demonstrative with the definite article are found in Phoenician. In Neo-Punic, standard Phoenician-Punic usage continued although there was an increased use of the definite article with the demonstrative adjective.

In all forms of Phoenician and Punic, the use of the definite article with the noun modified by a demonstrative pronoun was optional since the demonstrative rendered the noun determined. Thus, in Phoenician and Punic, "this city" was expressed freely as ***HQRT Z*** or ***QRT Z*** and, rarely, ***HQRT HZ*** or ***QRT HZ***.
While in the larger corpus of inscriptions in general the use of the definite article with the noun was inconsistent, the author of any given inscription was himself generally consistent. The following examples illustrate the several variant expressions of the noun with demonstrative adjective.

HQRT Z

This usage is characteristic of the Aztwadda inscription (*KAI* 26), its author generally consistent in his use of the definite article with the noun:

26 A II 9, 17 ***WBN 'NK HQRT Z*** "And I built this city."

26 A III 7 ***WKN HQRT Z B'LT ŠB'***, "And may this city become the possessor of abundance."

26 A III 14/15 ***YḤMD 'YT HQRT Z WYS' HŠ'R Z*** "He loves this city, yet, pulls up this gate."

26 A III 15, 17/18 ***YS' HŠ'R Z*** "He shall tear out this gate."

But in 26 A III 7/8, the author does not use the definite article with the noun: ***W'M Z . . . YKN B'L 'LPM,*** ("And may this people become the possessor of oxen.").

The use of the definite article with the noun is extremely well represented throughout Phoenician and Punic:

15, 16 (Sidon) ***'YT HBT Z BN L'LY,*** "He built this temple for his god."

18.3/4 ***'YT HŠ'R Z . . . P'LT,*** "I made this gate."

24.15 ***MY YŠḤT HSPR Z*** "Whoever shall damage this inscription."

Pu 80.1 ***ḤDŠ WP'L 'YT HMṬBḤ Z*** "They rebuilt this slaughtering table."

NPu 101.5 ***ṬN'M 'L HMLKT Z 'ŠYN . . . W'RŠ,*** "Put in charge of this work were 'SYN and Aris."

This same usage is also characteristic of the Byblian Phoenician inscription of Yehawmilk (*KAI* 10), with the difference however that its author normally suppresses the use of the definite article when the noun is preceded by a preposition:

10.3-5 ***P'L 'NK . . . HMZBḤ NḤŠT ZN . . . WHPTḤ ḤRṢ ZN . . . WH'RPT Z',*** "I made this bronze altar . . . and this gold engraving . . . and this portico."

But Preposition + ***QRT Z***:

10.5 ***H'PT ḤRṢ 'Š BTKT 'BN 'Š 'L PTḤ ḤRṢ ZN,*** "The gold *bird* that is on the stone *tkt* that is on/next to this gold engraving."

10.11/12 ***LP'L ML'KT 'LT MZBḤ ZN . . . W'LT 'RPT Z',*** "To do work on this altar . . . and on this portico."

10.14 ***[WTS]G 'T PTḤY Z DL YSDH 'LT MQM Z*** "If you move this engraving of mine, together with its base, from this spot."

Observe however that this same author is not entirely consistent; for sometime he fails to use the definite article even when no preposition precedes the noun:

10.10/11 ***'M 'RṢ Z*** "The people of this land." *Obs.* Perhaps the definite article is not used with a noun governed by a construct noun.

10.13/14 ***'M TSR M[L']KT Z*** "If you remove this work."

QRT Z

The inconsistency with regard to the use or non-use of the definite article with the noun modified by a demonstrative adjective is well illustrated by the usage of the contemporary Sidonian inscriptions *KAI* 13 and *KAI* 14. The author of the latter (the Esmunazor inscription) does not use the article; but in contrast the author of the former inscription, written in the preceding reign (the Tibnit inscription) does prefer the article:

14.4 ***'L YPTḤ 'YT MŠKB Z*** "Let him not open this resting-place!"

14.7, 10 ***YPTḤ 'LT MŠKB Z*** "He shall open this resting-place."

14.10/11 ***YŠ' 'YT ḤLT Z*** "He shall carry off this coffin."

But 13.3 ***TPQ 'YT H'RN Z*** "You shall acquire this coffin."

The general inconsistency in the use of the definite article is graphically illustrated in the large corpus of Phoenician inscriptions from Kition in Cyprus: of the thirteen instances of the noun with demonstrative pronoun, ten have the noun without the article (*FK* A 1.2, A 2.2, A 29.2, A 30.2, B 5.1, B 6.1, B 45.1, B 47.2, E 2.2, F 1.2) and three with the article (F 1.4, B 2.1, B 40.1).

HQRT HZ

Twice only in Phoenician is the definite article found with the demonstrative adjective in the manner of Classical Hebrew ***HMQWM HZH*** *ham-maqōm haz-ze* "this place"). It is perhaps significant that both instances of this uncommon usage in Phoenician occur in inscriptions from Kition-Idalion in Cyprus, suggesting that it may have been unique to Cypriote Phoenician or even to the Phoenician of Kition-Idalion:

FK D 35 (Kition) ***H-'GN H-Z '[Š YTN PN L-DN],*** "This bowl th[at PN presented to DN]."

40.3 (Idalion) ***H-SMLM H-'L 'Š YṬN' BTŠLM,*** "These statues which Bitsalom erected."

QRT HZ

In Neo-Punic, standard Phoenician-Punic usage was generally respected, especially in formal literary prose. Peculiar, however, to late Neo-Punic is the occasional use of the definite article with the demonstrative adjective. The Neo-Punic usage differs however from that of Kitionite Phoenician ***HSML HZ*** in that the noun does not normally receive the definite article; this is however not greatly significant since the use of the definite article with the noun was always optional and inconsistent:

NPu 151.1/2 ***ṬN' HBN '-ST LSWL' BN ḤMLKT,*** "This stone was erected to SWL' bin Himilco."

NPu *IRT* 828.2/3 **Bur y-soth . . . fel,** "He built this tomb."

NPu *IRT* 879.1/3 **adom unim ys y-sy Bodsychun Chalia,** "This man, Bodsychun Chalia, was a person of substance."

NPu *Poen.* 937T **Ythem anech nasothi li yth irs aelichoth i-sith,** "With him I shared this shard of hospitality."

NPu *CIS* i 151.2 ***P'L T-H-M'Š '-ST,*** "He made this statue."

2b. Expressing the Anaphoric Adjective/Pronoun

The demonstrative functions in the same manner as the independent personal pronouns of the third person to refer back to someone or something earlier mentioned ("that, the aforementioned"):

NPu 137.1/5 ***L'DN LB'L WLTNT-PNB'L MQDŠM ŠNM <'L> 'Š P'L B'L TNSMT . . . B' H'LNM 'L 'LT HMQDŠM 'L B'SR WŠB' LYRḤ MP' LPNY,*** "Belonging to Baal and to Thinnith-Phanebal are these two sanctuaries which the citizens of Thinissut built . . . These/those (the aforementioned) gods entered these sanctuaries on the seventeenth of the month of First Mufa."

2c. Expressing Location ("Here")

Frequently, the demonstrative adjective must properly be rendered as a locative adverb "here," rather than a deictic.

Byb 4.1/3 ***BT ZBNY YḤMLK MLK GBL H'T ḤWY KL MPLT HBTM 'L,*** "<This is> the temple that Yehimilk, King of Byblos, rebuilt. It was he who restored all the ruined temples hereabouts." *Obs.* This use of the demonstrative is found in Hebrew in Numbers 27:12 ***WY'MR YHWH 'L-MŠH 'LH 'L-HR H'BRYM HZH WR'H 'T-H'RṢ,*** "YHWH said to Moses, "Ascend to <the top of> Mount Abarim here, and view the region!"

3. *The Quasi Enclitic Character of the Demonstrative Adjective*

In the Kilamuwa Inscription (KAI 24, 8th century), the demonstrative used as an adjective is written as quasi enclitic to the noun, as indicated by the absence of the word-divider:

24.14 ***WYZQ . SPR Z,*** "If he shall damage this inscription."

24.15 ***WMY . YŠḤT . HSPR Z,*** "Whoever shall destroy this inscription."

Elsewhere, however, in inscriptions that also use word-dividers, the demonstrative is written as a separate word:

Byb 1.2 ***YGL / 'RN / ZN,*** "If he shall remove this coffin."

30.2 ***L QBR / Z',*** "His is this grave."

30.2 ***Y'L / HGBR / Z',*** "This man came up."

33.2 ***[S]MLT . '[Z] . 'Š . YTN,*** "This statue which he presented."

C. *The Byblian Phoenician Demonstrative Pronouns*

The demonstrative pronouns of Byblian are different from those of Tyro-Sidonian. Byblian possesses two sets of demonstratives: Set A, used in all inscriptions but Yehawmilk (*KAI* 10) to express simple near deixis ("this, that"), and Set B, unique to the Yehawmilk (*KAI* 10) inscription. Set B appears to have been used only when co-occurring with Set A: when occurring in the same literary context, Set A expressed near deixis ("this one here" = the location of the speaker) and Set far deixis ("that one there," "yonder"). No comparable contrastive deixis is attested in Tyro-Sidonian Phoenician although Classical Hebrew did possess the contrastive sets ***ZH*** *ze* ("this") and ***HLZH*** *hallaze* ("that" = "yonder").

1. *Morphology*

Set A

Forms

Sg. M.
ZN 1.2; 2.3; 9A 1,3,5; 10.4 (bis),5,12; 11.1; 13

Sg. F.
Z' 10.6,12,14

Pl.
'L 4.3; 12.1

Set B

Forms

Sg. M.
Z 10.4, 5, 14 (bis)

Sg. F
Z 10.10, 11

Set A resembles morphologically the demonstrative pronouns ***ZN***, ***ZNH*** ("this," masculine sg.) and ***Z'*** ("this," feminine sg.) of Old Aramaic (Segert, par. 5.1.4.2, 5.1.4.3). Set B resembles the demonstratives of Tyro-Sidonian Phoenician.

2. *Syntax and Usage*

2a. Set A Occurring Alone

1.2 ***WYGL 'RN ZN TḤTSP ḤTR MŠPṬH,*** "If he shall move this coffin, his imperial sceptre shall break."

2.2/3 ***HNY B'LK TḤT ZN,*** "I, your king, am at the bottom of this (shaft)."

4.2/3 ***H'T ḤWY KL MPTLT HBTM 'L,*** "It was he who restored all the ruined temples hereabouts."

9A1 ***['NK] . . . P'LT LY HMŠKB ZN,*** "I made this coffin for myself."

9A2 ***BMŠKB ZN 'Š 'NK ŠKB BN,*** "In this coffin in which I lie."

9A5 ***['L TPT]Ḥ '[LT MŠKB] ZN,*** "Do not open this resting-place!"

11 ***B'RN ZN 'NK . . . ŠKBT,*** "I lie in this coffin."

12.1/2 ***HḤNWṬM 'L P'LT 'NK,*** "I made these *ḥnwṭm*."

13.1 ***WKN HN 'NK ŠKB B'RN ZN,*** "And so here do I lie, in this coffin."

13.2 ***['L TPTḤ 'L]T 'RN ZN,*** "Do not open this coffin!"

2b. Sets A and B Co-occurring in *KAI* 10

The following passages illustrate the contrastive deixis of Sets A and B. The narrator (Yehawmilk himself) points out the objects in the temple that he has made from the vantage point of "this inscription of mine here" ("this inscription of mine" being *KAI* 10 itself) and the spot upon which it stands. These, together with the temple itself and the city in which it is located (Byblos), constitute the "here" of the narration and are accordingly designated by means of the deictic pronoun ***Z*** ("this one here"); all other objects are designated by the pronouns ***ZN, Z'*** ("that one there, yonder"):

First Passage (lines 3/6)

WP'L 'NK LRBTY B'LT GBL HMZBḤ NḤŠT ZN 'Š BḤṢRH Z WHPTḤ ḤRṢ ZN 'Š 'L PN PTḤY Z WH'PT ḤRṢ 'Š BTKT 'BN 'Š 'L PTḤ ḤRṢ ZN WH'RPT Z' W'MDH

"For my Lady Baalat of Byblos did I make that (***ZN***) bronze altar there which is in this (***Z***) temple of hers here, and that (***ZN***) gold engraving that is opposite this (***Z***) inscription of mine, and the gold *bird* that is <perched> on the stone *pillar* that is next to that (***ZN***) gold engraving there."

Second Passage (lines 9/11)

WTTN [LY HRBT B]'LT GBL ḤN L'N 'LNM WL'N 'M 'RṢ Z WḤN 'M 'RṢ Z, "May the Lady Baalt of Byblos grant me favor on the part of the gods and on the part of the people of this (*Z*) land, and may she grant favor to the people of this (*Z*) land!"

Third Passage (lines 11/16)
[MY ’T] KL MMLKT WKL ’DM ’Š YSP LP‘L ML’KT ‘LT MZBḤ ZN [W‘LT PT]Ḥ ḤRṢ ZN W‘LT ‘RPT Z’ ŠM ’NK YḤWMLK MLK GBL [TŠT ’T]K ‘L ML’KT H’ W’M ’BL TŠT ŠM ’TK W’M TSR M[L’]KT Z’ [WTS]G ’T PTḤY Z DL YSDH ‘LT MQM Z WTGL MSTRW TSRḤ HRBT B‘LT GBL ’YT H’DM H’ WZR‘W ’T PN KL ’LN G[BL]
"Whoever you may be, any royal person or any commoner who shall continue to do work on that (*ZN*) altar there and on that (*ZN*) gold engraving and on that (*Z’*) portico, you shall place my name – Yehawmilk, King of Byblos – with yours on the aforementioned work. If you do not place my name with yours <on it> or if you remove that (*Z’*) work or if you move this (*Z*) inscription of mine here and its base from this (*Z*) spot and reveal its hiding-place, the Lady Baalt of Byblos shall make stink the aforementioned person and his seed before all the gods of Byblos."

II. The Definite Article

A. *Morphology*

Forms

Standard

H-	Ph	46.4 ***H-’Š*** ("the people"); 30.2 ***H-GBR*** ("the man"); 26 A II 9 ***H-QRT*** ("the city"), *et passim*
	Pu	69.1 ***H-’Š;*** 74.1 ***H-MŠ’TT;*** 76 b 4 ***H-LḤM,*** *et passim*
	NPu	119.4 ***H-NḤŠT,*** 120.1 ***H-MŠLM***, 130.1 ***H-YŠBM,*** *et passim*

Punic and Neo-Punic

’-	Pu	*CIS* i 5510.3,7 ***’-MTNT*** ("the presentation"); 112.6 ***’-MMLKT*** ("the kings")
	NPu	145 I 3 ***’-YŠB*** ("who dwells"); 151.1 ***’-ST***

		("this"); 160.1 -***KTRT*** ("the crown"), 160.3 ***'-Š'T*** ("the sodality")

Neo-Punic Pre-Vocalic Form

Ḥ-a-	NPu	126.9 ***Ḥ-'T*** *a-et* ("the time") but line 6 ***H-TMT*** *it-timmot* ("perfect"); 118.1 ***Ḥ-['\]RP'T*** *a-orpôt* ("the portico")

Punic and Neo-Punic Form after the Accusative Particle ***T-***

Ø-	Pu	79.7/8, 141.1 ***T-'BN*** ("the stone"); 101.1 ***T-MQDŠ*** ("the sanctuary")
	NPu	129.2 ***T-'KSNDR'*** ("the exedra"); 129.2 ***T-'RPT*** ("the portico"); 165.2 ***T-P'S*** ("the inscription")

Punic and Neo-Punic in Latin and Greek Letters

FORM B

a-	Pu	*Poen.* 947 **a-helicot** ("hospitality"); *Poen.* 946 **a-u** ("that")
	NPu	D 6.10 **a-ab** ("the enemy"); *Poen.* 937 **a-elichoth** ("hospitality"); *PBSR* 23 no. 5.10 **a-urys** ("the engraver"); *IRT* 893.1 **a-ys** ("which")

FORM B

a-	NPu	*IRT* 893.1 **a-nasib** ("the stele")
e-	NPu	Augustine to Psalm 136:7 **e-dom** ("blood")
ε-	NPu	Dioscurides (Vattioni p. 526 no. 51) σιθιλ εσ-σαδε ("shoot of the field")
i-	Pu	*Poen.* 940P **i-macum** ("the city")
	NPu	*Poen.* 947T **i-ith** ("this")
y-	NPu	*AI* 1 p. 233 **y-bur** ("the tomb"); *Poen.* 930 **y-macom** ("the city"); *IRT* 873.1, *Poen.* 939 **y-mu** ("which"); *IRT* 828.2 **y-soth** ("this"); *IRT* 879.1 **y-sy** ("this")

Comments

The definite article ***H-*** *han-* of standard Phoenician and Punic was an unstressed proclitic originating in the second-millennium Canaanite demonstrative pronoun/adjective *han-* ("this/that"). The original deictic use of the pronoun is attested in archaic Hebrew in Numbers 23:9b: ***HN-'M LBDD YŠKN*** ("This/that people shall dwell in isolation."); Numbers 23:24a ***HN-'M KLBY' YQWM*** ("This/that people shall rise/attack like a lion."); as a true article, the archaic form ***HN-*** in Genesis 44:8: ***HN KSP 'ŠR MṢ'NW BPY 'MTḤTYNW HŠYBNW 'LYK*** ("We brought back to you the silver that we found inside our money-bags."). In Phoenician itself, the earliest attested use of the definite article is in texts of the tenth and ninth centuries B.C.: ***H-***: 4.2/3, Byblos, *ca.* 950 B.C ***HBTM 'L*** ("these temples, the temples here"); 30.2, Cyprus, *ca.* 850 B.C. ***HGBR Z'*** ("this man"); 46.4/5, Nora, *ca.* 850 B.C. ***H'Š LMṢB*** ("the people of the colony"); 24.9/10, *ca.* 825 B.C. ***HMLKM HLPNYM*** ("the kings who preceded me").

As may be readily inferred from Greek and Latin-letter spellings, the definite article had two, complementary forms, both reflexes of the etymon *han-*:

FORM A: (*h)ā-*, an open unstressed syllable, with lengthening of vowel before a word beginning with a pharyngeal or laryngeal /' *h ḥ* '/: Pu *Poen.* 947 **a-helicot** *ā-helīkót* ("hospitality"). With the loss of the pharyngeals and laryngeals in late Punic and Neo-Punic, Form A came to be the form used before a word beginning with a vowel: NPu *PBSR* 28 p. 53 no. 5.10 **a-urys** *ā-ūrís* ("the engraver" = ***H-ḤRŠ***) and *Poen.* 937 **a-elichoth** *ā-elīkot* ("hospitality" = ***H-HLKT***).

FORM B: *(h)à-*, a closed unstressed syllable, with gemination of following consonant, the gemination being the assimilation of the final *-n* of *han-* to the initial consonant of the word following; this is the form before a word beginning with a non-pharyngeal/laryngeal consonant: NPu *IRT* 893.1 **a-nasib** *an-naṣīb* (***H-NṢB*** "the stele"). More common however was the pronunciation *(h)e-* / *(h)i-* + gemination, with the characteristic Phoenician sound-change /*a* > *i*/ in a closed unstressed syllable: Pu *Poen.* 940P **i-macum** *im-maqūm* ("the city"); NPu Augustine **e-dom** *ed-dóm* ("blood"); and *AI* 1 p. 233 **y-bur** *ib-būr* ("the tomb").

In Punic, the article was not aspirated. It continued for the most part to be written "historically" in the Phoenician manner as ***H-***; but early it was also occasionally spelled "phonetically" as **'-**. In Carthaginian inscription *CIS* i 5510, written in 406 B.C., both spellings co-occur: ***H-'DMM*** ("the men," lines 1, 2), ***H-RB*** ("the great," lines 8, 9, 10) but ***'-MTNT*** ("the stele," lines 3,7).

In Neo-Punic, in the formal inscription *KAI* 126 from Lepcis Magna, alongside ***H***- and **'**- the contrastive spelling ***Ḥ***- appears for prevocalic *a-*:: ***H-TMT*** *it-timmót* ("perfect," line 6), ***'-LPQY*** *il-Lepqi* ("Lepcis," line 7, 2x) but ***Ḥ'T*** *a-ét* ("the time," line 9). The latter spelling is also attested in Neo-Punic in formal inscription 118.1 ***H-['JRP'T*** *a-orpót* ("the portico").

Also peculiar to Punic and Neo-Punic is the common spelling **Ø**- of the definite article after the aphetic proclitic form ***T***- (Latin-letter **th-**) of the accusative particle (*nota accusativi*): 79.7/8 ***KL 'Š LSR T-'BN Z*** ("Anyone who shall remove this stone."); 101.1 ***T-MQDŠ Z BN'*** ("They built this sanctuary."); 165.1/2 ***QR' T-P'S,*** ("Read the inscription!"). The presence of the definite article in these defective spellings is certain, inferable from the many Neo-Punic Latin-letter examples of this same usage: *AI* 1 1927 p. 233 line 1 **fel th-ybur** ("He made the/this tomb."); *Poen.* 930 **th-ymlachun th-yacum syth** ("You rule over this city."). However, the definite article was on occasion indicated orthographically in Neo-Punic after the particle ***T***-: 138.3-6 ***T-HMZBḤ . . . ḤYDŠ W'YQDŠ*** ("He rededicated the altar."); 160.1 ***YTN' LY 'KTRT*** ("They awarded me the crown."); 161.3 ***ṬN' T-HM'Š ST*** ("He erected this statue.").

B. *Syntax and Usage*

1. *The Article Renders the Noun Definite (Determined)*

The most common use of the definite article was to render an indefinite noun definite (determined). This function, which arose from the use of the article as a true demonstrative, is already found in the earliest Tyro-Sidonian and Byblian inscriptions of the tenth and early ninth centuries B.C., among them the following:

10th cent. B.C. Byb 4.1 ***KL MPLT HBTM 'L,*** "All the ruined temples hereabouts."

Early 9th cent. B.C. 30.1/3 ***WH'Š 'Š [. . .]M L QBR Z' Y'L HGBR Z' [']L]ŠY,*** "The mana who [lead] them, his is this tomb. This warrior came up to Alasiya . . . "

Early 9th cent. B.C. 46..4/5 ***H'Š LMṢB,*** "The people of the colony."

Mid 9th cent. B.C. 24.15 ***WMY YŠḤT HSPR Z,*** "Whoever shall destroy this inscription."

The article was always used erratically. In some syntactic structures its use with the noun was optional as, for instance, if the noun was already rendered definite by (i) a descriptive adjective carrying the definite article, (ii) a demonstrative pronoun or (iii) an anaphoric pronoun:

14.22 ***'LNM HQDŠM***, ("The holy gods"). But in line 9 of the same text, the article is used with the noun: ***H'LNM HQDŠM,*** ("The holy gods").

26 A III 7/8 ***'M Z*** ("This people") but with the article in 26 A II 9 ***HQRT Z*** ("This city"). In all periods of the language, the constructions ***HQRT Z*** and ***QRT Z*** were free variants.

14.11 ***'DMM HMT,*** ("Those persons") but also with the article in line 22 of the same text: ***H'DMM HMT,*** ("Those persons"). As with the demonstrative pronoun, the constructions ***HQRT H'*** and ***QRT H'*** were free variants.

2. *The Article with Abstract Nouns*

An abstract concept may be conveyed by the means of the definite article. This usage is illustrated by the noun Pu **a-helicot** (NPu **a-elichoth**) *a-(h)elīkot* ("hospitality"): *Poen.* 947 **Itt esde anec nasote hers ahelicot,** ("With him I shared a shard of hospitality.") = *Poen.* 937. (Neo-Punic) **Ythem anech nasothi li yth irs a-elichoth i-sith,** ("With him I shared this shard of hospitality."). This same usage appears with the noun ***H-D'T*** *id-dá'at* ("friendship"): NPu 121,1;126,6 in the expression ***D'T H-TMT***, *literally*, ("perfect friendship/understanding") rendered **concordia** in Latin.

3. *The Article with Place-Names*

Place-names may receive the definite article. In the examples that follow, the article is set off in order to emphasize its presence:

NPu 126.7 ***'DR' '-LPQY W'M '-LPQ[Y],*** "The senate of Lepcis and the people of Lepcis."

Pu M. Ghaki, "Textes libyques et puniques," *REPPAL* 1 (1985), pp. 174-75 ***ND'R 'Š N'DR' B'L' H-M[D]DM LB'LḤMN,*** "<This is> the vow that the citizens of Medidi made to Baalhammon."

Pu *De Carthage a Kairouan. 2000 ans d'arts et d'histoire en Tunisie.* Musée du Petit Palais (Paris, 1982) cat. No. 152.2/3 ***B'LYTN BN D'B'R BN YTNB'L B'L H-MKT'RYM,*** "Baliathon son of Dabar son of Iathonbal, a citizen of Mactar."

NPu 172.2/3 ***PRṬ 'L MYṬB' RŠ' H-SLKY LBN'T T-HMQDŠ***

ST, "He undertook to build this sanctuary with the consent of the senate of Sulcis."

4. *The Article with the Descriptive Adjective of a Determined Noun*

If the noun is definite, the descriptive adjective carries the definite article: 14.9 ***H'LNM HQDŠM*** ("The holy gods"); 14.19 ***'RṢT DGN H'DRT*** ("The great grain regions"); 24.9/10 ***HMLKM HLPNYM*** ("The earlier kings"). *Obs.* If the adjective receives the definite article, the article need not be used with the noun: 14.12 ***'LNM HQDŠM*** ("The holy gods"); NPu 121.1 ***D'T HTMT*** ("Perfect friendship", rendered **concordia** in Latin).

5. *The Article Used Rarely with the Adjectival Demonstrative*

Only rarely is the definite article used with the demonstrative adjective. Significantly, Phoenician itself yields two examples only, both in texts from Cyprus, raising the question if dialect is perhaps a factor. Characteristic of Phoenician and Punic, the definite article is optional with the noun itself. Compare the optional suppression of the definite article with the noun when a qualifying adjective carries the definite article: 14.12 ***'LNM H-QDŠM,*** ("The holy gods") but 14.9 ***H-'LNM H-QDŠM***: Ph *FK* D 35 ***H-'GN H-Z,*** ("This bowl"); Ph 40.3 ***H-SMLM H-'L,*** ("These images"); NPu 151.1 ***HBN '-ST,*** ("This stone"); NPu *CIS* i 151.2 ***H-M'Š '-ST,*** ("This statue"); NPu *IRT* 828.2 **bur y-soth,** ("This tomb"); NPu *IRT* 879.2/3 **ys y-sy,** ("this man"); NPu *Poen.* 937T **irs a-elichoth i-sith** ("This shard of hospitality"). See the chapter on the Demonstrative Pronouns.

6. *Article Used Rarely with the Anaphoric Pronoun*

The definite article with the anaphoric pronoun is found a single time, in Punic. In normative usage, the anaphoric pronoun, like the demonstrative adjective, does not receive the article: Pu *Poen.* 944/46A **Alem ys duber ce fel dono Mittun et cil cumu {comu} con liful alt banim au,** ("I am told that his father Mittun did everything for that son of his, as he was to do it for him."). But *cf.* normative usage, without the article: Byb 10.15 ***H'DM H'*** ("That person"); 13.6 ***HDBR H'*** ("That thing"); 14.22 ***H'DMM HMT*** ("Those persons"), *et passim.*

7. *The Article Used with Relative Pronoun in Late Neo-Punic*

In late Neo-Punic, the relative pronoun may receive the definite article when the antecedent of the pronoun is definite. This usage is unknown in standard Phoenician and Punic. See chapter on the relative pronoun.

NPu *IRT* 893.1 **A-nasib a-ys fel Sudru,** "<This is> the stele that Sudru made."

NPu *IRT* 873.1/4 **Myntsyfth y-mu fel Bibi Mythunilim,** "<This is> the stele that Bibi Mythunilim made."

NPu Poen. 939 **Bod i(ly) a(nech) lythera y-mu ys lomyn choth iusim,** "Let me inquire of these men who are coming out from here."

8. *The Article Expresses the Relative Pronoun*

In Phoenician-Punic, the verbal relative clause, regardless of the form of the verb in the clause, is normally introduced by the relative pronoun ***'Š.*** Rarely, the definite article is used:

8a. The Verb is an Active Participle

CIS i 91.2 ***NṢḤT 'T 'BY HYṢ'M W'ZRNM,*** "I defeated my enemies who came forth <in battle against me> and their allies."

NPu 161. ***KL 'N'SP L'***, "All who were gathered to him."

NPu 145 I 3 ***L'M 'YŠB 'DMT,*** "For the people that inhabit the land."

See the chapter on the relative pronouns for the normal use of ***'Š*** to introduce a verbal relative clause.

8b. The Verb is the Suffixing Form Past Perfective

26 A I 1/2 ***'NK 'ZTWD HBRK B'L 'BD B'L,*** "I am Aztwadda, whom Baal blessed, the servant of Baal."

172.1/3 ***[LḤ]MLKT . . . HPRṬ . . . LBN'T T-HMQDŠ ST,*** "To Himilco, who undertook to build this sanctuary." = Latin **Himilconi . . . quei hanc aedem . . . faciundam coeravit.**

This use of the definite article is found also in Hebrew: see Waltke-O'Connor, par. 19.7.

9. *Use as a Vocative Particle*

NPu 164.1/3 ***TBQY ʾʾLK WQRʾ T-Pʿ S ʾŠ ʿL HMNṢBT ST,*** "Tarry, O passer-by, and read the inscription that is on this stele!"

CHAPTER SIX

THE RELATIVE AND DETERMINATIVE PRONOUNS

I. Relative Pronouns

A. *Morphology*

Forms

Archaic

***Z*-** *zū*-	Byb	1.1; 4.1; 6.1; 7.1

Standard Phoenician and Punic

'Š *'is*	Ph	13.3; 14.4,7,9,10,15,17,19; 18.4; 19.2,9,10, *et passim*
	Byb	9 A 3, B 3; 10.2, 4, 5, 6, 7
	Pu	61 A 2; 63.1; 64.1; 66.1; 69.1, 13,14,15,16,18,19,20, *et passim*
	NPu	126.7; 130.2; 137.1; 141.4, *et passim*
es	Pu	*Poen.* 949
is	Pu	*Poen.* 940P
	NPu	*Poen.* 930, 940A
ys	NPu	*Poen.* 939; *IRT* 893.1
υς	Pu	*EH* Gr 1

Late Neo-Punic

FORM A

M' *mū*	NPu	Trip. 77.1/2;
mu	NPu	*IRT* 828.1; 863; 873.2, 877.2; 901.1,4

FORM B

M' 'Š *mū 'is*	NPu	Trip. 79.1/2
mu ys	NPu	*Poen.* 939

Comments

The earliest Phoenician relative pronoun, the proclitic *zū*- (spelled *Z*-), is attested in Byblian inscriptions *KAI* 1-7, dating to the years

1000-900 B.C. It is not evident however that this pronoun was normative of the standard literary language of that period or a preferred archaism. The reflex of Proto-Canaanite *dhū-*, the pronoun *zū-* is historically related to the relatives relative ***D-*** *dū-* of literary Ugaritic (archaic Ugaritic ***Ḏ-*** *dhū-*) and archaic/archaizing ***ZW*** *(zū)*, ***ZH*** *(ze)* of the language of the Biblical Psalms (Tsevat p. 51 no. 157). No example of the pronoun is as yet attested in Tyro-Sidonian Phoenician texts.

By the early ninth century B.C., the proclitic *zū-* had been replaced in all dialects of Phoenician by the relative pronoun *ʾīs* (spelled ***ʾŠ***) which, from this time on, became normative of standard Tyro-Sidonian Phoenician, Punic and Byblian. The origin of the relative *ʾīs* is obscure; its vocalization is however certain from the *plene* spelling ***ʾYŠ*** and Roman and Greek letter spellings **es, is, ys,** υς. This same relative pronoun was also used in the Lowlands (Shephelah) Canaanite dialect of Lachish, attested in a 4th -century B.C. frankincense altar inscription from that site (*NESE* i 487 f.): ***LBNT ʾYŠ BN MḤLY*** ("<This is> the incense altar that Mahli built/erected."). It is also found twice in a passage in non-Judaean Canaanite, perhaps the Lowlands dialect, preserved in Numbers 1:4: ***YHYW ʾTKM ʾYŠ ʾYŠ LMṬH ʾYŠ RʾŠ LBT ʾBTYW HWʾ***, ("<Conduct ye a census of the entire confederation of the Bane-Israel by the families of their clans>. Let assist you the man of each tribe who is the head of its clans."). Lowlands Canaanite may have taken this pronoun from the neighboring coastal Phoenician dialects; for in archaic Lachishite, as the Late Bronze II Lachish ewer inscription reveals (see below), the relative pronoun was ***Š-***.

No evidence exists in Phoenician or Punic for the existence of a relative pronoun of the shape ***Š-***. The pronoun ***Š-*** that does occur in Phoenician and Punic is not a relative but a determinative pronoun, serving primarily to express an indirect genitive relationship. There was however a relative pronoun ***Š-*** in the Canaanite of the Lowlands (Shephelah); it is attested in the dialect of Lachish of the Late Bronze Age, in an inscription (*ca.* 1300-1200 B.C.) on a ewer discovered in the Fosse Temple: ***MTN ŠYT[N . . .]TY LʾLT*** ("<This is> the gift that [. . .]tay presented to Elath."). This pronoun is also known from the non-Judaean passages in the Bible and in post-Biblical and Mishnaic Hebrew and in an oval seal inscription published by A. Avigad, *IEJ* 16 (1966) 247f: ***ʾBNDB ŠNDR LʿŠT(RT) BṢDN TBRKH***, ("Abinadab. <This is> what he vowed to Astarte of Sidon.

May she bless him!"). This seal inscription, often included among the Phoenician inscriptions, is linguistically, orthographically and stylistically not Phoenician.

The relative pronoun *ʾīs* remained standard in Phoenician into the late Neo-Punic (*ca.* 1st-5th centuries ad). In late Neo-Punic however there emerged a new relative pronoun, *mū* (spelled ***Mʾ*** **mu**) and its variant *mū īs* (***Mʾ ʾŠ*** **mu ys**), in origin the indefinite relative "what, that which" extended in use as a general relative with antecedent. Analogues to this common development are the Afrikaans relative pronoun **wat** and Viennese and Yiddish **was.** *Mū* and *mū īs,* which originated in the colloquial Punic of the late Roman period, eventually came also to be accepted in literary Neo-Punic, as evidenced by its use in *Poenulus* (Poen. 939) **Bod i(ly) a(nech) lythera ymu ys lomyn choth iusim** ("Let me ask these men who are coming out from here."), a line from the entrance monologue of Hanno from the Neo-Punic version of the comedy *Karkhedonios.* The original Punic version of this same line employed the earlier relative **es** (***ʾŠ***): *Poen.* 949 **Anec litor bod es iussim limin co.** In spite of its great currency in late Neo-Punic, the relative *mū* (*mū īs)* never entirely replaced standard Phoenician-Punic *ʾīs.*

It is possible that the use of the indefinite relative *mū* as a general relative may occur in an inscription on a goblet (*IEJ* 23 p. 120): ***QBʿ M ʾN ḤN ʿRBT LMRZḤ ŠMŠ,*** ("<This is> the goblet that I, Hanno, *presented* to the Sodality of Shemesh."). The translation of the text is however highly problematic; and aside from the matter of the authenticity of the inscription itself, it is not evident at all that the the dialect is Phoenician: the text has short form ***ʾN*** *ʾanī* of the independent personal pronoun "I," elsewhere found only in archaic Phoenician, and the verb ***ʿ-R-B*** ("to give"), otherwise unknown in Phoenician.

B. *Syntax and Usage*

1. *Introducing a Non-Verbal Relative Clause: Relative Clauses with Nominal, Adjectival or Adverbial Predicate*

When the relative clause was a non-verbal sentence with nominal or adjectival predicate, the subject of the relative clause was optionally expressed by the independent personal pronouns of the third person.

1a. Relative Clause with the Independent Pronoun

40.1/2 ***ŠNT 31 L'DN MLKM PTLMYS . . . 'Š H' ŠT 57 L'Š KTY,*** "Year 31 of the Lord of Kings Ptolemaios which is (*lit.,* which it is) year 57 of the people of Kition."

43.4/5 ***ŠNT 11 L'DN MLKM PTLMYŠ . . . 'Š HMT L'M LPṬ ŠNT 33,*** "Year 11 of the Lord of Kings Ptolemais which is (*lit.,* which it is) year 33 of the people of Lapethos."

1b. Relative Clause without Independent Pronoun

The expression of the subject of the non-verbal sentence with nominal or adjectival predicate by the independent personal pronouns of the third person was not obligatory, as the following examples indicate.

Ph 26 A III 13, IV 1 ***'DM 'Š 'DM ŠM,*** "A person who is a person of name/fame." Not ***'DM 'Š 'DM ŠM H'*** or ***'Š H' 'DM ŠM,*** "a man who he is a man of name."

Pu *Poen.* 944/45 **Ys es hulec silli balim esse lipane esse con,** "The man who was my guest-friend in this nation in the past." Not **es hu hulec silli . . . con.** "who he was my guest-friend."

26 A II 3/4 ***MQMM 'Š KN LPNM NŠT'M,*** "Places that were dangerous in the past." Not "that they were dangerous." Not ***'Š HMT KN LPNM NŠT'M.***

In a non-verbal relative clause with adverbial predicate, the third person independent personal pronoun was never used as subject.

Pu 80.1/2 ***H'ŠM 'Š 'L HMQDŠM,*** "The men who are in charge of sanctuaries." Not "the men who they are in charge of sanctuaries."

Pu 66.1 ***'KLYN . . . 'Š 'L HMMLHT,*** "Cleon, <the official> who is in charge of the salt revenues." = Greek Κλεων ο επι των αλων.

NPu 130.5 ***'RKT 'Š 'L HMḤZM,*** "The department which is in charge of marketplaces made four of the seats with fine monies."

2. *Introducing a Verbal Relative Clause*

2a. Used with the Participle (Active and Passive)

The relative pronouns are used to introduce all verbal relative clauses, including those in which the verb is a participle (active or passive). In contrast, Hebrew requires the use of the definite article with the participle, usage known in Phoenician as well but much less common.

14.9 ***MMLKT 'DR 'Š MŠL BNM,*** "The mighty king who rules them."

37 A 7 ***LŠRM B'R 'Š ŠKNM LMLKT QDŠT,*** "<Paid> to those who dwell in the city who were employed for the sacred liturgy."

60.9 ***H'DMM 'Š NŠ'M LN,*** "The persons who were elected by us."

Pu *CIS* i 3785.5/6 ***KL 'DM 'Š GNB T-MTNT Z,*** "Anyone who shall steal this stele."

Pu *Eph.* 3.55.1 ***[HPRKJ]T 'Š KST W'ṬPT 'YT [. . .] MQDŠ Z,*** "The [*curtain*] that covers and conceals the [*holy of holies*] of this sanctuary."

Pu *Poen.* 949 **Anec litor bod es iussim limin co,** "Let me inquire of <these men> who are coming out from here." = NPu *Poen.* 939 **Bod i(ly) a(nech) lythera ymu ys lomyn choth iusim,** "Let me inquire of these men who are coming out from here."

NPu Trip. 2 ***[P'L T-HPTḤ WH . . .]T 'Š 'DḤT 'L P'NY' WT-HTLY'M 'Š 'L HPTḤ,*** "[He made the *ptḥ* and the . . .]s that are . . . -ing in front of it (*or* on its surface) and the *hanging things* that are on/above the *ptḥ*."

Instances in Phoenician and Punic of the definite article functioning as relative pronoun with an active participle are the following:

CIS i 91.2 ***NṢḤT 'T 'BY HYṢ'M,*** "Would that I might defeat my enemies who come forth <to do battle with me>."

NPu 145 I 3 ***'M 'YŠB 'DMT,*** "The people who dwell on the land."

2b. Used with Finite Forms of the Verb

60.2 ***ŠM'B'L BN MGN 'Š NŠ' HGW 'L BT 'LM W'L MBNT ḤṢR BT 'LM,*** "Samobaal son of Magon, whom the community elected in charge of the temple and the building of the temple court." *Et passim.*

Pu 80.1/2 ***H'ŠM 'Š 'L HMQDŠM 'Š KN BŠT Š[PṬM] GRSKN WGR'ŠTRT . . . WBD'ŠTRT,*** "The men in charge of sanctuaries who were in office in the year of the Suffetes Gisco, Gerastart and Bodastart rebuilt this slaughtering table."

Pu 69.20 ***KL KHN 'Š YQḤ MŠ'T BDṢ L'Š ŠT BPS Z,*** "Any priest who shall accept a payment that is in excess of that set down in this inscription." *Et passim.*

Pu 79.6/8 ***KL 'Š LSR T-'BN Z,*** "Anyone who shall remove this stone."

3. *Resumptive Pronoun in the Relative Clause*

If the antecedent of the relative pronoun is the direct or indirect object of the verb in the relative clause, the antecedent may be referred back to by means of a resumptive pronoun. However, in Phoenician such resumption is not obligatory.

3a. With Resumption of the Indirect Object

Byb 9 A 3 ***BMŠKB ZN 'Š 'NK ŠKB BN,*** "In this resting-place in which I lie (*lit.*, which I lie in it)."

43.12/13 ***HDLT HNḤŠT . . . 'Š BN MNḤT ḤNY,*** "The bronze plaque in which are the details of my beneficence (*lit.*, which in it are the details of my beneficence)."

NPu 126.7/9 ***[ṬYBRY QLWDY] . . . 'Š LPNY . . . YTN' L'BD BṢP'T,*** "[Tiberius Claudius], to whom they granted (*lit.*, who to him they granted) <the right> to use the broad senatorial purple stripe."

Once, instead of resumption in the case of an indirect object, the preposition is used with the relative pronoun:

26 A I 13/15 ***BN 'NK ḤMYT 'ZT . . . BMQMM B'Š KN 'ŠM R'M B'L 'GDDM,*** "I built strong protective fortresses in places in which (*bi'īs*) there were bad men, bandits."

3b. Without Resumption of the Indirect Object

26 A I 15/16 ***'ŠM R'M . . . 'Š BL 'Š 'BD KN LBT MPŠ,*** "Bad men, none of whom was a vassal (*lit.*, who none was a vassal of the House of Mopsos)." Not "who none of them was a vassal."

3c. Resumption of the Direct Object in the Relative Clause

Resumption of the direct object in a relative clause by means of a suffixal object pronoun is also known in Phoenician, as in Hebrew, but it is extremely rare:

Byb 10.1/2 ***'NK YḤWMLK . . . 'Š P'LTN HRBT B'LT GBL MMLKT 'L GBL,*** "I am Yehawmilk, whom the Lady Baalt of Byblos made king (*lit.*, who the Lady Baalt of Byblos made me king) of Byblos."

Pu *RES* 891.1/3 ***[HPRK]T 'Š KST W'ṬPT ['YT TW H]MQDŠ Z 'Š NDR' MGN [BN . . .] BN MGN BN PLSMLQRT,*** "The [*curtain*] that covers and conceals the [*cella* of] this sanctuary which Mago [son of PN] son of Mago son of Pillesmilqart vowed [*lit.*, which Mago vowed it]."

NPu Trip. 79.1/2 ***BʾRM QNʾT ʾT Mʾ ʾŠ PʿLM MʿṢWKN,*** "You have acquired the tomb that Masauchan built (*lit.*, which Masauchan built them)." *Obs.* ***BʾRM*** is plural in form but singular in meaning; later in the same inscription, it is subject of the singular verb ***NPʿL*** ("it was made").

NPu 168.1/6 ***GʿY YL MNWLʿ ṬNʿ Lʾ ʿBN NʿSʿYʾ BRKT BT RGʿṬʾ,*** "<This is the tombstone of> Gaius Julius Manulus. Birikt daughter of Rogatus erected to him <this> stone <that> they pulled up (*lit.*, they pulled it up)."

4. *Ellipsis of the Antecedent of the Relative Pronoun*

Often the relative pronoun has an unexpressed antecedent which is evident from the context.

Byb 11 ***SWT WMRʾŠ . . . WMḤSM . . . KM ʾŠ LMLKYT ʾŠ KN LPNY,*** "A garment and head-piece and mouth-piece like <those> which belonged to the queens who preceded me."

Pu *Poen.* 949 **Anec litor bod es iussim limin co,** "Let me inquire of <these men> who are coming out from here." *Obs.* The Neo-Punic version of the line has the plural demonstrative **ily** ("these men") as antecedent of the relative pronoun: *Poen.* 939 **Bod i(ly) a(nech) lythera ymu ys lomyn choth iusim,** "Let me inquire of these <men> who are coming out from here."

54.2 ***ʾŠ YṬNʾT ʾNK DʿMSLḤ BN DʿMḤNʾ ṢDNY,*** "<This is the stele> that I, Domsalaoh son of Domhanno the Sidonian, erected."

59.1/2 ***ʾŠ YṬNʾ LY YTNBʿL BN ʾŠMNṢLḤ,*** "<This is the stele> that Yatonbaal son of Esmunsaloh erected to me."

The elliptic use of the relative pronouns is common in the expressions ***ʾŠ ʿL*** and ***ʾŠ B-*** ("he who is in charge of <some function>."). The former acquired the specialized meaning of "Governor."

NPu 141.1 ***WTḤ ʾŠ ʿL ʾRṢT TŠKʿT,*** "WTH, Governor of the Province of Thusca."

NPu D 2.1/10 **Iulius Masthalul. . . is [al C]leruch[ia A]dnim,** "Iulius Masthalul, Governor of the Colony of Adnim."

NPu D 5.1/13 **Iulius [. .]ibitua[n] . . . is a[l Cler]ruch[ia A]dnim,** "Iulius [xx]ibituan, Governor of the Colony of Adnim."

Pu 66.1 ***ʾKLYN ŠḤSGM ʾŠ BMMLHT,*** "Cleon SHSGM, <the official> who is in charge of the salt revenues." Greek Κλεων ο επι των αλων.

5. *The Use of the Definite Article with the Relative Pronoun in Neo-Punic*

In Late Neo-Punic, all forms of the relative pronoun may optionally receive the definite article when the antecedent of the relative is determined. This usage is unknown in Punic and Phoenician:

IRT 893.1/3 **A-nasib a-ys fel Sudru lobi[t]hem ulybane[m],** "<This is> the stele that Sudru made for his daughter and for his son."

NPu *IRT* 873.1/4 **Myntsyfth y-mu fel Bibi Mythunilim uintseb libinim Mythunilim,** "<This is> the stele which Bibi Mythunilim made and erected to his son, Mythunilim."

NPu *Poen.* 939 **Bod i(ly) a(nech) lythera y-mu ys lomyn choth iusim,** "Let me inquire of these men who are coming out from here."

6. *The Relative Pronoun Expresses the Locative "Where"*

26 A II 3/5 ***BMQMM ʾŠ KN LPNM NŠTʿM ʾŠ YŠTʿ ʾDM LLKT DRK,*** "In places that in the past were dangerous, where (*ʾīs*) one used to be afraid to walk the road." *Obs.* Phoenician does not use the preposition ***B***- + suffix pronoun or ***ŠM*** ("there") with the relative pronoun as we find in Hebrew ***ʾŠR . . . BW/ŠM*** ("where").

7. *Relative Pronoun as Adverbial Complement to the Jussive/Optative*

The relative pronoun functions as an adverbial complement to the optative and Jussive in Neo-Punic. This use of the pronoun is well known in Biblical and post-Biblical Hebrew: see E. Qimron, *The Hebrew of the Dead Sea Scrolls* (Harvard, 1986), §400.11.

NPu 147.2/4 ***[N]GD HŠMM NDR NDRʾ ʾŠ L[***CCC ***HʾL] . . . [ʾ]Š LʾTT HʾL ʾBBRKTM L[N] . . . ʾŠ Lʾʿ ZR [HʾL . . .],*** "Facing Heaven, they prayed: 'May God . . .! May God grant us of His blessings . . .! May God help [us]!'"

NPu Trip. 10.3/4 ***ʾŠ LKN ʾḤRT[M] BRY<K>ʾT,*** "May their afterlife be a happy one!"

8. *The Virtual Relative Clause*

A relative clause may be expressed without the use of a relative pronoun. The "virtual" relative clause corresponds to English: "The man I saw." Examples are rare:

29.1/2 ***ʾRN [Š]N MGN ʾMTBʿL . . . MTT LʿŠTRT ʾDTY,*** "<This

is> the ivory box Amotbaal presented as a gift to her Lady Astarte."

NPu 168.1/6 ***G'Y YL MNWL' ṬN' L' 'BN N'S'Y' BRKT BT RG'Ṭ',*** "<This is the tombstone of> Gaius Julius Manulus. Birikt daughter of Rogatus erected to him <this> stone they pulled up (*lit.*, they pulled it up)."

9. *In Fixed Expressions*

9a. In the Marker of the Indirect Genitive ***'Š L-*** ("of")

Phoenician and Punic often express the construct relationship indirectly by means of fixed markers, equivalent essentially in function to the English word "of." One such marker is the expression ***'S L-,*** literally, "which is of" or "which belongs to." In this marker, the relative pronoun is non-functional, being merely a member of the expression.

24.15 ***B'L ṢMD 'Š LGBR,*** "Baal-Semid of Gabbar" (*i.e.*, Baal-Semid, the personal god of Gabbar).

24.16 ***B'LḤMN 'Š LBMH,*** "Baalhammon of BMH" (*i.e.*, Baal-hammon, the personal god of BMH).

NSI 150.5 ***'Š 'LM 'Š LMLQRT BṢR,*** "The Man-of-the-God (Prophet) of Milqart of Tyre."

CIS i 88.4 ***HSLMT 'Š LMPQD Z,*** "The storerooms of this depository."

Obs. The indirect genitive is also expressed by means of the determinative pronoun ***Š-*** in Punic, by means of the compound ***ŠL-*** in Phoenician and in Neo-Punic and by means of the simple preposition ***L-***. See the section on the Determinative Pronoun and the chapter on Prepositions.

9b. In the Marker of Origin and Location ***'Š B-*** ("of, from, in")

Another common marker, serving to specify origin, provenience or location, is the expression ***'Š B-,*** literally, "who/which is of/from/in." Here, too, the relative is non-functional, being merely a member of the expression.

17.1/2 ***'ŠTRT 'Š BGW HQDŠ 'Š LY,*** "Astarte of GW, my goddess."

Caquot-Masson, *Syria* 45 (1968) 302-306 line 2 ***RŠP HMKL 'Š B'DYL,*** "Rasep the Destroyer of Idalion."

Head, 790 ***L'DK' 'Š BKN'N,*** "Laeodicaea in/of Canaan (Phoenicia)."

The non-functionality of the relative pronoun in this expression is indicated by the fact that it is frequently omitted:

18.2/3 ***‘BD’LM BN MTN BN ‘BD’LM BN B‘LŠMR BPLG L’DK,*** “Abdilim son of Mittun son of Abdilim son of Baalsamor of the district of Laodicaea.”

10. *In the Independent Possessive Pronoun* ***’Š LY***

Phoenician possesses an independent possessive pronoun ***’Š LY*** *’īs lī* (“my”) that is compounded of the relative pronoun and the preposition ***L-*** with suffixal pronouns: 18.3/4 ***HŠ‘R Z WHDLHT ’Š L*** (“This gate and its doors”); 17.1/2 ***‘ŠTRT . . . HQDŠ ’Š LY*** (“Astarte, my deity”). This pronoun is discussed at length in the following chapter.

11. *The Pseudo-Relative Clause*

The relative pronoun is sometimes precedes a finite verb in sentences in which the direct object is clause-initial and in sentences beginning with a prepositional phrase. In these senences, the relative pronoun is a feature of rhetoric and style rather than function.

26 C III 2 ***WZBḤ ’Š Y[LKT L]’LM KL HMSKT,*** “And I brought a sacrifice to the god (Baal-KRNTRYS) at all the sacrifices.” That ***ZBḤ*** is the direct object of the verb and not the antecedent of the relative pronoun is proved by the alternate version of this same line in 26 A II 19-III 1: ***WYLK <’NK> ZBḤ L KL HMSKT,*** “And I brought a sacrifice to him (Baal-KRNTRYS) at all the sacrifices.”

Pu *CIS* I 5689.1/5 ***LRBT LTNT-PNB‘L WL’DN LB‘LḤMN ’Š NŠ’ ‘BD’ŠMN HSPR BN ‘BDMLK HSPR ’YT ’RŠT ŠRY,*** “To the Lady Thinnith-Phanebal and to the Lord Baalhammon did Abdesmun the Scribe, the son of Abdmilk the Scribe, bring the first-born of his (own) flesh.” Not “who he brought to him.”

It is quite possible that all Phoenician-Punic dedications of the type NOUN + ***’Š*** + VERB + SUBJECT may be psudo-relative clauses. So, for example, a typical dedicatory statement like *KAI* 41.1/3 ***SML ’Z ’Š YTN WYṬN’ MNḤM . . . L’DNY L[RŠ]P ’LYYT*** should perhaps properly be rendered (“Menehhem presented and erected this statue to his Lord Rasap Eleeitai,”) and not literally, (“This statue that Menehhem presented and erected to his Lord Rasap Eleitai.”). This may be argued from the fact that although the Greek version of this same dedication mimics the Phoenician in rendering a relative clause (τον ανδριανταν τον-νυ εδοκεν κας ονεθεκεν Μανασες . . . τοι Απειλονι τοι Ελειται, ("The statue that Manases presented and set up to Apollo Eleitai"), the Greek also has the antecedent in the accusative case, as if it were the direct object of the two verbs. Confirmation of this analysis is perhaps to be found in the dedication of the Pyrgi inscription (*IFPCO* pp. 160-161): it is a sentence compounded of two independent clauses, the first a pseudo-verbal clause (for rhetorical and stylistic reasons), the second a simple declarative clause; both clauses should therefore perhaps be rendered as declarative sentences: ***LRBT L'ŠTRT 'ŠR QDŠ 'Z 'Š P'L W'Š YTN TBRY' WLNŠ MLK 'L KYŠR' . . . BMTN 'BBT WBN TW K 'ŠTRT 'RŠ BDY,*** ("For the Lady Astart did Tiberius Velianas, King of Caere, make and set up this sacred *aser* as a gift in [her] temple [*lit.*, this sacred *aser*, which he made and set up], and he [re]built the/her/its cella; because Astarte requested it of him.").

II. Determinative Pronoun

A. *Morphology*

Forms

FORM A		
Š- si-	Pu	49 36 Av.; 64.1/2; 77.1/2, *et passim*
		NPu 122.1; 124.3/4, *et passim*
su- (sy-)	Pu	*Poen.* 948
sy-	NPu	178.1; cf. *Poen.* 933 **syllochom** ("your")
si-	Pu	*cf. Poen.* 1141 **silli** ("my")
FORM B		
ŠL- silli-	Ph	Lapethos 3.4 ***QB'M ŠLKSP*** ("silver cups"); 51 reverse line 2 ***'Š ŠLḤ[RMNYM*** ("the men/people of HRMNYM').
	NPu	122.2 [. . .]***'YT ŠLṬBRY 'WGSṬS*** ("the . . . of Tiberius Augustus"); 122.2 ***Q'DRYG' ŠL[GRM'NY]QS*** ("the quadriga of Germanicus")

Comments

The determinative pronoun was a proclitic, uninflected for number, gender and case. Its shape, readily inferable from Latin-letter spellings, was *si-* + gemination of the consonant following: Pu *Poen.* 948:

mucom sussibti ("the place of his residence"). Vocalization and gemination are confirmed by the Latin-letter spellings of the independent possessive pronoun ***ŠL-***: Pu *Poen.* 1141 **silli** ("my") and *Poen.* 933 **syllochom** ("your"). The simple form ***Š-*** was unique to Punic and Neo-Punic. Phoenician knew only the extended form ***ŠL-*** of the pronoun, compounded with the preposition ***L-***. Historically, both in morphology and syntax, the pronoun is related to the Akkadian determinative pronoun ***ša*** (Ungnad-Matouš §30). Within the Canaanite family of languages, its only counterpart (syntactically, not morphologically) is the the literary Ugaritic inflected determinative ***D-*** (masc. sg.), ***DT*** (fem. sg.), ***DT*** (plural). Judaean Canaanite (Hebrew) possessed no morphologic counterpart although Late Hebrew (Biblical and Post-Biblical) had a syntactic counterpart in the indirect genitive marker ***ŠL***, a compound of the relative pronoun and the preposition ***L-***. While Phoenician ***ŠL*** and Late Hebrew ***ŠL*** are outwardly similar, they are quite different in their morphology.

The determinative pronoun ***Š-*** of Phoenician and Punic is not related to the Canaanite relative pronoun *še-*, attested in the Late Bronze II Lachish ewer inscription and in Late Hebrew, despite the outward similarity in morphology. As observed in the section on the relative pronoun, the relative ***Š-*** is unattested in any form of Phoenician and Punic.

B. *Syntax and Usage*

1. *Expressing the Indirect Genitive*

1a. Phoenician ***ŠL-***

The principal function of the determinative pronouns is to mark the indirect genitival relationship between two determined nouns. This is to say, the pronouns are essentially equivalent to the preposition "of" in English "the house of the mayor" or "the table of wood." In standard Phoenician, this function was commonly performed by ***'Š L-***: *NSI* 150.5 ***B'LYTN 'Š 'LM LMLQRT,*** ("Baalyaton, the Prophet of Milqart"). The use of ***ŠL-*** was rare, attested three times only in Phoenician, twice in the same inscription from Lapethos in Cyprus (Lapethos 3), raising the possibility that it may have been peculiar to Cypriote Phoenician. As earlier observed, Phoenician never used the simple pronoun ***Š-*** in this function as did Punic.

Lapethos 3 (Honeyman, *Le Muséon* 51 (1938) 285-298) line 4 ***QB'M***

ŠLKSP, "Cups of silver." *Obs.* In line 7 of this same inscription we find the direct genitive ***QB' KSP,*** "cups of silver."

Lapethos 3 lines 8/9 ***'NK PR[M . . . YTN]'T L['DNY LMLQRT] BL[P]Š W'L GBL Š[LL]PŠ [R]BT,*** "I PR[M erect[ed a – - –] for [my Lord Milqart of Lapthos and <for> the territorial gods of Great Lapethos." This restoration and rendering are problematic.

51 reverse line 2 (4th-3rd cent. Phoenician papyrus of unknown provenience): ***['L PN B]DB'L RB ḤRMNYM W'L PN 'Š ŠLḤR[MNYM],*** "*Before* Bodbaal, Governor of Hermonim, and *before* the people of Hermonim." *Obs.* It is possible that ***ḤRMNYM*** (if that is the correct reading) is the name of the ship that brought the cargo of goods listed in the papyrus. If so, Bodbaal may have been the captain (***RB***) of the ship and the ***'Š*** the "crew" of the ship. The place ***ḤRMNYM*** may occur in Psalm 42:7: ***M'RṢ YRDN WḤRMNYM,*** "From the region(s) of the Jordan and Hermonim." The location of the site is unknown.

The compounded determinative pronoun is essentially unknown in Punic although two instances, both in the same inscription, occur in Neo-Punic alongside ***Š-*** and ***L-*** in the same function: 122.2 [. . .]***'YT ŠLṬBRY 'WGSṬS WQDRYG' ŠL[GRM'NY]QS,*** ("The . . . of Tiberius Augustus and the quadriga of Germanicus.").

1b. Punic *Š*-

The use in Punic of the determinative pronoun to express the indirect genitival relationship between two nouns is exceedingly common. Often, the governing noun is not expressed, especially in headings and initial statements of identification.

1b-1. The Governing Noun Expressed

Pu 81.4 ***YB' 'LT HḤRZ ŠMQDŠM 'L,*** "They brought <them> into the custody of these sanctuaries."

Pu *CIS* i 5987.1 ***ḤNB'L HKHNT ŠKRW',*** "Hannabal, the Priestess of Korwa (Kore)."

Pu *CIS* i 5942 ***GRTMLQRT HKHNT ŠRBTN,*** "Gertmilqart Priestess of Our Lady."

Pu *CIS* i 4824.5/6 ***BYRḤ KRR ŠT Š'BD'ŠMN WḤN',*** "In the month of Kirur, in the year of Abdesmun and Hanno."

Pu 100.2/7 ***HBNM Š'BNM . . . HḤRŠM ŠYR . . . HNSKM ŠBRZL,*** "The builders of <buildings> of stone . . . the makers of <objects> of wood . . . the casters of <objects> of iron."

Pu *Poen.* 948 **<Esse> mucom sussibti,** "This is the place of his residence."

NPu J.G. Février, *JA* 1967 pp. 63-64 ***HMTNT ST ŠMTNB'L BN ŠPṬ***, "This gift is of (*i.e.*, this is the gift of) Mittunbal bin Sufet."

NPu 122.1 ***HNSKT Š'LM 'WGSṬS WKS'T ŠHNSKT L'LM 'WGSṬS,*** "The metal statues of the god Augustus and the thrones of the metal statues of the god Augustus."

NPu 124.3/4 ***KTBT DBR' HBT ŠG'Y BN ḤN',*** "The family history book [=family chronicle] of Gaius son of Hanno."

NPu 178.1.3 **Felioth iadem syRogate,** "<This is> the manufacture of (*i.e.*, was manufactured by) Rogatus."

Obs. The governing noun may carry a proleptic (anticipatory) possessive pronoun:

NPu 169.1/5 ***LŠBLT . . . 'ŠTM ŠYPT'N,*** "For SBLT, the wife (*lit.*, his wife) of Yupta." Cf. Song of Songs 3:7 ***MṬTW ŠLŠLMH*** *miṭṭato šelliŠlōmō* ("the bed of Solomon").

Obs. One putative instance of the pronoun ***Š-*** in Phoenician is alleged to occur in a seal from Anatolia from *ca.* ninth-eighth century B.C., published by A. Dupont-Sommer, *JKAF* 1 (1950/1) 43f ***ḤTM ŠṢRY*** "<This is> the seal of SRY." However, the correct reading of the seal is ***ḤTM MṢRY*** "<This is> the seal of Misri."

1b-2. With Ellipsis of the Governing Noun in Heading or Statement of Identification

NPu 117.1/2 ***Š'PWL'Y M'K[ŠM]' RYD'Y,*** "<This is the tomb> of Apuleus Maximus Rideus."

NPu NP 116.1f ***Š'ZRB'L,*** "<This is the tomb> of Hasdrubal."

Pu *CIS* I 5947.1 ***Š'M'ŠTRT,*** "<This is the tomb> of Amastart."

Pu Manfredi, *Monete,* 330-332 ***ŠYWB'Y,*** "<Coinage> of Juba."

Obs. In contrast to Punic usage, Phoenician, which does not have the determined pronoun ***Š-***, always uses in this function the preposition ***L-:*** 36.1/2 ***L'ṬHR BT 'BD'ŠMN,*** "<This is the tomb> of 'THR daughter of Abdesmun"; *CIS* I 50.1 ***L'ŠMNŠLK BN GRMLK,*** "<This is the tomb> of Esmunsillek son of Germilk." Head, *Historia Nummorum,* p. 790f ***LL'DK' 'Š BKN'N,*** "<Coinage> of Laodicaea in Phoenicia"; Head, p. 739 ***LṢDQMLK,*** "<Coinage> of Sidqmilk (King of Lapethos)." *Et passim.*

2. *Expressing Personal Relationship*

The determinative pronoun is commonly used to express association or relationship between two persons, the precise nature ofwhich is not entirely clear. The relationship might be that of father and son, in which case ***Š***- could be synonymous with ***BN*** ("the son of"), or that of slave to his master, in which case one might translate "the slave of." It is however more likely that the pronoun is an abbreviation of the longer expression ***Š'ZRT*** PN ("a member of the family of ") which occurs in Punic in *CIS* i 4873.3: ***BD'ŠMN HGRR Š'ZRT B'LYSP*** ("Bodesmun the Sawyer, a member of the family of Baalyasop."). This usage is characteristic of Punic only: the one alleged instance of the pronoun in Phoenician, in a graffito (*KAI* 49 36 Av) from Abydos, is perhaps Punic; all other occurrences are in Punic sources.

49 36 Av ***'NK MGN BN BD' ŠḤPṢB'L MNF,*** "I am Mago son of Bodo, <the X of> of Hipsibaal of Memphis."

Pu 64.1/2 ***B'LḤN' ŠBDMLQRT,*** "Balanno, member of the family of Bomilcar."

Pu 77.1/2 ***BRKMLQRT Š'ZRB'L BN GRSKN,*** "Birikmilqart, member of the family of Hasdrubal son of Gisco."

Pu *CIS* i 4872.3/4 ***'RŠ BN 'KBR Š'BD'ŠMN,*** "Aris bin Akbor, member of the family of Abdesmun."

Pu *CIS* i 5510.11 ***B'L'ZR BN ZBG ŠḤ[N'],*** "Baalazor son of Zabog, member of the family of Hanno."

Pu *CIS* i 5594.4/5 ***ḤŠQM HMRGL Š'DRB'L,*** "HSQM the Footman, member of the family of Adherbal."

Pu M. Fantar, "Une inscription exposee au Musee d'Utique," *Cahiers de Tunisie* 20, 79-80 (1972), pp. 9-15 ***QBR PRK' ŠBDMLQRT BN 'ŠMN'MS BN BDMLQRT,*** "<This is> the tomb of PRK', member of the family of Bomilcar son of Esmunamos son of Bomilcar."

CHAPTER SEVEN

THE INTERROGATIVES, INDEPENDENT POSSESSIVE PRONOUNS, THE INDEPENDENT OBJECT PRONOUNS AND OTHER PRONOUNS

I. The Personal Interrogative Pronoun

A. *Morphology*

Forms

MY *mī*	Ph	13.3; 14.4, 11, 12, 20, 24.14,15
	NPu	Trip. 49.1 in the name ***MYK'***
me	Pu	*Poen.* 1010
mi	Pu	*Poen.* 1002; *IRT* 827.1/2 in the name **Micebal**

Comments

The pronoun, pronounced *mī*, is the reflex of archaic Canaanite *miya* attested in the 14th century B.C. Amarna letters (EA 85.63; 94.12; 116.67). The spelling ***MY*** is historical, reflecting the pronunciation *miya*, the final *yod* being consonantal, not a vowel-letter.

B. *Syntax and Usage*

1. *Interrogative*

WHO?

Pu *Poen.* 1010 **Mi u?,** "Who is he?"

Pu *Poen.* 1002 **Me sem abuca?,** "What is/was your father's name?" *Cf.* the use of ***MY*** in Hebrew in Judges 13:17: ***MY ŠMK,*** "What is your name?"

NPu *IRT* 827.1.2 in the personal name **Mi-ceBal** *mī k^eBa'al*, "Who is like Baal?" The hypocoriston of this same name appears in NPu Trip. 49.1 ***MY-K'*** *mī-ka* (feminine).

2. *Indefinite Relative*

WHO, HE WHO

14.10/11 ***W'NK LMY KT 'B WLMY KT 'M WLMY KT 'Ḥ,*** "But as for me, to him who <had no father> I was a father, and to him who <had no mother> I was a mother, and to him who <had no brother> I was a brother."

24.15 ***WMY YŠḤT HSPR Z YŠḤT R'Š B'LṢMD,*** "As for him who shall destroy this inscription, Baal-semed shall smash his head."

24.11/12 ***MY BL ḤZ PN Š ŠTY B'L 'DR WMY BL ḤZ PN LP ŠTY B'L BQR,*** "I made him who had never owned a sheep the owner of a flock, and I made him who had never owned an ox the owner of cattle."

WHOEVER, WHICHEVER

13.3/4 ***MY 'T KL 'DM 'Š TPQ 'YT H'RN Z 'L 'L TPTḤ 'LTY,*** "Whoever you may be, anyone <at all>, who shall acquire this coffin, do not, do not open it!"

14.4 ***QN MY 'T KL MMLKT WKL 'DM 'L YPTḤ 'YT MŠKB Z,*** "O acquirer <of this resting-place>, whoever you may be, any person of royal lineage or any commoner, let him not open this resting-place!"

14.13/14 ***MY BBNY 'Š YŠB TḤTN WYZQ BSPR Z MŠKBM 'L YKBD LB'RRM,*** "As for whichever of my sons who shall sit <on the throne> in my stead, if he shall damage this inscription, the *mškbm* shall no longer respect the *b'rrm.*"

II. The Neuter Interrogative

A. *Morphology*

Forms

M	Ph	Indefinite: 24.4 (*M 'Š*)
M'	NPu	Relative: Trip.77.1;
		Indefinite: *BAC* NS 1-2 (1965) 229 (Bulla Regia); *Teboursouk* 8.2/3
mu	Pu	Interrogative: *Poen.* 1010; 1141b
	NPu	Relative: *IRT* 828.1; 865; 873.2; 877.2; 901.1, 4
M' 'Š	Ph	Indefinite: 24.4

	NPu	Relative: Trip. 79.1/2
mu ys	NPu	Relative: *Poen.* 939

Comments

The etymon of the pronoun appears was *mā*. The Phoenician reflex *mū* evidences the vocalic sound-change *ā* > *ō* > *ū* under stress. The relative *mū ʾīs* is compounded of the interrogative and the relative pronoun.

B. *Syntax and usage*

1. *Interrogative*

WHAT?

Pu *Poen.* 1010 **Mu? Pursa. Mi u?,** "What? Explain! Who is he?"

Pu *Poen.* 1141b **Mu <dobrim>?,** "What are they saying?" *Obs.* The Punic corresponds to Latin *Poen.* 1143 **quid illu locuti sunt inter se?**

2. *Indefinite Relative*

WHAT = THAT WHICH

24.4/5 ***M ʾŠ PʿLT BL PʿL <HMLKM> HLPNY{H}M***, "The kings who preceded me did not accomplish what I accomplished!"

NPu J. Fevrier, *BAC* NS 1-2 (1965-66) 229 (Bulla Regia 2): ***NDʿR ʾT Mʾ NʿDR***, "He vowed [fulfilled] what he vowed." *Cf. Téboursouk* 4.2/3 ***NDʿR ʾŠ NʿDR,*** "He vowed [fulfilled] what he vowed."

NPu *Téboursouk* 8.2/3 ***PYGʾ ʾT Mʾ NʿDR LBʿL,*** "He fulfilled what he had vowed to Baal."

3. *General Relative*

In Neo-Punic, the indefinite pronouns ***M*** and ***M ʾŠ*** ("what, that which") were extended to use as general relatives with antecedent. The pronouns are very common in late Neo-Punic alongside Standard Phoenician-Punic ***ʾŠ***. The forms ***M*** and ***M ʾŠ*** were free variants. Both forms could receive the definite article when the antecedent was determined.

_Mʾ_ = mu

NPu Trip. 77.1/2 ***MNṢBT Mʾ PʿLʾ BN[Yʾ] LʾBNʾM NYMRʿN,*** "<This is> the stele that his [Nimmira's] sons made for their father Nimmira."

NPu *IRT* 828.1 **Mintsyf[th m]u fel Baricbal Typafi,** "<This is> the stele that Baricbal Tapapius made."

NPu *IRT* 865 **Isfositio Nubo mu felun Flaban Ebean Numerian Sihhanc baneo,** "<This is> the *isfositio* of Nubo that his sons Flavianus, Ebean, Numerianus <and> Sihhanc made <for him>."

NPu *IRT* 877.1/6 **Centenari mu fel Thlana Marci Cecili byMupal efsem <M>acer byn banem,** "<This is> the *centenarium* (fortified farmhouse) that Thlana Marcius Caecilius son of Mupal made in the name of Macer, his grandson."

NPu *IRT* 901.1/4 **Memoria mu fela Thualath byth Nasif,** "<This is> the memorial that Thualath daughter of Nasif made."

NPu *LA* 1 1964/65 no. 3.3/6 **Castru[m] mu in[tseb u]fel [Math]lich,** "[This] fortified farmhouse is that which [Math]lich ere[cted and] built."

The relative pronoun may carry the definite article if its antecedent is determined:

NPu *IRT* 873.1/4 **Myntsyfth y-mu fel Bibi Mythunilim uintseb libinim Mythunilim,** "<This is> the stele which Bibi Mythunilim made and erected to his son, Mythunilim."

M’ ’Š **= mu ys**

NPu Trip. 79.1/2 ***B’RM QN’T ’T M’ ’Š P‘LM M‘ṢWKN,*** "You have acquired the tomb that Masauchan made."

The relative may carry the definite article if its antecedent is determined:

NPu *Poen.* 939 **Bod i(ly) a(nech) lythera ymu ys lomyn choth iusim,** "Let me inquire of these men who are coming out from here."

4. *Indefinite*

ANY(THING) (Latin **ecquid**)

Pu *Poen.* 1023 **Mu Ponnim sucartim?** "Do you remember anything of Punic?" *Obs.* The Punic corresponds to Poen. 985 **ecquid commeministi Punice?** Cf. the use of Hebrew *ma* in 1Samuel 19:3 ***WR’YTY MH,*** "If I learn anything," and Job 13:13 ***Y‘BR ‘LY MH,*** "Let anything befall me."

III. Independent Possessive Pronouns

A. *Morphology*

Phoenician and Punic ***'Š LY***

Forms

Sg. 1. C.		
'Š LY *'is lī*	Ph	17.1/2 ***'ŠTRT 'Š BGW HQDŠ 'Š LY*** ("Astarte of GW, my deity"); 43.9 ***L'DN 'Š LY LMLQRT*** ("for my Lord Milqart"); 50.4/5 ***KL KSP 'Š LY,*** ("all my money")
Sg. 3. M.		
'Š L *'is lo*	Ph	18.3/4 ***HŠ'R Z WHDLHT 'Š L,*** ("This gate and its doors"); Umm el-Awamid 19.2 ***'B Š L*** ("his father"); *RES* 56=1954 ***BNT 'Š L*** ("his daughters")
Pl. 1. C.		
'Š LN *'is lon(u)*	Pu	*RCL* 1966 p. 201 line 7 ***HMḤŠBM 'Š LN*** ("Our treasurers")

Phoenician and Neo-Punic ***ŠLY*** *sillī*

Forms

Sg. 1. C.		
silli *sillī*	Pu	*Poen.* 943/4 **hulec silli** ("my host"); *Poen.* 1141 **done silli** ("my father"); *Poen.* 1141 **amma silli** ("my other"); *Poen.* 1141 **bene silli** = var. **bane silli** ("my son")
Sg. 3. M.		
ŠL' *sillo*	Pu	100.5 ***'ZRT ŠL'*** ("his family")
	NPu	150.3 *[. . .]**M ŠL'*** ("his . . ."); *Punica* p. 153 no. 155.2/3 ***B'LM ŠL'*** ("his gods")
Sg. 3. F.		
ŠL' *silla*	NPu	143.3 ***'Š <Š>L'*** ("her husband")

Pl. 2. M.

syllochom *sillokom*	NPu	*Poen.* 933 **bymarob syllochom** ("in your custody")

Pl. 3. M.

ŠLM *sillom*	Pu	89.4 ***KSP . . . ŠLM*** ("their money")

Comments

The Phoenician and Punic independent possessive pronouns were used freely alongside the more common suffixal possessive pronouns. Phoenician and Punic used the independent possessive pronoun ***'Š LY*** *'īs lī* ("my"), compounded of the relative pronoun and the inflected form of the preposition ***L-***. Punic alone possessed the form ***ŠLY*** *sillī* ("my"), compounded of the determinative pronoun and the inflected form of the preposition. Both possessive pronouns, related to ***'Š L-*** and ***ŠL-*** respectively, are used to express the indirect genitive.

B. *Syntax and Usage*

The independent possessive pronouns follows the noun in the absolute state; the noun may carry the definite article or the article may be suppressed by reason of redundancy inasmuch as the possessive pronoun rendered the noun determined. The independent possessive pronouns could also follow and complement a suffixal possessive pronoun. Both pronouns were also expressed as simple ***LY,*** with suppression of the relative or determinative pronoun.

1. *The Noun Carries the Definite Article*

18.3/4 ***'YT HŠ'R Z WHDLHT 'Š L P'LT BTKLTY BNTY,*** "I built this gate and its doors at my own expense."

2. *The Noun is without the Definite Article*

Umm el-Awamid no. 9.1/2 ***LB'LŠMR RB Š'RM BN 'BD'SR SKR 'Š ṬN' L 'B 'Š L 'BD'SR RB Š'RM,*** "<This is> the memorial of Baalsamor Chief of Gatekeepers son of Abdosiri which his father, Abdosiri Chief of Gatekeepers, erected to him."

Pu *Poen.* 943/4P **Hulec silli . . . Antidamas con,** "Antidamas was my guest-friend."

NPu *Punica* p. 153 no. 15.1/3 ***ND'R 'Š NDR YKNŠLM . . . LB'L WLTNT B'LM ŠL',*** "The vow that Yakun-Salom vowed to Baal and to Thinnith, his gods."

NPu *Poen.* 932/933 **Yn byn ui bymarob syllochom, alonim, uybymysyrthochom,** "My nephew is in your custody, O gods, and under your protection."

3. *The Noun Carries the Suffixal Possessive Pronoun*

Pu *Poen.* 1141 **Hauo done silli,** "May my father live long!"
Pu *Poen.* 1141 **Hauo bene silli,** "May my son live long!"

4. *Possessive Pronoun Abbreviated to* ***LY***

46.5/8 ***'M L KTN . . . WNGD L PMY,*** "Its (the colony's) mother-city is Kition; its leader is Pumay."

NPu *JA* 1916/2 p. 495f no. 13.3 ***MNṢBT L',*** "His stele."

Pu *Poen.* 941A **Al bet lo cu cian bate,** "I have just now arrived at his house here."

IV. Independent Object Pronouns

Phoenician

The pronominal direct object of a verb is normally expressed by the suffixal pronoun. Phoenician does, however, possess an independent direct object pronoun, expressed by preposition ***'LT*** *'alt* + Suffixal Pronoun. The pronoun is related to the use in common Phoenician (Byblian and Tyro-Sidonian) of the preposition ***'LT*** to introduce the defined direct object of an active transitive verb in the manner of the particle ***'YT***: Byb 9 A 5 ***['BL LPT]Ḥ '[LT MŠKB] ZN,*** ("Do not open this resting-place!"); 14.7 ***YPTḤ 'LT MŠKB Z,*** ("He shall open this resting-place."); *cf.* the use of the accusative particle ***'YT*** in the latter statement in the same inscription in line 4: ***YPTḤ 'YT MŠKB Z***. The use of the preposition ***'LT*** to mark the determined direct object of an active transitive verb is entirely comparable to the use of the preposition ***L-*** in this same function in Aramaic (Segert, par. 6.5.2.3.6).

The independent object pronoun is attested in Tyro-Sidonian in two inscriptions, Tibnit = *KAI* 13 and Esmunazor = *KAI* 14, in all instances in the Sg. 3.M. ***'LTY*** *'altêyo* ("him/it"):

13.3/4, 5/6 ***’L TPTḤ ‘LTY***, “Do not open it (the coffin: ***’RN***)!”

14.20 ***’L YPTḤ ‘LTY***, “Let him not open it (the resting-place: ***MŠKB***).”

14.21 ***’L Y‘R ‘LTY***, “Let him not empty it (the resting-place) out!”

Punic

The Phoenician independent object pronoun ***‘LTY*** (“him”) is not attested in Punic, which uses instead the accusative particle ***’T*** + suffix pronoun; this pronoun, unknown in Phoenician, corresponds to Hebrew ***’TW*** *’ōto* (“him”). There are two examples only of the Punic independent object pronoun:

Pu *CIS* i 6001.1/2 ***‘BDMLKT ’L TŠ’ <’>T’***, “<This is the funerary urn of> Abdmilkot: do not carry it off!” The *aleph* in ***TŠ’*** is a haplography of two, contiguous *alephs*. *Obs.* The inscription is written in ink on a clay jar (funerary urn) found in 1895 in the Douimes necropolis at Carthage: Delattre, *Mem. Soc. des Antiquaires de France tome* LVI p. 257; Berger, *Musee Lavigerie* p. 67; Lidzbarski, *Ephemeris* I p. 295/96.

Pu *CIS* i 580.3 ***’RŠT BT BD‘ŠTRT ŠM‘ QL’ BRK ’T’***, “Arisut bit Bod'astart. He heard her voice; he blessed her”!

V. Other Pronouns

’DM *’adom*

ONE (German *man*, French *on*), A PERSON

26 A II 4/5 ***YŠT‘ ’DM LLKT DRK***, “One used to be afraid to walk the road.”

See also the related pronouns ***KL ’DM*** (“anyone”) and ***’DMM*** (“people”).

’DMM *’adamīm*

PEOPLE (in general)

14.6 ***’P ’M ’DMM YDBRKNK ’L TŠM‘ BDNM***, “Even if people tell you <to open my coffin>, do not be persuaded by them!”

’ḤD *’eḥḥad*

EACH ONE, EACH

Pu 69.3 ***B’LP KLL . . . LKHNM KSP ‘ŠRT 10 B’ḤD***, “In payment for an entire ox, the priests shall receive ten 10 silver for each one (animal).”

ʾŠ *ʾīs*

ONE (German *man*; French *on*)

Pu *Poen.* 944/946 **Ys duber ce fel dono . . . et cil comu con liful alt banim au,** "I am told (*lit.*, one says) that his father did everything for that son of his as he was to do <it for him>."

Pu *Poen.* 946 **Ys duber ci hen hu,** "I am told (*lit.*, one says) that he is here." = NPu *Poen.* 936 **Ys dubyr ch'innochoth u.**

Pu *Poen.* 948 **Alem us duber limir <esse> cumom sussibti,** "I am told (*lit.*, one says) that this is the place where he resides." = NPu *Poen.* 938 **Ynny i(s) d(ubyr) ch'ily gubulim lasibithim.**

See also the related pronoun ***BL ʾŠ*** ("no one, none").

EACH, EACH ONE

NPu 159.8 ***ʾŠ H'Lʾ [L]ʾ 'LTʾ WM[N]ḤT BMQDŠ,*** "Each offered up to Him his burnt offering and *minḥīt*-offering in the sanctuary."

NPu *AI* 1 p. 233 lines 1/4 **Fel th-ybur Licini Piso lybythem ulysthim ulys arun,** "Licinius Piso made <this> mausoleum for his daughter, for his son and for his wife, and for each a coffin."

BL ʾŠ *bal ʾīs*

NO ONE, NONE

26 A I 15/16 ***ʾŠM R'M B'L ʾGDDM ʾŠ BL ʾŠ 'BD KN LBT MPŠ,*** "Bad men, bandits, none of whom was a vassal of the House of Mopsos."

See the related pronoun ***ʾŠ*** ("one").

BT- *bitt-*, free variant ***BNT-*** *binat-*

The etymology of this pronoun, the basic meaning of which is "self, one's self," is obscure. The pronoun is used in Phoenician and Punic with the (i) the independent personal pronoun, (ii) the suffixal possessive pronoun and (iii) the anaphoric pronoun to form other pronouns.

ONE, ONE'S SELF, following an complementing a independent personal pronoun:

NPu 72 B 4 ***WB'L ḤRŠ Hʾ BTM,*** "He himself was the architect."

ONE'S OWN, following and complementing a suffixal possessive pronoun:

18.3/4 ***'YT HŠ'R Z . . . P'LT BTKLTY BNTY,*** "I built this gate at my own expense."

Pu 107.4 ***MLK 'DM BŠRM BN'TM,*** "The sacrifice of a human being of his own flesh."

Pu 105.3 ***MLK 'DM BŠ'RM BTM,*** "The sacrifice of a human being of his own flesh."

NPu 126.11 ***MZBḤ WP'DY P'L LMBMLKTM BT,*** "He built the altar and the podium at his own expense."

See the chapter on the Suffixal Possessive Pronoun for discussion and numerous other examples of the pronoun in this function.

THAT VERY, THAT SAME, following and complementing an anaphoric pronoun:

Kition lines 3/4 ***WYṢ' . . . L'GD LM MLḤMT BMQM 'Z BYM H' BNTY,*** "They came forth to do battle with them at this place on that same day."

KL *kil*

EACH (ONE), EVERYONE. The pronunciation of this pronoun is known from the Latin-letter spellings (Punic) **cel** and **cil** (*Poen.* 945) and (Neo-Punic) **chil** and **chyl** (*Poen.* 935).

24.5/6 ***KN BT 'B BMTKT MLKM 'DRM WKL ŠLḤ YD LL[Ḥ]M,*** "My royal house was in the midst of those of more powerful kings, and each one undertook to fight <me>."

Pu 89.2/3 ***'TK 'NK MṢLḤ 'YT 'M'ŠTRT W'YT 'MRT W'YT KL 'Š L',*** "I, Meslih, commend to you Amastart and Omrit and everyone who is <related> to her."

ANYONE

Pu 79.6/7 ***KL 'Š LSR T-'BN Z,*** "Anyone who shall remove this stele."

EVERYTHING

60.3/4 ***K BN 'YT ḤṢR BT 'LM WP'L 'YT KL 'Š 'LTY,*** "Because he built the temple court and did everything with which he was charged."

Pu 81.1 ***LRBT L'ŠTRT WLTNT BLBNN MQDŠM ḤDŠM <'L> KM KL 'Š BN[M],*** "<Dedicated> to the Lady Astarte and to Thinnith of Lebanon are these two sanctuaries as well as everything that is in them."

Pu *Poen.* 944/46 **Ys duber ce fel dono . . . et cil** (var. **cel**) **cumu** (var. **comu**) **con liful alt banim au,** "I am told that his father did everything for that son of his as he was to do it <for him>."= NPu *Poen.* 935/36 **Dobrim chy fel yth chil ys chon ythem liful yth binim,** "I am told that he did everything for his son that he was to do for him."

KL 'DM kil 'adom

ANYONE

13.3/4 ***MY 'T KL 'DM 'Š TPQ 'YT H'RN Z 'L 'L TPTḤ 'LTY,*** "Whoever you may be, anyone who shall come into possession of this coffin, do not, do not open it!"

EVERYONE

Pu 89.5/6 ***[. . .] 'M 'YT KL 'DM 'Š 'LṢ 'LTY BRḤT HKSP Z,*** "[Take away], O Mother, everyone who took pleasure with regard to me because of the loss of that money!"

NPu 165.3 ***KL 'DM KN NḤR,*** "He *treated* everyone honestly."

KL MNM

EVERYTHING

Pu 81.2 ***KL MNM '[Š BMQDŠM 'L],*** "Everything that is in these sanctuaries."

Pu 81.3 ***MLKT HḤRṢ WDL KL MNM '[Š . . .] WDL KL MNM BM'ZNM HMQDŠM 'L,*** "The goldwork and everything tha[t is in . . .] and everything <that is> in the *storerooms* of these sanctuaries."

ANYTHING AT ALL, NOTHING AT ALL

13.5 ***KL MNM MŠD BLT 'NK ŠKB B'RN Z,*** "Nothing of value but for me lies in this coffin."

See the related pronoun ***MNM*** ("something, anything").

MNM

SOMETHING, ANYTHING, NOTHING; cf. Ugaritic ***MNM*** (Aistleitner, par. 1592).

14.4/5 ***'L YBQŠ BN MNM K 'Y ŠM BN MNM,*** "Let him not look for anything in it [my coffin], for they did not put anything <of value> in it."

Pu 74.6 ***BKL ZBḤ ʾŠ YZBḤ DL MQNʾ WDL ṢPR BL YKN LKHN MNM,*** "Of any sacrifice that a man who owns no livestock nor fowl shall sacrifice, the priest shall not receive anything."

See also the related pronoun ***KL MNM*** ("everything").

CHAPTER EIGHT

THE NOUN AND ADJECTIVE

I. The Noun

A. *Morphology*

Inflection

Sg. M.
Absolute and Construct

-Ø	Ph	14.1 ***MLK*** *mílik* ("kings"), *et passim*
	Pu	*Poen.* 940 **macom** *maqōm* ("city"), *et passim*
	NPu	*Poen.* 937 **irs** *(ḥ)irs* ("shard"), *et passim*

Sg. F.
Absolute and Construct

FORM A

-T *-ot*	Ph-NPu	18.1 ***ʻRPT*** *ʻurpót* ("portico"), *et passim*
-'*T*	NPu	118.1, 122.2 ***ʻRP'T*** ("portico")
-ot	Pu	*Poen.* 937 **helicot** *h^{e}līkót* ("hospitality")
-oth	NPu	*Poen.* 947 **elichoth** ("hospitality"); 178.1 **felioth** ("work"); *Poen.* 934 **thymmoth** *timmót* < *tammót* ("finished, past")
-ut(h)	NPu	In personal names: *RES* 520 **Arisuth**; *CIL viii* 4850.2, 16768.2 **Birihut**; *CIS viii* 16955.1 **[Bi]ricut**
With Suffixal Pronouns		
-T *-at-*	Ph	174.6 αμαθη *ʼamaté* ("his female slave," gen.).
	Pu	*EH* Greek 1.1 ρυβαθων *ribbatón* ("Our Lady").

FORM B

-T *-t*	Ph	14.3 ***ʻTY*** *ʻittī* < *ʻintī* ("my time"); 19.5 , 60.1 ***ŠT*** *sat* < *sant* ("year")
	Pu	*Poen.* 948 **sibti** ("his residence")
-th	NPu	*IRT* 901.3 **byth** *bit* < *bint* ("daughter");

		mintsifth ("stele"); *IRT* 828.1, 873.1 **myntsyfth** ("stele"); **sath** ("year"); *Poen.* 933 **mysyrth** *miṣṣirt* ("protection"); *Poen.* 934 **yth** ("time")
With Anaptyctic Vowel		
-ith *-ìt*	NPu	*LA* 1 p. 45 no. 4.6 **myith** *mí'ìt* ("hundred"); *Poen.* 938 **sibithim** ("his residing")
FORM C (Nouns III*y*)		
-*T* *-īt* (*-iyt*)	Ph	26 A I 21 ***QṢT*** *qaṣīt* ("outlying area")
	Pu	69.14, 159.8 ***MNḤT*** *minḥīt* ("offering")
Dual		
Absolute State		
-***M*** *-êm*	Ph	34.4 ***ʿNM*** *ʿênêm* ("eyes")
	Pu	64.1 ***NṢBM WḤNWṬM*** *naṣībêm weḥanūṭêm* ("two stelai and two *ḥnwṭm*")
	NPu	141.5 ***M'TM*** *mi'(a)têm* ("two hundred")
-em	NPu	**iadem** *yadêm* ("two hands")
Construct State		
-***Ø*** *-ê*	Ph	Byb 10.10 ***L-ʿN*** *li-ʿênê* ("in the eyes of")
Pl. M.		
Absolute State		
FORM A		
-***M*** *-īm*	Ph-NPu	14.17 ***BTM*** *bāttīm* ("temples"), *et passim*
	Pu	81.4 ***MQDŠM*** *miqdasīm* ("sanctuaries"), *et passim*
	NPu	137.1 ***ŠPṬM*** *sōfṭīm* ("suffetes"), *et passim*
-***'M***	Pu	101.6 ***BN'M*** *būnīm* ("builders")
-***YM***	NPu	140.3 ***K'ʿSYM*** *kōʿsīm* ("undertakers"), 140.6 ***BʿNYM*** *būnīm* ("builders"); 161.6 ***KHNYM*** *kōhnīm* ("priests").
-em	NPu	*S* 24.3 **ai{a}em** *(ḥ)ayyīm* ("life"), *S* 24.3 **bunem** ("builders"), *IRT* 828.2 **mythem** *mitīm* ("dead persons")
-im	Pu	*Poen.* 947 **alonim** *'allōnīm* ("gods"); *Poen.* 947 **iussim** *yūṣīm* ("those coming out")

	NPu	*Poen.* 937 **alonim** ("gods"); *Poen.* **dobrim** ("they say"), *Poen.* 998 **donnim** ("gentleman"), *Poen.* 939 **iusim** ("those coming out"); *IRT* 893.4/5 **ilim sebuim** *ilīm* z^e*bū(ḥ)īm* ("sacrificed gods")
FORM B		
-***M*** *-êm*	Ph	***MM*** *mêm* ("water"), 14.16,17 ***ŠMM*** *samêm* ("sky")
-em	Pu	*Poen.* 1142 **mem** ("water"); *Poen.* 1027 **samem** *samêm* ("heavens")
-ημ	Ph	Sanch. 9 Σαμημ-ρουμος **samêm rūmīm* ("High Heavens")
Construct State		
-Ø *-ê*	Ph	*14.15* ***BT 'LNM*** *battê ʾallōnīm* ("the houses of the gods"); 26 A III 5 ***KL 'LN QRT*** *kil ʾallōnê qart* ("all the gods of the city")
	Pu	101.1 ***B'L' TBGG*** ("the citizens of Thugga")
	NPu	118.3 ***BN'*** ("sons"); 119.4, 126.7 ***'DR'*** ("senators"); 124.3 ***DBR'*** ("affairs")
-e	NPu	*S* 24.4 **b[e]ne** ("sons"); cf. *IRT* 865 **baneo** ("his sons")
-ε	Pu	*EH* Gr. 1.2 φανε ("face") in the divine name Φανεβαλ
-η	Pu	*EH* Gr. 3.2/3 φενη ("face") in the divine name Φενηβαλ
Pl. F.		
FORM A		
-***T*** *-ūt*	Ph	14.19 ***'RṢT*** *ʾaraṣūt* ("regions"), *et passim*
	Pu	68.5 ***P'MT*** ("times"); *CIS* I 6000.7 ***T'ṢMT*** ("great deeds"), *et passim*
	NPu	151.3 ***ŠNT*** *sanūt* ("years"), *et passim*
-*'T*	NPu	122.2 ***MSWY'T*** ("garments")
-ut	Pu	*Poen.* 940 **alonut** *ʾallōnūt* ("goddesses")
-uth	NPu	*Poen.* 930 **alonuth** ("goddesses")

FORM B

-HT *-hūt*	Ph	18.4 ***DLHT*** *dalahūt* ("doors"; sg. ***DLT*** *dalt, delt*); Hasan-Beyli 3 ***QRHT*** *qarahūt* ("cities"; sg. ***QRT*** *qart*)

FORM C

-YT *-yūt*	Ph	Byb 11 ***MLKYT*** ("queens"); 26 A I 13, 17 ***ḤMYT*** *ḥūmiyūt* ("walled fortresses"; sg. ***ḤMT*** *ḥūmīt)*; 26 A I 4 ***QṢYT*** *qaṣiyūt* ("outlying areas"; sg. ***QṢT*** *qaṣīt*); *CID* 8B ***ŠDYT*** *sadiyūt* ("fields")

1. *General Comments*

Sg. M.: The masculine singular exhibited no inflectional ending in the Absolute State. This is largely true as well of the noun in the Construct State with the exception of the nouns *ʾab* ("father") and *ʾaḥ* ("brother") and *pe* ("mouth; order, authorization"). In the case of *ʾab* and *ʾaḥ*, the construct forms in Phoenician exhibited the final vowel *-ū* for the nominative and accustive case and *-ī* for the genitive: *ʾabū* (nominative and accusative) and *ʾabī* (genitive); in Punic, at least by the 3rd century B.C., the form with final *-ū* came to be used for all cases in the construct: **Lymyth Icsina Micebal . . . au Mylthe,** ("<This is the tombstone> of the deceased Icsina Micebal, the brother of Mylthe."). The same inflection and development of these nouns was true of the presuffixal forms also: older Phoenician had *ʾabūyo* ("his father") for the nominative and accusative but *ʾabīyo* for the gentive; *cf.* Old Byblian ***LʾBH*** *liʾabīhu* ("for his father"); Old Tyro-Sidonian (9th cent. B.C.) ***ʾBY*** *ʾabīya* ("my father," gen.); but in Punic all cases exhibit final *-ū:* **auia** *ʾa(ḥ)ūya* ("her brother," nom.) but also **abuca** *ʾabūka* ("your father," gen.). The only other noun exhibiting a special form in the construct is ***P*** *pe* ("mouth"), which has the vestigial genitive case form *pī* with the preposition ***LPY*** *lipī* ("according to"). Case-inflection was also vestigial in place-names that end in *-ō*, such as ***YP*** *Yapō* ("Joppa, Jaffa") and ***ʿK*** *ʿAkkō* ("Acco, Acre"), which exhibit the case ending ***-Y*** *-ī* in the genitive: 14.19 ***YPY*** *Yapī* (genitive, governed by the particle ***ʾYT***); 49 34 At ***ʿKY*** *ʿAkkī* (genitive, in the construct relatioship ***YŠB ʿKY*** "a resident of Akko").

The masculine singular bisyllabic construct noun exhibited, as in Hebrew, pretonic vowel-reduction: **sidy** *s*ⁱ*di*, the construct of **sady,** in the place-name D 21 **Sidy Lybim** ("Land of the Libyans");

mucom *m^u^qōm,* the construct form of **macom,** in *Poen.* 948 **mucom syssibti** ("the place of his residing"). Note that in Hebrew, too, the noun *maqōm* has the construct form *m^e^qōm* before the relative pronoun *ʾašer* (Genesis 39:20, Leviticus 4:24) and *še-* (Qoheleth 1:7).

In marked contrast to bisyllabic construct nouns, masculine (and feminine) singular monosyllabic nouns, such as ***BN*** ("son"), ***ŠM*** ("name") and ***RB*** ("master"), were essentially proclitic in the construct. The virtual proclitic nature of the latter two nouns is indicated by the assimilation of the final consonant to the initial consonant of the governed noun: *IRT* 877.2/3 **Thlana Marci Cecili byMupal** ("Thlana Marcius Caeciliius son of Mupal *bimMupal*"); *cf.* Byblian 6.1, 7.3 ***BYḤMLK*** ("son of Yahimilk *biyYaḥīmilk*"); *IRT* 877.1/5 **Centenari mu fel . . . efseMacer byn banem** ("Fortified farmhouse that he built in the name of Macer *efsemMaker,* his grandson."). In the case of the noun ***RB*** *rab* < **rabb,* the virtual proclitic character of the construct form is evidenced by the construct sound-change *a* >*i* in closed unstressed syllable, indicating that the noun is in fact the initial syllable of the following word: D 2.4/5 **ryb mith** *rìbmít* ("commander of a hundred" = ***RB M'T***). In *LA* 1 p. 45 no. 4.4 **ryb <M>ycnim** *ribBiqnim* ("Governor of Miqnim"), the bound noun shows the sound-change *a* > *i* but also assimilation of the final **b** of the first noun to the initial **m** of the second, with resultant *-bb-*; this same phenomenon is attested already in Phoenician with the monosyllabic construct noun *milk* ("the king of") in *FK* A 1.2 ***MLKTY*** *milkKit(t)ī* for ***MLK KTY*** *milkKit(t)ī,* the haplography ***K*** for ***KK*** indicating proclitic character of the monosyllabic bound noun; *cf.* Neo-Punic **efseMacer** *evsemMaqer* ("in the name of Macer") for **efsem-Macer.**

Sg. F.: The feminine singular exhibits the free variant inflectional endings *-ót* (Canaanite stress-lengthened *-át)* and *-t.* The form *-ót* appears with the noun in the absolute and in the construct state; it possesses the complementary variant (allomorph) unstressed *-àt-*, used with stressed suffixal pronouns: absolute and construct *ribbót* but presuffixal *ribbató* ("his Lady"). In Neo-Punic *-ot* also had the pronunciation *-ut,* with lowering of the vowel, although this pronunciation is attested only in feminine personal names. The form *-t* has the occasional variant *-ìt,* with anaptyctic vowel: *Poen.* 938 **sibith-** *síbit* ("residing") and *LA* 1 p. 45 no. 4.6 **myith** *míʾit* ("hundred").

The polysyllabic construct noun normally retained its own (independent) stress, as indicated by the stressed form **felioth** *felīót* in the direct genitive 178.1 **felioth iadem** ("manufacture," *lit.*, "work of the hands"). Had the noun lost its independent stress in construct, it would have exhibited the unstressed feminine afformative *-àt* found in the presuffixal forms Pu *EH* Gr 1.1 ρυβαθων *ribbatón* ("our Lady") and Phoenician 174.6 αμαθη *ʾamaté* ("his slave woman"). This same pattern of independent stress is frequently evidenced in the stressed construct form **amot** *ʾamót* in the sentence-names like **Amot-Micar** (*ʾMT MLQRT*, "Servant of Milqart" *CIL* viii 12335).

Pl. M.: The masculine plural exhibits the inflectional ending *-īm* and its complementary variant *-êm*, the latter used with two nouns only, both from stems ending in *-ay*: *mêm* < *maym* ("water") and *samêm* < *samaym* ("sky"); the morphology of these two nouns is related to that of the Aramaic masculine plural active participles of verbs III*y*, *e.g.*, *bānayn* (Syriac *bāneyn*). The construct plural of both forms exhibited the inflectional ending *-ê* < *-ay*, in origin the construct ending of the masculine dual in the oblique case: *S* 24.4 **b[e]ne M[. .]chan** ("the sons of M[. .]chan"). The construct form is also that used with the suffixal (possessive) pronouns: *IRT* 865 **baneo** *banêyo* ("his sons"). The polysyllabic masculine plural construct noun retained independent stress but exhibited the same pattern of pretonic reduction characteristic of the Hebrew construct: *f*^{e}*nê*, the construct plural of *fanīm* ("face") in the divine name *EH* Greek 3.2/3 Φενη-Βαλ ("Face-of-Baal").

Pl. F.: The feminine plural inflectional ending was *-ūt* < *-ōt*. The form *-yūt* appears principally with feminine nouns from III*y* singular forms with the feminine afformative *-īt* (*-iyt*). But also the plural *CID* 8B ***ŠDYT*** ("fields") of the III*y* noun ***ŠD*** *sade*. However, note the rare exception Byb 11 ***MLKYT*** ("queens"; sg. ***MLKT*** *milkot*). The feminine afformative *-(a)hūt* is found only for the plural forms of monosyllabic feminine nouns of the shape *CaCt* like *delt* ("door, tablet") and *qart* ("city").

2. *Unusual Plural Forms*

Some masculine plural nouns have plural forms different from those in Hebrew or not attested in Hebrew. ***ʾŠ*** *ʾīs* ("man") has the regular plural ***ʾŠM*** *ʾīsīm* (26 A I 15), not *ʾanašīm* as in Hebrew. The noun

'DM *'adóm* ("man, person") had a plural form ***'DMM*** *'adamīm* (14.6, 60.7 "people") not known in Hebrew. ***MQM*** *maqōm* ("place") has the regular masculine plural ***MQMM*** *maqūmīm* (26 A II 3), not *m^eqōmōt* as in Hebrew.

The word "god" (***'LM*** *'ilīm*) has several plurals: ***'LM*** *'ilīm* (26 A II 6), ***'LNM*** *'allōnīm* (10.10; 14.9, 22; *Poen.* 930, 920) and ***BN 'LM*** *banê 'ilīm* (26 A III 19). The latter two plural yield the rare "back-form" singulars ***'LN*** *'allōn* (104.1/2; *EH* 5.1).

The masculine singular noun ***RB*** *rab* had the feminine plural ***RBT*** in titles, such as Pu 101.2 ***RBT M'T*** ("commanders of a hundred"; sg. ***RB M'T***); and when the noun means ("proprietary god"): NPu 119.1 ***LŠDRP' WLMLK'ŠTRT RBT 'LPQY,*** ("For Satrapes and for Milkastart, the proprietary gods of Lepcis."). But the word had the plural ***RBM*** *ribbīm* when it means "generals of the army" (Pu *CIS* i 5510.9).

Some feminine nouns of the type *CVCt* have the plural *CVCahūt*: ***DLHT*** (18.3 "doors") is the plural of ***DLT*** *delt*, and ***QRHT*** (Hassan-Beyli 3 "cities") is the plural of ***QRT*** *qart* ("city"). However, the feminine noun ***'ŠT*** *'ist* ("wife, woman") has the regular plural form ***'ŠTT*** *'isatūt* (37 A 14; B 5), never *našīm* as in Hebrew; this plural follows the pattern of Hebrew ***DLTWT*** *d^elatōt* ("doors"), the plural of *délet;* and ***QŠTWT*** *q^ešatōt* ("bows"), the plural of *qéšet*.

The noun ***MLKT*** *milkot* ("queen") has the plural ***MLKYT*** (11); contrast the regular plural ***MLKWT*** *m^elakōt* of Hebrew. The singular noun ***'LM*** *'ilīm* ("goddess") has the feminine plural form ***'LNT*** *'allōnūt* ("goddesses," *Poen.* 930, 940) when female gender need be indicated specifically .

3. *Common Noun Patterns*

Given here is a small selection of the more common noun patterns, illustrated by vocalized examples, most from the Tripolitanian Latin-letter Punic inscriptions and the Punic and Neo-Punic passages preserved by Plautus in the *Poenulus*.

3a. Monosyllabic Nouns

qal: **ab** *'ab* (***'B*** "father," *CIL* viii 21481). Fem. **sath** *sat* < *sant* (***ŠT*** "year," *LA* 1 p. 45 no. 4.2)

qil: **byn ban- ben- bin- byn-** ("son," see Special Classes); **myth** *mit* (***MT*** "dead person," *IRT* 827.1); **et** *ʿeṣ* (***ʿṢ*** "wood," *Poen.* 1142); **sem** *sem* (***ŠM*** "name" *Poen.* 1002; *IRT* 877.4). Fem. **byth** *bit* < *bint* (***BT*** "daughter," see Special Classes); **myith** *míʾit* (***MʾT*** "one hundred," *LA* 1 p. 45 no. 4.; **sibt-** *sibt* (***ŠBT*** "residing," *Poen.* 948); **yth** *ʿit* < *ʿint* (***ʿT*** "time," *Poen.* 934)

qīl: **ys** *ʾīs* (***ʾŠ*** "man": *IRT* 879.1)

qōl: κουλ- *qūl* (***QL*** *qūl* "voice," *EH* Gr. 1.4); **bur** *būr* (***BR*** "tomb," *AI* 1 p.233 line 1)

qūl: **lua** *lūᵃh* (***LḤ*** "tablet," *LA* 1 p. 45 no. 3.1/.2)

qall: **amma** *ʾamma* (***ʾM*** "mother," *Poen.* 1141A); **ryb-** *rib* < *rab* < *rabb* (***RB*** "master")

qill: **cel** and **cil** *kil* < *kill* ("everything," *Poen.* 945); **chyl** *kil* < *kill* ("everything," *Poen.* 937)

qatl: αλφ *ʾalp* (***ʾLP*** "ox," Vattioni p. 325 no. 41); αφδε *ʿabde* (***ʿBDY*** "his slave," Ph 174.8); **arb** *ʿarb* (***ʿRB*** "evening," *LA* 1 p. 45 no. 4.7); **hers** var. **irs** *ḥerś* (***ḤRŠ*** "shard, pottery," *Poen.* 937; 947); **ars** *ḥarš* (***ḤRŠ*** "craftsmanship," *IRT* 889.3)

IIʿ: **bal** *baʿl* (***BʿL*** "master," *IRT* 889.3); **nar** *naʿr* (***NʿR*** "son," *IRT* 889.3)

II*w*: **on** *ʾôn* < *ʾawn* (***ʾN*** "inquity," D 6.5/6)

II*y*: **bet** *bêt* < *bayt* (***BT*** "house," *Poen.* 941A); **bit** *bīt* < *bayt* (***BT*** "house," *Poen.* 941P); **byth** *bīt* < *bayt* (***BT*** "house," *Poen.* 931)

III *ḥ* ʿ: **iyra** *yíraḥ* (***YRḤ*** "month," *LA* 1 p. 45 no. 4.1/2, 8

qutl: **umer** var. **umir** *ʾúmir* (***ʾMR*** "word," *Poen.* 1017)

qitl: **ix** *ʿiqs* (***ʿQŠ*** *ʿiqs* "deception," *Poen.* 1033)

3b. Bisyllabic Nouns

qatal: **adom** *ʾadom* (***ʾDM*** "person," *IRT* 879.1). Fem. αμαθη *ʾamate* (***ʾMTY*** "his female slave," Ph 178.6)

qatil: **sady** *sadi* (***ŠD*** "field, country," D 2.7/8; D 5.10/11)

qutul: **becor** *bᵉkor* (***BKR*** "firstborn son," *Poen.* 942)

qatīl: **iaed** *yaḥīd* (***YḤD*** "only son," *Poen.* 932); **nasib** *naṣīb* (***NṢB*** "stele," *IRT* 893.1). Fem. **helicot** *hᵉlīkot* (***HLKT*** "hospitality," *Poen.* 947); **felioth** *felīot* ("work," 178.1)

qatōl: λασουν *lasūn* (***LŠN*** "tongue," Vattioni p. 525 no. 41); **salus** *salūs* (***ŠLŠ*** "three," Vattioni p. 533 no. 7)

qutūl: **gubul-** *gᵘbūl* (***GBL*** "district," *Poen.* 939)

qōtel: **hulec** *hūlek* (***HLK*** "host," *Poen.* 943); **urys** *(ḥ)ūris* (***ḤRŠ*** "engraver," *PBSR* 28 p. 53 no. 5.10)

qawtal: **guzol** *gûzol* (***GZL*** "dove," Vattioni p. 529 no. 7)
quttāl: **umman** *ʾummān* (***ʾMN*** "artisan," 178.2/3)
qattīl: **addir** ("mighty," *CIL* viii 21481)
qittīl: ***QYDŠ*** *qiddīs* ("holy, holy one," 145 I 4)
qittūl: κισσου *qissūʾ* (***QŠʾ*** "cucumber," Vattioni p. 525 no. 39)

3c. Nouns with Preformatives and Afformatives

3c-1. Preformative ***M-***

maqtal: **[mi]gdal** *migdal* (***MGDL*** "tower," *PBSR* 28 p. 54 no. 7.3); **macom** *maqōm* (***MQM*** "place," *Poen.* 930; *Poen.* 940). Fem. **mysyrth** *miṣṣirt* < *maṣṣart* (***MṢRT*** "protection," *Poen.* 933)
maqtil: Fem. **myntsyfth** *mintsivt* < *mantsibt* (***MNṢBT*** "stele," *IRT* 828.1; *IRT* 873.1)
maqtōl: **marob** *maʿrōb* (***MʿRB*** "custody,":*Poen.* 933)

3c-2. Preformative ***N-***

naqtal: Fem. ***NʾSPT*** ("assembly," 60.1)

3d-3. Preformative ***T-***

taqtal: Fem. **thychleth** *tiklīt* (***TKLT*** *tiklīt* "expenditure," *IRT* 906.4)

3c-4. Afformative *–ōn*

qatlōn: **allon-** (**allonim, allonut**) *ʾallōnim ūallōnut* (***ʾLNM WʾLNT*** "gods and goddesses," *Poen.* 940; NPu *Poen.* 930)

4. *Special Classes of Nouns*

Requiring special comment are several nouns that are frequently attested in sources of all periods and whose morphophonology is therefore comparatively well known. To this group belong the morphologically related nouns *ʾab* ("father") and *ʾaḥ* ("brother") that have the extended forms *ʾabū* and *ʾaḥū* respectively in construct and before suffixal pronouns; the monosylabic nouns *ʾam* ("mother"), *bin* ("son"), *bit* ("daughter"), *ʾist* ("woman, wife") and *sem* ("name").

ʾB and ʾḤ

In the earlier period, sometime before the middle of the first millennium B.C., the nouns *ʾab* and *ʾaḥ* in the construct singular and before possessive pronouns retained a two-case inflection: *ʾabū* and *ʾaḥū* in the nominative and accusative, *ʾabī* in the genitive. It is possible that the genitive form is represented by ninth-century Tyro-

Sidonian ***'BY*** *ʾabīy(a)* ("my father") and Byblian ***L'BH*** *liʾabīhu* ("for his father"); the genitive inflection was in fact always retained (vestigially) in the case of the noun ***P*** *pe* ("mouth") in the preposition ***LPY*** *lipī* ("in accordance with," Pu 69.13) and in the genitive case construct form ***PY*** *pī:* Pu 79.9 ***BY PY 'DM*** ("without the permission/authorization of someone").

In the second half of the first millennium B.C., if not earlier, the construct form and form with possessive pronouns of the nouns *ʾab* and *ʾaḥ* was *ʾabū* and *ʾaḥū* respectively, regardless of the case of the noun. Thus, in third century B.C. literary Punic one finds the form *ʾabūka* in the genitive in **me sem abuca** *mī sem ʾabūka* ("What is/was your father's name?: *Poen.* 1003); and in Neo-Punic the form *abūnom* in the genitive: *S* 24.2 **felu labunom Iyllul** *felū labūnom Yillul* ("They built it for their father Iyllul."); cf. the Neo-Punic form *a(ḥ)ūya* in the genitive: *IRT* 826.1/3 **fela l<a>uia Ocles** *fela l(a)ūya Ocles* ("She made <it> for her brother Ocles.").

In late Neo-Punic of the Roman period, the historical forms *ʾabī* ("my father") and *ʾaḥī* ("my brother") appear to have competed with new forms *(a)būyī* and *(a)ūyī.* In the latter, which are the result of paradigmatic analogy, the presuffixal forms *(a)bū-* and *a(ḥ)ū-* receive the possessive pronoun *-ī* of the first person singular, with the intervention of intervocalic glide *-y-* that was used in Phoenician with the possessive pronouns *-o* ("his") and *-a* ("hers") when affixed to a vowel: Phoenician *ʾabūyo* ("his father") and *ʾabūya* ("her father"). The sole example of this new form is **ui** *(ḥ)ūyī* ("my brother," which occurs twice in *Poen.* 932/933) **Liphoc anech yth byn ui iaed; yn byn ui bymarob syllochom, alonim, uybymysyrthochom,** ("I would get my brother's only son. My brother's son in is your custody, O gods, and under your protection.").

'B

Forms

Singular

Absolute State

'B *ʾab*	Ph	24.10; 26 A I 3
ab	Pu	In the divine name *CIL* viii 21481

		Abadir
	NPu	D 6.9, 10
With Possessive Suffixes		
1. Sg.		
Archaic		
'B *'abī*	Ph	24.10: nominative case
'BY *'abīya*	Ph	24.5,9: genitive case
Standard		
'BY *'abī*	Ph	26 A I 11
a-bi (Asarh. 60.61)	Ph	In the personal name **A-bi-ba-'a-li**
αβι	Ph	In the personal name Αβιβαλος
2. Sg. M.		
abuca *'abūka*	Pu	*Poen.* 1003 (gen.)
3. Sg. M. *'abūyo*		
'BY	Ph	34.2
'BY'	NPu	Trip. 79.2
'BY'	NPu	*NP* 63.2
buo	NPu	*IRT* 877.6
Byblian		
'BH *'abīhu*	Byb	1.1 (gen.)
3. Pl. M.		
'BNM *'abūnom*	Ph	40.5
'B'NHM	NPu	143.4
'BN'M	NPu	Trip. 77.2
abunom	NPu	*S* 24.2 (gen.)
Plural		
'BT *'abūt*	Ph	26 A I 12
With Suffix Pronouns		
3. Sg. M.		
'BTM *'ahūtim*	NPu	126.8

'Ḥ

Singular

Absolute		
'Ḥ *'aḥ*	Ph	24.11
Construct		
au *('a)ḥū*	NPu	*IRT* 827.2/3 (gen.)

With Suffix Pronouns

1. Sg.		
'Ḥ *'aḥī*	Ph	24.3 (nominative case)
a-ḫi	Ph	In the name ***A-ḫi-mil-ki*** (Assurb. II 84)
ḫi *('a)hī*	Ph	In the name ***Ḫi-ru-um-mu*** (Tigl. III 9.51)
hi	Pu	In the name **Himilco** (*CIL* viii 10525).
ui *('a)ḥūyī*	NPu	*Poen.* 931, 932 (2x)
3. Sg. M.		
'ḤY *'aḥūyo*	Ph	47.2.
'ḤY'	NPu	*NP* 2.2
3. Sg. F.		
auia *'aḥūya*	NPu	*IRT* 826.3 (nom.)
uia *('a)ḥūya*	NPu	*IRT* 826.2 (gen.)
3. Pl. M.		
unom *('a)ḥūnom*	NPu	*PBSR* 23 p. 141 no. 24.4 (nom.)

'ŠT

In Phoenician-Punic, the word for "woman, wife" was *'is(a)t* (*'ésat*), the feminine of the noun *'īs;* its plural was *'isatūt* (*'isatōt*), after the pattern of Hebrew *qéšet* ("bow"; plural *q*^{e}*šatōt*). The single vocalized example of the noun in the absolute case is Greek-letter Phoenician εσαθ, in which the a-vowel is secondary, deriving from the plural form *'isatūt.* The noun-form *'išša* < *'aššat* < *'anthat* does not exist in Phoenician-Punic. The construct form is attested in the presuffixal form **ysth-** in Latin-letter spelling.

Forms

Singular		
Absolute State		
'ŠT *'esat*	Ph	26 A II 5
εσαθ	Ph	174.7

Construct State

'ŠT *'est*	Pu	93.2

With Suffix Pronouns

3. Sg. M.

Nominative Case

'ŠT' *'isto*	NPu	117.4; 142.3

Genitive Case

'ŠTY *'isti(m)*	NPu	Trip. 79.4	
'ŠTM		NPu	169.4; 171.2; *NP* 22.2
ysthim	NPu	*AI* 1 1927 233 line 3; *IRT* 828.2	

Plural

Absolute and Construct

'ŠTT *'is(a)tūt*	Ph	37 A 14, B 5

BN

The exceedingly common noun ***BN*** ("son") had the form *bin* in the construct singular, always with the vowel *i.* In the presuffixal form, however, the noun is attested in vocalizations *bin-* and *ben-* but also often in the vocalization *ban-*; the latter is perhaps influenced by the plural form *banīm.* The a/i-vowel of the noun with suffixes is normally retained, even when the pattern of stress would dictate its reduction to zero: *e.g., IRT* 828 **loby[ni]m** and *IRT* 873.3 **libinim** ("for his son"); cf. the full reduction of the vowel in Hebrew ***LBNW*** *livnó* ("for his son"); a single instance of full reduction is however recorded: *AI* 1 1927 233 **lifnim** *livním* ("for his son"). The plural form absolute was *banīm* and the construct form *banê* or *b^{e}nê,* with vowel reduction.

Forms

Singular

Absolute State

BN	Ph	14.8

Construct State

BN	Ph, Pu, NPu *Passim*	
B'N	Pu	*CIS* i 5522.4
bn	NPu	D 9.2
bin	Pu	*Poen.* 943

by-	NPu	*IRT* 877.4
byn	NPu	*Poen.* 932 (2x); *Poen.* 995A; D 2.3; D 5.20; *IRT* 877.5; *IRT* 906.2
βυν	Pu	175.4;177.3
With Suffixes		
1. Sg.		
bene	Pu	*Poen.* 1141P
bane	Pu	*Poen.* 1141A
3. Sg. M.		
Nominative Case		
BN' *bino*	Pu	161.9
BNY	NPu	153.4.
binim	NPu	*IRT* 889.1
[by]no	NPu	*PBSR* 28 53 no. 6.1/2
byne	NPu	*IRT* 906.1
by[ni]m	NPu	*IRT* 828.1/2
Genitive Case		
BNY *bini(m)*	NPu	Trip. 79.4
banem	NPu	*IRT* 877.5/6; *IRT* 893.3/4
banim	Pu	*Poen.* 946A
benim	Pu	*Poen.* 946P
binim	NPu	*IRT* 873.2; *Poen.* 936
ifnim	NPu	*AI* 1 1927 233 line 2
3. Sg. F.		
BNY *bini(m)*	Ph	40.4 (gen.)
3. Pl. M.		
Nominative Case		
BNM *binom*	Ph	Umm el-Awamid 6.3
bynom	NPu	*PBSR* 28 53 no. 5.1
Genitive Case		
bannom	NPu	*PBSR* 28 53 no. 5.11
Plural		
Absolute State		
BNM *banīm*	NPu	162.5
Construct State *banê*		
BN	Ph	26 A III 19; 27.11; 40.4

BN'	NPu	118.3; 126.5,6; Trip. 51.4
b[e]ne	NPu	*PBSR* 23 p. 141 no. 24.4

With Suffix Pronouns

1. Sg. *banay*

BNY	Ph	24.13

3. Sg. M.

BNY' *banêyo*	NPu	Trip. 8.2
baneo	NPu	*IRT* 865

3. Sg. F.

B'N[Y'] *banêya*	NPu	117.5
B'NY'	NPu	*JA* 1918 254,4

BT

The noun ***BT*** had the shape *bit* in the construct singular; this was doubtless its shape in the absolute singular as well. As the Latin-letters spelling clearly indicate, the sound-change *i>a* in a doubly closed stressed syllable seen in the Hebrew form *bat* (absolute and construct) was not characteristic of Phoenician phonology. As in Hebrew, the noun had the shape *bitt-* with affixed possessive pronouns. The plural was *banūt* < *banōt* as in Hebrew.

Forms

Singular

Construct State

BT *bit*	Ph	14.15; 29.1; 50.1
	Pu	*NP* 4; NP 12.2; *EH* 55.3
B'T	NPu	*NP* 36.3
byth	NPu	*IRT* 901.3

With Suffix Pronouns

3. Sg. M.

Nominative Case

BT' *bitto*	NPu	JA 1916/2 515: 38,2

Genitive Case

bythem *bitti(m)* NPu AI 1 1927 233 lines 2

3. Sg. F.
bythi *bitti(m)* NPu *IRT* 901.5

Plural
Absolute
BNT *banūt* Ph RES 56.3
NPu 162

B. *Syntax and Usage*

1. *Collective Singular Nouns*

There are several nouns that are morphologically singular but have plural meaning. These generally denote a body of persons. Most common of this group of nouns is ***'Š*** *'īs* ("people"): 46.3/5 ***ŠLM H'Š LMṢB,*** ("May the people of the colony prosper!"). Other examples are ***'DM*** *'adom* ("people, population") and ***B'L*** *bá'al* ("citizenry"): 30.4 ***BN YD B'L WBN YD 'DM,*** ("From it [the island of Cyprus] he drove out <its> citizenry, and from it he drove out <its> people."). Here also belongs ***'M*** *'am,* used as the plural of ***'Š*** *'īs* in Müller 2.74/75 ***'M MḤNT*** *'am maḥnīt* ("members of the army"), the plural of ***'Š MḤNT*** (*CIS* i 5866).

2. *Plural with Singular Meaning*

There are several nouns that occur in the morphologic plural but with singular meaning. The common noun ***'DN*** *'adōn* ("lord, master"), normally used in the singular, is also attested in the plural form ***'DNM*** *'adūnīm* ("the Lord") in the personal name *CIS* i 4551.7, 5274.4 ***ŠM-'DNM*** ("The Lord is <my>name [god]."). This same noun in this usage is also characteristic of Hebrew: Is 19:4 ***'DNYM QŠH*** ("a hard master"); and, more important, is the common use of this noun in Hebrew when referring to God (***'DNY*** *'adonay* "My Lord").

The normal word for "god" and "goddess" was ***'LM*** *'ilīm* 59.2 ***'LM NRGL*** ("the god Nergal"); 48.2 ***'LM 'DRT 'S*** ("the great goddess Isis"). Like Hebrew ***'LHYM*** *'elōhīm* ("God") the noun is plural and, indeed, used in Phoenician as a plural meaning "gods": 26 A II 6 ***BYMTY 'ŠT T<L>K LḤDY DL PLKM B'BR B'L W'LM,*** ("In my time, a woman is able to travel alone, without bodyguards, thanks to Baal and the gods.").

The divine name ***B'L*** ("Baal") is attested in the plural form ***B'-LYM*** *Ba'alīm* ("Baal") in the personal name *CIS* i 135.5 ***Y-B'LYM*** ("Where is Baal?"). It is this plural form with singular meaning that is imitated in Biblical *hab-Be'alīm* (Ju 2:11, 3:7, 8:33, 1): (6,10; 1 S 7:4, 12:10 *et cet.*) = *hab-Ba'al* ("Baal").

The common term *būr* ("tomb, mauseoleum") is found in both the singular and plural (with singular meaning). ***B'RM*** *būrīm* ("tomb") is found in NPu Trip. 79.1/2 ***B'RM QN'T 'T M' 'Š P'LM M'ṢWKN,*** ("You have acquired the tomb that Masauchan built."). That the noun is in fact singular is assured by the use of a singular verb in line 6 of this same inscription: ***NPL'*** (for ***NP'L***) ***BTṢTY BTY,*** ("It was built at his own expense."). The same word in the morphological singular occurs in NPu *IRT* 8282/3 **Bur ysoth . . . fel,** ("He built this tomb."). The use of the plural with singular meaning with architectural terms is common usage in Ugaritic, in which the plurals ***BHTM*** and ***HKLM*** express the singular "temple".

3. *Feminine Singular Abstract Noun with Concrete Meaning*

The feminine noun ***MMLKT,*** in origin meaning "kingship, kingdom," denotes "king" or "prince": 14.9 ***MMLK<T> 'DR*** ("whichever mighty king."); Pu 111.4/5 ***MSNSN HMMLKT*** ("King Masinissa"). Compare the Ugaritic feminine singular abstract nouns ***D'T*** (originally "knowledge, friendship") and ***T'DT*** (originally "witness") with concrete meaning "friend" and "messenger" respectively.

4. *Abstract Noun Expressed by the Plural Noun*

The plural ***'BT*** *'abūt* of the noun *'ab* ("father") expresses the concept of "fathership": 26 A I 12 ***W'P B'BT P'LN KL MLK*** ("And every king adopted me as his father."). Compare the plural ***BNM*** *banīm,* literally "sons," with the meaning "sonship."

'DNM *'adūnīm,* the plural of *'adōn* ("lord, king"), expresses the concept of "lordliness, royalty," used as an adjectival noun: 26 A I 10 ***BT 'DNY*** *bêt 'adūnay* ("my royal house"); 26 A I 10 ***ŠRŠ 'DNY*** *suris 'adūnay* ("my royal stock"). Compare the similar use of the abstract nouns ***MLK*** ("kinship") and ***MŠPṬ*** ("imperium") in 1.2 ***ḤṬR MŠPṬH . . . KS' MLKH*** ("his imperial scepter . . . his royal throne").

Like the plural ***'BT*** *'abūt* ("fathership"), the plural ***BNM*** *banīm* of ***BN*** ("son") has the abstract meaning of "sonship": NPu 124.2/3 ***B'LYTN QMD' 'Š 'L' BBNM 'T M'QR BN G'Y*** ("Balitho Commodus, who was adopted in sonship alongside Macer son of Gaius."). This same usage is attested in Hebrew in Jeremiah 3:19: ***'ŠYTK BBNYM*** ("I shall adopt you as son, *lit.*, I shall place you in sonship.").

As in Hebrew the plural noun ***YMM*** *yamīm* has the meaning "time": 26 A III 4/6 ***LTTY B'L KRNTRYŠ WKL 'LN QRT L'Z-TWD 'RK YMM WRB ŠNT*** ("Baal-KRNTRYS and all the gods of the city give to Aztwadda a long time [*lit.*, longness of time] <of rule> and many years <of rule>!").

The plural noun ***MṬBM*** *mêṭabīm* has the meaning "approval": NPu 172.1/4 ***PRṬ 'L MYṬB' RŠ' HSLKHY LBN'T T-HMQDŠ ST*** ("He undertook to build this sanctuary with the approval of the senate of Sulcis.").

5. *Common Gender Nouns*

The plural noun with singular meaning ***'LM*** *'ilīm* is common gender, denoting both "god" and "goddess," the gender of the noun indicated by the gender of the deity to whom it refers or by the gender of the descriptive adjective: 59.2 ***'LM NRGL*** ("the god Nergal"); 60.6 ***'LM B'L ṢDN*** ("the god Baal of Sidon"); but 48.2 ***'LM 'DRT 'S 'LM 'ŠTRT*** ("the great goddess Isis <and> the goddess Astarte"). Similarly, although not common, the noun ***QDŠ*** *qiddīs* ("deity=god or goddess"): 17.1/2 ***'ŠTRT 'Š BGW HQDŠ 'Š LY*** ("Astarte of GW, my goddess"). The term ***R'Š*** *rūs* ("head") is used of either a man or woman: NPu 136 ***WKN' Š'NT 'SR WŠMN R'Š 'M Š'RT*** ("For eighteen years she was head of the service personnel.").

6. *Secondary (False) Feminine Gender Nouns*

A masculine noun denoting an object associated with a woman may receive the feminine afformative *-(o)t*. For instance, the masculine noun ***SML,*** when denoting the statue of a woman or goddess, appears as ***SMLT:*** 33.2/3 ***[S]MLT '[Z] 'Š YTN WYṬN' MNḤŠT Y'Š 'ŠT [B'L]YTN . . . LRBTY L'ŠTRT*** ("This statue <of the goddess Astarte> is that which Y'S, the wife of Baalyaton, presented and erected to her Lady Astarte."). Similarly, Philo Byblius (cited by Eusebius, *Praeparatio Evangelica*. I 10.43), when comparing and equating the Phoenician god Χουσωρ (***KŠR***) and the Israelite goddess (!) Θουρω ("Torah"), renders the divine name Khousor feminine as Χουσαρθις, properly to be understood as "Female Khousor." This same convention is also employed in Hebrew poetry in Song of Songs

6:10: the poet likens a woman in her beauty to the figures (goddesses) ***LBNH*** ("Moon") and ***ḤMH*** ("Sun"); she is also likened in her awesomeness to the goddess (!) ***NRGLWT*** ("Nergaloth," or "Female Nergal"; the received text has ***NDGLWT***).

7. *Adverbial Uses of the Noun*

The noun in the accusative case was extensively used adverbially, to express direction, location, manner, *etc.* This use survived even when the accusative case-vowel *-a* was merely vestigial. The noun in the accusative expresses the following:

IN, ON, AT, expressing location

14.16 ***WYŠBN 'YT 'ŠTRT ŠMM 'DRM*** "And we caused Astarte to reside in the Great Heavens."

14.16/17 ***'NḤN 'Š BNN BT L'ŠMN-ŠD QDŠ 'N YDLL BHR,*** "It was we who built a temple for holy Esmun-SD at En-YDLL in the mountains."

14.17 ***YŠBNY ŠMM 'DRM,*** "We caused Him (Esmun) to reside in the Great Heavens."

49 no. 7 G ***'NK PSR BN B'LYTN HMT PP,*** "I am Posiri, the son of Baalyaton who died at Paphos."

Pu 115.1/2 ***ŠLM BD'ŠTRT . . . 'YT NDRM BT B'L'DR,*** "Bostar fulfilled his vow in the temple of Baaladdir."

Pu *CIS* i 6000.7/8 ***'DR ŠPḤ SK[R YRḤ MD] YRḤ BT 'S,*** "His family has magnified/ honored his memory monthly in the temple of Isis."

Pu *CIS* i 247-9 Pu ***BT ṢD-TNT M'RT,*** "The temple of Sid-Thinnith in Megara."

OF, FROM, expressing provenience of a god or person

37A 5 ***'ŠTRT KT,*** "Astarte of (*lit.*, in, from) Kition."

48.2 ***['Š]RT ŠMRN,*** "Ashirta of (*lit.*, in, from) Samaria."

RES 921 (A.M. Honeyman, *Iraq* 6 1939 105) line 4 ***'ŠTRT PP,*** "Astarte of (*lit.*, in, from) Paphos."

Pu *CIS* i 140.1 ***[']ŠTRT 'RK,*** "Astarte of (*lit.*, in, from) Eryx."

The above divine names are not in construct relationship with the place-name. Rather, the locative accusative here is syntactically related to the designation of the place of the cult by means of the more common expression **Divine Name 'Š *B*- Place.** See Relative Pronouns. In Ugaritic, the locative is expressed by means of the archaic locative morpheme *-**umma**:* ***AṮRT ṢRM*** "Ashirta of (*lit.*, in) Tyre" // ***ILT ṢDYNM*** ("Ilat of (*lit.*, in) Sidon."

49 36 ***’NK MGN BN BD’ ŠḤPṢB‘L MNP,*** "I am Mago son of Bodo of the family of Hipsibaal of Memphis."

TO, expressing movement to a place.

49 (34 At) ***’NK P‘L’BST BN ṢDYTN BN GRṢD HṢRY YŠB ‘KY B‘T MṢRM BPṬRT ‘BDMLQRT H’NY,*** "I, Paal-Basti son of Sidyaton son of Ger-Sid the Tyrian, a resident of Akko, came to Egypt *at the invitation* of Abd-Milqart the Heliopolitan."

CIS i 112 (Abu Simbel) B lines 1/2 ***GRHKL BN ḤLM ’Š ‘L ŠD KŠ LḤMH,*** "<I am> Gerhekal bin HLM, who sailed upstream to the Land of Kush, to LHMH (=Abu Simbel)."

CIS i 112 C lines 1/2 ***KŠY BN ‘BDP‘M ’Š ‘L [Š]D KŠ LḤMH,*** "<I am> KSY bin
Abdpa'm, who sailed upstream to the Land of Kush, to LHMH."

IN, AT, DURING, of time

14.2/3 ***NGZLT BL ‘TY,*** "I was snatched away not at my time."

26 A II 19-III 1 ***WYLK <’NK> ZBḤ L KL HMSKT***, "And I brought to him (the god Baal-KRNTRYS) a sacrifice at all the sacrifices." = 26 C IV 2/3: ***WZBḤ ’Š Y[LKT L]’LM KL HMSKT,*** "And I brought to the god a sacrifice of fire at all the sacrifices."

Pu *CIS* i 5510.7/8 ***ṬNT ’MTNT Z BḤDŠ [P]‘LT ŠT ’ŠMN‘MS . . . WḤN’,*** "This stele was erected on the new moon of <the month of> P'LT in the year of <the suffetes> Esmunamos and Hanno."

Pu *CIS* i 5510.9/11 ***WYLK RBM ’DNBL BN GRSKN HRB WḤMLKT BN ḤN’ HRB ‘LŠ WTMK HMT ’YT ’GRGNT WŠT [H]MT ŠLM,*** "<And on the new moon of Paaloth, in the year of Esmunamos and Hanno>, the generals Idnibal son of Gisco the Great and Himilco son of Hanno the Great marched at dawn (***‘LŠ*** = Ar. *ghalasan*) and seized Agrigentum, and they (the Agrigentines) made peace (*i.e.*, they surrendered)."

OF, expressing material

26 A III 2/4 ***WBRK B‘L KRNTRYŠ ’YT ’ZTWD ḤYM WŠLM W‘Z ’DR ‘L KL MLK,*** "May Baal-KRNTRYS bless Aztwadda with long life and health and strength greater than that of any other king." *Cf.* the use of the preposition ***B-*** (of means) instead in 26 C III 16/18: ***BRK B‘L KRNTRYŠ ’YT ’ZTWD BḤYM WBŠLM WB‘Z ’DR ‘L KL MLK.***

AS, expressing respect or manner

14.2/3, 12/13 ***K NGZLT BL ‘TY BN MSK YMM ’ZRM,*** “I was snatched away before (*lit.,* not at) my time, at too young an age (*lit.,* at the age of a few days), like a child sacrificial victim (*’zrm*).”

29.1/2 ***’RN [Š]N MGN ’MTB‘L . . . MTT L‘ŠTRT ’DTY,*** “(This is) the ivory box Amotabaal presented as a gift to her Lady Astarte.”

60.3 ***P‘L ’YT KL ’Š ‘LTY MŠRT,*** “He accomplished everything that was incumbent upon him as a public service.”

8. *Nouns in the Direct Genitival Relationship*

The direct genitival relationship was expressed by a governing noun (the *nomen regens*) in the construct state followed directly by the governed noun (the *nomen rectum*). Normally, this genitival relationship requires (i) that the construct noun not carry the definite article and (ii) that the construct relationship be *direct*, that is, that nothing intervene between the governing and the governed noun. Typical representative examples of the direct genitive are 13.2 ***MLK ṢDNM*** *milk Ṣīdōnīm* (“the king of the Sidonians”); 14.19 ***’RṢT DGN H’DRT*** *’arṣūt dagon ha-’iddīrūt* (“the great regions of grain”); 24.9 ***KS’ ’BY*** *kisse ’abī* (“the throne of my father”); 90.1 ***QBR B‘LḤN’*** *qeber Ba‘alḥanno* (“the tomb of Baalhanno”); 121.1 ***MḤB D‘T HTMT*** *me(ḥ)eb da(‘)at it-timmot* (“the lover of Perfect Accord” = *amator Concordiae*); 124.3/4 ***KTBT DBR’ HBT*** *kᵉtōbit dibrê ib-bêt* (“the book of the affairs of the family” = “the family register and chronicle”). Examples are legion.

There are however several anomalous direct genitival relationships in Phoenician-Punic that diverge from the classic type in (i) permitting the governing noun to receive the definite article; (ii) permitting a compound to govern a noun; or (iii) permitting the direct construct chain to be interrupted by a so-called “proleptic” suffixal pronoun on the governing noun.

8a. The Governing Noun is Determined

The governing noun may receive the definite article when it is in construct with a noun denoting the material of which it is crafted.

Byb 10.4 ***HMZBḤ NḤŠT ZN*** “This altar <of> bronze.”

Byb 10.4 ***HPTḤ ḤRṢ ZN*** “This inscription <of> gold.”

Byb 10.5 ***H‘PT ḤRṢ*** “The bird <of> gold.”

8b. The Governing Noun is a Compound

The governing noun may itself be a construct chain, governs without use of an intervening indirect genitive marker.

59.2 ***YTNB'L BN 'ŠMNṢLḤ RB KHNM 'LM NRGL,*** "Yatonbaal son of Esmunsaloh, Chief of Priests <of> the god Nergal." Compare the use of the indirect genitive marker ***'Š L-*** after a governing compound in *NSI* 150.5 ***B'LYTN 'Š 'LM 'Š LMLQRT,*** "Baalyaton, the Man-of-God of the god Milqart."

8c. The Governing Noun Carries a Proleptic Suffixal Pronoun

This construction is employed when the governed noun is a proper name. The proleptic pronoun on the governing noun anticipates the governed noun. The construction is very common.

14.1 ***ŠNT 'SR W'RB' 14 LMLKY MLK 'ŠMN'ZR,*** "Year fourteen 14 of the reign (*lit.*, of his reign) of King Esmunazor."

Pu 111.3/5 ***ŠŠT 'RB'M ŠT LMLKY MSNSN,*** "The forty-sixth year of the reign (*lit.*, of his reign) of Masinissa."

Pu 112.4/5 ***ŠŠT ḤMŠM ŠT LMLKNM MKWSN WGLSN WMSTN'B',*** "The fifty-sixth year of the reign (*lit.*, of their reign) of Micipsa, Gulussa and Mastanaba."

Pu *Poen.* 948 **<Esse> mucom sussibti A(charist)ocle,** "This is the place of the residing (*lit.*, of his residing) of Acharistocles." That is, "This is the place where Acharistocles resides."

9. *The Meaning of the Genitival Relationship*

9a. Expressing Possession

The governing noun expresses the object possessed, the governed noun the possessor. This is the most common use of the genitive:

14.15/5 ***BT 'LNM,*** "The temples of (belonging to) to the gods."

26 A I 6 ***'QRT P'R,*** "The granaries of (belong to) <the city of> Paar." E*t passim.*

9b. Expressing Relationship, Authority, Jurisdiction

14.1 ***MLK ṢDNM,*** "The king of the Sidonians."

43.2 ***RB 'RṢ***, "The Governor of the Region."

NPu 126.7 ***'DR' 'LPQY W'M 'LPQY,*** "The senators of Lepcis and the people of Lepcis."

9c. Objective

43.7 ***MŠ PN 'BY,*** "The bust of (portraying) my father." *Cf.* 43.2 ***HSML Z MŠ 'NK YTNB'L,*** "This image is a statue of (portraying) me, Yatonbaal."

Umm el-Awamid no. 6.1 ***Z MṢBT B'LŠMR,*** "This is the tombstone of (commemorating) Baalsamor."

9d. Governed Noun Expresses Material

29.1 ***'RN [Š]N,*** "Box <made> of ivory."

NPu 137.5/6 ***NBL NSKT,*** "Vessels of metal."

9e. Governed Noun Expresses the Direct Object

19.6 ***P'L N'M,*** "Doer of good," *i.e.,* "He who does good."

NSK BRZL, "Caster of iron <objects>," *i.e.,* "He who casts iron objects."

NPu 126.4/5 ***MḤB BN' 'M,*** "Lover of his fellow citizens," *i.e.,* "He who loves his fellow citizens."

Pu 106.1/2 ***MLK 'DM BŠRM BTM,*** "Sacrifice of a human being of his own flesh."

9f. Governed Noun Expresses Recipient (Indirect Object)

Pu 61 A 1/2 ***MLK B'L,*** "A *molk*-sacrifice to Baal." *Obs.* This is the name of the sacrifice itself: lines 1/4 ***NṢB MLK B'L 'Š ŠM NḤM LB'LḤMN 'DN,*** "<This is> the stele commemorating the *Molk*-to-Baal that Nahhum gave to Baalhammon, his Lord."

14.6 ***T'BT 'ŠTRT,*** "An abomination of (to) Astarte."

9g. Governed Noun Expresses Author/Actor

50.2 ***'MR 'ḤTK,*** "<This is> the message of (authored by) your sister."

NPu 78.1/2 **Felioth iadem syRogate,** "<This is> the manufacture of (by) Rogatus." That is, "<This was> manufactured by Rogatus."

9h. Governed Noun is a Verbal Noun: Expressing a Relative or

Adverbial Clause

14.21 ***ḤLT MŠKBY,*** "The coffin in which I rest," *lit.*, "The coffin of my resting."

Pu *Poen.* 948 **mucom syssibti,** "The place where he resides," *lit.*, "The place of his residing."

9i. Governing or Governed Noun Expresses Adjective

26 A I 13 ***NʿM LBY,*** "My fine mind," *lit.*, "The goodness of my mind."

Byb 1.2 ***KSʾ MLKH,*** "His royal throne," *lit.*, "The throne of his kingship."

34.5 ***MŠKB NḤTNM,*** "Their peaceful resting-place," *lit.*, "The resting-place of their peace."

This usage, which is very common, is discussed in detail under Adjectives.

9j. Specification

26 A II 8 ***NḤT LB,*** "Peace of mind."

9k. Identification

14.18 ***ṢDN ʾRṢ YM,*** "Maritime Sidon," *lit*, "Sidon, land of the sea."

14.19 ***ŠD ŠRN,*** "The Sharon region."

26 A II 8/9 ***ʿMQ ʾDN,*** "The Adana Valley."

II. The Adjectives

Phoenician possesses both (i) true adjectives and (ii) adjectival nouns. The former are used to express both the descriptive adjective and the predicate adjective; the adjectival is limited to expressing the descriptive adjective.

1. *The True Adjective*

The number of true adjectives is small or, more precisely stated, few occur in the inscriptions. The following is a concise list of those most frequently attested: ***ʾDR*** *ʾaddīr* ("large, great, major"); ***ʾRK*** *ʾarrīk* ("long, tall"); ***BRK*** *barīk* ("blessed, happy"); ***DRY*** *dūrī* ("lasting, enduring");

ZR *zor* ("another = different from the first"); ***N'M*** *na'īm* ("good, excellent"); {***YP*** *yafe* ("appropriate, seemly"); ***YŠR*** ("good, righteous"); ***KBR*** *kibbīr* ("great, large"); ***KLL*** *kalīl* ("entire"); ***LPNY*** *lifanī* ("former, earlier, past, preceding, prior"); ***NŠT'*** *nista'* ("dangerous, fearsome"); ***'Z*** *'az(z)* ("strong"); ***ṢDQ*** *ṣiddīq* ("good, righteous"); ***Ṣ'R*** *ṣa'īr* ("small, minor, lesser"); ***QDŠ*** *qiddīs* ("holy, sacred"); ***RB*** *rab(b)* ("many"); ***R'*** *ra'(')* ("bad, evil"); ***ŠLM*** *salem* ("whole, intact"); ***ŠPR*** *sippīr* ("beautiful"); ***TM*** *tam(m)* ("perfect, good; complete").

In addition to these adjectives, the participles, especially the passive participle, function as true adjectives: *e.g.*, ***ZBḤ*** *sabūh* ("sacrificed"); ***MḤṢB*** *meḥaṣṣab* ("settled"); ***MYLL*** *m^{e}yullal* ("mourned, lamented"); ***PSL*** *pasīl* ("sculpted"), etc.

1a. Used as Descriptive Adjective

When used as a descriptive adjective, the adjective follows the noun and agrees with it in number and gender: 18.6 ***ŠM N'M*** ("a good name"); Pu 69.3 ***'LP KLL*** ("an entire ox"); NPu 178.2/3 **umman nai(m)** ("a good artisan"); NPu D 6.7
sem ra ("a bad name"); Pu 78.5 ***'BN 'RKT*** (" tall stele/stone"); Pu 78.4 ***MNṢBT PSLT*** ("a sculpted stele"); 26 A II 7/8 ***ŠBT N'MT*** ("good living"); NPu *Poen.* 935 **yth thymmoth** ("time past"); NPu *IRT* 893.4/5**ilim sebuim** ("sacrificed gods"); NPu 161.2 ***'RṢT RBT*** ("many lands").

Rules governing the use of the definite article with the descriptive adjective are difficult to formulate for want of a sufficient repertory of examples. The following is a partial description based on the extant evidence:

If the noun is determined, the descriptive adjective carries the definite article; the noun itself need not receive the article inasmuch as the determined adjective renders the noun determined: 14.9 ***H'LNM HQDŠM*** ("The holy gods"); 24.9 ***HMLKM HLPNYM*** ("The kings who preceded <me>."). The noun without the definite article: NPu 145 I 4 ***'LM 'QYDŠ*** ("The holy god"); 14.22 ***'LNM HQDŠM 'L*** ("These holy gods").

The descriptive adjective receives the definite article when it modifies a construct chain, the latter grammatically equivalent to a determined noun: 14.19: ***'RṢT DGN H'DRT*** ("The great grain regions"); NPu 161.1/2 ***MLK [M]ŠLYYM HMYLL*** ("The lamented king of the Massylii").

The descriptive adjective need not receive the definite article when modifying a determined noun if the noun is modified by a demonstrative pronoun; for the demonstrative renders both the noun and the adjective determined: NPu 118.1 ***MŠ 'LM ŠP'R ST*** ("This beautiful statue of the god"). Compare however the use of the optional use of the definite article with the adjective in the following: 14.22 ***'LNM HQDŠM 'L*** ("These holy gods").

If the descriptive adjective modifies a divine or place name, it need not receive the definite article: 58 ***'SKN 'DR*** ("Great Sakun"); B.V. Head 791 ***GBL QDŠT*** ("Holy Byblos").

1b. Descriptive Adjective: Comparative Degree

The adjective is not declined. Comparative degree is expressed by the simple adjective followed by the preposition ***'L*** ("more than, greater than"):

26 A III 4 ***'Z 'DR 'L KL MLK,*** "Strength/might greater than that of any <other> king."

1c. The Predicate Adjective

The predicate adjective agrees in number and gender with the noun. It may precede or follow the noun:

24.7 ***'DR 'LY MLK D[N]NYM WŠKR 'NK 'LY MLK 'ŠR,*** "More powerful than I was the king of the Danunians, so I hired the king of Assyria against him."

26 A II 3/4 ***MQMM 'Š KN LPNM NŠT'M,*** "Places that were dangerous in the past."

NPu Trip. 10.3 ***LKN 'ḤRT[M] BRY<K>'T,*** "May their end/afterlife be blessed/happy!"

2. *Adjectival Nouns*

The adjectival noun is an abstract noun which, when used in construct with another noun, functions as a descriptive adjective. The adjectival noun is either the governing noun (*nomen regens*) or the governed noun (*nomen rectum*) in this construct relationship.

2a. Governing Noun

'ḤRYM (plural)

OTHER (plural), *lit.*, OTHER ONES, REMAINING ONES

19.9 ***KM 'Š BN 'YT KL 'ḤRY [HMQDŠ]M 'Š KN B'RṢ,*** "Just as they also (re)built all the other [sanctuari]es that are in the region."

'RK

LONG (of time), *lit.*, LONGNESS

26 A III 4/6 ***LTTY B'L KRNTRYŠ WKL 'LN QRT L'ZTWD 'RK YMM WRB ŠNT,*** "Baal-KRNTRYS and all the gods of the city give to Aztwadda a long time <of rule> and many years <of rule>!"

'ŠR

HAPPY, *lit.*, HAPPINESS

NPu 145 II 11 ***KYLN B'ŠR LB P'LN BYT TŠB'T,*** "All of us with happy hearts rendered <this> *eulogy.*"

KL

ALL, ENTIRE, WHOLE, EVERY, ANY, *lit.*, TOTALITY, ENTIRETY

4.2/3 Byb ***H'T ḤWY KL MPLT HBTM 'L,*** "It was he who repaired all the ruined temples hereabouts."

26 A III 19 ***KL DR BN 'LM,*** "The entire family of the gods."

50.4/5 ***KL KSP 'Š LY,*** "All my silver."

NPu 145 II 11 ***KYLN B'ŠR LB P'LN BYT TŠB'T,*** "All of us with happy hearts rendered <this> *eulogy.*"

M'SP

ALL, *lit.*, COLLECTION, ENTIRETY

NPu 122.1 ***M'SP HNSKT Š'LM 'WGSṬS,*** "All the metal objects of the god Augustus."

MPḤRT

ALL, *lit.*, COLLECTION, ENTIRETY

Byb 4.3/6 ***Y'RK B'LŠMM WB'L<T> GBL WMPḤRT 'L GBL QDŠM YMT YḤMLK WŠNTW 'L GBL,*** "Baalsamem and Baalt of Byblos and all the holy gods of Byblos grant Yehmilk a long time and many many years <of rule> over Byblos!"

MPLT

RUINED, *lit.*, RUINS

Byb 4.2/3 ***H'T ḤWY KL MPLT HBTM 'L,*** "It was he (King Yehimilk) who restored all the ruined buildings/temples hereabouts."

MSK

FEW, *lit.*, RESTRICTED (SMALL) NUMBER

14.2/3 ***NGZLT BL ʿTY BN MSK YMM ʾZRM,*** "I was snatched away before my time, at the age of a few days, like a child sacrificial victim."

Nʿ M

GOOD, EXCELLENT, *lit.*, GOODNESS, EXCELLENCE

26 A I 12/13 ***WʾP BʾBT PʿLN KL MLK BṢDQY WBḤKMTY WBNʿM LBY,*** "Moreover, every king adopted me as father because of my honesty, my cleverness and my good intellect."

43.15/16 ***WYSKRN MLQRT [WYTN LY] Nʿ M ŠRŠ,*** "Milqart remember me and give me good progeny!"

RʾŠT

FINEST, BEST, *lit.*, FIRST QUALITY

31.1 ***ʾZ YTN LBʿL LBNN ʾDNY BRʾŠT NḤŠT,*** "This <cup>, made of the best copper, did he present to his Lord, Baal of Lebanon."

RB

MANY, *lit.*, GREAT NUMBER, LARGE AMOUNT

26 A III 4/6 ***LTTY BʿL KRNTRYŠ WKL ʾLN QRT LʾZTWD ʾRK YMM WRB ŠNT,*** "Baal-KRNTRYS and all the gods of the city give to Aztwadda a long time <of rule> and many years <of rule>!"

2b. Governed Noun

ʾDN(M)

ROYAL, *lit.*, KINGLINESS, LORDLINESS

26 A I 9/10 ***WYṬNʾ ʾNK BT ʾDNY BNʿM WPʿL ʾNK LŠRŠ ʾDNY Nʿ M,*** "I established by royal house out of good intent, and I did what is good for my royal progeny."

ʾN

EVIL, WICKED, CRIMINAL, *lit.*, INIQUITY

D 6.5/7 **Badinim garasth is on, / mySyrthim bal sem ra**, "From Adnim I expelled the wicked fellow, / From the Syrthis, him of ill repute."

MLK

ROYAL, *lit.*, KINGSHIP, ROYAL POWER

Byb 1.2 ***TḤTSP ḤṬR MŠPṬH THTPK KSʾ MLKH,*** "His imperial sceptre shall break, his royal throne shall overturn."

MŠPṬ

IMPERIAL, *lit.*, IMPERIUM, ROYAL POWER

Byb 1.2 ***TḤTSP ḤṬR MŠPṬH THTPK KS' MLKH,*** "His imperial sceptre shall break, his royal throne shall overturn."

III. The *Nisbe* Noun and Adjective

A. *Morphology*

Inflection

Sg. M.		
-Y *-ī*	Ph	53.2. 54.2 ***ṢDNY*** ("Sidonian"); 54.1 ***'ŠQLNY*** ("Ascalonian")
-'	Pu	*CIS* i 359.4/5 ***ŠN'*** ("second"); *RES* 910 ***ŠLŠ'*** ("third"); ***DR'*** *dūrī* ("enduring")
Sg. F.		
-T *-īt*	Ph	59.1 ***ṢDNT*** ("Sidonian")
Pl. M.		
-YM *-īm*	Ph	26 A I 5/6 ***DNNYM*** ("Danunians"); *FK* A 9 A/B; B 40.2;F 1.3,5,6 ***KRSYM*** ("Corsic"); 60.7 ***ṢDNYM*** ("Sidonians")
	NPu	118.2 ***LWBYM*** ("Lybians"); 153.4 ***LBYM*** ("Lybians")
-M	Ph	13.1, 14.14 ***ṢDNM*** ("Sidonians")
-em	NPu	D 2.8, 5.11 **[Lyb]em** ("Libyans")
-im	Pu	*Poen.* 1023 **Ponnim** ("Phoenician")
	NPu	*LA* 1 p. 45 no. 4.5 **Sorim** ("Tyrians")
Pl. F.		
-YT *-iyyūt*	Ph-Pu-NPu	Not recorded

Comments

The Sg. M. form- *ī* is the reflex of original *-iyy;* reflected in the retained historical spelling ***-Y***. In Punic, the Sg. M. was occasionally spelled phonetically with *aleph*. The Sg. F. *-īt* is the reflex of *-iyt*. The Pl. M. *-īm* is the reflex of original *-iyyīm*. Already in the first half of the first millennium B.C., the masculine plural had the pronunciation *-īm;* however, the historical spelling ***-YM***, which reflects the primitive pronunciation *-iyyīm,* was retained alongside the phonetic spelling ***-M.***

B. *Syntax and Usage*

1. *Forming Gentilic from Place-Name*

The *nisbe* is used primarily to form a gentilic from a place-name:

14.1 ***'ŠMN'ZR MLK ṢDNM,*** "Esmunazor, King of the Sidonians."

54.1 ***'NK ŠM BN 'BD'ŠTRT 'ŠQLNY,*** "I am Sem son of Abdastart the Ascalonian."

NPu 118.2 ***RB T'ḤT RB MḤNT BŠD LWBYM,*** "Commander <of the Army> in the Stead of the Commander of the Army (=Proconsul) in the region of the Libyans (=Libya)."

2. *Expressing Names of Languages (Masculine Plural)*

Names of languages are expressed by the masculine plural gentilic:

FK B 40.1/2 ***'ŠMN'DNY ŠRDL BN 'BDMLQRT BN RŠPYTN MLṢ HKRSYM,*** "Esmunadoni the Sardin, the son of Abdmilqart sonof Rasapyaton, Interpreter of the Corsic Language." *Obs.* Corsic was the language of the Corsi, a people of Northern Sardinia; Esmunadoni was an ethnic Sardin from Sardinia and perhaps himself a native speaker of Corsic. The post of ***MLṢ (H)KRSYM*** *melīṣ hik-Korsīm* ("Translator of the Corsic Language") is often mentioned in the inscriptions of Kition, a city which apparently boasted a substantial Corsic and Sardin elment. In this regard, one should note that in the archaic inscription from Nora in Sardinia (*KAI* 46), the colony itself (called ***TRŠŠ***) claims ***KTN*** (Kition) as its mother-city.

Pu *Poen.* 1023 **Ponnim sycartim?,** "Do you remember any Punic?" This is the Punic translation of the line Plautus translated **Ecquid commeministi Punice?** (*Poen.* 985).

The masculine plural gentilic ***KRSYM*** expressing the name of the language is merely an abbreviation of the fuller ***DBRM KRSYM*** ("Corsic language," *lit.,* "Corsic words"); *cf.* Hebrew *d^{e}barīm* = *śapa* ("language, speech," Genesis 11.1).

3. *Forming Cardinal Numbers from Ordinals*

Pu 76 B 1 ***YM HʾRBʿY,*** "The fourth day." *Obs.* In Phoenician, the cardinal is formed directly from the ordinal: ***ʾRBʿ*** *ʾarbaʿ* ("four") > ***ʾRBʿY*** *ʾarbaʿī* ("fourth"). See the chapter on Numerals.

4. *Forming Adjectives from Nouns*

NPu 128.2/3 ***[SK]R DRʾ LʾLM LʾB,*** "<This is> a permanent memorial forever to a <good> father." *Obs.* The adjective ***DRY*** *dūrī* ("permanent, enduring") is formed from the noun ***DR*** *dūr* < *dōr* ("eternity"); *cf.* Akkadian ***dārīu.***

5. *Forming Nouns and Adjectives from Prepositions*

LPNY *lip(a)nī* ("first, earlier, former, past") < ***LPN*** *lip(a)nê* ("before"):

24.9/10 ***LPN HMLKM HLPNYM YTLKN MŠKBM KM KLBM,*** "Before the kings who preceded me (*lit.*, the earlier kings) the *mškbm* used to go about like dogs." That is, "The kings who preceded me treated the *mškbm* like dogs."

24.4/5 ***M ʾS PʿLT BL PʿL HLPNY{H}M,*** "I accomplished what my predecessors (*lit.*, the preceding ones) did not accomplish."

NPu 137.5 ***BʿSR WŠBʿ LYRḤ MPʿ LPNY,*** "On the seventeenth of the month of First Mufa."

CHAPTER NINE

THE VERB: INTRODUCTION AND THE SUFFIXING FORM

I. Introduction

A. *The Forms, Tense and Aspect*

The Phoenician verb possesss three Moods: (i) Indicative, (ii) Non-indicative (subjunctive, optative, jussive, cohortative), (iii) Imperative. There are four Voices: (i) Active (Transitive and Intransitive); (ii) Passive; (iii) Stative and (iv) Reflexive. There are two Aspects: Perfective and Imperfective. There are six Tenses: (i) Past Perfective; (ii) Past Imperfective; (iii) Pluperfect; (iv) Present Perfective; (v) Present Imperfective; (vi) Future.

The verbal system consists of six Stems (also known as Patterns, Conjugations, Themes; *Binyanim* in Hebrew): (i) Qal (*qatol* < *qatal*), the so-called "simple" stem, itself having an active form and an inner passive form; (ii) Nip'al (*niqtal*), the external passive of the Qal; (iii) Pi'el (*qittel*), the so-called "intensive" stem, and its inner passive form Pu'al (*quttal*); (iv) Yip'il (*yiqtel*), the so-called "causative" stem, and its inner passive form Yop'al; (v) Yitpe'el (*yitqettel*), the so-called "reflexive" form; and (vi) the Yipta'al (*yiqtatal*), the intransitive of the Qal, this stem occurring in Byblian Phoenician only.

Each Stem possesses all of the following nine Forms: (i) Suffixing Form (*qatol*); (ii) Prefixing Form A (Old Canaanite *yaqtulu*); (iii) Prefixing Form B (Old Canaanite *yaqtul*); (iv) Prefixing Form C (Old Canaanite *yaqtula*); (v) Active Participle; (vi) Passive Participle; (vii) Imperative; (viii) Infinitive Absolute; (ix) Infinitive Construct.

Tense, Aspect and Mood in Phoenician are entirely a function of syntax, not of morphology. This is to say, there is no one-to-one correlation between any given Form of the verb and a specific Tense, Aspect or Mood. Rather, in and of themselves, the Forms are entirely unmarked for tense, aspect and mood. The reference (tense, aspect and mood) of any given Form is determined by (i) the type of syntactic structure in which the Form is embedded; (ii) the position (syntactically restricted or non-restricted) of the Form within that syntactic structure. Take for instance the Suffixing Form of the verb.

The Suffixing Form is not marked for past perfective action. This is to say, the form ***QR'*** *qaró'* < *qará'* does not mean "he called out." Inherently, that is, not in context, the form is purely a morphological entity, unmarked for tense, aspect or mood. Its tense, aspect and mood references are several, each a function of syntax:

(i) When the Suffixing Form is the main (principal) verb of a simple independent (non-subordinate) clause (declarative sentence), the Suffixing Form has past perfective tense/aspect-reference. So used in standard literary Phoenician prose, the Form is syntactically restricted to non-sentence initial position. The syntactically restricted sentence-initial Forms expressing the Past Perfective are (a) the Infinitive Absolute and (b) Prefixing Form B, both of which in turn may not assume sentence-initial position in a simple declarative statement.

(ii) When the Suffixing Form is not the main (principal) verb of a simple declarative sentence but is consecutive to (follows) the main verb, the Suffixing Form assumes the tense and aspect reference of the main verb. This subform of the Form is the "Suffixing Form Consecutive."

(iii) When the Suffixing Form is the main (principal) verb of the result clause of a temporal sentence, the Suffixing Form has past perfective tense/aspect-reference but is syntactically restricted to clause-initial position.

(iv) When the Suffixing Form occupies sentence-initial position in an independent (non-subordinate clause), its tense/aspect/modal reference is (i) Present Perfective or (ii) Jussive Optative. In Phoenician, it is never Past Perfective. Punic however loosens this syntactic restriction, permitting the Suffixing Form to stand sentence-initial and yet function with Past Perfective reference.

(v) When the Suffixing Form is clause-initial in the main (resumptive) clause of a sentence with anticipatory clause, it has Future tense-reference.

The corollary to no one-to-one correlation between a specific Form and a specific tense, aspect or mood is that a specific tense, aspect or mood may be expressed by more than one Form. Take, for instance, the expression of the Future Tense: in Phoenician, the Future Indicative is expressed by (i) Prefixing Form A *yiqtol* < *yaqtulu*; (ii) Prefixing Form B *yiqtol* < *yaqtul* in the result clause of a conditional sentence; (iii) Infinitive Construct *liqtōl*; (iv) Suffixing Form *qatol* < *qatala* in resumptive clause of a sentence with anticipatory clause and in the result clause of a conditional sentence. Similarly, an imperative is expressed by (i) the Imperative Form; (ii) second person of Prefixing Form B *tiqtol* < *taqtul*; (iii) Infinitive Absolute *liqtōl*.

Presented here is a preliminary summary of the correspondences between Form and Use (Tense, Aspect, Mood):

Form	**Use (Tense, Aspect, Mood)**
Suffixing Form	Present Perfective
	Past Perfective
	Future
	Jussive/Optative
	Consecutive (Unmarked)
Prefixing Form A	Past Imperfective
	Present Imperfective
	Future Imperfective
Prefixing Form B	Past Perfective
	Future Imperfective
	Jussive/Optative
	Subjunctive
Prefixing Form C	Jussive/Optative
	Subjunctive
Active Participle	Surrogate for the Active Verb (All Tenses)
	Participial (Action in Progress, all Tenses)
Past Participle	Surrogate for Past Perfective
Imperative	Imperative
Infinitive Absolute	Paranomastic
	Past Perfective
	Consecutive (Unmarked)
	Verbal Noun
Infinitive Construct	Infinitive (Object of Certain Verbs)
	Future
	Jussive/Optative
	Imperative
	Subjunctive
	Gerundial
	Expressing Temporal Clause

Tense, Aspect, Mood	**Form**
Present Perfective	Suffixing Form
Present Imperfective	Prefixing Form
Past Imperfective	Prefixing Form
Past Perfective	Suffixing Form Prefixing Form C Infinitive Absolute
Pluperfect	Verb *kon* + Suffixing Form
Future Indicative	Prefixing Form A Prefixing Form B Suffixing Form Infinitive Construct
Subjunctive	Infinitive Construct Prefixing Form B or C
Jussive/Optative	Prefixing Form B Prefixing Form C Suffixing form Infinitive Construct
Imperative	Imperative Form. Form B (second person) Infinitive Construct

B. *The Verbal Stems*

QAL

The verbal stem is also called by grammarians the verbal pattern, theme, conjugation; the Hebrew term is *binyan.* The QAL is the simple stem. It includes active transitive verbs of the form (Suffixing) *qatol,* such as 14.18 ***YTN*** *yaton* ("he gave"), as well as stative verbs, such as 60.1 ***TM*** *tam* ("it was good"). The Prefixing Form of the strong verb was *yiqtol* (*yiqtal*): Pu *Poen.* 940 **timlacun** *timlakūn* ("you rule"). The QAL had an inner passive form *qutel,* attested in Pu *Poen.* 1027 **gunebte** *gunebti* ("I have been robbed") and in Byblian 1.2 ***LPP*** *lupep* ("it will be twisted up"). The Active Participle of the strong verb was *qūtel*: Pu *Poen.* 948 **duber** *duber* ("says," masc. sg.); and the Passive Participle was *qatūl*: *IRT* 893.5 **sebuim** *zebūḥīm* ("sacrificed," masc. pl.). The Imperative was *q°tol* and *qutla (*in the masculine singular): Pu *Poen.* 1013 **lec** *lek* ("go!") and Pu *Poen.* 1010 **pursa** *pursa* ("explain!"). The Infinitive Absolute was *qatōl* (*qatūl*):13.6/7 ***PTḤ*** *patōḥ* ("open"); and the Infinitive Construct was *liqtūl*: Pu *Poen.* 945 **liful** *lifʿūl* ("to do").

NIP'AL

The NIP'AL is the external passive of the QAL: 14.2, 12 ***NGZLT*** *nigzalti* ("I was snatched away"); Pu 69.20 ***NʿN[Š]*** *neʿnas* ("he will be fined"); Pu *Poen.* 943 **neso** *neʿso* ("he was made"). The Prefixing Form appears in 14.8 ***ʾL YQBR*** *ʾal yiqqaberū* ("they shall not be entombed"). The NIP'AL participle is also the source of certain adjectives like 26 A II 4 ***NŠTʿ*** *nistaʿ* ("dangerous," *lit.*, "feared").

PI'EL and PU'AL

The Suffixing Form of the PI'EL strong verb was *qittel (qettel, qittil)*: NPu *IRT* 892.3 **bycys** *biqqis* ("he requested") and the Prefixing Form *yeqettel* (<*yeqattel*): 14.5 ***YBQŠ*** *yebeqqes* ("he seeks"); the PU'AL was *quttal* and *yequttal* respectively. In standard Phoenician orthography, the PI'EL and PU'AL are indistinguishable from the QAL. However, in Punic one finds also the occasional spelling C*Y*CC of the Suffixing Form, with the *mater lectionis* ***Y*** indicating the first of the thematic vowels: ***ḤYDŠ*** *ḥiddés* ("he restored"); 119.2; 123.2 ***ṬYNʾ*** *ṭinne(ʾ)* ("he erected"). The Active Participle was meqettel: Pu 66.1 ***MʾRḤ*** *meʾerreḥ* ("host," title of the god Esmun), found in Greek and Latin letters as Μηρρη and **Merre** respectively; the Passive Participle was *mequttal*: NPu 161.2 ***MYLL*** *meyullal* ("mourned"). The Imperative (masc. sg.) was qettel: NPu Augustine **messe** *messeḥ* ("anoint!"). The Infinitive Absolute was *qettel*: 26 A I 6 ***MLʾ*** *melle(ʾ)* ("fill"); and the Infintive Construct was liqettel: Pu *CIS* i 5510.6 ***LŠLM*** *lisellem* ("to greet").

YIP'IL

In Standard Phoenician and Punic, the Suffixing Form of the strong verb had the form ***Y***CCC *yiqṭél:* 14.17 ***YŠBNY*** *yûsebnuyo* ("we caused him to reside"); 42.4 ***YQDŠ*** *yiqdés* ("he dedicated"), with initial *yod* and the thematic vowels *i-e* (or *i-i*). The initial *yod* was characteristic of the entire paradigm, including the infinitives: 26 A I 20 ***YŠBM ʾNK*** *yûsebom ʾanīki* ("I caused them to dwell"); Pu *Poen.* 943 **iulec anec** *yūlek ʾanīk* ("I brought").

In Neo-Punic, the Suffixing Form was *iqtél*, written in the following ways:

(a) ***'Y*CCC**: Trip. 32.1 ***'YB'*** *ibī(')* ("he brought"); Trip. 67.1 ***'YDḤ*** *ideḥ* ("he enlarged," root *d-ḥ-ḥ*); 145 III 12 ***'YKRM'*** *ikremó* ("it honored him"); 121.2 ***'YQDŠ*** *iqdés* ("he dedicated").
(b) ***HY*CCC**: Mactar B II 2 ***HYKRM*** *ikrem* (?"he restored"); Mactar B III 3 ***HY'L*** *e'lo* ("he raised").
(c) ***H*CC(*Y*)C**: ***HṢDYQ'*** *iṣdíqa* ("she was good").
(d) ***Ḥ*CCC**: 124.4 ***ḤTM*** *itím* ("he completed," root *t-m-m*).
(e) ***Y*CC(*Y*)C**: 153.3 ***YPYQ'*** *ipīqó* ("he found it").
(f) **iCCeC**: *IRT* 873.3 **intseb** *inṣéb* ("he erected"); cf. D 5.19 **utseb** *ûṣéb* ("he erected," root *y-ṣ-b*).

The Prefixing Form of the strong verb was *yiqtil:* NPu *Poen.* 1027 **iyryla** *yir'ila* ("let him make tremble!"). The Active Participle was *miqtil:* Pu *Poen.* 1033 **migdil** *migdil* ("one who magnifies"). The Imperative was *yiqtel* (Pu *iqtel*): NPu Trip. 86.3 ***HKR*** *ikker* ("recognize!," root *n-k-r*). The Infinitive Absolute was *yuqtel:* Pu *Poen.* 943 **iulec** *yūlek* ("bring"); the Infinitive Construct was *liyeqtel* (Pu *leqtel*): Pu *CIS* I 5510.6 ***LYRḤ*** *liyerīḥ* ("to make welcome"); *cf.* later Pu 79.7 ***LSR*** *lesīr* ("to remove").

The YIP'IL has the inner passive form YOP'AL, corresponding to the Hebrew HOP'AL. It is attested once only, in the Prefixing Form: 14.6 ***'L TŠM' BDNM*** *'al tosma' bad^{e}nom* ("Do not be persuaded by them!").

YITPE'EL

Forms of this stem are not recorded in Phoenician. The precise shape of the form is therefore uncertain although one may speculate, in light of the Phoenician causative stem Yip'il, that the Suffixing Form had the shape Yitpe'el (=Hebrew Hitpael). In Neo-Punic, the stem is attested as Itpe'el, the preformative spelled ***HT-*** or ***'YT-***:

HT*CCC** 138.1 ***HTQDŠ *itqeddes* ("he sanctified himself"); *CIS* I 5522.2 ***HTRŠM*** ("he signed himself in").

'YT*CCC** 119.4 ***'YTKDW *ittekkedū* ("they mutually resolved").

The Suffixing Form of the Yitpe'el is attested but once, in Phoenician: 24.10 ***YTLK*** *yittallekū* ("they used to go about").

The attested functions in Phoenician of the YITPE'EL are to express (i) the reflexive ("he sanctified himself"), (ii) mutual action ("they mutually agreed") and (iii) continuity ("they used to go about").

YIPTA'AL

The YIPTA'AL (***YPT‘L***) is attested in Byblian Phoenician only and only in the Prefixing Form. It functions to express the intransitive of a transitive verb: ***TḤTSP*** (*tiḥtasap*) ***ḤṬR MŠPṬH THTPK*** (*tihta-pak*) ***KS’ MLKH,*** ("His imperial sceptre will break, <and> his royal throne will overturn."). The stem occurs in Ugaritic and Moabite with the same function.

C. *Voice*

There is active voice and passive voice. The passive is expressed in several different ways:

1. *By Inner Passive of the Verb Stem*

Byb 1.2 ***WH’ YMḤ SPRH LPP ŠBL,*** "If he shall erase its inscription, his royal robe shall be twisted up (*lupep*)."

Pu *Poen.* 1027 **Gunebte**!, "I have been robbed!" *Obs.* The verb is the inner passive (suffixing form) of the Qal.

NPu 134.1/2 ***ṬN’ ’BN Ẓ LPLKŠ BN ḤMT,*** "This gravestone has been erected to Felix son of HMT." The verb is the inner passive of the Pi'el (=Pu'al).

2. *By the Niphal*

14.2/3 ***NGẒLT BL ‘TY,*** "I was snatched away not at my time."

Pu *Poen.* 940/41 **Hu neso bin us es hulec silli balim esse lipane esse con,** "He was made the son of the man who was my guest-friend in this nation in the past."

NPu 130.1 ***NP‘L’ ŠŠ HYŠBM ’L’ BŠT HŠPṬM ‘BDMLQRT ṬBḤPY W’RŠ,*** "These six seats were made in the year of the Suffetes Abdmilqart Tapapius and Aris."

3. *By the Third Plural of the Active Voice*

14.5 ***’L YBQŠ BN MNM K ’Y ŠM BN MNM,*** "Let him not look for anything <of value> in it (my tomb), for nothing <of value> was placed in it," *literally*, "They did not place anything in it."

24.12/13 ***WMY BL ḤẒ KTN LMN‘RY WBYMY KSY BṢ,*** "As for him who had never owned an outer garment from the time of his youth, in my time he was dressed in byssus <garments>," *literally*, "They dressed him in byssus <garments>."

NPu *PBSR* 28 53 no. 5.9/11 **Bynom Mrausyn au[r]ys. Felu tabula y bud bannom,** "Their son Mrausyn was the engraver <of the preceding tablet>. That tablet was made by their son," *literally,* "They made the aforementioned tablet by their son."

4. *By the Indefinite*

4a. Expressed by the the Active Participle Singular

Pu *Poen.* 946 **Ys duber ci hen hu Acharistocle,** "I am told (*lit.,* "one says") that Acharistocles lives here." = Neo-Punic *Poen.* 936 **Ys dubyr ch'innochoth u Agorastocles,** "I am told (*lit.,* "one says") that Agorastocles lives here."

Pu *Poen.* 948 **Ys duber limur <esse> mucom sussibti A(charist)ocle,** "I am told (*lit.,* "one says") that this is the place where Acharistocles lives."

4b. Expressed by Active Participle Plural

NPu *Poen.* 935 **Dobrim chy fel yth chil ys chon ythem liful yth binim,** "I am told (*lit.,* "they say") that he did everything for his son that he was to do for him."

D. *Person, Number and Gender*

There is singular and plural. There is masculine and feminine gender. The plural of the active voice may be used to express the passive singular (see Voice above).

Polite forms or circumlocutions exist for the first person and for the second person. In addressing a superior, the plural of the second person is used; *cf.* French **vous parlez.** This usage is illustrated in a dialogue from the Punic version of the *Karkhedonios* in which a slave addresses his master in the second plural: 1023 **sycartim Ponnim** ("Do you remember Punic?"); but the master responds in the second singular: 1017 **bal umer iadata** ("Not a word! Do you know it?").

A superior or stranger is also addressed in the third person by means of the circumlocation ***'DNY*** ("my lord," *cf.* "mein Herr; monsieur"): Pu 1141 **hauo done silli** ("Live long!," *lit.,* "May my lord live long!). Also in the third person: Pu 1141 **hauo bene silli** ("Live long, my son!," *lit.,* "May my son live long!"); 1141 **haua**

amma silli ("Live long, my mother!," *lit.,* "May my mother live long!").

In polite address, the pronoun of the first person is ***‘BDK*** ("your servant(s)" = I, we), when speaking to one person; and ***‘BDKM*** ("your servant(s)" = I, we) when speaking to more than one person: 47.1/2 ***L’DNN LMLQRT B‘L ṢR ’Š NDR ‘BDK ‘BD’SR W’ḤY ’SRŠMR*** ("To our Lord Milqart is what we [*lit.,* your servants], Abdosiri and his brother Osirisamor, vowed."); *cf.* NPu D 6 **Un ath a[bdach]a** ("Show me mercy!," *lit.,* Show your servant mercy!").

II. The Suffixing Form

A. *Morphology*

Inflection

Sg. 1. C.		
-***T*** *-ti*	Ph	Byb 9 A 1 ***P‘LT*** *paʿalti* ("I built"); 14.2 ***NGZLT*** *nigzalti* ("I was snatched away"); 26 A I 8 ***ŠBRT*** ("I smashed"), *et passim*
-***TY***	NPu	145.6 ***K‘TBTY*** ("I have written down")
-te	Pu	*Poen.* 941 **bate** ("I have come"), *Poen.*1027 **gunebte** ("I have been robbed"), *Poen.* 947 **nasote** ("I have brought, I bring")
-ti	Pu	*Poen.* 940 **caruti** ("I call")
-thi	NPu	*Poen.* 930 **carothi** *qarōti* ("I call"); *Poen.* 931 **mysethi** ("I have come"); *Poen.* 937 **nasothi** ("I have brought, I bring")
-th	NPu	D 6.5/6 **garasth** *garast* ("I expelled"); D 6.9 **sath** *sat* ("I made")
Sg. 2. M.		
-***T*** *-ta*	NPu	Trip. 79.1 ***QN’T*** *qanīta* ("you have acquired")
-ta	Pu	*Poen.* 1017 **iadata** *yadaʿta* ("you know")
Sg. 2. F.		
-***T*** *-ti*	Pu	50.3 ***ŠLḤT*** *salaḥti* ("you will send")

Sg. 3. M.

-Ø *-o*	Ph	41.6 ***ŠMʿ*** *samoʿ* ("hear, heard"); 60.1 ***TM*** *tam* ("it was good"), *et passim*
	Pu	64.1 ***NDR*** *nador* ("he vowed"); *Poen.* 942 **con** *kon* ("he was") *et passim*
	NPu	121.2 ***PʿL WʾYQDŠ*** *fel uʾiqdes* ("he made and dedicated"); *IRT* 873.2/3 **fel . . . uintseb** *fel uʾinṣeb* ("he made and erected"), *et passim*

Sg. 3. F.

FORM A

-Ø *-a*	Byb	10.8 ***ŠMʿ*** *šimʿa* ("she heard"), 10.8 ***PʿL*** *peʿla* ("she made"); *cf.* archaic EA 106.10/11 ***šiḫtat*** ("it has been destroyed")
	Ph	33.2 ***YTN*** *yitna* ("she presented")
-ʾ	Pu	*CIS* i 5945 ***PʿL*** ("she made"); *CIS* i 4937.4 ***ŠPṬ*** ("she will adjudge"); *CIS* I 5510.3 ***ʾML*** *ʾamla* ("it will wither"), *et passim*
-ʿ	NPu	136.2 ***MTʿ*** *méta* ("she died"), 136.4 ***KNʿ*** *kóna* ("she was")
-a	Pu	*Poen.* 1141 **haua** *ḥawa* ("may she live long!")
	NPu	*AI* 2 1926 no. 29 **aua** ("she lived"); *IRT* 826.1/2, 901.2/4 **fela** ("she made")

Form with Affixed Object Pronouns.

-T *-at-*	Byb	10.2 ***PʿLTN*** *peʿlatni* ("she made me")
	Ph	*RB* 1916 p. 576-9, Pl. IV ***ḤWT*** *ḥiwwato* ("may she make him live long!")
	Pu	*CIS* i 3783.6 ***NKST*** *niksato* ("she will cut him off"); *CIS* i 4945.4/6 ***QBT*** *qibbato* ("she will curse him")

Pl. 1. C.

-N *-nu*	Ph	14.15, 17 ***BNN*** *banīnu* ("we built"); 14.16, 17 ***YŠBN*** *yûsibnu* ("we caused to dwell"); 14.19 ***YSPN*** *yasapnu* ("we an-

		nexed")
	NPu	145.11 ***P'LN*** ("we made"); 159.5 ***YSPN*** ("we added").
-*N'*	NPu	Mactar B ***KN'*** *kannu* ("we were")
Pl. 2. M		
-*TM* *-tim*	NPu	163.1 ***KNTM*** *kantím* ("you were")
-tim	Pu	*Poen.* 1023 **sycartim** *s'kartím* ("you remember")
Pl. 3. C.		
-Ø *-ū*	Ph	47.1 ***NDR*** *nedrū* ("they vowed")
	Pu	*CIS* i 5510.10 ***TMK*** ("they seized")
-'	Pu-NPu	130.5 ***P'L'*** ("they made")
-u	NPu	*IRT* 889.2, 906.1 **felu** *fe(ʿ)lū* ("they made")
-un *-ūn*	NPu	*IRT* 865 **felun** *fe(ʿ)lūn* ("they made")

Sg. 1. C.: The inflectional ending was *-ti* in all periods. The two instances of *-t* in Neo-Punic occur in a poem in iambic rhythm that required *metri causa* the suppression of the final unstressed *i*-vowel. See C.R. Krahmalkov, *BASOR* 294 (1994), 69-82.

Sg. 2.: The masculine inflectional ending is attested in the vocalization *-ta,* like the singular of the first person retaining the final short unstressed vowel; *cf.* also the retention of the final unstressed a-vowel of the Sg. 2. M. suffix pronoun *-ka.* While the feminine singular is not attested, one may confidently surmise that it was *-ti,* with retained final unstressed vowel; *cf.* also the retention of the final unstressed vowel in the Sg. 2. F. suffix pronoun *-ki.*

Sg. 3. M. The inflection of the masculine singular is identical to that of Hebrew, displaying no inflectional ending.

Sg. 3. F. The third feminine inflectional ending was *-a* as in Hebrew and, as in Hebrew, and *-at-* with affixed direct object pronoun. The Qal form was *CiCCá,* with full reduction of the penultimate vowel of the etymon *CaCaCá* and sound-change *a* > *i* in the initial closed unstressed syllable; this form is seen in 14th century B.C. Byblian *šiḥtat* and in Neo-Punic **fela** *felá* < *feʿlá* < *faʿala.* Requiring special comment is the third singular of III*y* verbs in Phoenician: this form displayed the form *CaCá*, the feminine inflectional ending affixed directly to the second consonant of the root; this form was different from the corresponding Hebrew *CaCatá*, compounded of the archaic Sg. 3. F. *CaCát* + feminine inflectional ending *-a*. Thus the contrastive morphology: Hebrew *ban^{e}tá* ("she built") as against Phoenician *baná* (but Phoenician *banat-* with affixed object suffix pronouns).

P. 1. C.: The first plural inflectional ending was *-nu*. The retention of the final unstressed u-vowel is indicated by the Neo-Punic *plene* spelling ***KN'*** *kánnu* ("we were") and by the fact that Form B of the direct object suffixal pronouns is used with the verb, *e.g.*, ***YSPNNM*** *yasapnu-nom* ("we annexed").

Pl. 2. M.: The second masculine plural inflectional ending was *-tim*, of which we possess a vocalized example. The feminine plural ending is not recorded.

Pl. 3. C.: The third plural ending is universally attested as *-ū*. In very late Neo-Punic, however, we find a single instance of the form *-ūn*, with final n, in analogy to the third person plural inflectional ending of the Prefixing Form A *yiqtolūn*.

Examples

QAL

Sg. 1.		
Strong		
BRKT *barakti*	Ph	50.2 ("I bless")
garasth *garast(i)*	NPu	D 6.5/6 ("I expelled")
[K]TBT *katabti*	Ph	43.13 ("I wrote")
NṢḤT *naṣaḥti*	Ph	*CIS* i 91.2 ("I defeated")
P'LT *pa'alti*	Ph	24.4 ("I did")
SMRT *samarti*	Ph	43.13 ("I nailed")
TMKT *tamakti*	Ph	24.13 ("I took")
TRQT *taraqti*	Ph	26 A ("I rooted out")
y-t-n		
YTT *yatatti*	Ph	43.9 ("I placed")
I*y*		
YŠBT *yasabti*	Ph	24.9 ("I sat")

IIweak		
[B]'T bati	Ph	49 34 At ("I came")
bate *bati*	Pu	Poen. 941 ("I have come")
KT *katti*	Ph	24.6,10 ("I was")
ŠT *satti*	Ph	24.11; 26 A
sath *satt(i)*	NPu	D 6.9 ("I made")
III *'aleph*		
QR'T *qarōti*	Byb	10.7 ("I invoked")
caruti *qarūti*	Pu	*Poen.* 940 ("I invoke")
carothi *qarōti*	NPu	*Poen.* 930 ("I invoke")
nasote *nasōti*	Pu	*Poen.* 947 ("I carry; I share")
nasothi *nasōti*	NPu	*Poen.* 937
III*y*		
BNT *banīti*	Ph	14.4 ("I built")
'LT *'alīti*	Ph	*CIS* i 113.1 ("I sailed upstream")
Sg. 2. M.		
I*y*		
iadata *yada'ta*	Pu	*Poen.* 1017 ("you know")
III*y*		
QN'T *qanīta*	NPu	Trip. ("you have acquired")
Sg. 2. F.		
ŠLḤT *salaḥti*	Ph	50.5/6 ("you shall send!")
Sg. 3. M.		
Strong		
aros *'aros*	NPu	*S* 24.5 ("he requested")
P'L *pa'ol*	Ph	26 A III 15 ("he made")
σαμω *samo'*	Pu	175.4 ("he heard")
samo *samo'*	Pu	*CIL* I 2407; viii 12331 (**Balsamo**)
y-t-n		
YTN *yaton*	Ph	41.1 ("he gave")
iaton *yaton*	Pu	CIL viii 16011 (**Baliaton**)
iathon *yaton*	Pu	CIL viii 27155 (**Sidiathones**)
ιαθων *yaton*	Pu	CIS I 89 (Μιλκιαθων**ος**).
I*nun*		
NDR *nador*	Pu	79.3 ("he vowed")
ναδωρ *nador*	Pu	175.3 ("he vowed")

NŠʾ *nasoʾ*	Pu	*CIS* I 3781.1f ("he brought")
II*wy*		
KN *kon*	Ph	40.5
con *kon*	Pu	*Poen.* 946 ("it was")
chon *kon*	NPu	*Poen.* 936 ("it was")
II *ʾaleph*		
sal *sal* (Neo-Punic)	NPu	D 6.10 ("he asked")
II *ʿayin*		
PʿL *paʿol*	Ph	60.3
fel *fel*	Pu	*Poen.* 944
fel *fel*	NPu	*Poen.* 936; Trip. 828.1; *IRT* 877.2.
nem *nem*	Pu	In the name Giddenem ("My luck be good!")
IIgem.		
ḤN *ḥan*	Pu	*CIL* v 4920; viii 68 **Ammicar *ḤN-MLQRT*** ("Milqart show favor")
ann- *ḥann-*	Pu	*CIL* v 4920 **Annobal** ("Baal favor him!")
an- *ḥan-*	Pu	*CIL* viii 508 **Annibal** ("Baal favor me!")
sab *sab*	NPu	Dreder 6.8 ("it encircled")
TM *tam*	Ph	60.1 ("it was deemed good")
TM *tam*	NPu	134.3 ("he was righteous")
III*y*		
hauo *ḥawo*	Pu	*Poen.* 1141 ("may he live long!")
auo *awo* < *ḥawo*	NPu	*IRT* 879.3; IRT 894.4 ("he lived")
ḤZ *ḥazo*	Ph	24.11,12 ("he saw")
YD *yado*	Ph	30.4 ("he expelled")
ʿL *ʿalo*	Ph	*CIS* i 112 A 1, B 2, C 2 ("he sailed upstream")

Sg. 3. F.

Strong

ʾRŠ *ʾersa*	Pu	Pyrgi ("she requested")
PʿL *peʿla*	Byb	10.8 ("she made")
NʿDR *nedra*	Pu	87.4 ("she vowed")
NDRʾ *nedra*	Pu	88.23 ("she vowed")
šiḫtat *siḫtat*	Arch Byb	EA 106.10/11 ("it has been destroyed")
ŠMʿ *semʿa*	Ph	Byb 10.8 ("she heard")

With object pronoun:		
PʿLTN *peʿlat-ni (?)*	Byb	10.2 ("she made me")
NKST *neksat-o (?)*	Pu	*CIS* i 3783.6 ("she will cut him off")
II*yw*		
KNʿ *kóna*	NPu	136.4 ("she was")
MTʿ *méta*	NPu	136.2 ("she died")
II gem.		
ḤN *ḥanna*	Byb	10.10 ("may she show favor")
TMʾ *tamma*	NPu	NP 55.2 ("she was righteous")
With object pronoun:		
QBT *qabbato*	Pu	*CIS* i 4945.5 ("she will curse him")
III*y*		
haua *ḥawa*	Pu	*Poen.*1141 ("may she live long!")
aua *awa* < *ḥawa*	NPu	*AI* 2 1928 no. 29 ("she lived")
Pl. 1. C.		
Strong		
PʿLN *felnu* <	NPu	145.11 ("we made")
YSPN *yasapnu*	Ph	14.20 ("we added")
YSPN *yasapnu*	NPu	159.5 ("we added")
II*w*		
KNʾ *kannu*	NPu	Mactar B IV 1 ("we were")
III*y*		
BNN *banīnu*	Ph	14.17 ("we built")
Pl. 2. M.		
Strong		
sucartim *s^{i}kartim*	Pu	*Poen.* 1023 ("you remember")
II*wy*		
KNTM *kantim*	NPu	163.1 ("you were")
Pl. 3. C.		
Strong		
felu *fe(ʿ)lū*	NPu	*S* 24.2; *IRT* 906.1 ("they made")
III*y*		
BN *banō*	Ph	19.1,9 ("they built")
BNʾ *banō*	Pu	101.1 ("they built")
bano *banō*	NPu	*PBSR* 28 53 no. 6.4 ("they built")
Ph *paʿalnu*		
II*wy*		

B' *bóʾū*	NPu	137.4 ("they came")
KN *kónū*	Ph	11; 26 A I 14 ("they were"); 26 A II 1
KN *kónū*	NPu	165.4,6,8
KN' *kónū*	NPu	130.3; 137.2 ("they were")
ŠM *sómū*	Ph	14.5 ("they placed")
ŠT *sótū*	Ph	24.13 ("they placed")
II *ʿayin*		
PʿL *peʿlū*	Pu	80.1
PHL' *felū* <*peʿlū*	NPu	142.4
felu *felū*	NPu	*IRT* 889.2; IRT 906.1
felun *felūn*	NPu	*IRT* 865

QAL PASSIVE

Sg. 1. C.		
gunebte *gunebti*	Pu	*Poen.* 1027 ("I have been robbed")
Sg. 3.M.		
LPP *lupep*	Byb	1.2 ("it will be twisted up")

NIP'AL

Sg. 1. C.		
Strong		
NGZLT *negzalti*	Ph	14.2,12 ("I was snatched away")
Sg. 3. M.		
Strong		
NʿNŠ *neʿnos*	Pu	69.20 ("he will be fined")
NPʿL *nepʿal*	Ph	RES 1204.1 ("it was made")
NPLʿ(!) *nef'al*	NPu	Trip. 79.5 ("it was built")
III*y*		
NBN' *nebno*	Pu	146.1 ("it was built")
neso *neʿso*	Pu	*Poen.* 943 ("he was made")
Sg. 3. F.		
NPʿL' *nefʿala*	NPu	Trip. 78.1 (old no) ("it was made")
NTN *nettana*	Pu	69.18 ("it shall be given")
Pl. 3. C.		

NPʿL *nefʾalū*	NPu	137.5 ("they were made")
NPʿLʾ *nefʾalū*	NPu	130.1 ("they were made")
y-t-n		
NNTN *nintanū*	NPu	137.6 ("they were given")
l-q-ḥ		
NLQḤʾ *nelqa(ḥ)ū*	NPu	122.2 ("they were purchased")

PI'EL

Sg. 1. C.		
Strong		
ŠLMTY *sillemti*	NPu	NP 86.3 ("I fulfilled")
III *ʾaleph*		
ṬNʾT *ṭinne(ʾ)ti*	Pu	*CIS* i 600.4 ("I erected")
mysethi *miṣṣe(ʾ)ti*	NPu	*Poen.* 931 ("I have come")
Sg. 3. M.		
ʾDR *ʾidder*	Pu	*CIS* i 6000.7 ("it magnified")
bycys *biqqis*	NPu	*IRT* 892.3/5 ("he sought")
ḤDŠ *ḥiddes*	Pu	62.1 ("he restored")
ḤYDŠ *iddes* < *ḥiddes*	NPu	138.6 ("he restored")
ṬNʾ *ṭinne(ʾ)*	NPu	NP 62.2 ("he erected")
ṬYNʾ *ṭinne(ʾ)*	NPu	119.2; 123.2; 127; 143.2
νεσε *nesse(ʾ)*	Ph	174,1/7 (***NŠʾ*** "he gave")
ŠYLK *sillek*	NPu	In name 138.2) ***BʿLŠYLK*** ("Baal save!")
sillec *sillek*	Pu	In name *CIL* v 4919 **Balsillecis.** and *CIL* viii 1249 **Balsillec**.
silech *sillek*	Pu	In name *CIL* viii 16 **Balsilechis** ()
σελημ *sillem*	Pu	In name *CIS* i 119 Εσυμσελημου (***ʾŠMNŠLM***)
Sg. 3. F.		
MGN *miggena*	Ph	29.1 ("she presented")
Pl. 3. C.		
ḤDŠ *ḥiddesū*	Pu	80.1 ("they restored")

PU'AL

Sg. 3. F.		
ṬN' *ṭunna'a*	NPu	134.1 ("it was erected")
Ṭ'N' *ṭunna'a*	NPu	133.1 ("it was erected")

YIP'IL

Sg. 1. C.		
Strong		
YṬN'T *yiṭne(')ti*	Ph	35.2 ("I erected")
YQDŠT *yiqdesti*	Ph	43.9,14 ("he dedicated")
y-š-b		
YŠBT *yūsebti*	Ph	26 A II 1 ("I caused to dwell")
II*y*		
YŠT *yisitti*	Ph	43.7 ("I made to be placed")
Sg. 3. M.		
Strong		
YṬN' *yiṭne(')*	Ph	41.1/2 ("he erected")
'YKRM *ikrem*	NPu	145 III 12 ("it honored")
HYKRM *ikrem*	NPu	Mactar B II 2/3 ("he restored")
intseb *intseb*	NPu	*IRT* 873.3 ("he erected")
YQDŠ *yiqdes*	Ph	42.4 ("he dedicated")
'YQDŠ *iqdes*	NPu	118.1; 121.2; 129.2; 138.6
I*y*		
utseb *ûtseb*	NPu	D 5.19 ("he erected"); *IRT* 892.5; *IRT* 893.6/7
uxeb *ûtseb*	NPu	*IRT* 893.6/7 ("he erected")
II*wy*		
'YB' *ibī(')*	NPu	Trip. 32 ("he brought")
YPYQ- *ipīq-*	NPu	153.3 ("he found; he acquired")
III*y*		
H'L *i'lo*	NPu	Mactar B II 2/3 ("he raised").
II gem.		
YGN *igin*	NPu	124.2 ("he roofed")
ḤTM *itim*	NPu	124.4 ("he completed it")
Sg. 3. F.		
YṬN' *yiṭne'a*	Ph	40.3 ("she erected")
Pl. 1. C.		
y-š-b		

YŠBN *yûsebnu*	Ph	14.16,17 ("we caused to dwell")

Pl. 3. C.
II*wy*

YB' *yibī'ū*	Pu	81.4 ("they brought")

YITPE'EL

Pl. 3. C.
y-k-d

'YTKDW *ittekkedū*	NPu	119.4 ("they mutually resolved")

Comments

The morphology of the Phoenician-Punic verb is essentially the same as the Hebrew. The differences are as follows. Final *yod* verbs in the Qal have the forms *bano* ("he built"), *bana* ("she built") and *banô* ("they built"): the feminine singular is formed in paradigmatic analogy to the strong verb Sg. 3.F. *qetla*; the masculine plural is a development from original *banaw*, like Syriac *bnaw* (Biblical Aramaic *bnô*), although the evidence is not particularly good.

Verbs II *'aleph* and II *'ayin* in Punic and Neo-Punic had the monosyllabic forms *CaC* and *CeC* in the Qal stem: *e.g.*, D 6 **sal** (***Š'L*** "he asked") and *IRT* 873.2 **fel** (***P'L*** "he made"); *IRT* 826.1/2 **fela** ("she made"); *S* 24.2 **felu** ("they made"). The masculine singular forms are "back-formations" from the feminine singular and plural forms *fe'la* and *fe'lū*: when the laryngeals and pharyngeals were lost, came to be pronounced *fela* and *felū* respectively, giving rise by analogy to the masculine singular *fel*, which replaced original *fa'ol*. These new monosyllabic roots underlie new nominal forms like Neo-Punic 178.1 **felioth** *felīót* ("work"), created in analogy to nouns such as *Poen.* 947 **helicot** *helīkót* ("hospitality").

Verbs IIIgem. in the Qal are all based on the form *CaC(C)*, never on the form *CaCaC*. Thus one finds D 6 **sab** *sab* < *sabb* (***SB*** "he encircled"), not *sabab*.

The verb "to give" in the Qal Suffixing Form is *y-t-n*. However, in the Prefixing Form and in the derived stems, the root is *n-t-n*, as can be seen from the Qal Prefixing Form 50.3/4 (Daphnae) ***TNTN*** *tintenī* ("you gave") and in the Neo-Punic Niph'al Suffixing Form 137.6 ***NNTN*** *nintenū* ("they were given").

Verbs I*y* exhibit loss of the initial *y* in the Hitpe'el: NPu 119.4 ***'YTKDW*** *ittekkedū* ("they mutully resolved"). An analogous develoment is seen with the root *h-l-k/y-l-k* in the Prefixing Form of the Hitpe'el: 24.10 ***YTLKN*** *yittellekūn* ("they used to go about").

B. *Syntax and Usage*

1. *Past Perfective: Phoenician*

1a. Non Clause-Initial

In formal literary prose, past perfective action was expressed by three forms: (i) Infinitive Absolute, (ii) Prefixing Verb B and (iii) Suffixing Verb. For purposes here of convenient reference, one may call these expressions of the Past Perfective Past Perfective I, Past Perfective II and Past Perfective III respectively.

In Phoenician, Past Perfective III (Suffixing Form) occurs in complementation to Past Perfective I and II: Past Perfective I and II are syntactically restricted to sentence-initial position in the simple declarative sentence, Past Perfective III to non sentence-initial position. Past Perfective III can however be the past perfective tense of choice, as for example in the Esmunazor Inscription (*KAI* 14) and the Yatonbal bin Gerastart Inscription (*KAI* 43), to the exclusion of Past Pefective I and II; but it must always be used non sentence-initial.

In a simple declarative sentence, when the Suffixing Form is used to express past perfective action, it is syntactically restricted in the following two ways: (i) it must be the main verb of the sentence; and (ii) it may never occupy sentence-initial position, the sentence-initial form expressing past perfective action being always Past Perfective I or Past Perfective II.

A Suffixing Form that is not the main verb in the simple declarative sentence is the "consecutive" subform, which takes its tense and aspect reference from the main verb. See Consecutive. A Suffixing Form that occurs in sentence-initial position in a simple sentence cannot be Past Perfective III although the situation in Cypriote Phoenician is ambiguous. Past Perfective III does however occupy initial position in the main clause of a complex sentence. See Complex Sentence.

The following examples illustrate non sentence-initial Past Perfective III as the main verb of a simple declarative sentence in literary Phoenician and Punic prose.

1a-1. Subject (Noun or Pronoun) Precedes

24.6 ***WKL ŠLḤ YD,*** "Each extended his arm."

24.13 ***’NK TMKT MŠKBM LYD,*** "I took the *mškbm* by the hand."

24.13 ***WHMT ŠT NBŠ,*** "And they disposed their feelings."

Pu *Poen.* 943 **Hu neso bin us esse,** "He was made the son of this man."

26 A I 15/16 ***BL ’Š ‘BD KN LBT MPŠ,*** "None was a vassal of the House of Mopsos."

26 A II 10/11 ***B‘L WRŠP . . . ŠLḤN LBNT,*** "Baal and Rasep commissioned me to build it".

1a-2. Direct Object Precedes

31.1 ***’Z YTN LB‘L LBNN ’DNY,*** "He gave this to Baal of Lebanon, his Lord."

18.3 ***’YT HŠ‘R Z WHDLHT ’Š L P‘LT BTKLTY BNTY,*** "I built this gate and its doors at my own expense."

26 A I 21-II 1 ***WDNNYM YŠBT ŠM,*** "And I settled Danunians there."

43.12/13 ***HDLT HNḤŠT [Z K]TBT WSMRT BQR,*** "So, too, did I inscribe that bronze plaque and nail it to the wall."

1a-3. Relative Pronoun Precedes

24.4/5 ***M ’Š P‘LT BL P‘L HLPNY{H}M,*** "My predecessors did not accomplish what I accomplished."

26 A I 14/15 ***BMQMM B’Š KN ’ŠM R‘M,*** "In places in which there were bad men."

26 A I 19 ***HMLKM ’Š KN LPNY,*** "The kings who were before me."

1a-4. Prepositional Phrase Precedes

43.7 ***’BḤY ’BY YŠT BMQDŠ MLQRT ’YT MŠ PN ’BY BNḤŠT,*** "When my father was still alive, I had the bronze bust of my father placed in the sanctuary of Milqart."

24.10 ***LMY KT ’B LMY KT ’M,*** "To him who <had no father> I was a father, to him who <had no mother> I was a mother."

24.12/13 ***BYMY KSY BṢ,*** "In my days, they dressed him in byssus."

26 A I 12/13 ***B’BT P‘LN KL MLK BṢDQY WBḤKMTY WBN‘M LBY,*** "Every king adopted me as father because of my honesty, my cleverness and the excellence of my mind."

26 A II 15/16 ***BYMTY KN . . . ŠB‘ WMN‘M,*** "In my days there was abundance and prosperity."

1a-5. Adverb or Conjunction Precedes

14.18/19 ***W‘D YTN LN ’DN MLKM ’YT D’R WYPY,*** "Moreover, the Lord of Kings ceded to us Dor and Joppa."

60.3 ***K BN ’YT ḤṢR BT ’LM,*** "Because he built the temple court."

1a-6. Presentative Particle Precedes

CIS I 4.3/5 ***K BN BD‘ŠTRT MLK ṢDNM ’YT ŠRN ’R[. . .Z] L[’]LY L‘ŠTRT,*** "Bodastart, King of the Sidonians, built [this] *šrn* for his goddess Astarte."

1a-7. Negative Particle Precedes

14.5 ***’Y ŠM BN MNM,*** "They put nothing in it."

26 A II 19 ***BL ‘N KL HMLKM ’Š KN LPNY*** "<I conquered mighty lands that> all the kings before me did not conquer."

1a-8. Particle ***L’MR*** Precedes

14.2/3 ***DBR MLK ’ŠMN‘ZR MLK ṢDNM L’MR NGZLT BL ‘TY,*** "<This is the final> statement of King Esmunazor, King of the Sidonians, 'I was snatched away not at my time!'"

1b. Clause-Initial Past Perfective III (Suffixing Form)

Past Perfective III is obligatory in certain types of main clauses of a complex sentence (sentence with subordinate clause and main clause). In such clauses, it is syntactically restricted to clause-initial position:

1b-1. In the Main Clause of a Temporal Sentence

In this usage, the clauses are marked off by the conjunction *w*-, which introduces the main result clause.

Byb 10.7/8 ***KM ’Š QR’T ’T RBTY B‘LT GBL WŠM‘ QL,*** "When I called my Lady Baalt of Byblos, she heard my voice."

Kition, lines 1/3 ***BMṢ’NM ’BN W‘ZRNM HPPYM L’GD LN MLḤMT . . . WYṢ’ ‘LNM MḤ]NT ’Š KTY L’GD LM MLḤMT BMQM Z,*** "When our enemies and their Paphian allies came to wage war with us, the army of the people of Kition went forth against them to wage war with them in this place."

CID 7AB-8AB ***WKM ’Š YGL ’YT MSNZMŠ BYMT ’ZWŠŠ W YSB MLK WRYK<LY> LMSN’ZMŠ KL HŠDYT ’L,*** "When they exiled MSNZMS in the time of 'ZWSS, the king of WRYKLY turned over all these fields to MSN'ZMS."

In this same sentence-type in Classical Hebrew, the Suffixing Form may not be introduced by the conjunction *w-*.

1b-2. In the Main (Result) Clause of a Sentence with Anticipatory Clause

In this usage, the clauses are not marked off by the conjunction *w-*.

24.11 ***WMY BL ḤZ PN Š ŠTY B'L 'DR,*** "As for him who had never owned a sheep from the time of his youth, I made him the owner of a herd."

24.11/2 ***WMY BL ḤZ PN 'LP ŠTY B'L BQR,*** "And as for him who had never owned an ox, I made him the owner of cattle."

2. *Cypriote and Punic Usage*

It is not at all certain that in Phoenician the Suffixing Form with past perfective reference was ever used in sentence-initial position. Putative examples of this usage are extremely few and always ambiguous, readily susceptible to interpretation as "consecutive" subforms of the Suffixing Verb. One possible instance is perhaps found in Cypriote Phoenician: *FK* B 46.2 (4th cent.) ***P'L Z Y[. . .],*** ("Y[. . .] made this."). However, the verb ***P'L*** could just as well be understood as an Infinitive Absolute (Past Perfective I). Ambiguous are the following three examples of the Suffixing Form in the first singular, the first two with independent personal pronoun, in Cypriote Phoenician:

43.13/14 ***WP'LT 'NK 'LT [HMQDŠ] . . . . 'PDT BK[S]P MŠQL KR 100 W 2,*** "And I made a ephod of silver for [the sanctuary], its weight 102 *kor.*"

Kition line 4 ***WYṬN'T 'NK WKL 'M KTY 'YT HTRPY 'Z,*** "And I and the entire nation of Kition erected this trophy."

CIS I 91.2 ***NṢḤT 'T 'BY HYṢ'M,*** "?I defeated my enemies who came forth <to battle against me>."

The first two examples may be the consecutive form of the Suffixing Form, each occurring in a string of statements couched in the first person Past Perfective; the third example may be of the clause-initial cohortative use of the Prefixing Form. More examples are required to determine if Cypriote Phoenician of the second half of the first millennium B.C. permitted, in marked contrast to general

Phoenician usage, the Suffixing Form in sentence (clause)-initial position with past perfective meaning.

Punic and Neo-Punic, although essentially the same as Phoenician, did allow Past Perfective III in sentence-intitial position. The vocalized forms in Neo-Punic in Latin letters indicate the sentence-initial verb is the Suffixing Form, not the Infinitive Absolute (Past Perfective I).

Pu 80.1 ***ḤDŠ WP'L 'YT HMṬBḤ Z*** "They rebuilt this slaughtering altar."

Pu 115.1/2 ***ŠLM BD'ŠTRT BN BD'ŠMN 'YT NDRM,*** "Bostar son of Bodesmun fulfilled his vow."

Pu *RCL* 1961 p. 201 line 1 ***PTḤ WP'L 'YT HḤṢ Z*** "They opened and made this street."

NPu 130.1 ***NP'L' ŠŠ HYŠBM 'L' BŠT HŠPṬM 'BDMLQRT ṬBḤPY W'RŠ,*** "These six seats were made in the year of the suffetes Abdmilqart Tapapius and Aris."

NPu 140.1 ***BN' B[T] Z [Q]W'R[Ṭ]H BT NPTḤN,*** "Quarta daughter of Nyptane built this tomb."

NPu 141.1 ***ṬN' T-'BN Z WTḤ 'Š 'L 'RṢT TŠK'T,*** "WTH, Governor of the province of Tusca, erected this milestone."

NPu *AI* 1 p. 233 lines 1/2 **Fel th-ybur Licini Piso,** "Licinius Piso built this tomb."

NPu D 5.19/20 **Utseb sy lo Machrus byn Rogate,** "Machrus son of Rogatus erected this to him."

NPu D 6 **Sab siben Mycne,** "Our militia surrounded Mycne."

3. *Pluperfect (kon pa'ol)*

The Pluperfect is expressed by the Suffixing Form of the verb *k-w-n* + the Suffixing Form of the principal verb, *e.g., hū kon pa'ol* ("he had made"), in the manner of Classical Arabic *kāna fa'ala.* A single example occurs, in Phoenician:

40.3/5 ***HSMLM H'L 'Š YṬN' BTŠLM . . . 'L BN BNY . . . ŠLŠT BN MRYḤY . . . HNDR 'Š KN NDR 'BNM MRYḤY BḤYY L'DNNM LRŠP MKL,*** "These statues are what Bitsalom erected for her grandsons, the three sons of <her son> MRYHY. <This is> the vow that their father MRYHY had made to their Lord Rasap-Mekalle when he (MRYHY) was alive."

4. *Present Perfective*

Present Perfective expresses a singular action confined within the present moment in time ("here and now, this once") or a simple generalization in present time. With verbs of cognition, such as "to know, to remember," the Present Perfective conveys a simple statement of fact in present time. In Latin translations of Punic, this use of the suffixing form is captured by the Latin Present Indicative.

The Suffixing Form with Present Perfective meaning is not restricted syntactically within the sentence but may freely occupy sentence-initial or non- sentence-initial position.

50.2/3 ***BRKTK LB'L ṢPN,*** "I bless (greet) you in the name of Baalsaphon."

Pu *Poen.* 940 **Et alonim ualonut caruti *(QR'T)* is timlacun alt imacum esse** = NPu *Poen.* 930/31 **Yth alonim ualonuth carothi is ymacom syth thymlachun,** "I invoke you gods and goddesses who rule over this city." *Obs.* This verse illustrates the contrast in aspect between the Present Perfective **carothi** and the Present Imperfective, expressed by Prefixing Form A **thymlachun**, a plural action not confined within a specific moment in time.

Pu *Poen.* 947 **Itt esde anec nasote** (***NŠ'T***) **hers ahelicot,** "I bring to him <this> shard of hospitality." = NPu *Poen.* 937 **Ythem anech nasothi li yth irs aelichoth isith,** "I bring to him this shard of hospitality on my behalf." *Obs.* The Latin translation of the Neo-Punic is: *Poen.* 958 **ad eum hospitalem hanc tesseram mecum fero.**

Pu *Poen.* 1023 **Mu Ponnim sucartim** (***SKRTM***) **?,** "Do you remember any Punic?" *Obs.* The Punic corresponds to *Poen.* 985 **Ecquid commeministi Punice?**

Pu *Poen.* 1023 **Iadata *(YD'T)*?,** "Do you know <it>?" *Obs.* The Punic corresponds to *Poen.* 991 **an scis**?

5. *Cohortative, Optative*

This use of the Suffixing Verb is restricted to sentence-initial position in formal literary prose. This syntactic restriction is respected in all periods of the language. Non sentence-initial optative/jussive must be expressed by Prefixing Verb B.

26 A III 2/3 ***BRK B'L . . . 'YT 'ZTWD,*** "Baal bless Aztwadda!"

26 A III 7 ***WKN HQRT Z B'LT ŠB' . . . W'M Z 'Š YŠB BN YKN B'L 'LPM,*** "May this city be(come) the possessor of plenty

. . . and may this people who dwell in it become possessors of cattle!" *Obs.* Note the sequence ***KN . . . YKN,*** in which the first verb is clause-initial Suffixing Verb optative and the second non clause-initial Prefixing Verb B optative.

CIS i 91.2 (Kition) ***NṢḤT 'T 'BY HYṢ'M,*** "Would that I might defeat my enemies who have come forth." *Obs.* On the use of the sentence-initial Suffixing Verb as cohortative (a wish in the first person), cf. Hebrew Genesis 47:30 ***WŠKBTY 'M-'BTY,*** " I would lie with my ancestors <in the land of Canaan>."

Pu *Poen.* 1141 **Auo donnim,** "May the gentlemen live long!"

Pu Poen.1141 **Hauo done silli,** "May my lord/father live long!"

Pu *Poen.* 1141 **Haua amma silli,** "May my mother live long!"

Pu *Poen.* 1141 **Hauo bane** (var. **bene**) **silli** "May my son live long!"

6. *Future*

The Suffixing Form has future tense reference in the main clause of a complex sentence. The complex sentence may be one of three types: (i) a sentence with anticipatory clause or (ii) a temporal sentence or (iii) a conditional sentence. Common to these sentence types is the syntactic restriction of the Suffixing Form to initial position in the main (resumptive, result) clause.

6a. In Result Clause of a Sentence with Anticipatory Clause

The verb is often preceded by the conjunction *w*-, which functions solely to mark off the main clause from the preceding, anticipatory clause; this use of the conjunction *w*- is non-obligatory.

26 A III 12-19 ***'M MLK BMLKM . . . 'Š YMḤ ŠM 'ZTWD BŠR Z . . . WMḤ B'LŠMM . . . 'YT HMLK H',*** "As for any king who shall erase the name of Aztwadda from this gate, Baalsamem shall erase that king!"

Pu 69.18 ***KL MŠ'T 'Š 'YBL ŠT BPS Z WNTN LPY HKTBT 'Š [. . .],*** "As for any payment that is not listed in this inscription, it shall be given/paid in accordance with <what is listed in> the book that <is held by the officials in charge of payments>."

Pu 69.4 ***BṢW'T QṢRT WYṢLT WKN H'RT WHŠLBM WH-P'MM W'ḤRY HŠ'R LB'L HZBḤ,*** "Of the *ṣw't* and the *qṣrt* and the *yṣlt* <of a slaughtered animal>, the skin and the flanks and the feet and the rest of the meat shall belong to the sacrificer."

Pu 69.20 ***KL KHN 'Š YQḤ MŠ'T BDṢ L'Š ŠT BPS Z WN'N[Š],*** "As for any priest who shall take a payment in excess of that listed in this inscription, he shall be fined."

Pu 79.6/11 ***WKL 'Š LSR T-'BN Z . . . WŠPṬ TNT-PNB'L BRḤ 'DM H',*** "As for anyone who shall remove this stele, Thinnith-Phanebal shall adjudge the intent of that person."

Pu *CIS* i 4945.4/6 ***W'Š YRGZ T-MTNT Z WQBT TNT-PNB'L,*** "As for anyone who shall disturb this stele, Thinnith-Phanebal shall curse him!"

Pu *CIS* i 3783.5/7 ***WKL 'DM 'Š GNB T-MTNT Z NKST TNT-PNB'L,*** "As for any person who shall steal this stele, Thinnith-Phanebal shall cut him off!"

Pu *CIS* i 5510.2/3 ***WKL 'DM 'Š LKP 'YT 'MTNT Z WL'KR WLŠBTY 'ML YD,*** "As for any person who shall knock down this stele or disturb or remove it, his hand shall wither."

Pu *CIS* i 5510.4 ***WKL 'DM 'Š 'YBL MŠRT WKPT RBTN TNT-PNB'L W'DN B['L]ḤMN 'YT 'DMM HMT,*** "As for any person who will not render service, Our Lady Thinnith-Phanebal and the Lord Baalhammon shall bind those persons."

Obs. In these same kinds of sentences, future tense in the main clause may also be expressed by means of Suffixing Verb A:

24.15 ***WMY YŠḤT HSPR Z YŠḤT R'Š B'L ṢMD,*** "As for him who shall erase this inscription, Baal of the Club shall smash his head!"

Pu *CIS* i 3784.1/3 ***KL 'Š LGNB T-'BN Z B'LḤMN YQṢY',*** "As for anyone who shall steal this stone, Baalhammon shall cut him off."

6b. In the Result Clause of a Conditional or Temporal Sentence

This syntactic structure is closely related to the preceding in both the suffixing verb restricted to clause-initial position in the main clause of a sentence with preceding clause.

Byb 1.2 ***WH' YMḤ SPRH LPP ŠBL,*** "But if he shall erase its [the coffin's] inscription, his long royal robe shall be twisted up."

50.5/6 ***'D 'Š 'D' BM'[. .]T WŠLḤT LY 'T SPR HNQT,*** "When I *pay you back*, you shall send me the quittance."

Pu *CIS* i 5510.7 ***[M]ŠRT LQN' WKN L' ḤL WŠLM,*** "<If> he who serves shall be zealous, wealth and prosperity shall be his!"

7. *The Consecutive Subform*

When consecutive to the main verb of a sentence or clause, the Suffixing Form, by itself unmarked for mood, aspect and tense, assumes the mood, aspect and tense of the main verb. The consecutive form is always syntactically restricted to follow the main verb of the sentence and clause.

7a. Past Perfective + Suffixing Form (=Past Perfective)

14.18/19 ***W'D YTN*** (*yaton*) LN ***'YT D'R WYPY . . . WYSPNNM*** (*yasapnunom*) **'LT *GBL 'RṢ,*** "Moreover, he gave to us Dor and Joppa, and we annexed them to the territory of the state."

24.6/7 ***KN BT 'BY BMTKT MLKM 'DRM WKL ŠLḤ*** (*saloḥ*) ***YD LL[Ḥ]M WKT*** (*katti*) ***BYD MLKM <HMT> KM 'Š,*** "My state was in the midst of those of more powerful kings, each <of whom> extended his hand to fight <me>, but in the hands of <those> kings I was like fire."

26 A I 21-II 2 ***WDNNYM YŠBT*** (*yûsebti*) ***ŠM WKN*** (*konū*) ***BYMTY BKL GBL 'MQ 'DN,*** "And I settled Danunians there, and so they [the Danunians] lived throughout the territory of Amq Adana in my time."

26 C I 11/17 ***WP'L 'NK SS 'L SS . . . WŠBRT MLṢM . . . WTRQT KL R' 'Š KN B'RṢ WYṬN'T BT 'DNY BN'M,*** "I acquired horse upon horse and smashed dissenters and I rooted out all the evil that was in the land and equipped my royal house with what is good."

43.9 ***BḤY 'BY YTT*** (*yatatti*) ***WYQDŠT*** (*yiqdesti*) ***ḤYT ŠGYT BGBL ŠD NRNK L'DN 'Š LY LMLQRT,*** "When my father was still alive, I gave and dedicated many *shrines* throughout the territory of the Land of Narnaka to my Lord Milqart."

43.13/15 ***WP'LT*** (*pa'alti*) ***'NK . . . 'PDT BK[S]P . . . WYQDŠT*** (*yiqdesti*) ***L'DN ['Š LY LMLQ]RT,*** "And I made an ephod of silver and dedicated it to my Lord Milqart."

60..3/4 ***K BN*** (*bano*) ***'YT ḤṢR BT 'LM WP'L*** (*pa'ol*) ***'YT KL 'Š 'LTY,*** "Because he built the temple court and did everything with which he was charged."

Pu *CIS* i 5510.9/11 ***WYLK*** (*yelekū*) ***RBM 'DNB'L BN GRSKN HRB WḤMLKT BN ḤN' HRB 'LŠ WTMK*** (*tamkū*) ***HMT 'YT 'GRGNT WŠT*** (*sotū*) ***HMT ŠLM,*** "Generals Idnibal son of Gisco the Great and Himilco son of Hanno the Great marched at dawn, and they seized Agrigentum, and they (the Agrigentines) made peace."

7b. Future + Suffixing Form (=Future)

26 A III 13/14 ***YMḤ*** *(yimḥe)* ***ŠM 'ZTWD BŠ'R Z WŠT*** *(sot)* ***ŠM,*** "He shall erase the name of Aztwadda from this gate and place his own name <on it>."

26 A III 16 ***YP'L*** *(yip'al)* ***L Š'R ZR WŠT*** *(sot)* ***ŠM 'LY,*** "He shall make another gate for it and place his own name upon it."

26 C III 14/16 ***Y'MR*** *(yūmar)* ***LMḤT ŠM 'ZTWD BSML 'LM Z WŠT*** *(sot)* ***ŠM,*** "He shall think to erase the name of Aztwadda from this statue and shall place his own name <upon it>."

26 C III 17/18 ***'P'L*** *('ep'al)* ***SML ZR WŠT*** *(satti)* ***ŠMY 'LY,*** "I shall make another statue and shall place (*satti*) my own name upon it."

60.4/5 ***'YT R'T Z LKTB*** (*liktōb:* future periphrastic) ***H'DMM . . . 'LT MṢBT ḤRṢ WYṬN'Y*** (*yiṭni'ū*ya) ***B'RPT BT 'LM.,*** "The men shall inscribe this resolution upon a stele of gold and shall erect it and shall erect it in the portico of the temple."

Pu 69.7/8 ***WBṢW'T YK[N*** *(yakūnū)* ***LM 'LT PN HMŠ'T Z QṢRT] WYṢLT WKN*** *(konū)* ***H'RT WHŠLBM WHP'MM W'ḤRY HŠ'R LB'L HZBḤ,*** "Of the dismembered parts <of the sacrificial animal>, the *qṣrt* and the *yṣlt* shall belong to them (the priests) in addition to this payment, but the skin/hide and the *šlbm* and the legs and the rest of the meat shall belong to the sacrificer."

7c. Jussive/Optative + Suffixing Form (=Jussive/Optative)

Byb 10.9/11 ***WTTN*** *(titten)* ***[LY HRBT B]'LT GBL ḤN . . . WḤN*** *(ḥanna)* ***'M 'RṢ Z,*** "May the Lady Baalt of Byblos grant me favor, and may she show favor to the people of this land!"

CHAPTER TEN

THE VERB: THE PREFIXING FORMS

Introduction

The Prefixing Form of the verb comprises three distinct subforms: (i) Prefixing Form A, the reflex of West Semitic *yaqtulu*, (ii) Prefixing Form B, the reflex of West Semitic *yaqtul* and (iii) Prefixing Form C, the reflex of West Semitic *yaqtula*. In Phoenician, as in Classical Arabic and Old Aramaic, the three prefixing forms were mutually distinct in morphology: Form A in the Pl. 2. M. and Pl. 3. M. exhibited the inflection *-ūn* (**-*N***); in contrast, Forms B and C ended in *-ū* (**-Ø**; Pu **-ʾ**). This difference in inflection was consistently and scrupulously maintained, in marked contrast to Ugaritic and Hebrew, in which the forms were often used in free variation. Form C differed from Forms A and B in the Sg. 1. C. and Sg. 3. M. exhibiting word-final *-a*, but this inflectional ending appears in the writing of the form only in the Punic and Neo-Punic Latin-letter orthography.

I. Prefixing Form A

A. *Morphology*

Forms

BT *bit*	Ph	14.15; 29.1; 50.1
QAL		
Sg. 1. C.		
Strong		
ʾPʿL *ʾepʿal*	Ph	26 C III 17 ("I shall make")
ʾŠʾL *ʾesʾal*	Ph	48.2/3 ("I ask")
III*y*		
ʾʾL *ʾedle*	Ph	13.4 ("I possess")
este *ʾeste*	Pu	*Poen.* 1141 ("I shall drink")
y-t-n		
ʾT(N)- *ʾetten*	Pu	89.2 ("I give")

Sg. 2. M.		
Strong		
TP['L] *tip'al*	Ph	Byb 9 B 3 ("you shall make")
TPTḤ *tiptaḥ*	Ph	13.7 ("you shall open")
II*w*		
TPQ *tipūq*	Ph	13.3 ("you shall acquire")
TŠT *tisīt*	Ph	Byb 10.13 ("you shall place")
Sg. 3. M.		
Strong		
Y'MR *yûmer*	Ph	26 C III 14/15 ("he shall contemplate")
YZBḤ *yizbaḥ*	Pu	69.15 ("he shall sacrifice")
YḤMD *yaḥmod*	Ph	26 A III 14 ("he loves")
Y'MS *ya'mos*	Ph	14.7 ("he shall carry off")
YP'L *yip'al*	Ph	26 A III 16 ("he shall make")
YPTḤ *yiptaḥ*	Ph	14.7 ("he shall open")
YŠT' *yista'*	Ph	26 A II 4 ("he used to fear")
I*n*		
YŠ' *yissa(')*	Ph	14.7 ("he shall take away")
YS' *yissa'*	Ph	26 A III 15,17 ("he shall pull out")
II*wy*		
YKN *yakūn*	Ph	26 A IV 2 9 ("it shall be")
III*y*		
YMḤ *yimḥe*	Ph	Byb 1.2; 26 A III 13 ("he shall erase")
Sg. 3. F.		
h-l-k		
TLK *telek*	Ph	26 A II 5 ("she walks")
Pl. 1. C.		
III*y*		
neste *neste*	Pu	*Poen.* 1142 ("we shall drink")
Pl. 2. M.		
Strong		
timlacun *timlakūn*	Pu	*Poen.* 940P ("you rule")
thymlachun *timlakūn*	NPu	*Poen.* 931 ("you rule")

Pl. 3. M.
Strong

YDBRN *yidborūn*	Ph	14.6 ("they shall say")
YSGRN *yisgorūn*	Ph	14.9, 21 ("they shall lock up")
I*n*		
YŠ'N *yissa'ūn*	Ph	60.6 ("they shall withdraw")

PI'EL
Sg. 2. M.
III*y*

TGL *tegelle*	Ph	Byb 10.14 ("you shall disclose")

Sg. 3. M.
III*y*

YQṢ- *yeqeṣṣe*	Pu	*CIS* i 3784.3 ("he shall cut off")

Pl. 3. C.
III*y*

YQṢN *yeqeṣṣūn*	Ph	14.22 ("they shall cut off")

YIP'IL
Sg. 2. M.
I*w*

TSR *tisīr*	Ph	Byb 10.13/14 ("you shall remove")

Sg. 3. M.
Strong

YŠḤT *yisḥit*	Ph	24.15,16 9 ("he will destroy")
I*y*		
YSP *yûsip*	Ph	Byb 10.10 ("he will continue")
I*n*		
YZQ *yizziq*	Ph	24.14 9 ("he shall damage")

Sg. 3. F.

TSRḤ *tisriḥ*	Ph	Byb 10.15 ("she shall make stink")

YITPE'EL
Pl. 3. M.
h-l-k

YTLKN *yittellikūn*	Ph	24.10 ("they used to go about")

YIPTA'AL
Sg. 3.M.

YḤTSP *yiḥtasap*	Ph	Byb 1.2 ("it will break")
YHTPK *yihtapak*	Ph	Byb 1.2 ("it will overturn")

Comments

The morphology of the verb is generally consistent with that of Classical Hebrew. The salient differences are as follows: (i) the second and third masculine plural regularly display the plural morpheme -*ūn*, as earlier observed; (ii) the prefixed morphemes of all Stems were *ʾi- ti* and *yi-*, with an i-vowel, as indicated by the Prefixing Form B Latin-letter spellings *Poen.* 933 **l-iphoc** (*l-ipoq*)and *Poen.* 949 **l-itor** (*l-itor*) of the first singular Qal forms of Verbs II*w* (contrast Hebrew *yaqom*, with a-vowel) and the first person singular Yip'il Prefixing Form C *Poen.* 939 **l-ythera** (*l-itīra)*; (iii) the thematic I-vowel of the Yip'il is short in both the Prefixing and Suffixing Form, as is clear from Prefixing Form C *Poen.* 1027A **ierasan** (*yer*^{ʿa}*sa-n*), with pretonic reduced and *a*-colored thematic vowel; (iv) the verb *h-l-k* in the Yitpe'el had the form *yittellek*, with assimilation of the initial root-letter to the inflectional prefix; this same phenomenon is seen in Phoenician in the case of Verbs I*y*, as indicated by the Yitpe'el Suffixing Form 119.4 ***ʾYTKDʾ*** *ittekkedū* ("they mutually resolved," root *y-k-d*).

B. *Syntax and Usage*

1. *Expressing the Present Imperfective*

13.4/5 ***ʾY ʾDLN KSP ʾY ʾDLN ḤRṢ,*** "I do not possess silver, I do not possess gold."

26 A II 5/6 ***ʾŠT T<L>K LḤDY DL PLKM,*** "<In places that were dangerous in the past, where one was afraid to walk the road, in my time> a woman walks alone without bodyguards."

26 A III 14/5 ***ʾM ʾP YḤMD ʾYT HQRT Z,*** "Even if he loves this city."

48.2/3 ***LʾLNM ʾŠʾL [TB]RK ʾYT ʾRBʿT BNY,*** "I ask of you gods: Bless ye my four sons!"

Pu 89.2 ***ʾTK ʾNKY MṢLḤ ʾYT ʾMʿŠTRT,*** "I, Meslih, commend (*lit.*, give) to you Amastarte." *Obs.* ***ʾTK*** (= ***ʾTNK***) corresponds to **commendo tibi** in related texts in Latin.

Pu *Poen.* 940P **Et alonim ualonut caruti is timlacun (*TM-***

***LKN*) alt imacum esse,** "I call you gods and goddesses who rule over this city." = NPu *Poen.* 940A **Yth alonim ualonuth carothi is thymlachun th-ymacum syth** = *Poen.* 930 **Deos deasque ueneror** (=**carothi**) **qui hanc urbem colunt** (=**thymlachun**). Observe the aspectual contrast in this statement between the present perfective **caruti** and the present imperfective **timlacun**.)

2. *Expressing the Past Imperfective*

24.9/10 ***LPN HMLKM HLPNYM YTLKN MŠKBM KM KLBM,*** "In the presence of earlier kings, the *mškbm* used to go about like dogs." *Obs.* The non-literal translation of this statement is: "The *mškbm* (members of the lower class) were treated like dogs by the kings who preceded me."

26 A II 3/6 ***BMQMM 'Š KN LPNM NŠT'M 'Š YŠT' 'DM LLKT DRK WBYMTY 'NK 'ŠT T<L>K LḤDY DL PLKM,*** "In places that were dangerous in the past, where one used to be afraid to walk the road, in my time a woman walks alone, without bodyguards."

3. *Expressing the Future*

3a. In an Independent Clause (Sentence)

14.21/22 ***'L YŠ' 'YT ḤLT MŠKBY LM YSGRNM 'LNM HQDŠM 'L,*** "Let them not carry off the coffin in which I lie; if they do, these holy gods shall imprison them."

14.22 ***WYQSN HMMLKT H',*** "And they (he holy gods) shall cut off that king."

24,13/14 ***MY BBNY 'Š YŠB TḤTN,*** "Whichever of my sons shall sit on the throne in my stead."

26 A III 12/13 ***'DM . . . 'Š YMḤ ŠM 'ZTWD BŠ'R Z . . . WYS' HŠ'R Z . . . WYP'L L Š'R Z,*** "A person who shall erase the name of Aztwadda from this gate and shall tear out this gate and shall make for it another gate."

26 A III 17/18 ***'M BḤMDT YS' 'M BR' YS' HŠ'R Z,*** "Whether he shall tear it out out of love or shall tear out this gate out of malice."

26 C III 17/18 ***'P'L SML ZR,*** "I shall make another statue."

60.6 ***YŠ'N BKSP 'LM B'L ṢDN DRKMNM 20,*** "They shall withdraw twenty drachmas from the silver of the god Baal of Sidon!"

Pu *Poen.* 1142 **Neste ien. Neste dum et. Al. Anec este mem!,** (*Statement*) "We shall drink wine. We shall drink the blood of the vine." (*Answer*) "No! I shall drink water!"

3b. In the Protasis (*if*-clause) of a Conditional Sentence

13.6/7 ***W'M PTḤ TPTḤ ʿLTY . . . 'L YKN LK ZRʿ,*** "But if you shall open it, you shall not have offspring."

14.6 ***'P 'M 'DMM YDBRNK 'L TŠMʿ BD
NM,*** "Even if people shall urge you <to violate my coffin>, do not listen to their words!"

3c. In the Future Result Clause (apodosis) of a Conditional Sentence

In this use, the apodosis is not marked off from the protasis by means of the conjunction *w*- before the prefixing verb.

Byb 10.13/15 ***W'M TSR M[L']KT Z' WTSG 'T PTḤY Z DL YSDH ʿLT MQM Z WTGL MSTRW TSRḤ HRBT BʿLT GBL 'YT H'DM H' WZRʿW,*** "If you remove that work or move this inscription of mine and its base from this spot or disclose its hiding place, the Lady Baalt of Byblos shall make stink that person and his offspring."

3d. In the Main Clause of a Sentence with Anticipatory Clause

This sentence type is similar to the conditional sentence described in C above; accordingly, the main resumptive clause is not marked off from the anticipatory clause by means of the conjunction *w*- before the suffixing verb.

24.15/16 ***WMY YŠḤT HSPR Z YŠḤT R'Š BʿL ṢMD . . . YŠḤT R'Š BʿLḤMN,*** "As for him who shall destroy this inscription, Baal-Semed shall strike his head, and Baalhammon shall strike his head."

Pu *CIS* i 3784.1/3 ***KL 'Š LGNB T-'BN Z BʿLḤMN YQṢY',*** "As for anyone who shall steal this tone, Baalhammon shall cut him off."

II. Prefixing Form B

A. *Morphology*

Forms

QAL

Sg. 1. C.

IIw

'PQ-N *ipoq-na*	Pu	50.3 ("I received")
l-iphoc (***L-'PQ***) *l-ipoq*	NPu	*Poen.* 933 ("I would acquire")

l-itor (***L-ʾTR***) *l-itor*	Pu	*Poen.* 949 ("let me inquire")
Sg. 2. M.		
Strong		
TPTḤ *tiptaḥ*	Ph	13.3/4,5.6 ("you open")
TŠMʿ *tismaʿ*	Ph	14.6 ("you hear")
I*n*		
TŠʾ *tissa(ʾ)*	Pu	*CIS* i 6001.1/2 ("you carry off")
Sg. 2. F.		
Strong		
TBRKY *tibrokī*	Ph	29.2 ("you bless!)
y-t-n		
TNTN *tintenī*	Ph	50.3/4 ("you gave")
Sg. 3. M.		
Strong		
YBRK- *yibrok*	Ph	38.2, 39.3, 40.5 ("may he bless!")
YPTḤ *yiptaḥ*	Ph	14.20 ("that he open")
II*w*		
YKN *yakūn*	Ph	14.8,13 ("it be")
III*y*		
YʿL *yaʿl(e)*	Ph	30.2 ("he came up")
Sg. 3. F.		
Strong		
TBRK *tibrok*	Ph	Byb 10.8 ("may she bless!")
y-t-n		
TTN *titten*	Ph	Byb 10.9 ("may she give")
Pl. 2. M.		
Strong		
TBRK *tibrokū*	Ph	48.3 ("may you bless!")
y-t-n		
TTN *tittenū*	Ph	48.4 ("may you give!")
Pl. 3. M.		
Strong		
YʾDR *yeʾdarū*	Ph	26 A III 10 ("may they be strong!")
YʿBD *yaʿbodū*	Ph	26 A III 10 ("may they serve")

YPʿL- *yipʿalū*	Ph	50.3 ("may they make")
Iy and *h-l-k*		
YDʿ *yedaʿū*	Ph	60.7 ("they know")
YLD *yeledū*	Ph	26 A III 9 ("may they bear")
YLK *yelekū*	Pu	*CIS* i 5510.9 ("they proceeded")
II*w*		
YBʾ *yabōʾū*	Ph	30.1 ("they came")
NIP'AL		
Pl. 3. M.		
Strong		
YQBR *yiqqaberū*	Ph	14.8 ("that they be buried")
PI'EL		
Sg. 2. M.		
TRGZ *tereggez*	Ph	13.14 ("you disturb")
Sg. 3. M		
YBQŠ *yebeqqes*	Ph	14.5 ("that he seek")
III*y*		
YʿR *yeʿar(re)*	Ph	14.21 ("that he empty out")
YIP'IL		
Strong Verb		
Sg. 1. C.		
II*wy*		
l-ythera (***L-ʾTR***) *l-itīra*	NPu	*Poen.* 939 ("let me inquire")
Sg. 3. M.		
YʾBD *yiʾbid*	Ph	30.3 ("he devastated")
YOP'AL		
Sg. 2. M.		
TŠMʿ *tosmaʿ*	Ph	14.6 ("you be persuaded")

Comments

Prefixing Form B is morphologically distinguishable from Prefixing Form A in the forms of the second feminine singular, second masculine plural and third masculine plural. See comments above to Prefixing Form A.

B. *Syntax and Usage*

1. *Expressing the Past Perfective*

Classical literary Phoenician possessed three forms of the verb capable of expressing past perfective action: (i) Prefixing Form B; (ii) the Infinitive Absolute and (iii) the Suffixing Form. For the sake of convenience, I shall here refer to these forms as (i) Past Perfective I (Prefixing Form B), (ii) Past Perfective II (Infinitive Absolute) and (iii) Past Perfective III (Suffixing Form) respectively.

Past Perfective I, the form used to express past perfective action in classical literary Hebrew and Moabite, is found in Phoenician in three extant inscriptions: (i) an archaic ninth-century B.C.E. text from Cyprus (*KAI* 30) recounting the Phoenician invasion of that island; (ii) in a sixth-century B.C.E. letter from Dapnae (***TḤPNḤS***) in Egypt (*KAI* 50); and (iii) in a Carthaginian Punic historical account (*CIS* i 5510.9/11), written in the year 406 B.C., of the taking of the city of Agrigentum in Sicily in the winter of 406 B.C.E. Past Perfective I, like its Hebrew counterpart, was syntactically restricted to sentence-initial position although it was used within the same sentence in sequence with a preceding Past Perfective I. Past Perfective I was complemented by Past Perfective III, which was syntactically restricted to non sentence-initial position.

Illustrated in the following subparagraphs is the complementary use in Phoenician of sentence-initial Past Perfective I and non sentence-initial Past Perfective III within the same literary composition.

1a. Old Cyprus Inscription (*KAI* 30), 9th Century B.C.E.

1a-1. Sentence-Initial Past Perfective I (Prefixing Form B)

30.1/2 ***YB' 'Y MPT WH'Š 'Š [NGD]M L QBR Z',*** "They came to the island (Cyprus), and the man who was their [leader], his is this tomb."

30.2/3 ***Y'L IIGBR Z' '[L]ŠY WY'BD H[. . .] Z' 'YT H'Y,*** "This warrior came up to Alasia [Cyprus], and this [. . .] devastated the island."

1a-2. Non Sentence-Initial Past Perfective III (Suffixing Form)
30.4 (2x) ***BN YD B'L BN YD 'DM,*** "From it (Cyprus) he drove *(yado)* out its king, from it he drove *(yado)* out its people."

1b. Daphnae Letter (*KAI* 50), Egypt, 6th Century B.C.E.

1b-1. Sentence-Initial Past Perfective I (Suffixing Form B)
50.3/4 ***'PQ-N HKSP 'Š ŠLḤT LY WTNTN LY,*** "I got the silver that you sent me and have given (lent) to me."

1b-2. Non Sentence-Initial Past Perfective III (Suffixing Form)
50.3 ***HKSP 'Š ŠLḤT LY,*** "The silver that you sent me."

1c. Carthage Inscription (*CIS* i 5510), 406 B.C.E.

Pu *CIS* i 5510.9/11 ***WYLK RBM 'DNB'L BN GRSKN HRB WḤMLKT BN ḤN' HRB 'LŠ WTMK HMT 'YT 'GRGNT WŠT [H]MT ŠLM,*** "Generals Idnibal son of Gisco the Great and Himilco son of Hanno the Great marched at dawn, and they seized Agrigentum; and they (the Agrigentines) made peace (surrendered)." *Obs.* The forms ***TMK*** and ***ŠT*** are both Suffixing Form Consecutive, not Past Perfect III; they receive their past perfective tense-reference from the main verb of the sentence, Past Perfective I *yelekū*.

This is the sole extant specimen of Phoenician historical (historiographic) prose. It is from the closing part of a longer account of the siege of Agrigentum, corresponding roughly to the source used by Diodorus Siculus (xiii, 90.1) in his description of the capture of Agrigentum by the Carthaginians after its abandonment by the Greeks: Ο δ Ιμιλκας αμα τω φωτι την δυναμιν εντος των τειχων παρεισαγαγων σχεδον απαντας τους εγκαταλειφθεντας ανειλεν, "Imilkas (=Himilco), leading his army at dawn within the walls, put to death almost all who had been left behind inside <the city>."

2. *Expressing the Subjunctive*

Prefixing Form B is found once in a clause of purpose after ***LMḤT LKN*** ("in order that"). The more common expression of the subjunctive in Phoenician is by means of the Infinitive Construct.

60.6/8 ***YŠ'N BKSP 'LM B'L ṢDN DRKMNM 20 LMḤT LKN YD' HṢDNYM K YD' HGW LŠLM ḤLPT 'YT 'DMM 'Š P'L MŠRT 'T PN GW,*** "They shall withdraw 20 drachmas from the silver of the god Baal of Sidon in order that the Sidonians might know that the community knows to recompense persons who have performed community service."

3. *Expressing the Jussive, Optative and Cohortative*

3a. Word-Order: Subject – Verb

Byb 12.4 ***B'L YBRK WYḤWW,*** "Baal bless him and grant him long life!"

18.7/8 ***B'LŠMM L'LM YBRKN,*** "Baalsamem bless me always!"

26 A III 7/8 ***W'M Z 'Š YŠB BN YKN B'L 'LPM,*** "And may this people who dwell in it (the city) become owners of cattle!"

43.15 ***PQT WN'M YKN LY,*** "Good fortune and prosperity be mine!"

52.1/2 ***ḤRPKRṬ YTN ḤYM L'BDY L'BD'ŠMN,*** "Harpocrates grant long life to his servant Abdesmun!"

R.D. Barnett, *BMQ* 27 (1963/4) 85 ***ḤRPKRṬ YTN ḤYM L'MS BN 'ŠMNYTN,*** "Harpocrates grant long life to Amos bin Esmunyaton!"

Pu *Poen.* 1027P **Bal samem ierasan,** "Baal shake the heavens!" = NPu 1027A **Bal samem iyryla.**

3b. Word-Order: Verb – Subject

Byb 10.8 ***TBRK B'LT GBL 'YT YḤWMLK,*** "Baalt of Byblos bless Yehawmilk!"

Byb 10.9/10 ***WTTN LY HRBT B'LT GBL ḤN,*** "The Lady Baalt of Byblos grant me favor!"

43.15/16 ***WYSKRN MLQRT [WYTN LY] N'M ŠRŠ,*** "Milqart remember me and grant me good stock!"

3c. Prefixing Form B (Jussive/Optative) with the Proclitic Particle ***L-***

NPu EH 32.3 ***L-YŠM' QL',*** "May he hear (*lisma'*) his voice!"

NPu EH 216.3 ***LŠM' QL',*** "May he hear his voice!"

NPu NP 15.3 ***LŠ'M['] 'T QL[M],*** "May he hear his voice!"

The historical spelling, with the initial *yod* of the Suffixing Form indicated, is ***LYŠM'***. The spelling ***LŠM'*** is "phonetic," indicating the actual pronunciation with elision of intervocalic *yod*. ***LŠ'M[']*** is merely a spelling error for ***LŠM'[']***.

The proclitic particle is also used with Prefixing Form B expressing the Cohortative. See below. *Obs.* In Phoenician, the jussive and optative are also commonly expressed in Phoenician by means of clause-initial Suffixing Form and Infinitive Construct.

4. *Cohortative*

In the first person, Suffixing Form B may express the cohortative, a wish or strong future declarative assertion. The verb may receive the proclitic particle *l-*, which is also used with Form B expressing the Jussive/Optative.

Pu *Poen.* 949 **Anec l-itor (*L'TR)* bod es iussim limin co**, "Let me inquire of these men who are coming out from here." *Obs.* In the Neo-Punic version of this same line, the verb is expressed by Prefixing Form C: NPu *Poen.* 939 **Bod i(ly) a(nech) l-ythera ymu ys lomyn choth iusim.**

NPu *Poen.* 942 **L-iphoc (*L'PQ)* anech yth byn ui iaed,** "I would get my brother's only son."

5. *Expressing the Imperative*

In the second person, Suffixing Form B may be used to express the imperative.

29.2 ***TBRKY BYMY 'DNN,*** "Bless thou (*tibrokīyo*) our master during his lifetime!"

48.3/4 ***[TB]RK 'Y[T 'RB'T B]NY . . . [WT]TN LM ḤN WḤYM,*** "Bless ye (*tibrokū*) my four sons, and grant (*tittenū*) them favor and long life!"

Pu 77.3/4 ***TŠM' QLM,*** "Hear thou (*tisma'*) their voice!"

Pu *CIS* i 3604 ***TŠM'' 'YT QLM,*** "Hear ye (*tisma'ū*) his voice!"

6. *Following the Negative Particle* **'L** *'al*

6a. Prohibition (Negative Jussive/Optative)

14.20 ***'L YPTḤ 'LTY,*** "Let him not open it!"

14.21 ***'L Y'R 'LTY,*** "Let him not empty it out!"

14.21 ***'L Y'MSN BMŠKB Z,*** "Let him not remove me from this resting-place!"

6b. Vetitive (Negative Imperative)

13.3/4 ***'L TPTḤ 'LTY,*** "Do not open it!"

14.6 ***'L TŠM' BDNM,*** "Do not permit yourself to be persuaded by them!"

Pu Rep. 16.2 ***'L TŠ' <'>T',*** "Do not carry it (this urn) off!"

6c. Expressing Negative Future Result

6c-1. In the Resumptive Clause of a Sentence with Anticipatory Clause

In the main (resumptive) result clause of a sentence with anticipatory clause, Prefixing Form B introduced by the particle *ʾal* expresses the negative Future. This type of clause is closely related to the result clause (apodosis) of a conditional sentence (see below). *Obs.* This use of Prefixing Form B is found in Classical Arabic in the result clause of the conditional sentence.

14.6/8 ***WKL 'DM 'Š YPTḤ 'LT MŠKB Z . . . 'L YKN LM MŠKB 'T RP'M W'L YQBR BQBR W'L YKN LM BN WZR',*** "As for anyone who shall open this resting-place, they shall not have rest with the infernal deities, they shall not be buried in a tomb, and they shall not have son(s) nor offspring."

14.11/12 ***'M 'DMM HMT 'L YKN LM ŠRŠ LMṬ WPR LM'L,*** "As for those persons <who shall open my coffin and remove me from it and carry off my coffin>, they shall not have root below nor fruit above!"

6c-2. In the Result Clause (Apodosis) of a Conditional Sentence

13.6/7 ***W'M PTḤ TPTḤ 'LTY WRGZ TRGZN 'L YKN LK ZR' BḤYM,*** "But if you shall open it (my coffin) and disturb me, you shall not have offspring among the living!"

24.14/15 ***WYZQ BSPR Z MŠKBM 'L YKBD LB'RRM WB'R-RM 'L YKBD LMŠKBM,*** "If he shall damage this inscription, the *mškbm* shall no longer show respect to the *bʿrrm*, and the *bʿrrm* shall no longer show respect to the *mškbm*."

III. Prefixing Form C

A. *Morphology*

Prefixing Form C *yiqtola(n)* is the reflex of Canaanite *yaqtula* and its extended form *yaqtulana,* with the post verbal particle *-na*. Prefixing Form C is indistinguishable from Prefixing Form B in texts in Phoenician letters; its existence in the language is certain however from examples in Latin-letter Punic and Neo-Punic. Like Prefixing Form B, it is used to express the cohortative and the jussive/optative and like Prefixing Form B, it may also receive the proclitic verbal particle *l-*.

Forms

YIP'IL

Sg. 1

l-ythera *itīra*	NPu	*Poen.* 939 ("let me inquire")

Sg. 3.M.

ierasa *yerʿ^a^san*	Pu	*Poen.* 1027A ("may he make tremble")
iyryla *yirʿila*	NPu	*Poen.* 1027P ("may he make tremble")

Comments

The Punic and corresponding Neo-Punic forms in *Poen.* 1027 indicate that the particle *-n* (Old Canaanite *-na*) was separable and its use optional. The particle was also used in Phoenician with Prefixing Form A (Present Indicative) 13.4 (bis) ***'DL-N*** *'edle-n* ("I possess") and with Prefixing Form B (Past Perfective) 50.3 ***'PQ-N*** *'apoq(a)-n* ("I received"). In *Poen.* 1017A **ierasan** *yerʿ^a^sa-n*, the thematic vowel *a* is an *a*-colored *shewa*, indicating that in Phoenician the thematic *i*-vowel of the causative stem was short, as in Arabic and Aramaic, and thus susceptible to reduction.

B. *Syntax and Usage*

1. *Cohortative*

NPu *Poen.* 939 **Bod i(ly) a(nech) lythera ymu ys lomyn choth iusim,** "Let me inquire of these men who are coming out from here." *Obs.* In the Punic version of this same line in *Poen.* 949, the cohortative is expressed by Prefixing Form B*:* **Anec litor bod es iussim limin co.** The Latin translation of *Poen.* 939 renders the verb as Future Indicative: *Poen.* 960. **Hos percontabor qui hinc egrediuntur foras,** "I shall ask these men who are coming out from here."

2. *Jussive and Optative*

Pu *Poen.* 1027A **Bal samem ieresa-n,** "Baal shake the heavens!"
NPu *Poen.* 1027P **Bal samem iyryla,** "Baal shake the heavens!"

Like Prefixing Form B Jussive/Optative, Form C was not syntactically restricted. The two extant examples cited here follow their subject, with the direct object of the verb intervening: Subject-Direct Object-Verb.

CHAPTER ELEVEN

THE VERB: THE IMPERATIVE, THE PARTICIPLES AND INFINITIVES

I. The Imperative

A. *Morphology*

Inflection

Sg. M.			
Grade I	**-Ø**	Pu	*Poen.* 1013 **lec** *lek* ("go!"); D 6 **un** ("spare; show mercy!")
Grade II	*-a*	Pu	*Poen.* 1010 **pursa** *pursa* ("explain!")
Grade III	*-anna*	Pu	*Poen.* 1013 **lacanna** *l^{a}kanna* ("go away!")
Sg. F.			
	-ī	Ph	50.5 ***BṬḤ*** *biṭḥī* ("trust!")

Comments

The inflection of the masculine singular imperative is well documented in forms occurring in Latin-letter Punic and Neo-Punic sources. There were, as in Classical Hebrew, three grades of the imperative with regard to inflection: (i) Grade I, the simple form, represented by **lec** *lek* (***LK*** "go!") and **un** *(ḥ)un* (***ḤN*** "spare; show mercy!"), displayed *zero*-inflection; (ii) Grade II, represented by **pursa** *pursa* (***PRŠ*** "explain!"), displayed the extending morpheme *-a*; (iii) Grade III, represented by **lacanna** *lakanna* (***LK-N'*** "go away!"), the Grade II imperative *l^{a}ka* (*lek* + *-a*; Hebrew *l^{e}ka*) followed by the enclitic particle *-na* (***-N'***), with gemination of the initial *nun*; *cf.* Hebrew Genesis 32:30 ***HGYDH-N'*** *haggīdanna* ("tell!"); also Hebrew Ruth 2:2 ***'LKH-N'*** *'el^{e}kanna* ("let me go"); Genesis 18:21 ***'RDH-N'*** *'er^{e}danna* ("let me descend").

We possess no evidence for the pronunciation of the feminine singular and the masculine and feminine plural imperatives, but it is reasonable to assume they were identical to their Hebrew counterparts.

Forms

QAL

Sg. M.		
Strong Verbs		
'MR *ʾ^{o}mor*	Ph	50.2 ("say!")
NṢR *n^{o}ṣor*	Pu	*RES* 19.1, 20.1 ("protect!")
pursa *pursa*	Pu	*Poen.* 1010 ("explain!")
ŠMR *s^{o}mor*	Pu	*RES* 19.1, 20.1 ("guard!")
III*y*		
KRY *k^{e}re*	NPu	Trip. 86.3 (bis) ("buy!")
MN' *m^{e}ne*	NPu	Trip. 86.5 ("weigh out!")
h-l-k		
lec *lek*	Pu	*Poen.*1013 ("go!")
lacanna *l^{a}kanna*	Pu	*Poen.* 1013 ("go away!")
II*wy*		
ḤŠ *(ḥ)ūs*	NPu	Trip. 79.5 ("be considerate!")
KN *kūn*	NPu	Trip. 86.1, 8 ("be!")
Q'M *qūm*	Pu	Trip. 86.3/4 ("remain!")
Š'M *sīm*	NPu	Trip. 86.2 ("place!")
y-t-n		
TN *ten*	NPu	162.4/5 ("give!")
IIIgem.		
un (***ḤN***) *(ḥ)un*	NPu	D 6.11 ("spare; show mercy!")
Sg. F.		
Strong		
BṬḤ *biṭḥī*	Ph	50.5 ("trust!")

PI'EL

Sg. M.		
messe (***MŠḤ***) *messe(ḥ)*	NPu	Aug. on the Gospel of John 15:27 ("anoint!")

YIP'IL

I*n*		
HKR *akker* or *ikker*	NPu	Trip. 86.4 ("remember!")

B. *Syntax and Usage*

The subject of an imperative is frequently expressed by the independent personal pronoun; the pronoun may precede or follow the imperative. The use of the pronoun is optional.

50.5 ***ʾT BṬḤ BDBR[Y],*** "You trust in my word(s)!"

NPu Trip. 86.3/4 ***BʿT ʾTʾ ŠʿM ʾT QʾM BBʿT ʾT HKR S WʾT KRY KRY ʾT HŠD ŠBNʿ ḤNʾ,*** "Make a contract with him! You keep to the contract! You heed this! And you buy, buy the field belonging to the sons of Hanno."

NPu D 6.11 **Un ath ab[dach]a,** "Spare thou (show mercy to) thy servant!"

Obs. The imperative is also expressed by Prefixing Verb B, the Suffixing Verb and the Infinitive Construct.

II. The Active Participle

A. *Morphology*

Forms

QAL

Sg. M		
Strong		
duber *dūber*	Pu	*Poen.* 944, 948 ("says")
dubyr *dūbir*	NPu	*Poen.* 936 ("says")
urys *(ḥ)ūris*	NPu	*PBSR* 28 p. 53 no. 5.10 ("engraver")
KHN *kūhen*	Ph Pu NPu	13.2, *et passim* ("Priest")
MŠL *mūsel*	Ph	14.9 ("ruler")
ŠMR *sūmer*	Pu	62.7 ("watchman")
ŠPṬ *sūpeṭ*	Ph Pu NPu	78.8, *et passim* ("suf(f)es")
III *ʾaleph*		
RPʾ *rūpeʾ*	Pu	*CIS* I 4884.6; *CIS* I 4885.5 ("healer; physician")
III*y*		
BN *būne*	Ph	46.6 ("builder")
buny *būni*	NPu	*IRT* 906.4 ("builder")
IIIgem.		
GRR *gūrer*	Pu	*CIS* i 4873.3 ("sawyer")

Sg. F.			
Strong			
ʿṬPT	*ʿūṭept*	Pu	*RES* 891.1 ("covers")
ŠKBT	*sūkebt*	Byb	11 ("lies; rests")
III*w/y*			
KST	*kūsīt*	Pu	*RES* 891.1 ("covers; conceals")
Pl. M.			
Strong			
dobrim	*dōbrīm*	Pu	*Poen.* 935 ("they say")
MŠLM	*mōslīm*	NPu	120.1 ("rulers; tribunes")
PʿLM	*pōʿlīm*	Ph	37 A 13 ("they work")
SPRM	*sōprīm*	Ph	37 A 15 ("scribes")
III *ʾaleph*			
YṢʾM	*yōṣʾīm*	Ph	*CIS* i 99.2 ("they came forth")
iussim	*yūṣīm*	Pu	*Poen.* 949 ("they are coming out")
iusim	*yūṣīm*	NPu	*Poen.* 939 ("they are coming out")
III*y*			
BNM	*būnīm*	Ph	37 A 5 ("builders")
bunem	*būnīm*	NPu	*S* 24.3 ("builders")
IIIgem.			
GRM	*gōrrīm*	Ph	37 A 16, B 10 ("sawyers")

PI'EL

Sg. M.			
Strong			
MʾRḤ	*m^{e}ʾerreḥ*	Pu	66.1 ("host")
merre	*m^{e}ʾerreḥ*	Pu	66.1 ("host")
μηρρη	*m^{e}ʾerreḥ*	Pu	66.1 ("host")
Pl. M.			
MḤŠBM	*m^{e}ḥessebīm*	Pu	

YIP'IL

Strong			
MYŠQL	*misqil*	NPu	121.1; 126.5 ("beautifier")
migdil	*migdil*	Pu	*Poen.* 1033 ("magnifier")
		Pu	II*w/y*
MQM	*meqīm*	Ph	44.2 ("awakener")

	Pu	90.3 ("awakener")
MYQM *meqīm*	NPu	163.4/5 ("awakener")
MYQṢ *meqīṣ*	Pu	77.1 ("awakener")
IIIgem.		
MḤB *meḥib(b)*	NPu	121.1; 126.4 ("lover")
MḤQ *meḥiq(q)*	Ph	*CIS* i 51 ("?")

Comments

The morphology of the active participle is the same as that of the Hebrew, with one exception: the *e/I*-vowel of the Qal singular *CūCéC* is reduced to *zero* in the plural form *CōCCīm*, as indicated by the Latin-letter spelling of the masculine plural *Poen.* 935 **dobrim** *dōbrīm* (sg. **duber, dubyr**) and confirmed by the Punic-letter spelling of the masculine plural 37 A 16 ***GRM*** *gōrrīm* ("sawyers," sg. ***GRR*** *gūrer*).

B. *Syntax and Usage*

1. *Surrogate for Any Tense*

1a. Expressing the Present Perfective

13.1 ***ʾNK TBNT KHN ʿŠTRT MLK ṢDNM . . . ŠKB BʾRN Z*** "I, Tibnit, Priest of Astarte, King of the Sidonians, lie (rest) in this coffin."

Pu *Eph.* 3.55.1 ***[H . . .]T ʾŠ KST WʿṬPT [H . . .],*** "The [. . .] that covers and conceals (*or* that is covering and concealing) the [. . .]."

Pu *Poen.* 944/946A **Us duber ce fel dono . . . et cil comu con liful alt banim au**, "One says that his father did everything for that son of his as he was to do <for him>."

NPu *Poen.* 935/936 =944/946 **Dobrim chy fel yth chil ys chon ythem liful yth binim,** "They say that he did everything for his son that he was to do for him."

Pu *Poen.* 946A **Us duber ci hen hu ac Aristoclem,** "One says that Aristocles lives (*lit.*, is) here."

1b. Expressing the Future

Pu *CIS* I 3783.5/7 ***WKL ʾDM ʾŠ GNB T-MTNT Z NKST TNT-[P]NBʿL,*** "As for any person who shall steal this stele, Thinnith-Phanebal shall cut him off."

Pu *CIS* i 169.2 ***[HŠ]ʾR WHŠLBM WHPʿMM ʾŠ BL ʿLM ʿLT***

HMZBḤ, "To the sacrificer belongs the meat and the shanks and the legs <of a sacrificial animal> that shall not go up <in flame> upon the altar."

Pu *CIS* i 5632.7/10 ***KL 'DM 'Š N[S' 'Y]T HNṢB Z W'[Š . . . W]ŠPṬ B'LḤMN B[RḤ ']DM H',*** "As for any person who shall tear out this stele or who [shall . . . it], Baalhammon shall condemn that person."

2. *Participial*

The active participle expresses a concomitant action in progress within the time-frame of the main verb.

2a. Present Tense

Pu *Poen.* 949A **Anec litor bod es iussim limin co,** "Let me inquire of these men who are coming out from here."

2b. Future Tense

14.9 ***WYSGRNM H'LNM HQDŠM 'T MMLKT 'DR 'Š MŠL BNM,*** "And the holy gods shall imprison them, together with whichever mighty king is ruling them <at the time>."

Pu *CIS* i 5510.4/5 ***[WKL ']DM 'Š 'YBL MŠRT WKPT RBTN TNT-PNB'L W'DN B['L]ḤMN 'YT 'DMM HMT BḤYM 'L PN ŠMŠ,*** "As for any person who shall not serve, Our Lady Thinnith-Phanebal and the Lord Baalhammon shall bind those persons among those living under the sun."

2c. Past Tense

CIS i 99.2 ***NṢḤT 'T 'BY HYṢ'M W'ZRNM,*** "I defeated my enemies who came forth <to fight me> and their allies."

3. *Nominal*

The active participle is the form of many nouns: ***BN*** *būne* ("architect, builder"); **hulec** *hūlek* ("guest-friend"); ***MḤŠB*** *meḥesseb* ("treasurer"); ***RP'*** *rūfe(')* ("physician," *lit.,* "one who cures").

III. The Passive Participle

A. *Morphology*

Forms

Sg. F.		
ṬN(')T *ṭanū(ʾ)t*	Pu	*CIS* i 5510.7 ("was erected")
ṬN'T *ṭanūʾt*	NPu	153.1 ("was erected")
PSLT *pasūlt*	Pu	78.4 ("sculpted")
Pl. M.		
sebuim *z*^{e}*bū(ḥ)īm*	NPu	*IRT* 893.5 ("sacrificed")
ṬN'M *ṭ*^{e}*nūʾīm*	Pu	101.5 ("were placed")
NŠ'M *n*^{e}*sūʾīm*	Ph	60.4 ("were elected")
ŠKNM *s*^{e}*kūnīm*	Ph	37 A 7 ("were placed")

Comments

The morphology of the passive participle is the same as the Hebrew, with one possible exception: the feminine singular afformative was *-t*, not *-ot* < *-at*, as is evident from the Punic defective spelling *CIS* I 5510.7 *ṬNT*, which can only be understood as *ṭanūt* < *ṭanuʾt* ("was erected").

B. *Syntax and Usage*

1. *Surrogate for Finite Passive Past Perfective*

37 A 7 ***ŠRM B'R 'Š ŠKNM LMLKT QDŠT,*** "Those residing in the city who were employed for the Sacred Liturgy."

37 A 13 ***GLBM P'LM 'L ML'KT,*** "The barbers <who were> employed in the Liturgy."

60.4/5 ***H'DMM 'Š NŠ'M LN 'L BT 'LM,*** "The persons who were elected by us in charge of the temple."

Pu *CIS* i 5510.7/8 ***WṬN<'>T 'MTNT Z BḤDŠ P'LT,*** "This stele was erected on the new moon of <the month of> Paaloth."

Pu 101.5 ***ṬN'M 'L HMLKT Z 'ŠYN . . . W'RŠ,*** "Asyan and Aris were put in charge of this work project."

NPu 153.1 ***'BN Z ṬN'T LB'LḤN',*** "This stele was erected to Balanno."

2. *Adjectival-Nominal*

Pu 78.4/5 ***MNṢBT PSLT . . . ʾBN ʾRKT BKRŠ BʿLḤMN,*** "A sculpted stele, being a tall stone bearing the figure of Baalhammon."

NPu *IRT* 893.4/5 **ilim sebuim,** "The sacrificed gods (*i.e.,* deified sacrificed children)."

IV. The Infinitive Construct

A. *Morphology*

Forms

QAL

Strong Verb		
L-ʾMR *li(ʾ)mūr*	Ph	14.2 ("to say")
li-mur *li(ʾ)mūr*	Pu	*Poen.* 948 ("to say")
L-ZBḤ *lizbūḥ*	Pu	69.14 ("to sacrifice")
L-GNB *lignūb*	Pu	*CIS* i 3784.1 ("to steal")
L-KTB *liktūb*	Ph	60.4 ("to inscribe")
L-MLK-Y *limolk-i*	Ph	14.1 ("of his reign")
L-MLK-NM *limolk^e-nom*	Pu	112.5 ("of their reign")
B-MṢʾ-NM *bimoṣʾ^e-nom*	Ph	Kition line 1 ("when they came")
Lʾ-ʿZR *laʿzūr*	NPu	147.4 ("may he help")
L-PʿL *lipʿūl*	Byb	10.11; NPu 124.4 ("to do")
li-ful *lifʿūl*	Pu	*Poen.* 945 ("to do")
li-ful *lifūl*	NPu	*Poen.* 935 ("to do")
L-PTḤ *liptūḥ*	Pu	70.3 ("to open")
B-ŠPT-M *bisofṭ-im*	NPu	159.5/6 ("when he was suffes")
II *wy*		
L-KN-Y *likūn-i*	Ph	18.6; 26 A II 14 ("that it be")
L-KN-NM *likūn^e-nom*	Ph	19.10 ("that they be")
II gem.		
L-KP *lakop(p)*	Pu	*CIS* i 5510.3 ("to overturn")
III*y*		
L-BNT *libnūt*	Ph	26 A II 11 ("to build")
L-BNT-M *libnūt-im*	NPu	*CIS* I 151.6 ("to erect it")
L-MḤT *limḥūt*	Ph	26 C IV 15 ("to erase")
I*y* and *h-l-k, n-š-ʾ, y-t-n*		
L-DʿT *ladaʿat*	Byb	2.1 ("know!")
L-LKT *lalek(e)t*	Ph	26 A II 4 ("to walk")

by-rysth-*birist-*	NPu	D 6.3/4 ("when he expelled")
L-Š'T *lase(')t*	NPu	145.4 ("exalt!")
L-ŠBT-NM *lisibt*^{e}*-nom*	Ph	26 A I 17 ("that they dwell")
sibt-i *sibt-i*	Pu	*Poen.* 948 ("his residing")
sibith-im *sibit-im*	NPu	*Poen.* 938 ("his residing")
L-TT-Y *lititt-i*	Ph	26 A III 4 ("may he give!")
L'-TT *latet(t)*	NPu	147.3 ("may he give!")

PI'EL

Strong Verbs		
L-'ṬR *li'eṭṭer*	Ph	60.1 ("to crown")
L-'KR *li'ekker*	Pu	*CIS* i 5510.3 ("to disturb")
L-QN' *liqenne(')*	Pu	*CIS* i 5510.7 ("shall be zealous")
L-ŠLM *lisellem*	Pu	*CIS* i 5510.6 ("to pay back")
L-ŠBT-Y *lisebbet-i*	Pu	*CIS* i 5510.3 ("to remove/destroy it")
II*y*		
L-KNT *likennūt*	Ph	60.5 ("to name/appoint")
L-QṢT-NM *liqeṣṣūt*^{e}*-nom*	Ph	14.9/10 ("they shall cut off")

YIP'IL

II*wy*		
L-YRḤ-Y *li-yarīḥ-i*	Pu	*CIS* i 5510.6 ("to make him welcome")
L-SR *l-asīr*	Pu	*CIS* i 3785.7, 4937.3 ("to remove")

Comments

The forms of the Infintive Construct are essentially identical to those of Classical Hebrew. But note that the Yip'il infinitive ***LSR*** is not a contraction of ***L-YSR*** but of ***L-'SR,*** the Punic ***'YQTL*** *iqtel.* The Infinite Construct construed with the preposition ***B***- or ***L***-, being a verbal noun in the genitive case, always takes the B-Forms of the suffixal pronouns as its subject or direct object.

B. *Syntax and Usage*

1. *The Infinitive Construct as Direct Object of Certain Verbs*

1a. ***ʾ-M-R*** + Infinitive: "think to do something"

26 C IV 17/18 ***YʾM[R] LMḤT ŠM ʾZTWD BSML ʾ[L]M Z,*** "If he shall think to erase the name of Aztwadda from this divine image."

1b. ***B-Ṣ-Ṣ*** + Infinitive: "undertake to do something"

NPu *CIS* i 151.6 ***KMT BʿṢṢ LBNTM LM,*** "So did he undertake to erect it (the statue) to them."

1c. ***Y-D-ʿ*** + Infinitive: "know to do something"

60.7/8 ***YDʿ HGW LŠLM ḤLPT ʾYT ʾDMM ʾŠ PʿL MŠRT ʾT PN GW,*** "The community knows to compensate those persons who have performed service on behalf of the community."

1d. ***Y-S-P*** + Infinitive: "continue to do something"

Byb 10.11/12 ***KL ʾDM ʾŠ YSP LPʿL MLʾKT ʿLT MZBḤ ZN,*** "Any person who shall continue to do work on this altar."
Pu 5510.6/7 ***YSP ʿLTY LŠLM WLYRḤY BMQM [Z],*** "They shall continue to greet him and make him welcome in this city."

1e. ***Y-K-D*** (Yitpe'el) + Infinitive: "mutually resolve to do something"

NPu 119.4/5 ***ʾYTKDʾ ʾDRʿ ʾLPQY WKL ʿM ʾ[L]P[QY LŠLM] LʾDN Hʾ LʾDRBʿL,*** "The senate of Lepcis and the entire nation of Lepcis resolved mutually to compensate that gentleman, Adherbal, <for his benefactions>."

1f. ***Y-T-N*** + Infinitive: "grant the right to do something"

NPu 126.7/9 ***LPNY ʾDRʾ ʾLPQY WʿM ʾLPQ[Y] LPY MʾSʾ ʾBTY WMʾSM BTM YTNʾ LʿBD BṢPʾT KL ḤʿT,*** "The senate of Lepcis and the people of Lepcis granted him the right to make use of the senatorial broad purple stripe always."

1g. ***K-W-N*** + Infinitive: "be obliged to do something"

Pu *Poen.* 944-46 **Alem us duber ce fel dono Mittun et cil comu con liful alt banim au,** "I am told that his father Mittun did everything for that son of his, as he was to do <for him>."

NPu 163.1/2 ***ṬŠ K' KNTM LTT L'Y'B'L 'BMṢRT 'LM,*** "Be ye . . . , for ye were to place L'Y'B'L under the protection of the gods."

1h. ***K-'-S*** + Infinitive: "undertake to do something"

NPu 124.2/4 ***B'LYTN QMD' . . . K'S LP'L WḤTM,*** "Balitho Commodus undertook to build it and completed it."

1i. ***P-R-Ṭ*** + Infinitive: "undertake to do something"

NPu 172.1/3 ***[Ḥ]MLKT BN 'DNB'L BN ḤMLKT HPRṬ 'L MYṬB' RŠ' HSLKY LBN'T T-HMQDŠ ST,*** "Himilco son of Idnibal son of Himilco, upon the approval of the senate of Sulcis, undertook to build this sanctuary."

1j. ***Q-W-M*** + Infinitive: "persist in doing something"

Byb 9 A 2 ***'L TQM LŠT 'RN 'LT 'RN,*** "Do not persist in placing one coffin on top of another coffin."

1l. ***Š-T-'*** + Infinitive: "to fear to do something"

26 A II 4/5 ***YŠT' 'DM LLKT DRK,*** "A person used to be afraid to travel the road."

1m. ***T-M-M*** + Infinitive: "be deemed good to do something"

60.1/3 ***BYM 4 LMRZḤ . . . TM BD ṢDNYM BN'SPT L'ṬR 'YT ŠM'B'L . . . 'ṬRT ḤRṢ BDRK<M>NM 20,*** "On this fourth day of Marzih, it has been deemed good by the Sidonians in assembly to crown Samobaal with a gold crown worth twenty drachmas."

2. *Forming Periphrastic Tenses and Moods*

2a. Future Indicative

The grammatical subject of the infinitive is expressed by the suffixal pronouns of the B-type. The logical subject of the sentence, if a substantive, stands in apposition to the suffix pronoun. The "proleptic" suffix pronoun is not however obligatory.

14.9/10 ***LQṢTNM 'YT MMLKT 'M 'DM H',*** "They (the holy gods) shall cut off that king or that commoner." *Obs.* The verb is expressed by Prefixing Form A *(yiqtol)* in the variant version of this same statement in line 22 of the text: ***YQṢN HMMLKT H' WH'DMM HMT,*** "They (the holy gods) shall cut off that king and those commoners."

60.45 ***'YT R'T Z LKTB H'DMM 'Š NŠ'M LN 'L BT 'LM 'LT MṢBT ḤRṢ,*** "The men who were elected by us in charge of the temple shall inscribe this resolution upon a gold stele."

60.5/6 ***LKNT GW 'RB 'LT MṢBT Z,*** "The community shall appoint a custodian in charge of this stele."

Pu *CIS* i 5510.2/3 ***KL 'DM 'Š LKP 'YT 'MTNT Z WL'KR WLŠBTY 'ML YD,*** "As for any person who shall overturn this stele or disturb or destroy it, his hand shall wither."

Pu *CIS* i 5510.7 ***MŠRT LQN' WKN L' ḤL WŠLM,*** "If he who serves shall be zealous, wealth and prosperity shall be his."

Pu 79.6/11 ***KL 'Š LSR T-'BN Z . . . WŠPṬ TNT-PNB'L BRḤ_DM H',*** "As for anyone who shall remove this stele, Thinnith-Phanebal shall condemn that person."

Pu *CIS* i 3784.1/2 ***KL 'Š LGNB T-'BN Z,*** "Anyone who shall steal this stele."

Pu 69.14 ***KL ZBḤ 'Š 'DM LZBḤ,*** "Any sacrifice that a person shall sacrifice."

2b. Subjunctive

The grammatical subject of the infinitive is expressed by the suffix pronouns of the B-type. The logical subject of the sentence, if a substantive, stands in apposition to the suffix pronoun. The suffix pronoun expressing the subject is not, however, obligatory.

14.19/20 ***WYSPNNM LGBL 'RṢ LKNNM LṢDNM L'LM,*** "We annexed them to the territory of our state that they might belong to the Sidonians forever."

18.3/6 ***'YT HŠ'R Z WHDLHT 'Š L P'LT BTKLTY BNTY . . . LKNY LY LSKR,*** "I built this gate and its panels to be (*lit.,* that it might be) a memorial to me."

19.9/11 ***KM 'Š BN 'YT KL 'ḤRY [HMQDŠ]M 'Š B'RṢ LKNNM L[M LSKR],*** "Just as they built all the other sanctuaries in the region to be (*lit.,* that they might be) a memorial to them."

26 A I 17/18 ***WBN 'NK ḤMYT BMQMM HMT LŠBTNM DNNYM BNḤT LBNM,*** "And I built protective fortresses in those places so that the Danunians might live in peace of mind."

26 A II 11/14 ***WBNY 'NK . . . LKNY MŠMR L'MQ 'DN,*** "I built it (the city) to be (*lit.*, that it might be) a place of protection for the Valley of Adana."

26 A II 10/11 ***K B'L WRŠP . . . ŠLḤN LBNT,*** "Baal and Rasap commissioned me to build <this city>." *Obs.* The verb ***LBNT*** does not carry a suffixal pronoun to indicate its subject.

NPu *CIS* i 151.1/4 ***LPLKS KHRHṢY P'L T-HM'Š 'ST PHLY' 'GBR 'TM' BN MQR' LKN L' WL'MM B'N',*** "Of Felix Ceresius. Pullius 'GBR the General, the son of MQR', made this statue to be of him (Felix) and of his mother B'N'." *Obs.* In Neo-Punic, the infinitive construct does not carry the suffix pronoun expressing its subject.

Obs. The subjunctive is expressed in Phoenician by Prefixing Form B if it is preceded and governed by the conjunction ***LKN*** ("in order that") in a Final Clause: 60.6/8: ***YŠ'N BKSP 'LM B'L ṢDN DRKMNM 20 LMḤT LKN YD'*** (*yede'ū*, Prefixing Form B, Pl. 3.) ***HṢDNYM K YD' HGW LŠLM ḤLPT 'YT 'DMM 'Š P'L MŠRT 'T PN GW,*** "They shall withdraw 20 drachmas from the silver of the god Baal of Sidon in order that the Sidonian might know that the community knows to compensate those persons who haver performed service on behalf of the community."

2c. Jussive and Optative

The logical subject of the infinitive is expressed by the suffix pronouns of the B-type. The logical subject of the verb, if a substantive, stands in apposition to the suffix pronoun. The suffix pronoun expressing the subject is not however obligatory.

26 A III 4/5 ***LTTY B'L . . . L'ZTWD 'RK YMM,*** "May Baal give to Aztwadda a long reign."

NPu 146.2/3 ***[']Š L'TT H'L 'BBRKTM L[N],*** "May God grant us of his blessings!" *Obs.* Note the absence of the suffixal pronoun with the infinitive to express the subject of the verb.

2d. Imperative

When the infinite is used to expresses the imperative, it does receive the suffixal pronoun as its subect.

Byb 2.1/3 ***LDʿT HNY BʿLK TḤT ZN,*** "Be aware: I, your king, am at the bottom of this <shaft>."

Pu 76 B 8 ***LŠT ʿLT HḤDRT NPT,*** "Place honey upon the swollen area."

Pu 70.1/4 ***QBR ZYBQT HKHNT . . . ʾBL LPTḤ,*** "<This is> the tomb of ZYBQT the Priestess. Do not open!"

3. *Expressing a Temporal Clause*

The infinitive construct, governed by the preposition ***B-***, is used to express the *when*-clause of a temporal sentence. The logical subject of the infinitive is expressed by the suffixal pronouns of the B-type; the logical subject, if a substantive, stands in apposition.

Kition lines 1/3 ***BMṢʾNM ʾBN WʿZRNM HPPYM LʾGD LN MLḤMT . . . WYṢʾ ʿLN[M MḤ]NT ʾŠ KTY LʾGD LM MLḤMT BMQM ʾZ,*** "When our enemies and their Paphian allies came to do battle with us, the army of the people of Kition went forth to do battle with them in this place."

NPu Trip. 79.5/6 ***NPLʿ*** (sic) ***BTṢTY BTY BḤYTNM WBḤYT<M>,*** "It (the tomb) was built at his own expense when they (those resting in the tomb) were still alive and he (the tomb's builder) was <still> alive."

NPu D 6.3/4 **Byrysth[im] Irirachan,** "When he drove out Irirachan." *Obs.* This is the superscription of a poem, beginning with a temporal clause expressed by the infinitive construct as in the superscriptions of the Biblical Psalms: *e.g.*, Psalm 3:1 ***BBRḤW MPNY ʾBŠLWM BNW,*** "When he (David) fled from Absalom, his son."

4. *Abstract Verbal Noun*

14.1 ***BYRḤ BL BŠNT ʿSR WʾRBʿ 14 LMLKY MLK ʾŠMNʿZR MLK ṢDNM,*** "In the month of Bul, in year fourteen 14 of the reign (*lit.*, of his reign) of King Esmunazor, King of the Sidonians."

Pu 112.4/5 ***BŠŠT ḤMŠM ŠT LMLKNM MKWSN WGLSN WMSTNʿBʾ ʾMMLKT,*** "In year fifty-six of the reign (*lit.*, of their reign) of Micipsa, Gulussa and Mastanab, the princes."

NPu 159.5/6 ***BYRḤ KRR ŠT BLL HZBḤ . . . BŠPṬM MSHBʾ BN YZRM,*** "In the month of Kirur, in the year of BLL the Sacrificial Priest, during the suffetship of MSHB' son of YZRM (or, "when MSHB' son of YZRM was Suffes)." *Obs.* The logical subject of the infinitive is expressed by the proleptic suffix ponoun ***–M*** *-īm* of the third masculine singular.

Pu *Poen.* 948/49 **Alem us duber ci <esse> mucom sussibti A(charist)ocle,** "I am told that this is the place where Acharistocles resides (*lit.*, the place of the residing of Acharistocles)." = NPu *Poen.* 938 **Ynny i(s) d(ubyr) ch'ilyb gubulim lasibithim <Agorastocles>,** "I am told that this is the district where Agorastocles resides (*lit.*, the district of the residing of Agorastocles)."

V. The Infinitive Absolute

A. *Morphology*

The Forms

QAL

Strong		
MLK *malōk*	Ph	24.2
NḤL *naḥōl*	Ph	Byb 3.3
P'L *pa'ōl*	Ph	26 A I 6/7
PTḤ *patōḥ*	Ph	13.6/7
ŠKR *sakōr*	Ph	24.7
TRQ *tarōq*	Ph	26 A I 9
y-t-n		
YTN *yatōn*	Byb	9 A 4
IIwy		
KN *kōn*	Ph	24.3 (bis), 26 A II 3, 7
con *kōn*	Pu	Poen. 941
ŠT *sōt*	Ph	26 A II 9, 19
III*y*		
BN *banō*	Ph	26 A I 17, II 9,17
BN-Y *banō-ya*	Ph	26 A II 11

PI'EL

ML' *mellō(')*	Ph	26 A I 6
RGZ *reggōz*	Ph	13.7
III*y*		
N *'ennō*	Ph	26 A I 18

YIP'IL

Strong		
YṬN' *yeṭne(')*	Ph	26 A I 9
YRḤB *yerḥeb*	Ph	26 A I 4
III*y*		
YḤW *yeḥwê*	Ph	26 A I 3
y-r-d; y-š-b; h-l-k		
YLK *yûlek*	Ph	26 A II 19
iulec *yûlek*	Pu	*Poen.* 942
YRD *yûred*	Ph	26 A I 20
YŠB *yûseb*	Ph	26 A I 20. II 18

B. *Syntax and Usage*

1. *Cognate Infinitive*

The cognate infinitive, also called tautological or paranomastic, complements a finite verb. The complementation is purely rhetorical.

Byb 3.2/6 ***'M NḤL TNḤL MGŠTK 'LK WMGŠT 'LY,*** "If you shall come into possession of it (the money), your share is yours and my share is mine."

13.6/7 ***'M PTḤ TPTḤ 'LTY WRGZ TRGZN,*** "If you do open it (my coffin) and disturb me, <you shall not have descendants among those living under the sun>."

2. *Consecutive*

An infinitive absolute that follows (is consecutive to) the main verb of a sentence assumes the references (tense, aspect, person, number and gender) of the main verb. This function is analogous to that of the Suffixing Form Consecutive but less common:

26 C ***WP'L 'NK SS 'L SS WP'L*** *(pa'ōl)* ***MGN 'L MGN,*** "I acquired horse upon horse and acquired shield upon shield."

26 A II 18/19 ***YŠB 'NK BN B'L KRNTRYŠ WYLK*** *(yûlek)* ***ZBḤ L,*** "I caused Baal-KRNTRYS to dwell in it (the city) and brought sacrifice to Him."

Obs. It is also possible to explain the two examples adduced here as examples of the periphrastic Past Perfective (see below), with scribal omission by error of the independent personal pronoun ***'NK*** ("I") as subject.

3. *Past Perfective Periphrastic*

In literary Phoenician, the Past Perfective was expressed by (i) Prefixing Form B (Past Perfective I); (ii) the Infinitive Absolute (Past Perfective II); and (iii) the Suffixing Form (Past Perfective III). Past Perfective I and Past Perfective II were syntactically restricted in the same manner: each functioned exclusively as the main (first) verb of a simple declarative sentence and was restricted to sentence-initial position. Past Perfective III, syntactically restricted to non sentence-initial position, was thus complementary to both Past Perfective I and II.

Past Perfective I and its complementary form, Past Perfective III, were used in both Tyro-Sidonian (Phoenician and Punic) and Byblian Phoenician. The Phoenician texts in which they occur are *KAI* 24 (the royal Kilamuwa inscription, *ca.* 850 B.C.) and *KAI* 26 (the royal Aztwadda inscription, *ca.* 750 B.C.). In literary Punic, they occur in the entrance monologue of Hanno in the *Poenulus* (Act V, 940-946a, *ca.* 350-250 B.C.). The Byblian texts in which they occur are *KAI* 9 (the royal son of Sipitbaal inscription, *ca.* 500-450 B.C.) and *KAI* 10 (the royal Yehawmilk inscription, *ca.* 450-400 B.C.).

In the paragraphs that follow, I give both the occurrences of Past Perfective I and Past Perfective III in the same text in order to illustrate the manner of their complementation.

3a. Kilamuwa Inscription (*KAI* 24), *ca.* 850 B.C.E.

3a-1. Past Perfective I

24.2 ***MLK GBR ʿL Y'DY WBL P[ʿL] KN BMH WBL PʿL WKN ʾB ḤYʾ WBL PʿL WKN ʾḤ Šʾ L WBL PʿL WʾN[K] KLMW BR TM[.]M ʾŠ PʿLT BL PʿL HLPNY[H]M,*** "Gabbar ruled over Y'dy, but he did not accomplish anything. There was BMH, but he did not accomplish anything. There was my father Hayya, but he did not accomplish anything. There was my brother Sa'il, but he did not accomplish anything. But as for me, Kilamuwa son of TM[.], I accomplished what my predecessors did not accomplish." *Obs.* The sentence-initial verbs ***MLK*** and ***KN*** (3x) are Infinitive Absolute (Past Perfect I); the non sentence-initial verbs ***PʿL*** and ***PʿLT*** are the Suffixing Form (Past Periphrastic Perfect III).

24.5/6 ***KN BT ʾBY BMTKT MLKM ʾDRM,*** "My royal house was in the midst of those of more powerful kings."

24.7/8 ***WŠKR ʾNK ʿLY MLK ʾŠR,*** "I hired against him the king of Assyria."

3a-2. Past Perfective III

24.2,3,4 ***BL P'L,*** "He did not accomplish anything."

24.4/5 (2x) ***M 'Š P'LT BL P'L HLPNY[H]M,*** "My predecessors did not accomplish what I accomplished."

24.6 ***WKL ŠLḤ YD LL[Ḥ]M,*** "Each one undertook to fight <me>."

3b. Aztwadda Inscription (*KAI* 26), *ca.* 750 B.C.E.

3b-1. Past Perfective I

26 A I 3 ***P'LN B'L LDNNYM L'B WL'M,*** "Baal made me father and mother of the Danunians."

26 A I 3/4 ***YḤW 'NK 'YT DNNYM,*** "I kept the Danunians alive."

26 A I 4 ***YRḤB 'NK 'RṢ 'MQ 'DN,*** "I expanded the territory of the Valley of Adana."

26 A I 6 ***WML' 'NK 'QRT P'R,*** "I filled the reservoirs of P'R."

26 A I 6/7 ***WP'L 'NK SS 'L SS,*** "I acquired horse upon horse."

26 A I 9 ***WTRQ 'NK KL HR' 'Š KN B'RṢ,*** "I rooted out all the evil that existed in the land."

26 A I 9/10 ***WYṬN' 'NK BT 'DNY,*** "I established my royal house."

26 A I 10 ***WP'L 'NK LŠRŠ 'DNY N'M,*** "And I did what was good for my royal progeny."

26 A I 11 ***WYŠB 'NK 'L KS' 'BY,*** "I took my place upon my father's throne."

26 A I 11/12 ***WŠT 'NK ŠLM 'T KL MLK,*** "I made peace with every king."

26 A I 13, 17 ***WBN 'NK ḤMYT,*** "I built walled fortresses."

26 A I 18 ***W'N 'NK 'RṢT 'ZT,*** "I conquered powerful lands."

26 A I ***YRDM 'NK,*** "I deported them."

26 A I 20/21 ***YŠBM 'NK BQṢT GBLY,*** "I resettled them in the distant part of my territory."

26 A II 9,17 ***WBN 'NK HQRT Z,*** "I built this city."

26 A II 11 ***WBNY 'NK,*** "I built it."

26 A II 17/18 ***ŠT 'NK ŠM 'ZTWDY,*** "I named it (the city) Aztwaddiya."

26 A II 18/19 ***YŠB 'NK BN B'L,*** "I caused Baal to dwell in it (the city)."

3b-2. Past Perfective III

26 A I 1 ***'NK 'ZTWD HBRK B'L,*** "I am Aztwadda, whom Baal

blessed." *Obs.* The definite article here expresses the relative pronoun.

26 A I 12/13 ***B'BT P'LN KL MLK BṢDQY WBḤKMTY WB-N'M LBY,*** "Every king adopted me as his father because of my honesty, my cleverness and the excellence of my mind."

26 A I 14/15 ***BMQMM B'Š KN 'ŠM R'M,*** "In places in which there were bad men."

26 A I 15/16 ***BL 'Š 'BD KN LBT MPŠ,*** "None was a vassal of the House of Mopsos."

3c. Entrance Monologue of Hanno, *ca.* 300 B.C.E.

3c-1. Past Perfective I

Poen. 942 **Iulec anec cona, alonim balim, bane becor Bals[illem],** "I brought here, O proprietary gods, my firstborn son Bals[illem]."

3c-2. Past Perfective III

Poen. 943/4 **Hu neso bin us es hulec silli balim esse lipane esse con,** "He was made the son of the man who was my guest-friend in this nation in the past."

Poen. 944/46 **Alem us duber ce fel dono Metun et cil comu con liful alt banim au,** "I am told that his (adoptive) father Mettun did everythng for that son of his as he was to do <for him>."

3d. Son of Sipitbaal Inscription (*KAI* 9), *ca.* 500-475 B.C.E.

3d-1. Past Perfective I

9 A 4 ***WYTN 'NK '[YT . . .],*** "I placed the [. . .]."

3d-2. Past Perfective III

9 A 1 ***['NK . . . B]N ŠPṬB'L MLK GBL P'LT LY HMŠKB ZN,*** "I, PN son of Sipitbaal, King of Byblos, built this resting-place for myself."

9 A 2 ***'L KN P'LT ['YT MŠKB ZN],*** "For this reason did I build this resting-place."

3e. Yehawmilk Inscription (*KAI* 10), *ca.* 450 B.C.E.

3e-1. Past Perfective I

10.2/3 ***WQR' 'NK 'T RBTY B'LT GBL,*** "I invoked my Lady Baalat of Byblos."

10.3 ***WŠM' [H'] QL,*** "She heard my voice."

10.3/4 ***WP'L 'NK LRBTY B'LT GBL HMZBḤ NḤŠT ZN,*** "I made this bronze altar for my Lady Baalt of Byblos."

10.6/7 ***WP'L 'NK YḤWMLK MLK BL LRBTY B'LT GBL,*** "I, Yehawmilk, King of Byblos, made <these things> for my Lady Baalt of Byblos."

3e-2. Past Perfective III

10.1/1 ***'NK YḤWMLK MLK GBL . . . 'Š P'LTN HRBT B'LT GBL MMLKT 'L GBL,*** "I am Yehawmilk, King of Byblos, whom the Lady Baalt of Byblos made king over Byblos."

10.7/8 ***KM QR'T 'T RBTY B'LT GBL WŠM' QL,*** "When I invoked my Lady Baalt of Byblos, she heard my voice."

4. *Verbal Noun*

The Infinitive Absolute, like the Infinitive Construct, is used also as a verbal noun: NPu 137.2/3 ***KN' 'L MLKT HBN' 'Š BMQDŠM 'L,*** "Those in charge of these sanctuaries were in charge of the building project."

CHAPTER TWELVE

THE NUMERALS

I. Cardinal Numbers

A. *Morphology*

1. *The Numerals 1-10*

Forms

ONE		
M. **'ḤD** *'eḥḥad*	Pu	69.3; 74.7; *CIS* i165.7, *EH* 64.3
F. **'ḤT** *'eḥḥat*	NPu	120.1
TWO		
Masculine		
Absolute		
ŠNM *snêm*	Ph	*RES* 827
	Pu	64.1; 130.3,6; 137.1
'ŠNM *esnêm*	Ph	88.6; 32.3*CIS* I 10.3
Construct		
ŠN *snê*	Ph	47.3.
	Pu	*CIS* i 122 a 2, b 3
'ŠN *esnê*	Ph	*CIS* i 88.6
	Pu	4596.5
Feminine		
Absolute		
ŠTM *stêm*	Ph	Umm el-Awamid 13.1
Construct		
ŠT *stê*		Not recorded
THREE		
M. **ŠLŠT** *salūst*	Ph	*CIS* I 93.4; Eph 1.13 nr. 11
	Pu	*CIS* I 165.9, 11
F. **ŠLŠ** *salūs*	Ph	19.8; *RES* 453
	Pu	*CIS I* 132.1
	NPu	130.2; 134.2; *NP* 58.2; *NP* 69.3

	Š'LŠ	NPu	144.3
	salus	NPu	Aug. on Epistle to the Romans 13

FOUR

M.	***'RB'T*** *'arbá'at*	Pu	*RES* 336.5
F.	***'RB'*** *'arba'*	Ph	*CIS* i 3.1; 89.1
		Pu	130.5, 137.6

FIVE

M.	***ḤMŠT*** *ḥamist*	Pu	*CIS* I 165.5, 166 B 10
F.	***ḤMŠ*** *ḥames*	Ph	Lapethos 3.8
		Pu	RES 1552
		NPu	*NP* 63.6; *NP* 67.4; *EH* 57.3; *EH* 64.2
	'MŠ	NPu	*NP* 22.4; *NP* 23.3; *NP* 24.3
	amys	NPu	*AI* 1 p. 45 no. 4.7

SIX

M.	***ŠŠT*** *sésit*		Not recorded
F.	***ŠŠ*** *ses*	Pu	130.1 (masculine); *JA* 1916/1 458, 3
	Š'Š	NPu	142.2
	sys	NPu	*AI* 1 p. 45 no. 4.1

SEVEN

M.	***ŠB'T*** *sebá'at*		Not recorded
F.	***ŠB'*** *séba'*	Ph	27.17
		Pu	76 B 6
	ŠB'T	NPu	*EH* 59.4; *EH* 60.4

EIGHT

M.	***ŠMNT*** *samūnīt*		Not recorded
F.	***ŠMN*** *samūne*	Ph	*CIS* I 92.2
		Pu	*RES* 168.3
	ŠMN'	NPu	*JA* 1916/1 465,5

NINE

M.	***TŠ'T*** *tisá'at*		Not recorded
F.	***TŠ'*** *tésa'*	Pu	130.2

TEN

M.	***'ŠRT*** *'asert*	Pu	*CIS* I 165.3; *CIS* I 175.1

F.	***ʿSR*** *ʿasar*	Ph	14.1
		Pu	101.1, 120.1
	ʿSʿR	NPu	*NP* 64.3
	asar	NPu	*AI* 1 p. 45 no. 4.1, 5

2. *The Numerals 11-1*

The cardinal nunmbers 11-19 are expressed in standard Phoenician-Punic by the numeral ten followed by the unit; the two numerals are conjoined by the conjunction ***W-*** ("and"): *i.e.*, eleven is expressed as ***ʿŠRT WʾḤD*** in the masculine and ***ʿŠR WʾḤT*** in the feminine. Both the numerals agree in gender with the noun. In late Neo-Punic only, in analogy to the Latin numerals **undecim, duodecim, tredecim**, *etc.*, the numerals 11-19 are expressed by the unit followed directly, without the conjunction, by the numeral ten.

2a. Standard Phoenician-Punic

ʿŠR(T) W- + Unit
Lapethos 3.2 ***YM ʿŠRT WŠLŠT 13***. "Day thirteen 13."
14.1 ***ŠNT ʿSR WʾRBʿ 14,*** "Year fourteen 14."
NPu 144.2/3 ***ʿWʾ ŠʿNT ʿSR WŠʿLŠ,*** "He lived twenty-three years."
NPu 120.1 ***RB MḤNT PʿMʾT ʿSR WʾḤT,*** "Consul eleven times."

2b. Late Neo-Punic

Unit + ***ʿŠR***
AI 1 p. 45 no. 4.1/2 **[S]ys asar liiyra Chirur,** "The sixteenth of the month of Kirur." *Cf.* Latin **sedecim.**

3. *The Numerals 20, 30, 40,. 50, 60, 70, 80, 90*

TWENTY

ʿŠRM *ʿesrīm*		Not recorded
ʿSRM	Pu	*EH* 59.3
HŠR[M]	NPu	*NP* 20.3
esrim	NPu	*IRT* 826.4

THIRTY

ŠLŠM *salūsīm*	Ph	41.5
	Pu	*CIS* I 3917.1; *NP* 27.5, 68.3

FORTY

'RB'M *'arba'īm*	Pu	*NP* 65.3; *JA* 1917/2, 12:1, 2
'RBM *arbīm*	NPu	*NP* 23.3, 60.3

FIFTY

ḤMŠM *ḥamissīm*	Pu	101.4; *CIS* i 165.6; *NP* 53.3; *NP* 56.3
'MŠM *amissīm*	NPu	140.7; 165.7

SIXTY

ŠŠM *sissīm*	Pu	149.4; *NP* 66.3
ŠYŠM	NPu	157.3

SEVENTY

ŠB'M *sib'īm*	Pu	133.3; 171.4

EIGHTY

ŠMNM *samūnīm*	Pu	130.2; *NP* 130.6

NINETY

TŠ'M *tis'īm*	Byb	3.2
TŠM	NPu	*JA* 1918 252, 5
ṬYŠM *tissīm*	NPu	*NP* 55.1; *JA* 1916/1, 107

4. *The Numerals 21-29, 31-39,* etc.

The cardinal numbers 21-29, 31-39, etc., are formed in two ways: (i) The multiple of ten (20, 30, 40, 50, 60, 70, 80, 90) followed by the unit (1, 2, 3, 4, 5, 6, 7, 8, 9), the multiple and the unit conjoined by the conjunction *W-* ("and"): *i.e.,* twenty-one is expressed as ***'ŠRM W'ḤD*** ("twenty and one"); (ii) The unit precedes the multiple of ten, without conjoining by the conjunction: *i.e.,* twenty-one is expressed as ***'ḤD 'ŠRM*** ("one twenty"). In both instances, the unit agrees in gender with the noun.

4a. ***'ŠRM*** **W-** + Unit

Lapethos 3.4 ***ḤMŠM WḤMŠT WRB' DR(KMNM),*** "Fifty-five and one quarter drachmas."

NPu 141.3/4 ***ŠT 'SRM W'ḤT,*** "Year twenty-one."

NPu 143.4 ***ŠNT 'RBM WḤD,*** "Forty-one years."

NPu 152.3 ***ŠŠM ŠT WŠLŠ,*** "Sixty-three years."

4b. Unit + ***ʿŠRM***

19.8 ***ŠLŠ ḤMŠM ŠT,*** "Year fifty-three."
Pu *EH* 56.3 ***ʾḤT{T} ʾRBʿM ŠT,*** "Year forty-one."
Pu *EH* 57.4 ***[ḤMŠ]T ʾRBʿM ŠT,*** "Year forty-five."
Pu *EH* 58.3 ***ŠŠT ʾRBʿM ŠT,*** "Year forty-six."
Pu *EH* 59.4, 60.4 ***ŠBʿT ʾRBʿM ŠT,*** "Year forty-seven."
Pu *EH* 63.4 ***ŠŠT ḤMŠM ŠT,*** "Year fifty-six."

5. *The Numerals 100, 200, 1,000, 10,000*

ONE HUNDRED

MʾT	Ph	*RES* 1502
	Pu	101.3; *CIS* I 143.1, 165.6, 171.4,6
	NPu	30.2
myith	NPu	*AI* 1 p. 45 no. 4.6

TWO HUNDRED

MʾTM	Pu	76 B 9; 141.5

THREE HUNDRED

ŠLŠ MʾT	NPu	*CIS* I 165.3

FIVE HUNDRED

ḤMŠ M[ʾ]T	Pu	Lapethos 3.8

ONE THOUSAND

ʾLP	Ph	Lapethos 3.8

TEN THOUSAND

RB(ʾ)		Not recorded
rybo	NPu	*AI* 1 p. 45 no. 4

ONE HUNDRED THOUSAND

asar rybo	NPu	*AI* 1 p. 45 no.4

B. *Syntax and Usage*

1. *Gender Marking and Agreement*

1a. Phoenician and Punic

In standard Phoenician-Punic, as in Classical Hebrew and Arabic, the masculine numerals 3-9 exhibit the afformative ***-T,*** while the feminine numerals 3-9 exhibit the afformative **-Ø.**

1a-1. Masculine
40.4 ***ŠLŠT BN MRYḤY,*** "The three sons of MRYHY."
Pu 80.1 ***'ŠRT H'ŠM 'Š 'L HMQDŠM,*** "The ten men who are in charge of sanctuaries."

2a-2. Feminine
14.1 ***ŠNT 'SR W'RB' 14,*** "Year fourteen 14."
19.8 ***ŠLŠ ḤMŠM ŠT,*** "Year fifty-three."
CIS I 92 ***ŠNT ŠMN 8,*** "Year eight 8."
Lapethos 3.2 ***YM 'ŠRT WŠLŠT 13 LYRḤ [KR]RM,*** "Day thirteen 13 of the month of Kirurim."

In Neo-Punic, gender-marking as in Phoenician-Punic is still encountered:
NPu 120.1 ***P'M'T 'SR,*** "Ten times."
NPu 120.1 ***P'M'T 'SR W'RB',*** "Fourteen times."
NPu 120.1 ***P'M'T 'SR WḤMŠ,*** "Fifteen times."

1b. Late Punic and Neo-Punic

In late Neo-Punic, under the influence of Latin, the numerals 3-9 imitate the morphology and syntax of the Roman numerals: the masculine numeral exhibits the afformative **-Ø**, while the feminine numeral exhibits the afformative ***-T:***

1b-1. Masculine
120.1 ***'SR HMŠLM,*** "The eight tribunes."
130.1 ***ŠŠ HYŠBM 'L',*** "These three benches."
130.5 ***YŠBM 'RB' P'L',*** "They made four benches."
137.5/6 ***NBL NSKT 'RB',*** "Four metal vessels."

1b-2. Feminine
Pu EH 57.4 ***[ḤMŠ]T 'RB'M ŠT,*** "Year forty-five."

Pu EH 58.3 ***ŠŠT 'RB'M ŠT,*** "Year forty-six."
Pu EH 59.4, 60.4 ***ŠB'T 'RB'M ŠT,*** "Year forty-seven."
Pu EH 63.4 ***ŠŠT ḤMŠM ŠT,*** "Year fifty-six."
Contrast Phoenician usage: 19.8 ***ŠLŠ ḤMŠM ŠT,*** "Year fifty-three."

2. *The Position of the Numeral in Enumerations*

2a. Preceding the Determined Noun

47.3 ***ŠN BN 'SRŠMR,*** "The two sons of Osirisamor."
CIS i 88.6 ***'ŠN BN ['D]NŠMŠ,*** "The two sons of Adonisemes."
Pu *CIS* i 4596.3/4 ***'ŠN BN' MHRB'L,*** "The two sons of Maharbal."
40.4 ***ŠLŠT BN MRYḤY,*** "The three sons of MRYHY."
Pu 80.1 ***'ŠRT H'ŠM 'Š 'L HMQDŠM,*** "The ten men who are responsible for the sanctuaries."
Pu 101.4 ***'D[R] ḤMŠM H'Š MQL' BN 'ŠYN,*** "MQL' son of 'SYN was Prefect of the Fifty Men."
Pu *CIS* i 3917.1 ***ŠLŠM H'Š 'Š 'L HMŠ'[TT],*** "The thirty men who are responsible for tariffs."

2b. Following a Noun Determined by a Demonstrative Pronoun

In this common usage, the pronoun is often not expressed but implicit. In the examples that follow, the non-expressed demonstrative is indicated in triangular brackets.
RES 827 ***SMLM ŠNM 'L YTN 'B[D . . . L . . .],*** "Abd[. . .] presented these two statues [to . . .]."
CIS i 14.58 ***MNḤT 2 'L '[Š Y]TN W]YṬN' 'BD'L[M] . . . L'DNY L[RŠP],*** "These two *mnḥt* are what Abdilim presented and erected to his Lord Rasap."
Umm el-Awamid 13.1/2 ***LMLK'ŠTRT 'L ḤMN K[K]RT ḤRṢ ŠTM <'L> 'Š YTN 'BDK 'BD'DNY,*** "<Dedicated> to Milkastart, God of Hammon, are <these> two talents of gold that Your servant Abdadonay has presented."
32.2/4 ***MZBḤ '[Z] W'RWM 'ŠNM 2 <'L> 'Š YTN BD' . . . L'DNY LRŠP,*** "This altar and <these> two 2 lions that Bodo presented to his Lord Rasap."
Pu 64.2 ***L'DN LB'[L]ŠMM B'YNṢM NṢBM WḤNWṬM ŠNM <'L> 'Š NDR B'LḤN',*** "<Dedicated> to Balsamem of Inosim are <these> stelai and two *ḥnwṭm* that Balanno had vowed <to him>."

NPu 137.1 ***LʾDN LBʿL WLTNT-PNBʿL MQDŠM ŠNM <ʾL> ʾŠ PʿL BʿL TNSMT,*** "<Dedicated> to the Lord Baal and to Thinnith-Phanebal are <these> two sanctuaries which the citizens of Thinnissut built <for them>."

In Neo-Punic, the numeral may precede the noun:

NPu 130.1 ***NPʿL ŠŠ HYŠBM ʾL ŠT ŠPṬM ʿBDMLQRT ṬBḤPY WʾRŠ,*** "These two benches were made in the year of the suffetes Abdmilqart Tapapius and Aris."

2c. Following the Non-Determined Noun

Pu 80.1 ***HMṬBḤ Ẓ DL PʿMM ʿŠRT,*** "This ten-footed slaughtering table," *lit.*, "this slaughtering table which possesses ten feet."

NPu 120.1 ***PʿMʾT ʿSR,*** "Ten times."

NPu 120.1 ***PʿMʾT ʿSR WʾRBʿ,*** "Fourteen times."

NPu 120.1 ***PʿMʾT ʿSR WḤMŠ,*** "Fifteen times."

NPu 130.5 ***YŠBM ʾRBʿ PʿLʾ BʿNŠM,*** "They made four benches with money derived from fines."

NPu 130.2 ***DNʿRYʾ ŠMNM WKNDRM TŠʿ,*** "Eighty denars and nine quadrans."

NPu 130.3 ***DNʿRYʾ ḤMŠM WŠNM,*** "Fifty-two denars."

NPu 137.5/6 ***NPʿL NBL NSKT ʾRBʿ ʿLT HMQDŠM ʾL SPM ŠNM WẒBRM ŠNM,*** "Four metal vessels were made for these sanctuaries, two goblets and two bowls."

NPu 144.2/3 ***ʿWʾ ŠʿNT ʿSR WŠʿLŠ,*** "He lived twenty-three years."

NPu 120.1 ***RB MḤNT PʿMʾT ʿSR WʾḤT,*** "Consul eleven times."

In late Neo-Punic, the numeral may precede the noun:

LA 1 p. 45 no. 5.5/6 **Asar rybo den(ario),** "One hundred thousand denars."

2d. Preceding or Following the Word "Year" or "Day" in Date Formula

14.1 ***ŠNT ʿSR WʾRBʿ 14,*** "Year fourteen 14."

19.8 ***ŠLŠ ḤMŠM ŠT,*** "Year fifty-three."

Lapethos 3.2 ***YM ʿŠRT WŠLŠT 13 LYRḤ [KR]RM,*** "Day thirteen 13 of the month of Kirurim."

CIS i 92 ***ŠNT ŠMN 8,*** "Year eight 8."

II. Ordinal Numbers

A. *Morphology*

Forms

FIRST

M. ***LPNY*** *lipanī*	Ph	24.5, 10
	NPu	137.5
F. ***LPNT*** *lipanīt*		Not recorded

SECOND

M. ***ŠNY*** *senī*	Ph	14.6
ŠN'	Pu	*CIS* i 5692.4
ŠNH	Pu	*CIS* i 4859.4
F. ***ŠNT*** *senīt*		Not recorded

THIRD

M. ***ŠLŠY*** *salūsī*		Not recorded
ŠLŠ'	Pu	*RES* 910
F. ***ŠLŠT*** *salūsīt*		Not recorded

FOURTH

M. ***'RB'Y*** *'arba'ī*	Pu	76 B 1
F. ***'RB'T*** *'arba'īt*		Not recorded

M. ***ḤMŠY*** *ḥamissī*	Pu	76 B 7
F. ***ḤMŠT*** *ḥamissīt*		Not recorded

Comments

To judge from ***'RB'Y*** *'arba'ī* ("four"), the ordinals 3-9 were *nisbe* forms of the cardinal numbers, not including forms of the shape *CaCīCī* like Hebrew *r^{e}bī'ī* ("four"). The Hebrew ordinals are a mixed series of both types.

B. *Syntax and Usage*

LPNY

FIRST

NPu 137.4/5 ***B' H'LNM 'L 'LT HMQDŠM 'L B'SR WŠB' LYRḤ MP' LPNY,*** "These gods entered these sanctuaries on the seventeenth of the month of First Mufa."

FORMER, EARLIER, PRECEDING, PAST

24.9/10 ***LPN HMLKM HLPNYM YTLKN MŠKBM KM KLBM,*** "Earlier kings (the kings who preceded <me>) treated the *mškbm* like dogs."

24.4/5 ***M 'Š P'LT BL P'L <HMLKM> HLPNY{H}M,*** "Earlier kings (the kings who preceded <me>) did not accomplish what I accomplished."

ŠNY

SECOND in command

Pu *KI* 11 ***RB <MḤNT> ŠNY,*** "The Second General of the Army." A military rank.

OTHER, ANOTHER

14.5/6 ***'L Y'MSN BMŠKB Z 'LT MŠKB ŠNY,*** "Let him not transport me from this resting-place to another resting-place!"

ŠLŠY

THIRD in command

Pu *RES* 910 ***RB <MḤNT> ŠLŠ',*** "The Third General of the Army." A military rank.

'RB'Y

FOURTH

Pu 76 B 1/2 ***YM H'RB'Y ŠḤPR Y' HQDŠ,*** "The fourth day of the piercing of the sacred *y'*." Heading in a medical text.

ḤMŠY

FIFTH

Pu 76 B 7/8 ***YM HḤMŠY LŠT 'LT HḤDRT NPT,*** "The fifth day: Pour honey upon the swollen area." Heading and treatment in a medical text.

III. Other Numeric Designations

A. *Numeric Group Designations*

A group of a given number is expressed in Phoenician by a feminine singular noun.

'RB'T

GROUP OF FOUR

NPu Trip. 79.1/5 ***B'RM QN'T M' 'Š P'LM M'ṢWKN L'BY' . . . WL'MM . . . WL'BNY. . . WL'ŠTY . . . ḤŠ L'RBTNM,*** "You have acquired the tomb that Masauchan built for his father and for his mother and for his son and for his wife. Do nothing to the four of them!"

ŠŠT

GROUP OF SIX

Umm el-Awamid no. 10.1/3 ***Z MṢBT SKR ŠM 'BD'[NT] BN 'BDRBT '[Š T]N[' L] ŠŠT [Ṣ]RT[Y],*** "This is the stele, the memorial to the name of Abdanat son of Abdribbot, that the six of his co-wives erected to him."

B. *Fractions*

RB' *réba'*

ONE FOURTH

Lapethos line 4 ***QB'M ŠLKSP MSPRM 6 MŠQLM PRS WḤMŠM WḤMŠT WRB' DR(KMN),*** "Silver goblets; their number is 6, and their weight is one *prs* and fifty-five and one quarter drachmas."

MḤṢ *meḥṣe* and ***MḤṢT*** *meḥṣīt*

ONE HALF

Hill cxxvii ***MḤṢ K(SP),*** "One half silver." Denomination of Tyrian coin.

Betlyon p. 39f ***MḤṢT,*** "One half." Denomination of Tyrian coin. *Obs.* When "one half" of an concrete object is meant, the noun used is ***ḤṢY*** *ḥaṣī:* RES 1205.5 ***P'L 'YT ḤṢY HSP Z,*** "He made one half of this *sp*."

RB' ŠLŠT *réba' salūst*

THREE QUARTERS

Pu 69.11 ***LKHNM KSP RB' ŠLŠT B'ḤD,*** "The priests shall receive three quarters silver for each <animal>."

C. *Multiples*

P'MT *pa'amūt* + Numeral

X NUMBER OF TIMES

NPu 120.1 ***RB MḤNT P'M'T 'SR W'ḤT WMYNKD P'M'T 'SR W'RB' W[TḤT] MŠLT 'SR HMŠLM P'M'T 'SR WḤMŠ,*** "Consul eleven times, emperor fourteen times and tribune fifteen times."

'D P'MT BRBM *'ad pa'amūt biribbīm*

MANY TIMES

Pu 68.5 ***ŠM' QL' 'D P'MT BRBM,*** "He (the god) heard his voice (supplication) many times." The preposition *'ad* is used here adverbially to express multiplicity, in the manner found in Hebrew 2Kings 4:35 ***'D ŠB' P'MYM*** ("seven times"). For ***BRBM*** *biribbīm* ("very, much, many"), see Adverbs.

CHAPTER THIRTEEN

THE PREPOSITIONS

The prepositions of Phoenician-Punic are of five types: (i) simple proclitics, such as ***'B-***, ***B-***, ***L-*** and ***M-***; (ii) compounded proclitics, such as ***L-B-*** , ***L-M-*** and ***L-M-B-***; (iii) simple non-proclitic independent prepositions, such as ***'L***, ***'ṢL***, ***'T***, ***BD***, ***MN***, ***'D***, ***'L***, ***'LT***; (iv) compounded proclitic and non-proclitics, such as ***L-MN***; (v) prepositional phrases, such as ***'T PN***, ***B-GW***, ***B-DṢ L***, ***B-MTKT***, ***L-PN***, ***'L PN***, ***'LT PN***. In addition, there are co-ordinated prepositional phrases, such as ***L-M- . . . W'D*** and ***L-M-B . . . W'D 'T***. In the list which follows, all five types of prepositions are integrated.

'B- *'eb-*

Forms

'B-	Ph	43.3,7
	Pu	Pyrgi 5; *CIS* i 6000.8
	NPu	147.3
ef-	NPu	*Trip.* 877.4

The preposition ***'B-*** is a rare free variant of ***B-*** *bi-*, originating in the pronunciation *b-* of the latter (without vowel) proclitic to a word beginning with a consonant; this pronunciation gave rise to the prothetic e-vowel, serving to break up the initial consonant cluster. Three of the extant five instances of this form occur with words beginning with a bilabial (*b m*), suggesting that *eb-* may have been preferred over *bi-* in order to avoid the bilabial sequences like *bib-* and *bim-*. The Neo-Punic vocalized example evidences the same spirantisation of *b-* contiguous to a following consonant that is evidenced in the Roman-letter Neo-Punic **myntsyfth** (***MNṢBT*** "stele") and in **lifnim** (***LBNM*** "for his son"). See the discussion in the Chapter on Phonology.

Usage

In meaning and function, the preposition *eb-* was identical to *bi-*.

IN

43.2/3 ***HSML Z . . . ʾŠ YṬNʾT ʾBMQDŠ MLQRT,*** "This statue that I erected in the sanctuary of Milqart."

Pu Pyrgi lines 1/5 ***ʾŠR QDŠ ʾZ ʾŠ PʿL WYTN . . . BMTN ʾBBT,*** "This sacred *ʾšr*, which he made and presented as a gift in the temple."

Pu *CIS* i 6000.8 ***WʾBT SPRY KTB BPS,*** "And they wrote a biography of him in an inscription in the temple."

NPu *IRT* 877.1/5 **Centenari mu fel Thlana Marci Cecili byMupal efsem <M>acer byn banem,** "<This is> the fortified farmhouse that Thlana Marcius Caecilius son of Mupal built in the name of Macer, his grandson."

IN, DURING (temporal)

43.7 ***ʾBḤY ʾBY YŠT BMQDŠ MLQRT ʾYT MŠ PN ʾBY,*** "I had the bust of my father placed in the sanctuary of Milqart while he (my father) was still alive."

ʾL ʾel

This preposition, related to Hebrew ***ʾL*** *ʾel,* is rare in Phoenician, attested twice only, once in Byblian and once in Tyro-Sidonian, in both with highly specialized function. In Byblian the preposition serves to introduce an anticipatory clause, in Tyro-Sidonian in epistolary address (destination). Phoenician does not use the preposition to express direction "to" or dative "to, for"; direction is expressed in Phoenician by the prepositions ***ʿL*** and ***ʿLT*** and by the noun in the accusative case; the dative is expressed by the prepositions ***ʾT,*** ***L-*** and ***ʿL(T).***

Usage

TO (in epistolary address formula)

50.1/2 ***ʾL ʾRŠT BT ʾŠMNYTN ʾMR LʾḤTY ʾRŠT ʾMR ʾḤTK BṢTK BSʾ,*** "(address) To Arisuth daughter of Esmunyaton. (Opening of the letter) Say to my sister Arisuth: <This is> the statement of your sister BSʾ."

AS FOR, AS TO, introducing an anticipatory phrase in Byblian. Tyro-Sidonian uses the particle ***'M*** *'ammā* in this same function.

Byb 1.2 ***W'L MLK BMLKM . . . WYGL 'RN ZN TḤTSP ḤṬR MŠPṬH,*** "As for any king, if he should remove this coffin, his imperial sceptre shall break."

'ṢL *'eṣel*

Usage

NEXT TO, ADJACENT TO; Hebrew ***'ṢL*** *'eṣel.*

Byb 9 B 2 ***['L TP'L LK MŠK]B 'ṢL HMŠK[B ZN],*** "Do not build a tomb for yourself next to this tomb!"

'T *'et ('itt-)*

Forms

ett	Pu	*Poen.* 947P
itt	Pu	*Poen.* 947A
yth	NPu	*Poen.* 936

With suffix pronouns:

1. Sg.

iti	Pu	*CIL* viii 23372 (**Itibalis**)
'TK	Byb	10.13

3. M.Sg.

ιθο	Ph	In the name Ιθοβαλος (Jos., *Ap.* 1.123)
ιθω	Ph	In the name Ιθωβαλος (Jos, *Ap.* 1.156)
to < *'itto*	Ph	In the name ***Tu-Ba-'-lum*** (Senn. Ii 51)
ythem	NPu	*Poen.* 936, 937

The preposition is the reflex of Proto-Canaanite *'itti*; Hebrew ***'T*** *'et* (*'itt-* before suffix pronouns). Gemination of the *t* is indicated in the Roman-letter Punic spellings **ett** and **itt**, which occur immediately before a word beginning with a vowel, *viz.*, **ett esde** ("with/to him"). The form **to** is aphetic, with loss of the initial unstressed syllable; it is unclear however if this form was characteristic of actual usage or confined to personal names. In the late Neo-Punic form **ythem,** the

3.Sg.M. suffix pronoun **-em**, earlier used exclusively with the noun in the genitive case, is extended to the use with the preposition; this extension is found in late Neo-Punic with nouns in the nominative case, *e.g.*, *IRT* 889.1 **binim** ("his son") and *IRT* 906.1 **byne** ("his son").

Usage

WITH, TOGETHER WITH

Byb 10.13 ***TŠT ŠM 'TK,*** "Place <on it> my name with yours."

13.7/8 ***'L YKN LK . . . MŠKB 'T RP'M,*** "(If you open my coffin,) you shall not have rest with/among the infernal deities."

14.9 ***YSGRNM H'LNM HQDŠM 'T MMLKT 'DR 'Š MŠL BNM,***, "The holy gods shall imprison them, together with whatever great king is ruling them."

26 A I 11/2 ***WŠT 'NK ŠLM 'T KL MLK,*** "And I made peace with every king."

Pu *Poen.* 947A **Itt esde anec nasote hers ahelicot,** "With him I shared a shard of hospitality." = NPu *Poen.* 937 **Ythem anech nasothi li yth irs aelichoth sith,** "With him I shared this shard of hospitality."

In the Phoenician and Punic personal names **Itibalis** ("Baal be with me!" *CIL* viii 23372); ***To-Ba'l*** (*Tu-ba-'-lum* Senn. Ii 51), Ιθοβαλος (Jos., *Ap.* 1.123) = Ιθωβαλος (Jos., *Ap.* 1.156), all meaning "Baal be with him!"

TO

37 A 11 ***'T PRKM QP' 1[. . .],*** "<Paid> to the taskmasters: x number of *qp'*." *Obs.* In all other instances in this same inscription, the statement of recipient is begun with the preposition ***L-***.

Pu *Poen.* 947 (alternate translation) **Itt esde anec nasote hers ahelicot,** "To him I bring a/the shard of hospitality." = NPu *Poen.* 937 **Ythem anech nasothi li yth irs aelichoth sith,** "To him I bring in my behalf this shard of hospitality." = Latin Poen. 958 **ad eum hospitalem hanc tesseram mecum fero.**

NPu 137.5/7 ***NP'L NBL NSKT 'RB' 'LT HMQDŠM 'L . . . WNNTN 'T HKHNM 'T 'RŠ,*** "Four metal vessels were made for these sanctuaries and were given to the priests, to Aris and to Bostar."

Obs. This meaning of the preposition is attested in Byblian Phoenician of the 14th century B.C. in EA 82.15: ***uššira-mi awīlaka ittiya*** ("Send your man to me!). Cf. also EA 87.10 and the common use of the preposition *ʿM* with Ugaritic in this same meaning and function.

FOR the benefit of someone/something

NPu *Poen.* 935/936 **Dobrim chy fel yth chil ys chon ythem liful yth binim,** "I am told that he did everything for his son that he was to do for him." *Obs.* In the Punic version of this statement, the preposition **alt** is used for **yth**: *Poen.* 944/946 **Alem us duber ce fel dono . . . et cil comu con liful alt banim au,** "I am told that his father did everything for that son of his as he was to do <for him>."

ʾT PN *ʾet panê*

Usage

FOR, ON BEHALF OF

60.7/8 *ʾDMM ʾŠ PʿL MŠRT ʾT PN GW,* "People who have done service for the community."

TO, BEFORE, IN THE EYES OF

Byb 10.15/16 *TSRḤ HRBT BʿLT GBL ʾYT HʾDM Hʾ WZRʿW ʾT PN KL ʾLN G[BL],* "The Lady Baalt of Byblos shall make that person and his descendants stink before (be offensive to) all the gods of Byblos."

BEFORE, IN THE PRESENCE OF

Lapethos line 2 *[Y]TT SML MŠ Z BNḤŠT ʾT PN ʾDNY ʾT PNY MLQRT,* "I placed this bronze statue before my Lord, before Milqart."

B- *bi-*

Forms

B-	Ph Pu NPu	*Passim*
BH-	NPu	Trip. 86.3

Latin-letter Spellings

A. Before a Consonant

by-	NPu	*LA* 1 line 8; *Poen.* 934 (bis); *IRT* 906.3

B. Before a Vowel

b-	Pu	*Poen.* 943 (**balim esse** "in this nation")
	NPu	*IRT* 823.3; D 6.5; *Poen.* 934

BN- with Suffixal Pronouns

3.M.Sg.

BN	Ph	Byb 9 A 3; 14.5; 30.4 (bis)

3.F.S.

BN	Ph	26 A III 8

3.M.Pl.

BNM	Ph	14.9

In Neo-Punic, the preposition was *bi-* before a consonant but *b-* before a vowel; cf. Hebrew ***B-*** b^{e}- but *b-* in ***B'LHYM*** *belōhīm.* As yet, there is no evidence extant for the pronunciation of the form ***BN-*** used with the suffix pronouns, nor is the history of this form clear.

Usage

IN

14.3/4 ***WŠKB 'NK BḤLT Z WBQBR Z BMQM 'Š BNT,*** "I lie in this coffin and in this tomb, in the mausolem that I built."

Pu *Poen.* 943/4 **Hu neso bin us es hulec silli balim esse lipane esse con,** "He (my son) was adopted by the man who was my guest-friend in this nation in the past."

NPu *Poen.* 932/3 **Yn byn ui bymarob syllochom, alonim, uybymysyrthochom,** "My brother's son is in your custody, O gods, and under your protection."

IN, OF, specifying the region in which a city is located

B.V. Head, *Historia Nummorum* (London, 1963) p. 790f (legend on coinage of Beirut) ***L'DK' 'Š BKN'N,*** "Laodicaea in Canaan (Phoenicia)." *Cf.* ***'BL MṢRYM 'ŠR B'BR HYRDN,*** "Abel of the Egyptians in the Transjordan"; ***ŠYLH 'ŠR B'RṢ KN'N,*** "Shiloh in the region of Canaan (here, the Cisjordan)".

IN (temporal)

14.1 ***BYRḤ BL BŠNT ʿSR WʾRBʿ 14 LMLKY,*** "In the month of Bul, in year fourteen 14 of his reign."

26 A II 14/15 ***BYMTY KN LʾRṢ . . . ŠBʿ WMNʿM,*** "In my time, the land enjoyed abundance and prosperity." *Et passim.*

AMONG

13.6/8 ***ʾL Y<K>N L<K> ZRʿ BḤYM TḤT ŠMŠ,*** "You shall not have descendants among those living under the sun."

Pu *CIS* I 5510.4/5 ***[WKL ʾ]DM ʾŠ ʾYBL MŠRT WKPT RBTN TNT-PNBʿL WʾDN B[ʿL]ḤMN ʾYT ʾDMM HMT BḤYM ʿL PN ŠMŠ,*** "As for any person who will not serve, our Lady Thinnith-Phanebal and the Lord Baalhammon shall tie up those persons among those living under the sun."

ON

14.16/17 ***WʾNḤN ʾŠ BNN BT LʾŠMN-ŠD QDŠ ʿN YDLL BHR,*** "It was we who built a temple for holy Esmun-SD at En YDLL on the mountain (*or* in the mountains)."

FROM (motion)

14.5/6 ***WʾL YʿMSN BMŠKB Z ʿLT MŠKB ŠNY,*** "Let him not move me from this resting place to another resting place!"

60.6 ***YŠʾN BKSP ʾLM BʿL ṢDN DRKMNM 20,*** "They shall withdraw from the silver of the god Baal of Sidon twenty drachmas."

NPu D 6.5/6 **Badnim garasth is on, / MySyrthim bal sem ra,** "From Adnim I expelled the wicked fellow, / From the Syrthis, him of ill repute."

OF (FROM), expressing provenience or association, of a god or person

17.1/2 ***ʿŠTRT ʾŠ BGW HQDŠ ʾŠ LY,*** "Astarte of GW, my goddess."

18.2/3 ***ʿBDʾLM BN MTN BN ʿBDʾLM BN BʿLŠMR BPLG LʾDK.*** "Abdilim son of Muttun son of Balsamor of/from the district of Laodikaia."

Caquot-Masson, *Syria* 45 (1968) 302-306 line 2 ***RŠP HMKL ʾŠ BʾDYL,*** "Rasep the Annihilator of Idalion" *Cf.* 38.1/2 ***RŠP MKL BʾDYL.***

Lapethos 3=Honeyman, *Le Muséon* 51 (1938) 285-298 line 5 ***ʾSR***

BLPŠ, "Osiris of Lapethos."

NSI 150.5 ***MLQRT BṢR,*** "Milqart of Tyre"

Pu 64.1 ***B'<L>ŠMM B'YNṢM,*** "Baalsamem of Inosim."

Pu 81.1 ***LRBT L'ŠTRT WLTNT BLBNN MQDŠM ḤDŠM <'L>,*** "<Dedicated> to the Lady Astarte and to Thinnith of Lebanon are these new sanctuaries."

Pu 86.3/4 ***'BDMLKT BN 'STRTYTN 'Š B'M BT MLQRT,*** "Abdmilkot son of Astartyaton, a member of the personnel of the temple of Milqart."

NPu 118.2/3 ***NKSP . . . 'Š BBN' M'SNK'W,*** "NKSP, <a member> of the Bane Masanchaw."

NPu 170.2/3 ***'DNBL HŠKŠY 'Š B'M LKŠ,*** "Idnibal the Sexite, <a citizen> of the nation of Lixus."

NPu D 9.1/4 **Yriraban byn Isicuar [i]s ys bAbar Timsiuch,** "Yriraban son of Isicuar, a soldier from the Trans-Timsiuch."

OF, partitive, expressing one of many

26 A III 12 ***MLK BMLKM WRZN BRZNM,*** "Any king or any ruler," *lit.,* "a king among kings, a ruler among rulers."

24.13/14 ***WMY BBNY 'Š YŠB TḤTN,*** "Whichever of my sons shall sit on the throne in my stead."

ANY, SOME, OF, partitive, corresponding to French *de*

NPu 147.3 ***LTT H'L 'B-BRKTM L[N],*** "May God (the god) grant us of his blessings!"

NPu 162.4/5 ***TN L' BTRBT ŠQLT,*** "Give her/him some weighted out interest."

NPu 163.3 ***BL L' BṢMḤ Š'RM,*** "He has no offspring at all of his own flesh."

FOR, TOWARDS, ABOUT, expressing attitude

24.13 ***W'NK TMKT MŠKBM LYD WHMT ŠT NBŠ KM NPŠ YTM B'M,*** "I took the *mškbm* by the hand; and they felt <towards me> as an orphan feels towards a mother."

AT, BY MEANS OF, THROUGH

18.3/4 ***'YT HS'R Z WHDLHT 'Š L P'LT BTKLTY BNTY,*** "I built this gate and its panels at my own expense."

NPu 129.1/3 ***BN' W'YQDŠ T-'KSNDR' WT-'RPT ST BTṢ'TM***

BTM, "He built and dedicated this exedra and portico at his own expense."

WITH

Byb 13.1 ***WKN HN 'NK ŠKB B'RN ZN 'SP BMR WBBDL[Ḥ],*** "And so here do I lie in this coffin, <my bones> gathered <and covered> with myrrh and bdelium."

26 C III 17/18 ***WBRK B'L KRNTRYŠ 'YT 'ZTWD BḤYM WBŠLM WB'Z 'DR 'L KL MLK,*** "May Baal-KRNTRYS bless Aztwadda with long life, with health and with might greater than that of any king!"

NPu 130.5 ***YŠBM 'RB' P'L' B'NŠM 'RKT 'Š 'L HMḤZM,*** "The department of works in charge of marketplaces built <these> benches with money from fines."

NPu 121.2 ***BT'RM BTM P'L W'YQDŠ,*** "He made and dedicated it with his own money."

BECAUSE OF, BY REASON OF

26 A I 12/13 ***B'BT P'LN KL MLK BṢDQY WBḤKMTY WBN'M LBY,*** "And every king adopted me as father because of my honesty, because of my cleverness and because of the excellence of my mind."

OUT OF, expressing intent or purpose

26 A III 15/18 ***'M BḤMDT YS' 'M BŠN'T WBR' YS' HŠ'R Z,*** "Whether he shall tear it out out of love or tear out this gate out of hatred and malice."

OF, expressing material of manufacture

31.1 ***'Z YTN LB'L LBNN 'DNY BR'ŠT NḤŠT,*** "To Baal of Lebanon he presented this <cup> made of the finest bronze."

43.7 ***YŠT BMQDŠ MLQRT 'YT MŠ PN 'BY BNḤŠT.*** "In the sanctuary of Milqart I placed the bust of my father made of bronze."

WORTH

60.1/3 ***'ṬRT ḤRṢ BDRK<M>NM 20,*** "A gold crown worth 20 drachmas."

AT A COST OF

IRT 906.1/3 **Thanubda ubyne Nasif felu myn$yfth [ly]Masauchan byn Iyllul bydenario yl 2100,** "Thanubda and his son Nasif made <this> stele for Masauchan son of Iyllul at a cost *amounting to* 2,100 denars."

IN PAYMENT FOR, IN EXCHANGE FOR

24.8 ***'LMT YTN BŠ WGBR BSWT,*** "One used to give a young woman for a sheep, and a young man for a garment."

Pu 69.3 ***B'LP KLL . . . LKHNM KSP 'ŠRT 10 B'ḤD,*** "For a whole ox, the priests shall receive ten 10 silver for each one."

IN CHARGE OF

Pu 66.1 ***'KLYN . . . 'Š BMMLHT,*** "Cleon, who is in charge of the salt works." = Greek Κλεων ο επι των αλων.

Pu *RCL* 1966 p. 201, line 1 ***PTḤ WP'L 'YT HḤṢ Z LMQM Š'R HḤDŠ 'Š KN BḤ[ṢT],*** "Those in charge of streets opened and built this street of the quarter of Newgate."

AS

Pu Pyrgi lines 1/5 ***LRBT L'ŠTRT 'ŠR QDŠ 'Z 'Š P'L W'Š YTN TBRY' WLNŠ MLK 'L KYŠRY' . . . BMTN 'BBT."*** "<Dedicated> to the Lady Astarte is this sacred *aser* that Tiberius Velanas, King of Caere, made and presented as a gift in the temple."

Pu 69.14 ***[']L BLL W'L ḤLB W'L ḤLB W'L KL ZBḤ 'Š 'DM LZBḤ BMNḤ[T] Y[KN LKHNM . . .],*** "For mash or for fat or for milk or for any sacrifice that one shall make as a *minḥīt*-offering, the priests shall receive [. . .]."

NPu 34 ***N'Š' ŠDBR L'DN B'LMN BMLK 'ZRM 'YŠ,*** "SDBR brought a male sacrificial offering to the Lord Baalhammon as a *molk*-offering."

WITH, in the sense of wearing or bearing

Byb 11 ***B'RN ZN 'NK BTN'M . . . ŠKBT BSWT WMR'Š WMḤSM LPY,*** "In this coffin do I, Bitnoam, lie, wearing a garment and a head-piece and a mouth-muzzle."

Pu 78.4/6 ***MNṢBT PSLT . . . 'BN 'RKT BKRŠ B'LḤMN,*** "A sculpted stela, being a tall stone with/bearing the figure of Baalhammon."

B-GW *bigō*

Usage

INSIDE, WITHIN; cf. Aramaic ***B-GW'*** *b^egō'*.

NPu Trip. 86.3/4 ***W'T KRY KRY 'T HŠD ŠBN' ḤN' BN MTN 'Š LM BHGW ʿR BʿMQT ŠHTʿM'R,*** "Buy, buy the land of the sons of Hanno bin Muttun that they own inside the city in the Palm Valley."

BD *bod, bad-*

Forms

BD	Ph	60.3; Akko lines 1/2; *CIS* i 87.1/4
	Pu	*CIS* i 4901
bod	Pu	*Poen.* 949
	NPu	*Poen.* 939; *IRT* 892
bud	NPu	*PBSR* 28 p. 53 no. 5

With Prepositions

1.Sg.		
BDY *badí*	Pu	Pyrgi line 6
3.Pl.		
BDNM	Ph	14.6

The preposition ***BD*** is in origin a contraction of ***B-YD*** ("in/from/by the hand of someone"); accordingly, since it is a noun governed by a preposition, it must take the form of the suffixal pronoun affixed to the noun in the genitive case: *e.g.*, ***BD-Y*** ("of him"); ***BD-NM*** ("by them").

Usage

BY, OF, FROM, expressing human agency

1. Agent of an active transitive verb

Pu Pyrgi line 1/6 ***LRBT LʿŠTRT 'ŠR QDŠ 'Z 'Š PʿL . . . TBRY' WLNŠ MLK ʿL KYŠRY' . . . K-ʿŠTRT 'RŠ BDY,*** "<Dedicated> to the Lady Astarte is this sacred *aser* that Tiberius Velanas, King of Caere, made <for her>, because she requested it of him."

Pu *Poen.* 949 **Anec litor bod es iussim limin co,** "Let me inquire of these men who are coming out from here." = NPu *Poen.* 939 **Bod i(ly) a(nech) lythera ymu ys lomyn choth iusim.**

NPu *IRT* 892.3/5 **Bycys Cae(u)s en bod Dubren allonim,** "Gaius sought/seeks favor from Dubren, his god."

2. *Agent of an Intransitive or Passive Verb*

14.5 ***'P 'M 'DMM YDBRNK 'L TŠM' BDNM,*** "Even if people tell you <to violate this tomb>, do not be pesuaded by them!"

60.1/3 ***TM BD ṢDNM BN'SPT L'ṬR 'YT ŠM'B'L . . . 'ṬRT ḤRṢ,*** "It has been deemed good by the Sidonians in assembly to crown Samobaal with a gold crown."

Akko lines 1/2 ***BD TLBN ḤRŠ 'Š YTN 'GN WB'LŠ<'>LT 'Š 'L 'ŠRT,*** "<Received> by TLBN is the pottery that 'GN and Baalsa'alti, the officials in charge of temples, delivered <to him>."

NPu *PBSR* 28 p. 53 no. 5.10/11 **Felu tabula y bud bannom,** "That <inscribed> tablet was made by their son."

IN THE POSSESSION OF <SOMEONE>, OWNED BY"

Pu *CIS* i 4901.3/4 ***ŠPṬ 'Š ṢDN BD 'DNM BD MLKYTN,*** "Safot, a slave owned by his master Milkyaton."

Pu *CIS* i 4905.3/5 ***ŠPṬ BN MṢLḤ 'Š ṢDN BD 'DNY BD ḤMLKT,*** "Safot bin Meslih, a slave in the possession of his master Himilco."

IN THE CHARGE OF

CIS i 87.1/4 ***BD 'BD'LM . . . P'LM 145 BD MNḤM . . . P'LM 22,*** "In the charge of Abdilim are 145 workmen; in the charge of Menehhem are 22 workmen."

B-DṢ L-

Usage

CONTRARY TO; etymology obscure

Pu 69.20 ***KL KHN 'Š YQḤ MŠ'T BDṢ L'Š ŠT BPS Z WN'N[Š],*** "As for any priest who shall accept a payment that is contrary to what is set down in this inscription, he shall be fined."

BY *bī*

The preposition ***BY*** is in origin ***B-'Y,*** the preposition ***B-*** and the negative particle *'Y*, having as analogue Hebrew ***B-L'*** *b*^{e}*lō*. The preposition is attested in Punic only, Phoenician using ***DL.***

Usage

WITHOUT

Pu 79.6/11 ***KL 'Š LSR T-'BN Z BY PY 'NK WBY PY 'DM BŠMY WŠPṬ TNT-PNB'L BRḤ 'DM H',*** "As for anyone who shall remove this stele without my permission or without the permission of someone authorized by me, Thinnith-Phanebal shall condemn that person."

Pu *CIS* i 5522.4 ***HTRŠM BMYP'L 'DN . . . ḤNM BY KSP,*** "He signed himself back into the employ of his master of his own free will <and> without <payment of> silver."

BLT bilti

Usage

SAVE, EXCEPT, BUT; *cf.* Heb *bilti.*

13.5 ***KL MNM MŠD BLT 'NK ŠKB B'RN Z,*** "Nothing at all *of value* but me (my body) lies in this coffin."

B-MTKT ?bimatūkot

Usage

IN THE MIDST OF; cf. Hebrew ***BTWK*** *b*^{e}*tôk.*

24.5/6 ***KN BT 'BY BMTKT MLKM 'DRM,*** "My royal house was in the midst of those of more powerful kings."

B-'BR bi'abūr

Usage

BECAUSE OF, THANKS TO

26 A II 5/6 ***BYMTY 'ŠT T<L>K LḤDY DL PLKM B'BR B'L W'LM,*** "In my time, a woman is able to travel alone, without bodyguards, because (thanks to) of Baal and the gods."

BECAUSE OF, FOR THE SAKE OF; *cf.* Hebrew ***B'BWR*** *ba*$^{'a}$*abūr*

26 A II 10/12 ***B'L WRŠP ṢPRM ŠLḤN LBNT WBNY 'NK B'BR***

B'L WB'BR RŠP ṢPRM, "Baal and Rasap-SPRM commissioned me to build it (the city of Aztwaddiya), so I built it because of (for the sake of) Baal and because of (for the sake of) Rasap-SPRM."

DL *?dal < dall*

Usage

WITHOUT

26 A II 3/6 ***BMQMM 'Š KN LPNM NŠT'M . . . WBYMTY 'NK 'ŠT T<L>K LḤDY DL PLKM,*** "In places that were dangerous in the past, in my time a woman walks alone without bodyguards." *Obs.* For "without," Punic uses the preposition ***BY*** *bī.*

K- *k^e-*

Forms

K-	Ph	43.12
	Pu	69.17
ce-	NPu	*IRT* 827 in the personal name **Micebal**

It is uncertain whether the preposition is the reflex of Canaanite proclitic **ka-* as is Hebrew *k^e-* or is the reflex of the independent (non-proclitic) preposition **kī* used in Akkadian; the Neo-Punic Latin-letter spelling **ce** is ambiguous. In light however of the co-occurrence in Phoenician-Punic of the independent form ***KM*** *k^emū,* it is perhaps likelier that ***K*** is the proclitic *k^e-*. The preposition ***K-*** is relatively uncommon in Phoenician-Punic, which preferred the independent form ***KM.***

Usage

LIKE

NPu *IRT* 827.1/2 in the personal name **Micebal** (***MYKB'L***), "Who is like Baal?" Cf. the Hebrew personal name ***MYK'L*** *mī-kaʾel* ("Who is like God?").

ACCORDING TO, IN ACCORDANCE WITH

43.10/12 ***KM ZBḤT . . . YM MD YM . . . [BḤD]ŠM WBSKS'M YRḤ MD YRḤ 'D 'LM KQDM,*** "So, too, did I make sacrifice daily and monthly on the new moons and full moons, regularly, in accordance with ancient practice."

Pu 69.16/18 ***WKL 'DMM 'Š YZBḤ [ZBḤ WYTN] H'DMM HMT MŠ'T 'L ZBḤ KMDT ŠT BKTB[T 'Š BD ŠLŠM H'Š 'Š 'L HMŠ'TT],*** "As for all persons who shall offer a sacrifice, those persons shall pay a payment for a sacrifice in accordance with the amount set down in the document held by the Thirty Men in charge of Payments."

KM *k^{o}mū k^{u}mū*

Forms

KM	Ph-NPu	Byb 11; 24.10
comu	Pu	*Poen.* 945A
cumu	Pu	*Poen.* 945A

The preposition is the reflex of Canaanite **kamō*; Hebrew *k^{e}mō*. The Punic Latin-letter spellings **comu** and **cumu**, which co-occur as conflates in *Poen.* 945, display coloring of the *shewa* through forward assimilation to the final u-vowel.

Usage

LIKE

Byb 11 ***B'RN ZN 'NK BTN'M 'M MLK 'ZB'L MLK GBL BN PLṬB'L KHN B'LT ŠKBT BSWT WMR'Š 'LY WMḤSM LPY KM 'Š LMLKYT 'Š KN LPNY,*** "In this coffin lie I, Bitnoam, mother of King Azbaal, King of Byblos son of Pelletbaal, Priest of Astarte, I wearing a garment and head-piece and muzzle like those <worn by> the queens of Byblos who preceded me."

24.9/10 ***LPN HMLKM HLPNYM YTLKN MŠKBM KM KLBM,*** "Before the kings who preceded me the *mškbm* used to go about like dogs."

See also ***KM*** and ***KM 'Š*** under Conjunctions.

L- *li-* (vars. *lo-*, *la-*)

Forms

L-	Ph Pu NPu	*Passim*

Latin and Greek-letter Spellings

A. Before a consonant:

la-	NPu	*Poen.* 939 **lasibithim**
le-	Pu	*Poen.* 995 **leadrumit**
li-	NPu	*IRT* 873.3 **libinim**; *AI* 1 line 1 **lifnim**; *LA* 1 1964 p. 45 no. 4.1/2 **liiyra**; *Poen.* 1013 **limin**
lo-	NPu	*IRT.* 893.2/3 **loby[t]hem**; *IRT* 828.1/2 **loby[th]im**; *Poen.* 939 **lomyn**
ly-	NPu	*IRT* 893.3/4 **lybanem**; *IRT* 901.5 **lybythi**; *AI* line 2 **lybythem**; *IRT* 906.2 **[l]yMasauchan**) *IRT* 827.1 **lymyth**
λυ-	Pu	*EH* Gr. 1.1 λυΒαλαμουν

B. Before a vowel:

l-	NPu	S 24.2 **labunom**; *AI* line 3 **luia**; *AI* line 3 **lysthim**) *AI* line 3 **lys**
λ-	Ph	174.8 λαφδε
	Pu	*EH* Gr. 1.1 λαδουν

With Suffixal Pronouns

1.Sg.		
LY *lī*	Ph-NPu	Byb 9 A 1; 17.2
li	NPu	*IRT* 901.5; *Poen.* 937
3.M.Sg.		
L *lo*	Ph	Byb 12.3; 18.4
lo	NPu	D 5.19
3.F.Sg.		
L *la*	Ph	26 A III 16
L'	NPu	143.3 ***ŠL'***
1 Pl.		
LN	Ph	14.18; 60.4
2.M.Pl.		
lochom	NPu	*Poen.* 933 **syllochom**
3.M.Pl.		
LM	Ph	14.8, 11; Umm el-Awamid 6.3

The preferred form of the preposition was *li-* (**le-, li-, ly-**) and, in the Neo-Punic period, *l-* before a vowel. The origin of the vowel in the form **lo-** is uncertain. The most uncommon of the forms was **la-,** appearing once, in **lasibit-**; cf. however Hebrew ***LŠBT*** *lašébet*, with the same form of the preposition.

Usage

FOR

Byb 1.1 ***'RN ZP'L [']TB'L BN 'ḤRM MLK GBL L'ḤRM 'BH,*** "Coffin that Ittobaal son of Ahiram, King of Byblos, made for his father Ahiram."

Pu 101.1 ***T-MQDŠ Z BN' B'L' TBGG LMSNSN HMMLKT,*** "The citizens of Thugga built this sanctuary for King Massinissa."

NPu *IRT* 873.1/4 **Myntsyfth ymu fel Bibi Mythunilim uintseb libinim Mythunilim,** "<This is the stele> that Bibi Mythunilim made and erected to his son Mythunilim." *Et passim.*

TO

31.1 ***'Z YTN LB'L LBNN 'DNY,*** "He presented this to Baal of Lebanon, his Lord."

34.1/3 ***MṢBT 'Z 'Š YṬN' 'RŠ . . . L'BY . . . WL'MY,*** "<This is> the stele that Aris erected to his father and to his mother." *Et passim.*

174.1/8 Αφεθενναυ υιος Αφεσαθουν νεσε οθ αμαθη λεσαθ λαφδε Μα[. . .], "Abdthennau son of Abdsaphun gave his female slave as a wife to his slave Ma[. . .]."

OF, expressing the indirect gentive

14.1 ***BŠNT 'SR W'RB' 14 LMLKY MLK 'ŠMN'ZR,*** "In year fourteen 14 of the reign of King Esmunazor."

NPu *LA* 1 1964 p. 45 no. 4.1/2 **[Bys]ys asar liiyra Chirur,** "On the sixteenth of the month of Kirur."

53.1/2 ***MṢBT SKR BḤYM L'BDTNT BN 'BDŠMŠ HṢDNY,*** "<This is> the memorial stele among the living of Abdtinnit son of Abdsemes the Sidonian."

Pu *Poen.* 995 **Anno bin Mutumbal leadrumet anec,** "I am Hanno son of Mythumbal of Hadrumetum." = NPu **Anno byn Mythumbal le adremeth anech.**

53.1 ***MṢBT SKR BḤYM L'BDTNT,*** "Memorial stele among the living of Abdtinnit."

CIS i 59.1/2 ***MṢB BḤYM L'BD'ŠMN,*** "Stele among the living of Abdesmun."

Pu/NPu *Poen.* 995A **Anno byn Mytthumbal leadrumit anech** = *Poen.* 995P **Anno byn Mythumbal leadrebeth anech,** "I am Hanno son of Mittunbal of Hadrumetum."

46.35 ***ŠLM H'Š LMṢB,*** "May the people of the colony prosper!"

NPu *Poen.* 938 **Ily gubulim lasibithim,** "This is the quarter where he resides," *lit.*, "these are the environs of his residence." The Punic of this same line (*Poen.* 948) uses the determinative pronoun: **<esse> mucom sussibti,** "This is the place of his residence."

Obs. The indirect genitive marker ***L-*** had specific functions not exercised by the other markers of the indirect genitival relationship. It served to express a genitival relationship between two governing nouns and a governed noun: the first of the governing nouns is in direct genitive but the second in indirect genitive:

35.2/3 ***MŠKB NḤTY L'LM WL'ŠTY,*** "My and my wife's eternal resting-place," *lit.*, "My eternal resting-place and <that> of my wife."

Umm el-Awamid ***MṢBT B'LŠMR [WL]'MN 'ŠT,*** "The stele of Baalsamor and 'MN, his wife." *lit.*, "The stele of Baalsamor and <that> of 'MN, his wife."

It is also normal in date formula, serving to express an indirect genitive relationship between a numeral and year or month:

14.1 ***ŠNT 'SR W'RB' 14 LMLKY,*** "Year fourteen 14 of his reign."

19.8 ***ŠLŠ ḤMŠM ŠT L'M ṢR,*** "Year fifty-three of the nation of Tyre."

Pu 111.3/5 ***ŠŠT 'RB'M ŠT LMLKY MSNSN,*** "Year forty-six of the reign of Masinissa." *Obs.* Once, quite exceptionally, in Punic the determinative pronoun is used instead in this construction: 101.1 ***ŠT 'SR Š[MLKY] MKWSN,*** "Year ten of the reign of Micipsa."

The genitive marker ***L-*** is that used in the inverted indirect genitive. In the inverted indirect genitive, the governed noun (with ***L-***) precedes the governing noun; the latter may receive a possessive pronoun that refers back to the governed noun.

Umm el-Awamid 9.1 ***LB'LŠMR . . . SKR,*** "The memorial of Baalsamor," *lit.*, "Of Baalsamor, his memorial (*sikro*)."

43.5 ***L'M LPT ŠNT 33,*** "Year 33 of the nation of Lapethos," *lit.*, "Of the nation of Lapethos, year 33."

Pu Pyrgi line 7 ***LMLKY ŠNT ŠLŠ 3,*** "Year three 3 of his reign," *lit.*, "Of his reign, year three 3."

NPu 145.4 ***L’LM HQYDŠ LŠ’T ’ḤT ŠMM,*** “Exalt the name of the holy god!”, *lit.*, “Of the holy god, exalt his name!”

Obs. This inverted construction is found in Hebrew, Ugaritic and Akkadian: Hebrew ***LYHWDH NḤŠWN BN ‘MYNDB,*** “Nahshon son of Aminadab of Judah” (Numbers 1:7); Ugaritic ***DT YRQ NQBNM,*** “The trappings of gold,” *lit.*, “Of gold, the trappings”; Akkadian ***ša Tiāmat karassa,*** “the anger of Tiamat,” *lit.*, “Of Tiamat her anger.”

BY, expressing agent of a passive verb

60.4/5 ***R‘T Z LKTB H’DMM ’Š NŠ’M LN ‘L BT ’LM ‘LT MṢBT ḤRṢ,*** “The persons who were elected by us in charge of the temple shall inscribe this resolution on a gold stele.”

AS, LIKE, expressing predication

26 A I 3 ***P‘LN B‘L LDNNYM L’B WL’M,*** “Baal made me a father and a mother to the Danunians.”

Lapethos 3.2/3 ***[YT]T SML MŠ Z BNḤŠT ’T PN MLQRT . . . LSKRN BḤYM,*** “I placed this statue before Milaqart as a memorial among the living.”

NPu *JA* 1967 p. 63 lines 1/2 ***L’DN LB‘L HQDŠ BYM N‘M LMLK,*** “<This child sacrificial victim was presented> to the Lord Baal the Holy on the “Good Day” as a *molk*-offering.”

174.1/8 **Αφεθενναυ υιος Αφεσαθουν νεσε οθ αμαθη λεσαθ λαφδε Μα[. . .],** “Abdthennau son of Abdsaphun gave his female slave as a wife to his slave Ma[. . .].”

L-B- *libi-*

Usage

A single instance of this compound preposition occurs, in Punic. It is equivalent in function and meaning to the simple preposition ***B-*** and to the compound preposition ***LMB-***.

FOR, IN PAYMENT FOR

Pu 69.12 ***[‘]L ṢPR ’M QDMT QDŠT ’M ZBḤ ṢD ’M ZBḤ ŠMN LKHNM KSP ’[GRT] 10 LB’ḤD,*** “For a bird or a sacred *qdšt* or a sacrifice of game or a sacrifice of oil, the priests shall receive 10 *’grt* for each.” Elsewhere in this same text, the simple preposition ***B-*** is used in essentially identical statements: line 3 ***B’LP KLL . . . LKH-***

NM KSP ʿŠRT 10 BʾḤD, "For an entire ox, the priests shall receive ten 10 silver weight for each." *Cf.* also lines 7, 11.

L-L- *lili-*

Usage

A single instance of this compound preposition occurs, in late Neo-Punic. It is equivalent in function and meaning to the simple preposition ***L-*** **;** *cf.* Hebrew *mimmen-* < *min-min* in *mimmennī* ("from me").

NPu IRT 828.1/2 **Mintsyft[h m]u fel Baricbal Typafi loby[ni]m . . . ulilyst<h>im . . . mythem,** "<This is> the stele that Baricbal Typafi made for his deceased son and wife."

L-MN *limin*

Forms

LM-	NPu	145 III 14
limin	Pu	*Poen.* 949, 1014
lomyn	NPu	*Poen.* 939

Usage

FROM

NPu 145 III 12/14 ***ŠMʾT HMZRḤ ʾŠ ʾYKRMʾ T-HMNḤT QRʾ LMMʿL MTʾ,*** "<Here are> the names <of the members of> the sodality who honored him. Read what is set down from top to bottom."

Pu *Poen.* 949 **Anec litor bod es iussim limin co,** "Let me inquire of these men who are coming out from here." = NPu *Poen.* 939 **Bod i(ly) a(nech) lythera ymu ys lomyn choth iusim.**

Pu *Poen.* 1014 **Lec lacanna limin co,** "Go! Go away from here!"

L-MN . . . WʿD *limin . . . weʿad*

Usage

FROM . . . TO, expressing extent

26 A I 4/5 ***YRḤB ʾNK ʾRṢ ʿMQ ʾDN LMMṢʾ ŠMŠ WʿD MBʾY,*** "I enlarged the land of Adana Valley from East to West (*lit.*, from the place of the exit of the sun to the place of its entry)."

26 A II 1/3 ***BKL GBL ʿMQ ʾDN LMMṢʾ ŠMŠ WʿD MBʾY,*** "Throughout the territory of the Adana Valley form East to West."

FROM . . . TO, BOTH . . . AND, expressing inclusivity

Pu 65.2, 81.1/6 ***[LM]'DRNM W'D Ṣ'RNM,*** "The great and the small among them."

L-M(N)-B- limibbi-

Usage

This compound preposition is identical in all its meanings and functions to the simple preposition ***B-***.

IN

Pu 69.5 ***'GL 'Š QRNY LMBMḤSR,*** "A calf whose horns are absent (*lit.*, in absence)."

NPu 124.1/2 ***G'Y BN ḤN' LMBŠM G'Y BN BNM M'QR <YTN> T-'MDM WT-HM'Q'M YGN WT-HMḤZ RBD LMBMLKTM BTM,*** "Gaius son of Hanno presented the columns and roofed the structure and paved the forum at his own expense in the name of Gaius, the son of his son Macer." Compare ***LMBŠM*** to simple ***BŠM*** in *IRT* 877.1: **Centenari mu fel Thlana Marci Cecili byMupal efsem <M>acer byn banem Bucu buo,** "<This is> the fortified farmhouse that Thlana Marcius Caeciliuis son of Mupal built in the name of Macer, the son of his son Bucu, his (Macer's) father."

IN (temporal), DURING

35.1/2 ***MṢBT LMBḤYY YTN'T 'L MŠKB NḤTY,*** "I erected <this> stele at my resting-place during my lifetime."

Pu 81.1/6 ***LRBT L'ŠTRT WLTNT BLBNN MQDŠM ḤDŠM <'L> KM KL 'Š BM[M] . . . 'Š YB' 'LT HḤRZ ŠMQDŠM 'L . . . LMBYRḤ ḤYR ŠPṬM 'BDMLQRT W[. . .]Y,*** "<Belonging> to the Lady Astarte and to Thinnith of Lebanon are these new sanctuaries as well as everything that is in them that was brought into the custody of these sanctuaires in the month of Hiyyar <in the year of> the suffetres Abdmilqart and [. . .]ay."

Trip. 14.1/2 ***['B]DMLQRT BN ḤNB'L . . . P'L' . . . LMBMḤY',*** "Abdmilqart son of Annobal made it during his lifetime."

WITH, AT. BY MEANS OF

NPu 126.10/11 ***MZBḤ WP'DY P'L LMBMLKTM BTM,*** "He built the altar and the podium at his own expense."

NPu 130.2 ***TMNM DN'RY' ŠMNM WKNDRM TŠ' LMB'NŠM,***

"Their (the benches) cost of eighty denars and nine quadrans <was met with money derived> from fines."

L-M(N)-B- . . . WʿD ʾT *limibb- . . . weʿad ʾet*

Usage

FROM . . . TO, expressing distance between two objects

NPu ***LMBʾBN ʾŠ ʿL HSYWʿT WʿD ʾT ʾBN Z MRṢM MʾTM WʾRBʿM,*** "From the stone that is next to the *sywʿt* to this stone is <a distance of> two hundred *stadia.*"

L-ʿN *liʿênê*

Usage

ON THE PART OF, BY, FROM; *lit.,* IN THE EYES OF

Byb 10.9 ***[WTTN LY HRBT Bʿ]LT GBL ḤN LʿN ʾLNM WLʿN ʿM ʾRṢ Z.*** "May the Lady Baalt of Byblos grant me favor on the part of the gods and on the part of the people of this land."

48.4 ***[WT]TN LM ḤN WḤYM LʿN ʾLNM WBN ʾDM,*** "And grant ye to them favor and long life on the part of the gods and men."

LPY *lipī*

Usage

BECAUSE OF, BY REASON OF, ON ACCOUNT OF

NPu 126.7/9 ***LPNY ʾDRʾ ʾLPQY WʿM ʾLPQ[Y] LPY MʾSʾ ʾBTY WMʾSM BTM YTNʾ LʿBD BṢPʾT KL ḤʿT,*** "The senate of Lepcis and the people of Lepcis granted to him <the right> to make use of the broad senatorial purple stripe always."

IN ACCORDANCE WITH

Pu 69.18 ***[K]L MŠʾT ʾŠ ʾYBL ŠT BPS Z WNTN LPY HKTBT ʾŠ [BD ŠLŠM HʾŠ ʾŠ ʿL HMŠʾTT],*** "As for any payment that is not set down in this inscription, it shall be given in accordance <with what is set down in> the book that is in the possession of the thirty men who are in charge of payments."

L-PN lipanê

Forms

LPN	Ph	24.10
lipane	Pu	*Poen.* 943/44P

With suffix pronouns:

Sg. 1.		
LPNY *lipnay*	Ph	Byb 11
Sg.3.M.		
LPNY *lipnêyo*	Ph	CID 9 AB
	NPu	126.7

Usage

BEFORE, IN THE PRESENCE OF

24.9/10 ***LPN HMLKM HLPNYM YTLKN MŠKBM KM KLBM,*** "In the presence of the kings who preceded me the *mškbm* used to go about like dogs." Non-literal translation: "The *mškbm* (members of the lower class) were treated like dogs by the kings who preceded me."

BEFORE (temporal)

Byb 11 ***B'RN ZN 'NK BTN'M . . . ŠKBT BSWT WMR'Š 'LY WMḤSM LPY KM 'Š LMLKYT 'Š KN LPNY,*** "I, Bitnoam, lie in this coffin, wearing a garment and a head-piece and a mouth-muzzle like those of the queens who were before me."

TO (dative)

CID 9AB ***WMṢ' LPNY PHLŠ HML'K,*** "PHLS the messenger came to him."

NPu 126.7/9 ***[ṬYBRY QLWDY S'SṬY] . . . 'Š LPNY 'DR' 'LPQY W'M 'LPQ[Y] . . . YTN' L'BD BṢP'T KL Ḥ'T,*** "Tiberius Claudius Sestius, to whom the senate and people of Lepcis granted <the right> to make use of the broad senatorial purple stripe always."

MN *min-*

Forms

M-	Ph	33.2
min	Pu	*Poen.* 949 in **limin**
myn	NPu	*Poen.* 939 in **lomyn**
my-	NPu	D 6.5/7

The preposition ***MN*** is relatively uncommon in Phoenician-Punic; preferred is the compound preposition ***LMN.*** Both the proclitic form *mi(n)-* and the independent (non-proclitic) *min* occur.

Usage

FROM
NPu D 6.5/7 **Badnim garasth is on, // MySyrthim bal sem ra,** "From Adnim I expelled the wicked fellow, / From the Syrthis, him of ill repute."

OF, expressing material
33.2/3 ***[S]MLT '[Z] 'Š YTN WYṬN' MNḤŠT . . . LRBTY L'ŠTRT,*** "<It is> this statue made of bronze that he presented and erected to his Lady Astarte."

FROM, OF, expressing origin
Pu 116.2/4 ***'BD'ŠMN BN M'DR 'Š KN'N MQ̧RMN,*** "Abdesmun son of Me'edder, a Phoenician from Q̧erumin."

NGD *neged*

Usage

FACING, OPPOSITE; Hebrew ***NGD*** *neged.*
NPu 147.2 ***[N]GD HŠMM ND'R NDR',*** "Facing Heaven they (the members of the sodality) prayed."

ʿD ʿad

Usage

AS FAR AS, TO; Hebrew ***ʿD*** *ʿad.*

CIS I 113.1 ***ʾNK ʾŠMNYTN . . . ʿLT ʿD SHRW,*** "I, Esmunyaton, sailed upstream as far as SHRW."

UNTIL (temporal)

Pu *CIS* I 6000.5 ***KM KHN BḤYY QDŠM ʿBD WʾLNM ŠMŠ ʿD LʾTY,*** "During his lifetime he served the holy ones like a priest, yea, he served the gods until he became too weak <to do so>."

Pu 78.1 ***YBRKY WYŠMʿ QL ʿD ʿLM,*** "May he bless him and hear his voice (petitions) for ever."

See also the co-ordinated prepositional phrases ***L-MN . . . WʿD*** and ***L-M-B- . . . WʿD ʾT*** ("from . . . to"); and the conjunction ***ʿD ʾŠ*** ("as soon as, when").

ʿL ʿal

Forms

ʿLY *ʿála*	Arch Byb	1.2
ʿL *ʿal*	Ph Pu NPu	26 A I 7, *et passim*
al	Pu	*Poen.* 941
	NPu	*Poen.* 931

With suffix pronouns:

1.Sg.		
ʿLY *ʿalay*	Ph	Byb 3.6; 24.7
2.M.Sg.		
ʿLK *ʿalêka*	Byb	Byb 3.5
3.M.Sg.		
ʿLY *ʿalêyo*	Ph	24.8
3.M.Pl.		
ʿLN[M] *ʿalênom*	Ph	Kition line 3

The archaic form ***ʿLY***, found once, in Old Byblian (tenth century B.C.E.), was perhaps pronounced *ʿála*; cf. Arabic ***ʿLY*** *ʿála;* but compare also archaic Hebrew ***ʿLY,*** vocalized *ʿ^a^lê* by the Massoretes. The pre-suffixal allomorph of *ʿal* was, as in Hebrew, *ʿalê-*. In Phoenician-Punic, the preposition ***ʿL*** has the free variant form ***ʿLT*** *ʿalt,* with excrescent -t (see below).

Usage

IN CHARGE OF

Byb 1.1 ***ʾL MLK BMLKM SKN BS<K>NM WTMʾ MḤNT ʿLY GBL WYGL ʾRN Z TḤTSP ḤṬR MŠPṬH THTPK KSʾ MLKH,*** "As for any king or any governor or any general of the army in charge of Byblos, if he shall remove this coffin, his imperial sceptre shall break, <and> his royal throne shall overturn."

60.2 ***ŠMʿBʿL BN MGN ʾŠ NŠʾ HGW ʿL BT ʾLM Wʿ L MBNT ḤṢR BT ʾLM,*** "Samobaal son of Mago, whom the community elected in charge of the temple and in charge of the building of the temple court."

Pu 80.1 ***ḤDŠ WPʿL ʾYT HMṬBḤ Z . . . HʾŠM ʾŠ ʿL HMQDŠM,*** "The men who are in charge of the sanctuaries rebuilt this slaughtering table."

NPu 137/2/3 ***KNʾ ʿL MLKT HBNʾ ʾŠ BMQDŠM ʾL,*** "In charge of the building project were those who are in charge of these sanctuaries."

TO (direction)

Pu Poen. 941 **Al bet lo cu cian bate,** "To his house here have I now come." = NPu Poen. 941 **Al byth ybar ui mysethi,** "To the house of my brother's friend have I come."

FROM

Byb 1.2 ***WNḤT TBRḤ ʿL GBL,*** "And peace shall depart from Byblos."

FOR the benefit of, ON BEHALF OF

40.3/4 ***HSMLM HʾL ʾŠ YṬNʾ BTŠLM . . . ʿL BN BNY,*** "Bitsalom erected these statues for her grandsons."

Pu *EH* 122.1/3 ***NDR MTNYBʿL LBʿLʿMN ʿL ḤTMLKT BT YʾRḤM,*** "Mittanibaal vowed <this> on behalf of Otmilkot daughter of Yʾ RHM."

FOR (dative)

Byb 3.2/6 ***TŠ'M Š<Q>LM KSP NŠBT 'M NḤL TNḤL MGŠTK 'LK WMGŠT 'LY,*** "Let us *share/divide* the ninety sheqels of silver: when you come into possession of it (the silver), your share will be for you, and my share will be for me."

AT, ALONGSIDE

35.1/2 ***MṢBT LMBḤYY YṬN'T 'L MŠKB NḤTY L'LM,*** "<This is> the stele that I erected when I was still alive at/alongside my eternal resting-place."

IN ACCORDANCE WITH

NPu 172.2/3 ***HPRṬ 'L MYṬB' RŠ' HSLKY LBN'T T-HMQDŠ ST,*** "He undertook to build this sanctuary with the consent of the senate of Sulcis."

IN PAYMENT FOR

Pu 69.14 ***[']L BLL W'L ḤLB W'L ḤLB W'L KL ZBḤ 'Š 'Š 'DM LZBḤ BMNḤ[T] Y[KN LKHNM . . .],*** "For mash or for fat or for milk or for any sacrifice that a person shall sacrifice as a *minḥīt*-offering, the priests shall receive [. . .]."

BECAUSE OF, BY REASON OF, ON ACCOUNT OF

NPu 123.2/5 ***TYN' L'ḤT 'MM . . . SKR KBD 'L P'LT M'ŠRT.*** "He erected <this> as a memorial of honor to his mother's sister because of her accomplishment of public service."

NPu 145 I 5/6 ***B'L ḤRDT 'L GBRTM,*** "<The god Mescar is> one who commands fear because of his might."

NPu 165.4 ***W'L KL KTM M'Ṣ' L' QMT,*** "And because of all his honesty he acquired high respect for himself."

AGAINST

24.7/8 ***WŠKR 'NK 'LY MLK 'ŠR,*** "I hired the king of Assyria against him."

MORE THAN, expressing comparative degree

24.7 ***W'DR 'LY MLK D[N]NYM WŠKR 'NK 'LY MLK 'ŠR,*** "The king of the Danunians was more powerful than I, so I hired against him the king of Assyria."

26 A III 2/4 ***WBRK B'L . . . 'YT 'ZTWD . . . 'Z 'DR 'L KL***

MLK, "Baal bless Aztwadda with strength greater than that of any other king."

TOGETHER WITH, AND

NPu 117.3/5 ***B'N' T'NBR' 'ŠT['] 'L PWDNŠ WŠ'W'{W'}R' WM'K[ŠM]" B'N[Y'},*** "His wife Thanubra and his sons Pudens and Severus and Maximus built <this tomb>." The conjunction **et** is found in the corresponding Latin: **Thanubra coniunx et Pudens et Severus et Maxsimus f(ilii) piissimi p(atri) amantissimo s(ua) p(ecunia) f(ecerunt).**

UPON, expressing addition

26 A 6/8 ***WP'L 'NK SS 'L SS WMGN 'L MGN WMḤNT 'L MḤNT,*** "And I acquired horse upon horse and shield upon shield and army upon army."

'L PN *'al panê*

Usage

OPPOSITE, FACING

Byb 10.4/5 ***HPTḤ ḤRṢ ZN 'Š 'L PN PTḤY Z,*** "And yonder gold inscription that is in opposite this inscription of mine here."

Pu *CIS* i 5510.4/5 ***BḤYM 'L PN ŠMŠ,*** "Among those living facing [*i.e.*, under] the sun." *Cf.* 13.7/8 ***BḤYM TḤT ŠMŠ,*** "among those living under the sun."

IN FRONT OF

Pu 81.3 ***H'LM 'Š 'L PN HMQDŠ[M 'L],*** "The columns that are in front of these sanctuaries."

NPu 173.1 ***[HMQDŠ . . . W]HMZBḤM 'Š 'L PNY,*** "The sanctuary and the altars that are in front of it."

'LT *'alt*

Forms

'LT	Byb	9 A 2, B 4
	Ph	14.10; 43.13; 60.6, *et passim*
	Pu	81.4
	NPu	137.4
alt	Pu	*Poen.* 946

With suffix pronous:

1.Sg.
'LTY *'altay* Pu 89.4,5

3.M.Sg.
'LT *'altêyo* Ph 13.4,6,7; 14.20,21

The preposition ***'LT*** *'alt* is the preposition ***'L*** *'al* with excrescent *-t.* The two forms of the preposition are without difference in function and meaning, and are used freely in the same text as, for instance, in the Phoenician inscription from the Piraeus (*KAI* 60). The preposition perhaps had the form *'altê-* before suffixal pronouns.

Usage

ON, UPON

60.4/5 ***'YT R'T Z LKTB H'DMM . . . 'LT MṢBT ḤRṢ,*** "The men shall inscribe this resolution upon a gold stele."

TO, expressing addition

14.18/20 ***W'D YTN LN . . . D'R WYPY . . . WYSPNNM 'LT GBL 'RṢ,*** "Moreover, he ceded to us Dor and Joppa, and we annexed them to the territory of the state."

NPu 159.5 ***TW' YSPN 'LT MQDŠM,*** "We added his cella to his sanctuary."

INCUMBENT UPON, CHARGED WITH

60.3/4 ***P'L 'YT KL 'Š 'LTY,*** "He accomplished everything that was incumbent upon him (*i.e.*, with which he had been charged)."

TO

14.5/6 ***'L Y'MSN BMŠKB Z 'LT MŠKB ŠNY,*** "Let him not carry me out from this resting-place to another resting-place."

INTO

Pu 81.1/4 ***LRBT L'ŠTRT WLTNT BLBNN MQDŠ ḤDŠM <'L> KM KL 'Š BN[M] . . . 'Š YB' 'LT HḤRZ ŠMQDŠM 'L,*** "Belonging to the Lady Astarte and to Thinnith of Lebanon are these new sanctuaries, as well as everything that is in them that was brought into the custody of these sanctuaries."

NPu 137.4/5 ***B' H'LNM 'L 'LT HMQDŠM 'L B'SR WŠB' LYRḤ***

MP' LPNY, "These gods came into (entered) these sanctuaries on the seventeenth of the month of First Mufa."

FROM

Byb 10.14 ***TSG 'T PTḤY Z DL YSDH 'LT MQM Z,*** "<If> you move this inscription of mine and its base from this spot."

FOR the benefit of

43.13/14 ***WP'LT 'NK 'LT [HMQDŠ . . .] 'PDT BK[S]P MŠQL KR 100 W 2,***. "And I made for the sanctuary an ephod of silver weighing 102 *kr.*"

Pu *Poen.* 944/946 **Fel dono . . . et cil comu con liful alt banim au,** "His father did everything for that son of his as he was to do <it for him>." = NPu *Poen.* 935/936 **Fel yth chil ys chon ythem liful yth binim,** "He did everything for his son that he was to do for him."

NPu 138.5/7 ***NP'L NBL NSKT 'RB' 'LT HMQDŠM 'L . . . WNNTN 'T HKHNM,*** "Four metal vessels were made for these sanctuaries and handed over to the priests."

EXPRESSING THE ACCUSATIVE PARTICLE

This use of the preposition is found in Phoenician only; it is unknown in Punic.

Byb 9 A 5 ***['BL LPT]Ḥ '[LT MŠKB] ZN,*** "Do not open this resting-place!"

14.7 ***YPTḤ 'LT MŠKB Z,*** "He shall open this resting-place." *Obs.* Note the use of the accusative particle ***'YT*** in the same context in the same inscription: ***YPTḤ 'YT MŠKB Z*** (line 4).

13.3/4, 5/6 ***'L TPTḤ 'LTY,*** "Do not open it (the coffin)!"

14.20 ***'L YPTḤ 'LTY,*** "Let him not open it (the resting-place: *MŠKB*)."

14.21 ***'L Y'R 'LTY,*** "Let him not empty it (the resting-place) out!"

'LT PN 'alt panê

Usage

IN ADDITION TO

50.4/5 ***WML'T 'LT PNY 'YT KL KSP 'Š LY,*** "And I shall pay in addition to it (your money) all my money."

Pu 69.3 ***WBKLL YKN LM' 'LT PN HMŠ'T Z Š'R MŠQL ŠLŠ***

MʾT 300, "For an entire animal, they (the priests) shall receive in addition to this payment meat weighing 300."

ʿN ʾŠ *ʿênê ʾīs* = ***ʿNM*** *ʿênêm*

Usage

IN PUBLIC VIEW; *lit.*, WITHIN PEOPLE'S VIEW

60.5 ***WYṬNʾY BʿRPT BT ʾLM ʿN ʾŠ,*** "They shall erect it (the inscription) in the portico of the temple in public view."

34.1/5 ***MṢBT ʾZ ʾŠ YṬNʾ ʾRŠ . . . ʿNM ʿL MŠKB NḤTNM LʿLM.,*** "This stele is that which Aris erected in public view at their eternal resting-place."

PNT *panōt*

Usage

TO

Pu 69.13 ***KL ṢWʿT ʾŠ YʿMS PNT ʾLM,*** "All the parts <of a sacrificed animal> that are brought to a god." *Ditto* 74.8, where the preposition is misspelled ***BNT***.

TḤT *táḥat*

Forms

TḤT	Ph-Pu	*Passim*
TʾḤT	NPu	118.2

With suffix pronouns:

1.Sg.
TḤTN *taḥtêni* Ph 24.14

3.M.Pl.
TḤTNM *taḥtênom* Ph 14.9

Usage

AT THE BOTTOM

Byb 2.1/3 ***LDʿT HNY BʿLK TḤT ZN,*** "Be aware <that> I, your king, am at the bottom of this <shaft>."

BENEATH, UNDER

14.11/12 ***’M ’DMM ḤMT ’L YKN LM ŠRŠ LMṬ WPR LM‘L WT’R BḤYM TḤT ŠMŠ,*** “As for those persons, they shall have no root below nor fruit above nor wealth among those who are living under the sun.”

26 A I 16/17 ***W’NK ’ZTWD ŠTNM TḤT P‘MY,*** “But I, Aztwadda, placed them under my two feet (*i.e.,* I subjugated them).”

NPu *NP* 69.2 ***TḤT ’BN ST ‘BN,*** “He has been laid to rest beneath this gravestone.”

BELOW, SOUTH OF

CID 3B-5A ***W’P MTŠ YTN LKLŠ ŠD ZBL WKRMM BŠD ZBL TḤT QRT WKRMM ’Š TḤT ML,*** “MTS also gave to KLS <?land> in the district of ZBL and vineyards in the district of ZBL south of the city, and vineyards that are south of ML.”

POSSESSING AUTHORITY

NPu 120.1 ***MYNKD Q‘SR ‘WGSṬS BN ’LM RB MḤNT P‘M’T ‘SR W’ḤT WMYNKD P‘M’T ‘SR W’RB‘ W[TḤ]T MŠLT ‘SR HMŠLM P‘M’T ‘SR WḤMŠ,*** “Emperor Caesar Augustus, the son of God, head of the army (consul) eleven times, emperor fourteen times and possessing the authority of the ten rulers (tribune) fifteen times.” Corresponding to Latin **[Imp(erator) Caesar divi f(ilius) Augustus] co(n)s(ul) XI imp(erator) XIIII trib(unicia) pot(estate) XV.**

IN ONE’S STEAD

14.8/9 ***W’L YKN LM BN WZR‘ TḤTNM,*** “They shall not have sons nor offspring in their stead.”

24.13/15 ***WMY BBNY ’Š YŠB TḤTN,*** “As for whichever of my sons shall sit <on the throne> in my stead.”

NPu 118.2 ***RB T’ḤT RB MḤNT,*** “Commander <of the army> in place of the commander of the army (*Latin* **proconsul**).”

CHAPTER FOURTEEN

THE ADVERBS AND CONJUNCTIONS

I. The Adverbs

A. *Adverbs of Degree and Manner*

B-RBM *biribbīm*

EXCEEDINGLY, GREATLY; VERY, VERY MUCH; corresponding in use and function to Hebrew ***M'D*** *m^{e}'od,* which is unknown in Phoenician-Punic.

26 A III 9/11 ***BRBM YLD WBRBM Y'DR WBRBM Y'BD L'Z-TWD,*** "May they bear many children, may they become very great, and may they ardently serve Aztwadda."

MANY

Pu 68.5 ***K ŠMʻ QL' ʻD PʻMT BRBM,*** "For he heard his voice many times (often)."

ḤNM *ḥinnam*

GRATIS (WITHOUT THOUGHT OF REPAYMENT); Hebrew ***ḤNM*** *ḥinnam*

Pu *CIS* i 171.4 ***[YTN KS]P KKRM M'T BTRY ḤNM,*** "[He gave] one hundred talents of silver of his own money without thought of repayment."

VOLUNTARILY (OF ONE'S OWN FREE WILL)

Pu *CIS* I 5522.2/4 ***ḤNBʻL . . . HTRŠM BMYPʻL 'DN 'ŠMNḤLṢ . . . ḤNM BY KSP,*** "Hannibal signed himself back into the employ of his master Esmunhalos of his own free will, without <payment to him of> silver."

KMT

SO, THEREFORE; Ugaritic ***KMT***

NPu *CIS* I 151.5/6 ***K-ʻBD' HMT L' TḤNT KMT BʻṢṢ LBNTM LM,*** "Because they did him a favor, so (therefore) did he *undertake* to erect it (the statue) to them."

KN *ken*

SO, THEREFORE; Hebrew ***KN*** *ken*

Byb 13.1 *[. . .]**N* ***’NK LḤDY WKN HN ’NK ŠKB B’RN ZN,*** “I alone . . . -ed. And so here do I lie, in this coffin.”

L-ḤD *liḥūd*

ALONE, ONLY; cf. Aramaic *lḥōd, lḥūd.* The adverb, being in origin a noun governed by a preposition, receives the suffix pronouns of the third person used with the noun in the genitive case.

26 A II 5/6 ***WBYMTY ’NK ’ŠT T<L>K LḤDY DL PLKM,*** “But in my time (reign), a woman is able to travel alone, without body-guards!”

Byb 13.1 *[. . .]**N* ***’NK LḤDY WKN HN ’NK ŠKB B’RN ZN,*** “I alone. . . -ed; and so here do I lie, in this coffin.”

‘D *‘ôd*

MOREOVER, FURTHERMORE, IN ADDITION; cf. Heb ***‘WD*** *‘ôd* (“still, yet”).

14.18/19 ***W‘D YTN LN ’DN MLKM ’YT D’R WYPY,*** “In addition, the Lord of Kings ceded to us Dor and Joppa.”

‘L KN *‘al ken*

THEREFORE, FOR THIS REASON; Hebrew ***‘L KN*** *‘al ken.*

Byb 9 A 2 ***BL TQM LŠT ’RN ‘LT ’RN ‘L KN P‘LT*** *[. . .],* “<So and so said>, 'You shall not persist in placing one coffin upon another!' For this reason, I made/built [. . .].”

B. *Locative Adverbs and Adverbial Expressions*

’Y *’ī,* orth. var. ***Y***

WHERE?; cf. Ugaritic ***IY*** *(’iyyā)*; Hebrew ***’YH*** *’ayye.*

In the Phoenician personal name 1Kings 16:31, 18:4.13.19, 19.1f, 21.5-25, 2Kings 9:7-37 ***’Y ZBL*** *(’ī zebel),* “Where is Zebel (Baal)?”

Pu *EH* 141.2 in the personal name ***’Y B‘L,*** “Where is Baal?”

Pu *CIS* i 135.5 in the personal name ***Y B‘LYM*** *(’ī Ba‘alīm),* “Where is Baal?”

HN *hinnō, hen*

HERE, sentence-initial demonstrative locative (Lat **ecce**); Heb ***HN*** *hinne,* ***HN*** *hen.*

Byb *KAI* 2 ***HNY B‘LK TḤT ZN,*** “I, your king, am here, at the bottom of this (shaft).”

Byb 13.1 ***HN ʾNK ŠKB BʾRN ZN,*** "Here do I lie, in this coffin."

Pu *Poen.* 947 **Hen hu Acaristocle,** "Acharistocles lives (*lit.,* is) here." = NPu *Poen.* 937 **Innochoth u Agorastocles.**

NPu *NP* 130.6 ***HN*** *(hinna)* ***ŠKBT BT ŠMNM ŠT,*** "Here does he lie, at the age of eighty years."

NPu *Punica* pp. 124/26 no. 3.4/5 ***ʾN BʾMQM ST NʿSPʾ ʿṢMYʿ,*** "Here, in this place, have her bones been gathered."

NPu Mactar B IV 2 ***WʾNʾ ŠMʾTM,*** "Here are their names."

HN henna

HITHER(Phoenician); Heb ***HNH*** *henna.* Punic uses ***KN*** *(kōna).*

NSI 31d 1/2 ***ʾNK ʿBDʾBST BN ṢDYTN BʾT HN BYM 2 LYRḤ ḤYR,*** "I, Abdubast son of Sidyaton, came here on day 2 of the month of Hiyyar."

HNKT hinnokōt

HERE (Neo-Punic), compounded of the locative demonstrative adverb *hinnō* ("here") and the locative adverb (Neo-Punic) *kōt* ("here"). The adverb, like the simple form ***HN*** *hinne, hen,* appears originally to have been restricted to sentence-initial position; but the example in *Poen.* 934 indicates that this restriction came to be loosened.

NPu *NP* 67.4/5 ***HNKT ʿBNT TʿT HBN{T} ST QBRT,*** "Here has she been laid to rest; beneath this stone is she buried."

NPu *NP* 68.4/5 ***HNKT ṢWʾYT TḤT ʾBN Z ʿBNT,*** "Here is she buried; beneath this stone has she been laid to rest."

NPu *NP* 69.2 ***HNKT QYBR TḤT ʾBN ST ʿBN,*** "Here is he buried; beneath this stone has he been laid to rest."

NPu *Poen.* 934 **Byth thymmoth innochoth ulech <silli> Antidamas chon,** "Antidamas was my host here in the past." = *Poen.* 955 **Sed hic mihi antehac hospes Antidamas fuit.**

NPu *Poen.* 937 **Innochoth u Agorastocles,** "Agorastocles lives here." = Pu *Poen.* 947 **Hen hu Acharistocle,** "Acharistocles lives here."

K kō, kū

HERE; cf. Heb ***KH*** *kō.* Neo-Punic uses ***KT*** *kōt* below.

Pu *Poen.* 941 **Con cu Metun. Al bet lo cu cian bate**, "Here lived Mettun. To his home here have I now come."

Pu *Poen.* 949 **Anec litor bod es iussim limin co,** "I shall inquire of these men who are coming out from here." = Poen. 960

Hos percontabor qui hinc egrediuntur foras.

Pu *Poen.* 1013 **Lec. Lacanna limin co,** "Go! Go away from here!"

NPu *LA* 1 p. 45 no. 4.1/5 **[Ubam]ys asar liiyra Chirur sath Migin inseb mes Sis cho ryb <M>ycnim,** "And on the fifteenth of the month of Kirur, in the year of Miggin, the Governor of Myqnim (=Myqne) erected here the statue of Sis."

KN *kōna*

HITHER, Punic only, being the locative adverb ***K*** *kō* ("here"), with adverbial -a of direction and euphonic *-n-*. Phoenician uses ***HN*** *henna.*

Pu *Poen.* 942/3 **Iulec anec cona, alonim balim, bane becor Bals[illem],** "I brought hither, O proprietary gods, my first-born son Bals[illem]."

KT *kōt*

HERE, Neo-Punic only, being Phoenician-Punic ***K*** *kō* ("here") with excrescent *–t.*

NPu *Poen.* 939 **Bod i(ly) a(nech) lythera ymu ys lomjyn choth iiusim,** "I shall inquire of these men who are coming out from here." = Pu Poen. 949 **Anec litor bod es iusim limin co.**

See also Neo-Punic ***HNKT*** ("here").

L-MṬ *limaṭṭa*

BELOW. BENEATH; Hebrew ***LMṬH*** *lᵉmaṭṭa*

14.11/12 ***ʾL YKN LM ŠRŠ LMṬ WPR LMʿL,*** "They shall not have a root below nor fruit above."

L-MʿL *limaʿla*

ABOVE; Hebrew ***LMʿLH*** *lᵉmaʿla*

14.11/12 ***ʾL YKN LM ŠRŠ LMṬ WPR LMʿL,*** "They shall not have a root below nor fruit above."

L-M-MʿL MṬ *limimmaʿla maṭṭa*

FROM TOP TO BOTTOM

NPu 145 III 12/14 ***ŠMʾT HMẒRḤ ʾŠ ʾYKRMʾ T-HMNḤT QRʾ LMMʿLʾ MTʾ,*** "Here are the names of <the members of> the *mizraḥ*-sodality that honored him. Read what is put down, from top to bottom."

ŠM *sam*

THERE; Heb *ŠM* *šam.*

26 A I 18-II 1 ***W'N 'NK 'RṢT 'ZT BMB' ŠMŠ . . . YRDM 'NK YŠBM 'NK BQṢT GBLY BMṢ' ŠMŠ WDNNYM YŠBT ŠM,*** "I conquered mighty lands in the West, and I deported them (their populations) and resettled them in the far part of my territory in the East; and I settled Danunians there (in the depopulated western lands)."

C. *Adverbs and Adverbial Expressions of Time*

'Z *'iz*

THEN, AT THAT TIME; Hebrew *'Z* *'az.*

NPu D 6.8/9 **Sab siben Mycne, / Is ab syth sath syby,** "Our militia surrounded Miqne; / Then did I take that enemy captive."

B-LL *billêl*

AT NIGHT, DURING THE NIGHT; Hebrew ***BLYLH*** *ballayla.*

Pu 76 A 6/7 ***WMKS' TḤ[DŠ – – –] BLL WQDMT,*** "Renew the covering (bandage) [x times] during the night and in the morning."

B-'T TMT *bi'it timmot*

IN TIME PAST, EARLIER, FORMERLY

NPu *Poen.* 934 **Byth thymmoth ynnochoth ulech <silli> Antidamas chon,** "Antidamas was my guest-friend here in the past." *Obs.* In the Punic version of this same line, the adverb used is **lipane esse:** *Poen.* 943/944 **Hulec silli balim esse lipane esse Antidamas con,** "Antidamas was my guest-friend in this nation in the past."

H-ŠT Z *hissat ezdō*

THIS YEAR, IN THIS YEAR; the noun is in the accusative of time.

NPu 137.5 ***B'SR WŠB' LYRḤ MP' LPNY HŠT Z,*** "On the seventeenth of the month of Prior Mufa of/in this year."

YM MD YM *yūm middê yūm*

DAILY, *lit.* DAY BY DAY

43.10/11 ***KM ZBḤT L'DN 'Š LY LMLQRT 'L ḤTT W'L ḤY ZR'Y YM MD YM,*** "And I made sacrifice daily to my Lord Milqart for a long life for me and for my descendants."

YRḤ MD YRḤ *yeraḥ middê yeraḥ*

MONTHLY, *lit.* MONTH BY MONTH

43.10/12 ***KM ZBḤT L'DN 'Š LY LMLQRT . . . [BḤD]ŠM WBKS'M YRḤ MD YRḤ,*** "So, too, did I make sacrifice monthly to my Lord Milkqart at the time of the new moons and the full moons."

KL H-'T *kil ha'it*

ALL THE TIME, ALWAYS; the noun is in the accusative of time; cf. Hebrew ***BKL-'T*** *b'kol-'et* ("always," Exodus 18:22; Psalm 10:5)

NPu 126.4 ***ZBḤ LK[L Ḥ']T,*** "Sacrificial priest for always." = Latin **flamen perpetuus.**

NPu 126.9 ***LPNY . . . YTN' L'BD BṢP'T KL Ḥ'T,*** "They permitted me to make use of the senatorial broad purple stripe always." = Latin **cui . . . lato clavo semper uti conce[ssunt].**

K-'N *k^e'an*

NOW; cf. Aramaic *k^e'an.* Hebrew has ***'TH*** *'atta.*

NPu *NP* 41.2/3 ***K'N K'N ŠM' QL' [B]RK',*** "Hear his voice now, now! Bless him!"

NPu *NP* 42.3/4 ***KḤN KḤN ŠM' QL' BRK',*** "Hear his voice now, now! Bless him!"

Pu *Poen.* 941 **Al bet lo cu cian bate,** "To his house here have I now come."

L-PN Z *lipnê ^ezde*

IN THE PAST, EARLIER, BEFORE; *cf.* Hebrew ***LPNY MZH*** *lipnê mizze.*

Pu *Poen.* 943/944 **Hulec silli balim esse lipane esse Antidamas con,** "Antidamas was my guest-friend in this nation in the past." = Latin *Poen.* 955 **Sed hic mihi antehac hospes Antidamas fuit.** In the Neo-Punic version of this same line, the adverb used is **byth thymmoth** ("in time past"): *Poen.*934 **Byth thymmoth innochoth ulech <silli> Antidamas chon,** "Here in time past Antidamas was my guest-friend."

L-PNM *lipanīm*

IN THE PAST, EARLIER, BEFORE; Hebrew ***LPNYM*** *l^epanīm.*

26 A II 3/6 ***BMQMM 'Š KN LPNM NŠT'M . . . WBYMTY 'NK 'ŠT T<L>K LḤDY,*** "In places that were dangerous before (in the past), in my time a woman walks alone."

L-ʿLM *liʿūlom*

ALWAYS, FOREVER; Hebrew ***LʿWLM*** *l^eʿōlam*

18.7/8 ***BʿLŠMM LʿLM YBRKN,*** "Baalsamem bless me always!"

MTM *matêm(a)*

EVER, NEVER; cf. Akkadian ***matīma***. The pronunciation of the adverb is uncertain.

26 A II 15/17 ***K BYMTY KN LʾRṢ ʿMQ ʾDN ŠBʿ WMNʿM WBL KN MTM LDNNYM LL BYMTY,*** "In my days (time), the land of the Valley of Adana enjoyed abundance and prosperity, yea, the Danunians never knew famine in my days (time)."

ʿD ʿLM *ʿad ʿūlom*

ALWAYS; Hebrew ***ʿD ʿWLM*** *ʿad ʿōlam*

43.10/12 ***KM ZBḤT LʾDN ʾŠ LY LMLQRT . . . YM MD YM . . . YRḤ MD YRḤ ʿD ʿLM KQDM,*** "So, too, did I always make sacrifice daily and monthly to my Lord Milqart."

ʿD PʿMT BRBM *ʿad paʿamūt birabbīm*

MANY TIMES, FREQUENTLY, OFTEN; cf. Hebrew 2Kings 4:35 ***ʿD-ŠBʿ PʿMYM*** *ʿad šebaʿ p^eʿamīm* ("seven times")

Pu 68.5 ***K ŠMʿ QLʾ ʿD PʿMT BRBM,*** "He heard his voice many times."

ʿLŠ *ʿalas*

AT DAWN, IN EARLY MORNING; the noun is in the accusative of time; Arabic *ghalasan* ("before dawn, very early")

Pu *CIS* i 5510.9/10 ***WYLK RBM ʾDNBʿL BN GRSKN HRB WḤMLKT BN ḤNʾ HRB ʿLŠ WTMK HMT ʾYT ʾGRGNT,*** "Generals Idnibal son of Gisco the Great and Himilco son of Hanno the Great, marching at dawn, seized Agrigentum." *Obs.* In the Greek translation of this line, preserved by Diodorus Siculus (xiii, 90, 1), the adverb is rendered αμα τω φωτι: Ο δ' Ιμιλκας αμα τω φωτι την δυναμιν εντος των τειχων παρεισαγαγων, "Imilkas (Himilco), before dawn leading the army inside the walls <of Agrigentum>."

QDMT *qadmot*

IN THE MORNING; cf. Aramaic ***QDWM(ʾ)*** *qiddūm(a)* and ***QDMTʾ*** *qadm^eta* ("early morning"); the noun is in the accusative of time.

Pu 76 A 6/7 ***WMKSʾ TḤ[DŠ – – –] BLL WQDMT,*** "Renew

the covering (bandage) [x times] during the night and in the morning."

II. The Conjunctions

A. *Subordinating*

'ḤR 'Š *ʾaḥar ʾīs*

AFTER; Hebrew **'ḤR 'ŠR** *ʾaḥar ʾašer*

NSI 56.2/6 ***'ḤR 'Š P'L ṢYW'T LHḤYM H'Š ŠL' . . . 'M' L ŠRT ŠNT ḤMŠM,*** "After her husband had made his farewell to the living, his mother performed public service for (another) fifty years."

'M *ʾim*

IF; Hebrew **'M** *ʾim*

Byb 10.13/14 ***W'M 'BL TŠT ŠT ŠM 'TK W'M TSR M[L']KT Z',*** "But if you do not place my name <on it> with yours or if you remove that work . . . "

13.6/8 ***W'M PTḤ TPTḤ 'LTY WRGZ TRGZN 'L YKN LK ZR' BḤYM TḤT ŠMŠ,*** "But if you open it (the coffin) and disturb me, you shall not have descendants among those living under the sun!"

See also **'M 'P** and **'P 'M** ("even if").

WHEN; Arabic *ʾimmā* ("when")

Byb 3.2/5 ***TŠ'M Š<Q>LM KSP NŠBT 'M NḤL TNḤL MGŠTK 'LK WMGŠT LY,*** "Let us *share* the ninety weight of silver: when you take possession of it (the silver), your share is yours, and my share is mine." *Obs.* The translation is problematic.

'M 'P *ʾim ʾap*

EVEN IF, EVEN THOUGH = **'P 'M**; cf. Hebrew **'P KY** *ʾap kī*

KAI 26 A III 12/19 ***W'M MLK BMLKM . . . 'Š YMḤ ŠM 'ZTWD BŠ'R Z WŠT ŠM 'M 'P YḤMD 'YT HQRT Z . . . WMḤ B'LŠMM . . . 'YT HMMLKT H' W'YT HMLK H',*** "As for any king who shall erase the name of Aztwadda from this gate and place his own name (on it), even if he may love this city, Baalsamem shall eradicate the aforementioned royal person and the aforementioned king."

'P 'M *'ap 'im*

EVEN IF = ***'M 'P***

KAI 14.6 ***'P 'M 'DMM YDBRNK 'L TŠM' BD
NM,*** "Even if people urge you <to violate my tomb>, do not listen to their words!"

K- . . . KMT

BECAUSE . . . SO (THEREFORE); cf. Hebrew ***K- . . . KN*** *k^e- . . . ken;* cf. also Ugaritic ***KMT*** ("thus, therefore")

NPu *CIS* I 151.5/6 ***K-'BD' HMT L' TḤNT KMT B'ṢṢ LBTNM LM,*** "Because they did him a favor, so (therefore) did he *undertake* to erect it (the statue) to them."

K- *kī*

WHEN; Hebrew ***KY*** *kī*

Byb 1.1 ***'RN ZP'L [']TB'L BN 'ḤRM MLK GBL L'ḤRM 'BH KŠTH B<T>'LM,*** "<This is> the coffin that Ittoba'al son of Ahiram, King of Byblos, made for Ahiram, his father, when they placed him (Ahiram) in <his> tomb."

NPu *LA* 1 45 no. 4.7/9 **Ubai[um] amys chyrym[u]ia byiyra [Mu]fa chy [c]hil[o] ufel th-y[. . .],** "And on day five they honored her, in the month of Mufa, when he had completed building the [. . .]."

THAT, introducing a noun clause that is the direct object of a verb

60.7 ***YD' HṢDNYM K YD' HGW LŠLM ḤLPT,*** "That the Sidonians might know that the community knows to compensate."

Pu *Poen.* 938 **Ynny i(s) d(ubyr) ch'ily gubulim lasibithim,** "I am told that these are the environs where he resides."

BECAUSE, AS A RESULT OF

13.5/6 ***'L 'L TPTḤ 'LTY W'L TRGZN K T'BT 'ŠTRT HDBR H',*** "Do not, do not open it and do not disturb me, for that act would be an abomination to Astarte."

26 A II 9/11 ***BN 'NK HQRT Z . . . K B'L WRŠP ṢPRM ŠLḤN LBNT,*** "I built this city, because Baal and Rasep-SPRM commissioned me to build it."

NPu *LA* 1 45 no. 4.1/5 **[Bam]ys asar liiyra Chirur sath Migin inseb mes Sis cho ryb <M>ycnim chi ur Sorim y,** "On the fifteenth of the month of Kirur, in the year of Miggin, the

Governor of Myqnim erected here the statue of Sis; for she is the light of the Tyrians."

KM ʾŠ *$k^{ə}$mū ʾīs*

WHEN; Hebrew ***Kʾ ŠR*** *kaʾ^{a}šer*

Byb 10.7/8 ***KM ʾŠ QRʾT ʾT RBTY BʿLT GBL WŠMʿ QL,*** "When I called my Lady Baalt of Byblos, she heard my voice."

CID 7A/8B ***WKM ʾŠ YGL ʾYT MSNZMŠ BYMT ʾZWŠŠ WYSB MLK WRYK<LY> LMSNʾZMŠ KL HŠDYT ʾL,*** "But when they exiled MSNZMS in the days of 'ZWSS, the king of WRYKLY returned all these fields to MSNʾZMS."

JUST AS

19.1/9 ***ʿRPT KBRT MṢʾ ŠMŠ WṢPLY ʾŠ BN HʾLM MLʾK MLKʿŠTRT WʿBDY BʿL ḤMN . . . KM ʾŠ BN ʾYT KL ʾḤRY HMQDŠM ʾŠ BʾRṢ,*** "The god Mal'ak-Milkastart and his servants, the citizens of Hammon, built <this> large eastern portico and its columns just as they <also> built all the other sanctuaries in the region."

KM Š- *$k^{ə}$mū si-*

WHEN (Punic) = ***KM ʾŠ***; cf. Mishaic Hebrew ***KŠ-*** *k^{e}še-*

Pu 81.4 ***ʾŠ YBʾ ʿLT HḤRZ ŠMQDŠM ʾL KM ŠḤGR HŠMRT LHR Hʾ[LM],*** "<The objects> which were brought into the custody of these sanctuaries when the protected area of the temple mount was closed to public entry."

LM *lam(m)a*

LEST, followed by Prefixing Form A (Future Imperfective), introducing a statement of future consequence; Hebrew ***LMH*** *lamma* (Qoheleth 5:5, 7:16); Aramaic *l^{e}mā*

14.21/22 ***ʾL YŠʾ ʾYT ḤLT MŠKBY LM YSGRNM ʾLNM HQDŠM ʾL,*** "Let them not carry off the coffin in which I lie lest these holy gods lock them up."

L-MḤT K-

FOR THE REASON THAT, BECAUSE; the initial element ***LMḤT***, the etymology of which is obscure, seems to function as an adverbial complement to the simple conjunction ***K-*** *kī* ("because").

60.1/3 ***TM BD ṢDNYM BNʾSPT LʿṬR ʾYT ŠMʿBʿL . . . ʿṬRT***

ḤRṢ BDRK<M>NM 20 LMḤT K BN 'YT ḤṢR BT 'LM, "It has been deemed good by the Sidonians in assembly to crown Samobaal with a gold crown worth 20 drachmas, because he built the temple court."

L-MḤT L-KN

IN ORDER THAT; followed by Prefixing Form B (Jussive/Subjunctive). The initial element ***LMḤT***, the etymology of which is obscure, seems to function as an adverbial complement to the conjunction ***LKN*** ("in order that"); *cf.* Arabic *likay(mā)* ("in order that"). In this same function, Hebrew employs ***LM'N*** *lᵉmaʿan.*

60.6/8 ***YŠ'N BKSP 'LM B'L ṢDN DRKMNM 20 LMḤT LKN YD' HṢDNYM K YD' HGW LŠLM ḤLPT 'YT 'DMM 'Š P'L MŠRT 'T PN GW***, "They shall withdraw 20 drachmas from the money of the god Baal of Sidon in order that the Sidonians might know that the community knows to compensate persons who have performed service in behalf of the community."

'D 'Š *ʿad ʾis*

WHEN, AS SOON AS; Hebrew ***'D 'ŠR*** *ʿad ʾašer*

50.5/6 ***'D 'Š 'D' BM'[. . .]T WŠLḤT LY 'T SPR HNQT***, "As soon as I *shall have paid back what I owe*, you shall send me the quittance."

B. *Conjunctions and Disjunctions*

1. *Modal*

'M

BUT, expressing exception; cf. Hebrew ***'M*** *ʾim* ("but") in the co-ordinated expression ***L' . . . KY 'M*** *lō . . . kī ʾim* ("not . . . but"; German "nicht . . . sondern").

Pu *CIS* i 170.2 ***[LB'L HZBḤ Š]R WH'ŠLBM WHP'MM 'Š BL 'LM 'LT HMZBḤ 'M L[TT LKHNM 'YT . . .]***, "[To the sacrificer belong] the meat and the joints and the legs which do not go up (are not burnt) upon the altar, but one must give the [. . . to the priests]." Cf. ditto line 3.

Pu 74.3 ***[WKN H']RT LKHNM WTBRT LB'L HZBḤ '[M LTT LKHN 'YT . . .]***, "The skin shall belong to the priests and the *tbrt* shall belong to the sacrificer, but give [the . . . to the priest]."

’P *’ap*

AND TOO, AND ALSO; Hebrew ***’P*** *’ap*

50.2 ***ŠLM ’T ’P ’NK ŠLM,*** “<I hope> you are well. I, too, am well.”

MOREOVER; FURTHERMORE

26 A I 11/12 ***WŠT ’NK ŠLM ’T KL MLK W’P B’BT P‘LN KL MLK,*** “I made peace with every king. Moreover, every king adopted me as father.”

CID 3b-4AB ***W’P MTŠ YTN LKLŠ ŠD ZBL,*** “Moreover, MTS gave to KLS a field in ZBL.”

BUT, HOWEVER

CID 3AB ***W’P WLWY YTN LMTŠ WLKLS,*** “But WLWY gave <this same land> to MTS and to KLS.”

CID 5AB ***W’P B‘L KR YŠB BN WQB MTŠ QBT ’DRT,*** “But Baal-KR, who dwells in it, he cursed MTS with a great curse (*or* But the citizenry of KR, <who> dwell in it, cursed MTS with a great curse).”

’PS *’epes*

BUT, HOWEVER, expressing contrast

26 A IV 1/3 ***’PS ŠM ’ZTWD YKN L‘LM,*** “<The gods shall eradicate all who would erase the name of Aztwadda from this gate>. But (in contrast) the name of Aztwadda shall endure forever!”

KM

SO TOO, ALSO; the conjunction seems to function as does ***GM*** *gam* in Hebrew

43.10 ***KM ZBḤT L’DN ’Š LY LMLQRT,*** “So, too, did I make sacrifice to my Lord Milqart.”

43.12/13 ***KM HDLT HNḤŠT [Z K]TBT WSMRT BQR ’Š BN MNḤT ḤNY,*** “So, too, did I inscribe this bronze plaque, in which are the details of my benefaction, and nail it to the wall.”

2. *Simple Conjunctions and Disjunctions*

’M *’im*

OR; Hebrew ***’M*** *’im*

14.6/8 ***KL MMLKT WKL ’DM ’Š YPTḤ ‘LT MŠKB Z ’M ’Š YŠ’ ’YT ḤLT MŠKBY ’M ’Š Y‘MSN BMŠKB Z ’L YKN LM MŠKB***

'T RP'M, "As for any person of royal descent or any commoner who shall open this resting-place or who shall carry off the coffin in which I rest or who shall carry me out from this resting-place, they shall not have rest among the infernal gods."

26 A III 12/13 ***W'M MLK BMLKM WRZN BRZNM 'M 'DM 'Š 'DM ŠM,*** "As for any king or any ruler or any commoner who is a person of distinction."

Pu 69.15 ***[B]KL ZBḤ 'Š YZBḤ DL MQN' 'M DL ṢPR BL YKN LKHN[M MNM],*** "Of a sacrifice that a person who owns no cattle or a person who owns no fowl shall sacrifice, the priests shall not have anything."

'M . . . 'M *ʾim . . . ʾim*

WHETHER . . . OR

26 A III 15/18 ***WYS' HŠ'R Z 'Š P'L 'ZTWD . . . 'M BḤMDT YS' 'M BŠN'T WBR' YS' HS'R Z,*** "If he shall pull out this gate that Aztwadda made, whether he shall tear it out out of love or shall tear out this gate out of hatred and malice."

RES 922.2 ***[']M MLK H' 'M ['DM H'],*** "Whether he is king or commoner."

Pu *CIS* I 5511.6 ***[K]L 'DM 'M 'Š 'M 'ŠT,*** "Every person, whether man or woman."

Pu 69.3 ***B'LP KLL 'M ṢW'T 'M ŠLM KLL LKHNM KSP 'ŠRT 10 B'ḤD,*** "For an entire ox, whether cut in pieces or entirely intact, the priests shall receive ten 10 silver for each."

'T *ʾet*

TOGETHER WITH, the preposition "with" used as a conjunction

14.9 ***WYSGRNM H'LNM HQDŠM 'T MMLK<T> 'DR 'Š MŠL BNM,*** "The holy gods shall lock them up, together with whichever mighty king is ruling them."

DL ?*dūle*

TOGETHER WITH, INCLUDING; this conjunction, perhaps in origin the active participle of the verb ***D-L-Y*** ("possess, include"), governs the accusative case.

Byb 10.14 ***WTSG 'T PTḤY Z DL YSDH 'LT MQM Z,*** "And if you move this inscription of mine together with its base from this spot."

Pu *CIS* i 5510.4/6 ***WKPT RBTN TNT-PNB'L W'DN B['L]ḤMN***

'YT 'DMM HMT BḤYM 'L PN ŠMŠ DL 'ZRTM W'[. .]NM, "Our Lady Thinnith-Phanebal and the Lord Baalhammon shall tie up those persons among those living under the sun, together with their families and their [. . .]s."

Pu *CIS* i 5510.10/11 ***WTMK HMT 'YT 'GRGNT WŠT [H]MT ŠLM DL B'L NWS,*** "And they (the Carthaginians) seized Agrigentum, and they (the Agrigentines) made peace, including those who had fled." *Obs.* Reference is made here to the Agrigentines who had fled to the city of Gela the night before the Carthaginians seized Agrigentum.

AND ALSO, AS WELL AS, found also with the conjunction ***W-*** in the form ***WDL***

Pu 81.2/4 ***HḤRṬYT . . . WDL MLKT HḤRṢ WDL KL MNM 'Š {B . . .] WDL KL MNM BM'ZNM HMQDŠM 'L WDL H'LM 'Š 'L PN HMQDŠ[M],*** "The sculpture and the works of gold and also everything that is in the [. . .], and also everything <that> is in the *storerooms* of these sanctuaries and also the columns that are in front of the sanctuaries."

W- *wi-, w- (ū-)*

AND, conjoining individual items within a sentence

9 B 5 ***B'L'DR WB'LT,*** "Baaladdir and Baalt." *Et passim.*

OR, conjoining individual items within a sentence:

14.8 ***'L YKN LM BN WZR' TḤTNM,*** "They shall not have sons nor progeny in their stead." *Et passim.*

AND, conjoining independent declarative (non-subordinate) sentences:

Pu *CIS* i 5510.10/11 ***WTMK HMT 'YT 'GRGNT WŠT [H]MT ŠLM,*** "They (the Carthaginians) seized Agrigentum, and they (the Agrigentines) made peace." *Et passim.*

YEA, INDEED, conjoining independent complementary or parallel sentences

26 A II 15/17 ***K BYMTY KN L'RṢ 'MQ 'DN ŠB' WN'M WBL KN MTM LDNNYM LL BYMTY,*** "In my time the land of the Valley of Adana enjoyed abundance and prosperity, yea, the Danunians never experienced hunger in my time!"

Pu *CIS* I 6000.5 ***K KM KHN BḤYY QDŠM 'BD W'LNM ŠMŠ***

'D L'TY, "Like a priest did he serve the holy ones during his lifetime, yea, he served the gods until he became too weak <to do so>."

C. *W-* *as Clause Marker*

The conjunction ***W-*** is commonly used for purposes of punctuation, specifically, to mark and set off constituent clauses of complex sentences. In the examples that follow, the punctuating conjunction is underlined.

1. *Marking the Main Clause of a Sentence with Anticipatory Clause*

Byb 1.2 ***W'L MLK BMLKM WSKN BS<K>NM WTM' MḤNT 'LY GBL WYGL 'RN ZN TḤTSP ḤṬR MŠPṬH THTPK KS' MLKH WNḤT TBRḤ 'L GBL,*** "As for any king or any governor or any general of the army in control of Byblos <after me>, if he shall reveal this coffin, his imperial sceptre shall break, his royal throne shall overturn, and peace shall depart from Byblos."

24.12/13 ***WMY BL ḤZ KTN LMN'RY WBYMY KSY BṢ,*** "As for him who had never owned a tunic from the time of his youth, in my time he was dressed in byssus garments."

24.13/15 ***WMY BBNY 'Š YŠB TḤTN WYZQ BSPR Z MŠKBM 'L YKBD LB'RRM,*** "As for whichever of my sons shall sit on the throne in my stead, if he shall damage this inscription, the *mškbm* shall no longer respect the *b'rrm*."

26 A II 3/6 ***WBMQMM 'Š KN LPNM NŠT'M 'Š YŠT' 'DM LLKT DRK WBYMTY 'NK 'ŠT T<L>K LḤDY DL PLKM,*** "And in places that were dangerous in the past, where one used to be afraid to travel the road, in my time a woman is able to travel alone, without bodyguards."

Pu 79.6/11 ***WKL 'Š LSR T-'BN Z BY PY 'NK WBY PY 'DM BŠMY WŠPṬ TNT-PNB'L BRḤ 'DM H',*** "As for anyone who shall remove this stone without my permission or without the permission of someone authorized by me, Thinnith-Phanebal shall condemn that person."

Pu *CIS* i 4945.4/6 ***W'Š YRGZ T-MTNT Z WQBT TNT-PNB'L,*** "As for anyone who shall disturb this stele, Thinnith-Phanebal shall curse him."

Pu *CIS* i 5510.4 ***[WKL ']DM 'Š 'YBL MŠRT WKPT RBTN TNT-PNB'L W'DN B['L]ḤMN 'YT 'DMM HMT,*** "As for any person who shall not serve, our Lady Thinnith-Phanebal and the Lord Baalhammun shall bind those persons."

The conjunction, while common in this type of sentence, is not obligatory, as the following sentences indicate.

Pu *CIS* i 3783.5/7 ***WKL 'DM 'Š GNB T-MTNT Z NKST TNT-[P]NB'L,*** "As for any person who shall steal this stele, Thinnith-Phanebal shall cut him off."

Pu *CIS* i 5510.2/3 ***[WKL 'DM] 'Š LKP 'YT 'MTNT Z WL'KR WLŠBTY 'ML YD,*** "As for any person who shall upend this stele or disturb or destory it, his hand shall wither."

2. *Marking the Apodosis of a Conditional Sentence*

Pu *CIS* I 5510.7 ***[M]ŠRT LQN' WKN L' ḤL WŠLM,*** "If he who serves shall be zealous, wealth and prosperity shall be his."

3. *Marking the Result Clause of a Temporal Sentence*

The conjunction marks off the result clause of a temporal sentence from the *when*-clause when the result clause begins with the Prefixing Verb (*qatal*) with past perfect tense reference. In contrast, Hebrew disallows the conjunction.

Byb 10.7/8 ***KM 'Š QR'T 'T RBTY B'LT GBL WŠM' QL,*** "When I invoked my Lady Baalt of Byblos, she heard my voice (supplication)."

CID lines 7/8 ***KM 'Š YGL 'YT MSNZMŠ BYMT 'ZWŠŠ W YSB MLK WRYK<LY> KL HŠDYT 'L LMSN'ZMŠ,*** "When they exiled MSNZMS (?read MTS) in the days of 'ZWSS, the king of WRYK-LY returned all these fields to MSN'ZMS."

Kition lines 1/3 ***BMṢ'NM 'BN W'ZRNM HPPYM L'GD LN MLḤMT WYṢ' 'L[NM MḤN]T 'Š KTY L'GD LM MLḤMT,*** "When our enemies and their Paphian allies came to do battle with us, the army of the people of Kition went forth against them to do battle with them."

KM *k*^{e}*mū* and ***KM 'Š*** *k*^{e}*mū 'is*

AS WELL AS; Hebrew ***K'ŠR*** *ka'ăšer*

Pu 81.1 ***LRBT L'ŠTRT WLTNT BLBNN MQDŠM ḤDŠM <'L> KM KL 'Š BN[M],*** "<Dedicated> to the Lady Astarte and to Thinnith of Lebanon are these new sanctuaries as well as everything that is in them."

Pu 96.1 ***[. . .]HṢ’ KM KL ’Š P‘L BBT,*** “The [. . .] as well as everything <else> that he/they made in/for the temple.”

AS, JUST AS

19.1/10 ***‘RPT KBRT . . . ’Š BN H’LM ML’K-MLK‘ŠTRT W‘BDY B‘L ḤMN . . . KM ’Š BN ’YT KL’ḤRY [HMQDŠ]M ’Š B’RṢ,*** “<This is> the large portico that the god Mal’ak-Milkastart and his servants, the citizens of Hammon, built just as they built all the other sanctuaries in the land.”

Pu *Poen.* 944/46 **Alem us duber ce fel dono Metun et cil comu con liful alt banim au,** “I am told that his father Mettun did everything for that son of his as he was to do <for him>.”

CHAPTER FIFTEEN

THE PARTICLES

A. *The Particles of Anticipation*

'M *'ammā*

AS FOR, in Tyro-Sidonian Phoenician, serving to introduce an anticipatory clause; the particle is cognate with Arabic *'ammā*. The pronunciation of the particle in Phoenician is uncertain. In Byblian, the preposition ***'L*** *'el* is found in this same function.

14.11 ***'M 'DMM HMT 'L YKN LM ŠRŠ LMṬ WPR LM'L,*** "As for the aforementioned persons, they shall not have root below nor fruit above."

26 A III 12/18 ***W'M MLK BMLKM . . . 'Š YMḤ B'LŠMM 'YT HMLK H' ŠM 'ZTWD . . . WMḤ,*** "As for any king who shall erase the name of Aztwadda, Baalsamem shall erase the aforementioned king."

'L *'el*

AS FOR, the Byblian Phoenician counterpart of Tyro-Sidonian ***'M*** *'ammā*, serving to introduce an anticipatory clause. The particle is the preposition "to." In this same function, Hebrew employs the preposition ***'L*** *'al* (Genesis 41:32).

Byb 1.2 ***W'L MLK BMLKM . . . WYGL 'RN ZN TḤTSP ḤṬR MŠPṬH,*** "As for any king <who will rule Byblos after me>, if he shall remove this coffin, his imperial sceptre shall break."

B. *The Particles of Existence*

'Š *'īs;* var. *YŠ*

THERE IS; *cf.* Ugaritic. ***IṮ*** *'īthi;* Hebrew ***YŠ*** *yeš*. It is not clear whether ***'Š*** and ***YŠ*** are merely orthographic variants or if the latter, found only in personal names, reflects the pronunciaiton *yes*.

NPu Mactar B IV 1 ***DR' KN' ŠLM W'Š LN MZR' WŠP'T,*** "In his time we were prosperous: we possessed (*lit.,* there was to us) sown land and abundance."

IS ALIVE, LIVES

Pu *EH* 224.3 in the personal name ***YŠ BŠT,*** "Where is Bast (Baal)?";*cf.* 2 Samuel 2:8-4:12: the Benjaminite personal name ***'YŠ BŠT*** *'īš Bošet.*

Pu *CIS* i 4917.5/7 (PN) ***'Š B'L,*** "Baal is alive!" = Pu *CIS* i 159.3 ***YŠ B'L***; cf. 1 Chronicles 8:33, 9:39 (Benjaminite personal name) ***'Š B'L*** *'eš Ba'al* = 1 Chronicles 11:11 ***YŠ B'L*** *yiš Ba'al. Ob.* The particle ***YŠ*** is merely an othographic variant of ***'Š,*** not a morphologically distinct form.

BL bal

THERE IS/ARE NOT; the normal negative particle, here used also as a negation of existence; cf. the use of the negative particle ***L'*** in "Ephraimite" Canaanite (as in Arabic) to express the negative existential "there is/are not": 2 Samuel 20:1, 1 K 12:16 ***L' LNW NḤLH BBN YŠY,*** ("And there is no inheritance for us in the son of Jesse.")

NPu 163.2/3 ***BD'ŠTRT DL TRBT ŠQLT K BL L' BṢMḤ Š'RM,*** "Bostar is without *weighed out* increase, for he has no offspring of his own flesh."

C. *The Negative Particles*

Phoenician (Byblian and Tyro-Sidonian) and Punic possess three particles that serve to negate nouns, verbs and phrases: ***'Y, '(Y)BL, BL.*** The negative particle ***L'*** *lō* is not attested in Phoenician or Punic.

'Y 'ī

This negation is found only in Middle Phoenician inscriptions from Sidon (Tibnit and Esmunazor) and at Chytroi (Cyprus); the earlier Tyro-Sidonian inscriptions of Kilamuwa and Aztwadda use ***BL. 'Y*** is also found in the compound negative ***'(Y)BL*** of Byblian Phoenician and Punic.

1. *Negates the Past Perfective (Suffixing Form)*

4.4/5 (Sidon) ***'L YBQŠ BN MNM K 'Y ŠM BN MNM,*** "Let him not look for anything in it (my coffin), for they did not put anything in it."

2. *Negates the Present Imperfective (Prefixing Form A)*

13.4/5 (Sidon) ***'Y 'DLN KSP 'Y 'DLN ḤRṢ,*** "I do not possess any silver, I do not possess any gold."

RES 922.4 (Chytroi) ***['L TPTḤ 'LT H'RN] Z K 'Y '[DLN KSP 'Y 'DLN ḤRṢ],*** "[Do not open] this [coffin] for I do not possess [silver, I do not possess gold}."

'YBL *'ibal*; orthographic var. ***'BL***

This particle, compounded of the negatives ***'Y*** and ***BL,*** is especially well represented in Byblian and Punic.

1. *Negates the Past Perfective (Suffixing Form)*

Pu 69.18 ***KL MŠ'T 'Š 'YBL ŠT BPS Z,*** "Any payment (price) that they did not set down in this inscription."

2. *Negates the Present Imperfective and Future (Prefixing Form A)*

Byb 10.13 ***'M 'BL TŠT ŠM 'TK,*** "If you shall not place my name with yours <on this work> . . ."

Pu 69.21 ***[K]L B'L ZBḤ 'Š 'YBL YTN 'T K[L . .]L HMŠ'T 'Š [BPS Z WN'NŠ},*** "As for any sacrificer who shall not pay the full a[mount of] the payment that is stipulated in [this inscription, he shall be fined.]"

3. *Negates the Periphrastic Imperative (Infinitive Absolute)*

Pu 70.4 ***'BL LPTḤ,*** "Do not open <this tomb>!"

4. *Negates the Active Participle*

Pu *CIS* i 5510.4/5 ***KL 'DM 'Š 'YBL MŠRT WKPT RBTN TNT-PNB'L . . . 'YT 'DMM HMT,*** "As for any person who shall not serve, Our Lady Thinnith-Phanebal shall bind those persons."

Obs: In Phoenician and Punic, the active participle is regularly negated by means of the simple negative particles rather than by the negative existential particle as in Hebrew. See also the negative particle ***BL*** with this same function (below).

’L ’al

1. *Negates Prefixing Form B (Negative Command)*

13.3/4 ***’L ’L TPTḤ ‘LTY W’L TRGZN,*** “Do not, do not open it (the coffin), and do not disturb me!”

2. *Negates Prefixing Form B (Jussive and Optative)*

14.4/5 ***’L YPTḤ ’YT MŠKB Z W’L YBQŠ BN MNM,*** “Let him not open this resting-place, and let him not look for anything in it!”

3. *Negates Prefixing Form B (Future Result)*

As in the conditional sentence in Classical Arabic, a future result is expressed by means of Suffixing Form B. Accordingly, the negative future result clause in Phoenician and Punic is expressed by means of Prefixing Form B negated by the particle ***’L.***

13.6/8 ***’M PTḤ TPTḤ ‘LTY WRGZ TRGZN ’L Y<K>N L<K> ZR‘ BḤYM TḤT ŠMŠ WMŠKB ’T RP’M,*** “If you do open it (the coffin) and disturb me, you shall not have offspring among those living under the sun nor rest among the infernal gods.”

14.6/9 ***K KL MMLKT WKL ’DM ’Š YPTḤ ‘LT MŠKB Z . . . ’L YKN LM MŠKB ’T RP’M W’L YQBR BQBR W’L YKN LM BN WZR‘ TḤTNM.,*** “As for any king or any commoner who shall open this resting-place, they shall not have rest among the infernal gods, and they shall not be buried in a grave, and they shall not have sons nor progeny in their stead.”

14.11/12 ***’M ’DMM HMT ’L YKN LM ŠRŠ LMṬ WPR LM‘L WT’R BḤYM TḤT ŠMŠ,*** “As for those persons <who shall open the tomb and remove the coffin>, they shall not have root below nor fruit above nor wealth among those living under the sun.”

24.13/15 ***WMY BBNY ’Š YŠB TḤTN WYZQ BSPR Z MŠKBM ’L YKBD LB‘RRM WB‘RRM ’L YKBD LMŠKBM,*** “As for whichever of my sons shall sit upon the throne in my stead, if he shall damage this inscription, the *mškbm* shall no longer respect the *b‘rrm*, and the *b‘rrm* shall no longer respect the *mškbm*.”

4. *Expressing Refusal*

Pu *Poen.* 1142 **Al. Anec este mem,** “No, I will not! I shall drink water!” Response to the invitation **Neste ien, neste dum et,** “Let us drink wine; let us drink the blood of the vine!”

BL bal

1. *Negates the Suffixing Form Past Perfective*

24.2/5 ***MLK GBR ʿL YʾDY WBL P[ʿL] KN BMH WBL PʿL WKN ʾB ḤYʾ WBL PʿL WKN ʾḤ ŠʾL WBL PʿL WʾN[K] KLMW BR TM[.] M ʾŠ PʾLT BL PʿL HLPNY{H}M,*** "Gabbar ruled over Y'DY, but he did not accomplish anything. There was BMH, but he did not accomplish anything. There was my father Hayya, but he did not accomplish anything. there was my brother Sa'il, but he did not accomplish anything. But as for me, Kilamuwa son of TM[.], I accomplished what my predecessors did not accomplish."

24.4/5 ***M ʾŠ PʿLT BL PʿL HLPNYM,*** "<My> predecessors did not accomplish what I accomplished."

26 A I 19 ***BL ʿN KL HMLKM ʾŠ KN LPNY,*** "<I conquered mighty lands that> all the kings who preceded me did not conquer."

2. *Negates Prefixing Form A Future Indicative*

Pu 79.15 ***BKL ZBḤ ʾŠ YZBḤ DL MQNʾ ʾM DL ṢPR BL YKN LKHN[M MNM],*** "Of a sacrifice that someone owning no cattle nor fowl shall sacrifice, nothing shall be for the priests."

3. *Negates the Active Participle*

Pu *CIS* i 169.2 ***BL ʿLM ʿLT HMZBḤ,*** "<The parts of a sacrificial animal that> do not go up <in smoke> upon the altar."

See the negative particle ***ʾ(Y)BL*** with this same function (above).

4. *Negates a Noun*

26 A I 15/16 ***BL ʾŠ ʿBD KN LBT MPŠ,*** "None (*lit.,* no man) was a vassal of the House of Mopsos."

Pu *Poen.* 1017A **Bal umir**, "Not a word!" Response to the question, **Mu Ponnim sycartim?,** "Do you remember any Punic?"

5. *Negates an Adverbial Phrase*

14.2/3 ***NGZLT BL ʿTY BN MSK YMM ʾZRM,*** "I was snatched away not at (*i.e.,* before) my <appointed> time, at the age of a few days, like a child sacrificial victim!"

6. *Existential: "There is/are not"*

NPu 163.3 ***BL L' BṢMḤ Š'RM,*** "He does not have any offspring of his own flesh."

D. *The Accusative Particles*

The accusative particle or *nota accusativi* introduces a determined direct object of an active transitive verb. Its use was not obligatory and, in any given text erratic and unpredictable. In classical Phoenician usage, the particle had the complementary forms ***'T*** and ***'YT***, the former used immediately before a noun with possessive suffix, the latter used in all other instances. This complementation, characteristic both of Tyro-Sidonian and Byblian Phoenician, did not obtain in Punic.

The original pronunciation of ***'YT*** is not certain: in doubt is whether the internal *yod* was consonantal or a the vowel-letter e-vowel indicating the pronunciation *'et,* as we know the particle to have been pronounced in Punic: Pu *Poen.* 940 **et;** Neo-Punic *Poen.* 930; 945; 947) **yth.** The pronunciation of Phoenician ***'T***, used before a noun with possessive suffix, was *'ōt,* as indicated by the Greek-letter transcription οθ (174.5); this form is clearly related to the Hebrew form ***'T*** *'ōt-* used with suffixal pronouns, *e.g.,* ***'TY*** *'ōtī* ("me"), ***'TW*** *'ōto* ("him"), etc.

In Punic and Neo-Punic, the particle is frequently attested as an aphetic proclitic ***T-*** (Latin-letter **th-**) before the definitive article (normally with suppression of the writing of the article). This form is not attested in Phoenician.

In Phoenician and occasionally in Punic, the particle governs the genitive case. Accordingly, the noun receives the B-forms of the possessive pronouns of the first singular and third singular and plural, these being the forms regularly used with the noun in the genitive case.

1. *Phoenician Usage*

Complementation of Forms

In formal Phoenician usage, the form ***'T*** *'ōt* was used immediately before a noun carrying a possessive pronoun; the possessive pronoun was always the B-Form, the allomorph affixed to the noun in the genitive case since the accusative particle governed the genitive. In all other instances, the complementary form ***'YT*** *'et* was used before the noun. The following passages illustrate this complementary usage.

'T

Byb 9 B ***['L YŠT ']T 'RNW 'LT 'RN '[. . .],*** "[Let him not place] his coffin upon the coffin of . . .}!" *Obs.* The noun ***'RNW*** *'arōniw* ("his coffin") is genitive in case and, accordingly, carries the B-Form ***-W*** of the third masculine singular possessive pronoun. The pronoun "his" affixed to a noun in the accusative case was **-Ø** *-o.*

Byb 10.2/3 ***WQR' 'NK 'T RBTY,*** "I invoked my Lady." *Obs.* The noun ***RBTY*** *ribbatī* is in the genitive case and, accordingly, carries the B-Form ***-Y*** of the first person singular possessive pronoun. The pronoun "my" affixed to a noun in the accusative case was **-Ø** *-ī.* This is true as well of the following two examples:

Byb 10.7 ***KM 'Š QR'T 'T RBTY,*** "When I invoked my Lady."

Byb 10.14 ***TSG 'T PTḤY Z,*** "If you move this inscription of mine."

48.3 ***TBRK. . . 'T 'MNM,*** "Bless ye their mother!" *Obs.* The noun ***'MNM*** *'amm^e nom* ("their mother") is genitive in case and, accordingly, carries the possessive pronoun ***-NM*** of the third person masculine plural. The pronoun "their" affixed to a noun in the accusative case was ***-M*** *-om.*

CIS i 91.2 ***NŠḤT 'T 'BY HYṢ'M,*** "Would that I might defeat my enemies who have/will come forth <against me>."

174.1/8 Αφεθενναυ υιος Αφεσαθουν νεσε οθ αμαθη (***NŠ' 'T 'MTY***) λεσαθ λαφδε Μα[. . .], "Abdthennau son of Abdsaphun gave his female slave as a wife to his slave Ma[. . .]." *Obs*: The noun αμαθη is genitive in case and, accordingly, has the possessive pronoun -η (Phoenician-letter ***-Y***) of the third masculine singular. This same pronoun appears in Greek transcription as -ε in λαφδε (***L'BDY*** "for his slave"), the noun, governed by a preposition, also genitive in case. The pronoun "his" affixed to a noun in the accustive case was **-Ø** *-o* in Tyro-Sidonian Phoenician.

NPu 145 I 4 ***L'LM HQDYŠ LŠ'T 'ḤT ŠMM,*** "Exalt the name of the holy god!" *Obs.* The form ***'ḤT*** perhaps reflects the shape *'ōt.*

'YT

Byb 10.8 ***TBRK B'LT GBL 'YT YḤWMLK,*** "Baalt of Byblos bless Yehawmilk!"

Byb 10.15 ***TSRḤ HRBT B'LT GBL 'YT H'DM H' WZR'W,*** "The Lady Baalt of Byblos make stink that person and his seed!" *Obs.* The noun ***ZR'W*** *zar'iw* ("his seed"), governed by the particle, is accordingly genitive in case and must receive the possessive pronoun ***-W*** *-iw* of the third masculine singular.

13.3 ***TPQ 'YT H'RN Z,*** "You shall come into possession of this coffin."

14.4/5 ***'L YPTḤ 'YT MŠKB Z,*** "Let him not open this resting-place!"

18.3.4 ***'YT HŠ'R Z WHDlHT 'Š L P'LT BTKLTY BNTY,*** "I built this gate and its doors at my own expense."

26 A III 14/15 ***'M 'P YḤMD 'YT HQRT Z,*** "Even if he loves this city."

48.3 ***[TB]RK 'Y[T 'RB'T B[NY] . . . W'T 'MNM,*** "Bless ye my four sons and their mother!" *Obs.* Note the complementation of the particles ***'YT*** and ***'T*** in the same sentence in the manner described above: ***'T*** before a noun carrying a posessive pronoun; otherwise, ***'YT***.

Once only in Phoenician is this form of the particle written phonetically ***'T*** *et:* 50.5/6 ***WŠLḤT LY 'T SPR HNQT,*** "Send me the quittance!"

2. *Punic and Neo-Punic Usage*

'YT (**et, yth**)

The accusative particle of classical Punic and Neo-Punic was ***'YT***; but in contrast to Phoenician usage, it was used without restriction.

Pu *CIS* i 5510.2/3 (Carthage, 406 B.C.E.) ***[KL 'DM] 'Š LKP 'YT 'MTNT Z . . . 'ML YD,*** "As for any person who shall knock down this stele, his hand shall wither."

Pu 80.1 ***ḤDŠ WP'L 'YT HMṬBḤ Z . . . H'ŠM 'Š 'L HMQDŠM,*** "The men in charge of sanctuaries rebuilt this slaughtering table."

Pu *Poen.* 940 **Et alonim ualonut caruti is timlacun alt imacum esse,** "I invoke you gods and goddesses who rule over this city." = NPu *Poen.* 930 **Yth alonim ualonuth carothi ys thymlachun yth m(ac)um ysyth,** "I invoke you gods and goddesses who rule this city."

Poen. 937 **Ythem anech nasothi li yth irs aelichoth sith,** "To him I bring on my behalf this shard of hospitality."

The form ***'YT*** was used in Punic before a noun with suffixed possessive pronoun but it continued to govern the genitive case: Pu *CIS* i 3604 ***TŠMʻʼ ʼYT QLM*** *tisma*ʻ*ū* ʼ*et qūlim* ("Hear ye his voice!"); 115.1/2 ***ŠLM ʻBDʻŠTRT . . . ʼYT NDRM*** ("Abdastart fulfilled his vow."). In both examples cited, we see the use of the B-Form ***-M*** *-im* of the possessive pronoun of the third masculine singular, used exclusively with the noun in the genitive case.

ʼT

This form is found in Punic as a rare phonetic spelling of ***ʼYT***, which is known to have been pronounced ʼ*et* from the Latin-letter spellings **et** and **yth**.

Pu 69.21 ***[K]L Bʻ L ZBḤ ʼŠ ʼYBL YTN ʼT K[L . .]L HMŠʼT ʼŠ [ŠT BPS Z WNʻNŠ],*** "As for any sacrificer who shall not pay the full a[mount of the] payment that is stipulated in this inscripion, he shall be fined."

T-

The aphetic form ***T-*** (**th-**) was widely used in late Punic and Neo-Punic, including in literary prose. It did not however replace the formal literary form ***ʼYT***. The form was used exclusively before the definite article; in all other instances, the preferred form was ***ʼYT*** (**et, yth**). In Punic-letter inscriptions, the definite article is commonly although not always written **Ø** after the particle.

Pu 79.6/7 ***KL ʼŠ LSR T-ʼBN Z,*** "Anyone who shall remove this stele."

Pu 101.1 ***T-MQDŠ Z BNʼ BʻLʼ TBGG,*** "The citizens of Thugga built this sanctuary."

NPu 129.1/2 ***BNʼ WʼYQDŠ T-ʻKSNDRʻ WT-ʻRPT ST,*** "He built and dedicated this excedra and this portico."

NPu 161.3/4 ***ṬNʼ T-HMʼŠ ST BMBW<ʼ> ʼḤDR DLʼ QBRʼ,*** "He erected this statue at the entrance of the chamber containing his tomb."

NPu *AI* 1 1927 p. 233 lines 1/2 **Fel th-ybur Licini Piso,** "Licinius Piso built the tomb."

NPu *LA* 1 p. 45 no. 4.9 **chy [c]hil[o] ufel th-y[. . .],** "When he had finished building the [ ]."

NPu *Poen.* 940A **Thymlachun th-ymacom syth,** "You rule this city." *Obs.* The form **yth** is used in the variant reading of this same line, in which the noun does not carry the definite article: NPu *Poen.* 930 **Thymlachun yth m(ac)um ysyth.**

Compare and contrast the consistent use of **yth** in Latin-letter Neo-Punic before a noun that does not carry the definite article:

NPu *Poen.* 930 **Yth alonim ualonuth carothi,** "I invoke you gods and goddesses."

NPu *Poen.* 937 **Ythem anech nasothi li yth irs aelichoth sith,** "To him I bring on my behalf this shard of hospitality."

’T with Suffixal Pronouns

Unique to Punic is the use of the accusative particle with suffixal pronouns to express the independent object pronoun in the manner of Hebrew *’ōto* ("him"). Two instances are attested:

Pu *CIS* i 580.3 ***’RŠT BT BD‘ŠTRT ŠM‘ QL’ BRK ’T’,*** "Arisut daughter of Bostar. Hear her voice, bless her!"

Pu *CIS* I 6001.1/2 ***‘BDMLKT ’L TŠ’ <’>T’,*** "<This is the funerary urn of> Abdmilkot. Do not carry it off!" The inscription is written in ink on a clay jar (funerary urn) found in 1895 in the Douimes necropolis at Carthage.

Obs. This pronoun is not attested in Phoenician, which uses instead the preposition ***‘LT*** with suffixal pronoun to express the independent direct object pronoun:

13.3/4 ***MY ’T KL ’DM ’Š TPQ ’YT ’RN Z ’L ’L TPTḤ ‘LTY,*** "Whoever you may be, any person who shall come into possession of this coffin, do not, do not open it!"

14.20/21 ***MY ’T KL MMLKT WKL ’DM ’L YPTḤ ‘LTY W’L Y‘R ‘LTY,*** "Whoever you may be, any person of royal descent or any commoner, let him not open it (my resting-place) nor empty it out!"

E. *The Presentative Particles*

The presentative particles serve to introduce a simple, declarative sentence. Their use is always non-obligatory, and they are seldom attested.

HLM ?*hallīm*

The particle occurs only in the Roman-letter spelling **alem** in the literary Punic passages in the *Poenulus*; no instance of the particle is found in Punic-letter inscriptions. Its pronunciation and etymology are problematic; the vocalization *hallīm* given here is based on the possible relatedness of the Punic particle to the Ugaritic presentatives ***HL, HLK*** and ***HLM.*** That Punic **alem** is indeed a presentative particle is certain from its equivalence to **ynny** (Hebrew hinne) in the Neo-Punic of the *Poenulus.*

Pu *Poen.* 944/46 **Alem us duber ce fel dono Metun et cil comu con liful alt banim au,** "I am told that his father Mettun did everything for that son of his as he was to do <for him>."

Pu *Poen.* 948 **Alem us duber limur <esse> mucom sussibti A(charist)ocle,** "I am told that this is the place where Acharistocles resides." = NPu *Poen.* 938 **Ynny i(s) d(ubyr) ch'ily gubulim lasibithim <Agorastocles>,** "I am told that this is the district where Agorastocles resides."

HN hinne, hen

This presentative is the same particle as Hebrew *hinne* and *hen,* and Arabic *ʾinna.* This use of the particle must be differentiated from its use as the locative demonstrative "here" (see the chapter on the adverbs).

NPu *Poen.* 938 **Ynny i(s) d(ubyr) ch'ily gubulim lasbisithim <Agorastocles>,** "I am told that this is the district where Agorastocles resides." = Pu *Poen.* 948 **Alem us duber limur <esse> mucom sussibit A(charist)ocle,** "I am told that this is the place where Acharistocles resides."

NPu *Poen.* 932/33 **Yn byn ui bymarob syllochom, alonim, uybymysyrthochom,** "My brother's son is in your custody, O gods, and under your protection."

NPu D 6.10 **In aab sa[l]e(m) lo sal,** "The enemy asked for mercy for himself."

K- kī

The conjunction *kī* is commonly used in Phoenician as a presentative particle. This use must be differentiated from that of a subordinating conjunction "because."

14.2 ***K-ʾNK {NḤN} NGZLT BL ʿTY,*** "I was snatched away not at (*i.e.,* before) my appointed time." *Obs.* This same declarative statement occurs again in this same inscription in the form of a quote: ***DBR MLK ʾŠMNʿZR MLK ṢDNM LʾMR NGZLT BL ʿTY,*** "The statement of King Esmunazor, King of the Sidonians: 'I was snatched away before my appointed time!'"

14.13/16 ***K-ʾNK ʾŠMNʿZR . . . WʾMY ʾMʿŠTRT . . . ʾŠ BNN ʿYT BT ʾLNM,*** "It was I, Esmunazor, and my mother, Amastarte, who built the temples."

CIS i4.3/5 ***K-BN BD'ŠTRT MLK ṢDNM 'YT ŠRN 'R[Ṣ DGN] L['JLY L'ŠTRT,*** "Bostar, King of the Sidonians, built up the Sharon, the reg[ion of grain], for his goddess, Astarte."

26 A II 15/16 ***K-BYMTY KN L'RṢ 'MQ 'DN ŠB' WMN'M,*** "In my time, the land of the Valley of Adana enjoyed abundance and prosperity!"

F. *The Particle of Citation and Quotation*

L'MR *limūr*

As in Hebrew, the infinitive construct ***L'MR*** may be used to introduce a citation or quotation:

14.2/3 ***DBR MLK 'ŠMN'ZR MLK ṢDNM L'MR NGZLT BL 'TY,*** "<This is the final> statement of Esmunazor, King of the Sidonians: 'I was snatched away before my appointed time!'"

Pu 948 **Alem us duber limur <esse> mucom sussibti A(carist)ocle,** "I am told: 'This is the place where Acharistocles resides.'" *Obs.* In the Neo-Punic, revision of this line, the indirect statement introduced by **chy** ("that") is used: *Poen.* 938 **Ynny i(s) d(ubyr) ch'ily gubulim lasibithim <Agorastocles>,** "I am told that this is the district where Agorastocles resides."

Citation of direct speech may also be introduced by a zero-marker: 26 C III 17/18 ***Y'MR 'P'L SML ZR WŠT ŠMY 'LY,*** "He shall say, 'I shall make another image and place my own name upon it.'"

G. *The Verbal Proclitic and Enclitic Particles*

1. *Proclitic* ***L-***

The proclitic particle ***L-*** *li-* is used optionally in Punic and Neo-Punic with Prefixing Verbs A and B when these express the cohortative or jussive. Proclitic to the inflectional morpheme *i-* of the first person singular, the particle had the form *l*.

NPu *Poen.* 932 **L-iphoc** (***L-'PQ***) **anech yth byn ui iaded,** "Let me get my brother's only son."

Pu *Poen.* 949 **Anec l-itor** (***L-'TR***) **bod es iussim limin co,** "Let me inquire of these men who are coming out from here."

NPu *Poen.* 939 **Bod i(ly) a(nech) l-ythera ymu ys lomyn choth iusim,** "Let me inquire of these men who are coming out from here."

Proclitic to the the third masculine singular of the Prefixing Verb, the verb had the form *liqtol,* from original *liyiqtol.* The verb form was written either historically as ***L-YQTL*** or phonetically as ***LQTL***:

Pu *EH* 32.3 ***L-YŠMʿ*** (*lismaʿ*) ***QLʾ,*** "May he hear his voice!"

Pu *EH* 216.3 ***LŠMʿ*** (*lismaʿ*) ***QLʾ,*** "May he hear his voice!"

2. *Post-Imperative* ***–Nʾ*** *-na*

This particle is used after the imperative ending in *–a*. It is cognate with the Hebrew imperatival particle *–na* (***-Nʾ***) and, like the latter, evidences doubling of the initial consonant *n* after the extending *a*-vowel of the imperative.

Pu *Poen.* 1013 **Lec. Lacanna limin co,** "Go! Go away from here!" Here, **lachanna** is the imperative *lᵃka* (*lek* with extending morpheme *-a)* + particle *-na* with gemination. Compare the Hebrew imperative with the particle and the same gemination: Genesis 32:30 ***HGYDH-Nʾ*** *haggīdanna* ("Tell!"); observe also Hebrew cohortatives with the particle following and the gemination present: Genesis 18:21 ***ʾRDH-Nʾ*** *ʾerᵉdanna* ("I would descend") and ***ʾLKH-Nʾ*** *ʾelᵉkanna* ("I would go").

3. *Enclitic* ***-N***

The separable enclitic particle ***-n(a)***, the reflex of Old Canaanite ***-na,*** is found affixed to all forms of the Prefixing Verb. The use of this particle in Phoenician with the Prefixing Verb is attested already in 14th century B.C. Byblian Phoenician, as evidenced by Amarna forms like *īpušu-na* (Prefixing Form A) and *timaḫḫaṣa-na* (Prefixing Form B). On this particle, see Moran, p. 11.

3a. With Prefixing Form A Present Imperfective

13.3/5 ***ʾY ʾDL-N KSP ʾY ʾDL-N ḤRṢ,*** "I do not possess silver, I do not possess gold." Cf. Archaic Hebrew Numbers 24:9 ***YQM-N*** *yaqūm(u)-na* ("he will arise"): (emended orthographically) ***KRʿ ŠKB KʾRY // WKLBYʾ-MY YQWM-N,*** "He (Israel) crouches, lies like a lion, // And like a lion shall he arise (attack)!" Note the occurrence of this same half-verse with the verb without the particle in Numbers 23:24a: ***HN-ʿM KLBYʾ YQWM,*** "That people shall arise (attack) like a lion!"

3b. With Prefixing Form B Past Perfective

50.3/4 ***'PQ-N HKSP 'Š ŠLḤT LY,*** "I got the silver that you sent me." *Cf.* Archaic Hebrew Judges 5:26 ***TŠLḤ-NH*** *tišlaḥ-na* ("she extended"): ***YDH LYTD TŠLḤ-NH,*** "She (Jael) reached out for the tent-peg."

3c. With the Jussive/Optative (Prefixing Form C)

Pu *Poen.* 1027P **Bal samem ierasa-n,** "Baal shake the heavens!"

H. *Directional Ending -a*

The directional ending *-a* < *-ah* of Hebrew and Ugaritic is also found in Punic in the adverb **cona** ("hither"): *Poen.* 942/943 **Iule anec cona, alonim balim, bane becor Bals[*illem*],** "I brought hither, O proprietary gods, my firstborn son Bals*illem*." The adverb **cona** is the simple locative **co** ("here"), with the directional ending **-a** affixed to it by means of intervening euphonic **-n-.** Compare the use of this ending in the Hebrew adverb ***ŠMH*** *šámma* ("thither").

I. *Accusative Ending -am*

The archaic accusative ending *-am* < *-amma* is retained in the Punic adverb *CIS i* 171.4; *CIS i* 5522.3/4 ***ḤNM*** *ḥinnam* ("gratis; of one's own free will").

CHAPTER SIXTEEN

CLOSING OBSERVATIONS ON SYNTAX

A. *The Equational Sentence*

The syntax, specifically, the word-order, of the equational sentence with nominal predicate was determined largely by the nature, nominal or pronominal, of the subject of the sentence. As a general rule, an independent personal pronoun as subject occupied initial position in a non-subordinate clause: 24.1 ***ʾNK KLMW*** ("I am Kilamuwa."); 26 A I 1 ***ʾNK ʾZTWD*** ("I am Aztwadda."); 54.1 ***ʾNK ŠM BN ʿBDʿŠTRT ʾŠQLNY*** ("I am Sem son of Abdastart the Ascalonian."). Rarely did the pronominal subject follow the predicate, as in *Poen.* 940A **Anno byn Mytthumbal leAdrumet anec** ("I am Hanno son of Mytthumbal of Hadrumetum.") or when the sentence was a subordinate clause, requiring inversion of subject and predicate, as in 10.9 ***K MLK ṢDQ Hʾ*** (". . . for he was a good king.") and *LA* 1 p. 45 no. 4.4/5 **chi ur Sorim y** (". . . for she is the light of the Tyrians."). In marked contrast, in the majority of examples of this same sentence type but with nominal subject, it is the nominal predicate that occupies sentence-initial position: 40.2 ***KNPRS ʾRSNʾS PLDLP ʾMTʾSR*** ("Amot-Osiri was Kanephoros of Arsinoe daughter of Philadelphos."); NPu *IRT* 879.1 **Adom unim ys ysy Bodsychun Chalia** ("This man, Bodsychun Chalia, was a person of substance."); Pu *Poen.* 943/944 **Hulec silli . . . Antidamas con,** ("Antidamas was my guest-friend.") = NPu *Poen.* 934 **Ulech <silli> Antidamas chon.** Somewhat less often does the nominal subject precede the nominal predicate: 16 A I 15/16 ***BL ʾŠ ʿBD KN LBT MPŠ*** ("None was a vassal of the house of Mopsos."); *PBSR* 28 p. 53 no. 5.9/10 **Bynom Mrausyn au[r]ys** ("Their son Mrausyn was the engraver.").

B. *The Syntax (Position) of the Verb in the Clause or Sentence*

In Phoenician, tense and aspect reference was a function of syntax, not of form; therefore critical to understanding the language is an understanding of the syntax of the verb, specifically, the syntactic restrictions governing the position of the verb in the sentence or clause which, in turn, determine largely the tense and aspect reference of the verb. Restriction in the clause or sentence is related not merely to initial or non-initial position use but also to the position of the verb with regard to its nominal or pronominal subject.

1. *The Suffixing Form of the Verb*

The Suffixing Form expressing the Present Perfective was without syntactic restriction in the sentence; the verb could occupy sentence-initial or non sentence-initial position: 50.2/3 ***BRKTK LB'LṢPN*** ("I bless you in the name of Baalsaphon!"); Pu *Poen.* 947 **Itt esde anec nasote hers ahelicot** ("To him I bring a shard of hospitality.").

The Suffixing Form expressing the Past Perfective was governed by numerous syntactic restrictions. In literary Phoenician and Punic usage, when the Suffixing Form Past Perfective was the main verb of an independent (non-subordinate) clause of a non-complex sentence, it was restricted syntactically to non clause/sentence-initial position: 24.13 ***W'NK TMKT MŠKBM LYD*** ("I took the members of the lower class by the hand."); 26 A I-21-II 1 ***WDNNYM YŠBT ŠM*** ("And I resettled Danunians there."); Pu *Poen.* 943 **Hu neso bin ys esse** ("He was made the son of this man."), *et passim.* Clause/sentence-initial Past Perfective was expressed in literary Phoenician and Punic only by the Infinitive Construct Past Perfective or by Prefixing Form B Past Perfective. In Punic and Neo-Punic, however, the syntactic restriction regarding the position of the Suffixing Form Past Perfective was not operative: Pu 80.1 ***ḤDŠ WP'L 'YT HMṬBḤ Z. . . 'ŠRT H'ŠM 'Š 'L HMQDŠM*** ("The ten men who are in charge of the sanctuaries rebuilt this slaughtering altar."); NPu *AI* 1 1927 p. 233 lines 1/2 **Fel thy-bur Licini Piso** ("Licinius Piso built <this> tomb."), *et passim.*

A Suffixing Form that is not a main verb but follows the main verb of an independent clause or sentence is the Consecutive Form; the Consecutive possesses no inherent tense or aspect reference but, rather, assumes the tense and aspect reference of the main verb of the sentence: 26 A I 6/8 ***WP'L 'NK SS 'L SS . . . WŠBRT MLṢM*** ("I acquired horse upon horse . . . and smashed those who scorned me."); 26 A III 16 ***WYP'L L Š'R ZR WŠT ŠM 'L*** ("He shall make for himself another gate and place his own name on it."); 10.9/11 ***TTN [LY HRBT B]'LT GBL ḤN . . . WḤN*** (*w^eḥanna*) ***'M 'RṢ Z*** ("The Lady Baalt of Byblos grant me favor, and may she favor the people of this land!").

In complex sentences in literary Phoenician and Punic, the Suffixing Form Past Perfective could occupy clause-initial position in the main (result) clause of a temporal sentence or in the main clause of a sentence with anticipatory clause: 10.7/8 ***KM 'Š QR'T 'T RBTY B'LT GBL WŠM' QL*** ("When I called my Lady Baalt of Byblos, she heard my voice."); 24.11 ***WMY BL ḤZ PN Š ŠTY B'L 'DR*** ("As for him who had never owned a sheep, I made him the owner of a flock.").

A Suffixing Form occupying clause-initial position in the result clause of a sentence with anticipatory clause or in the result clause of a conditional sentence has future tense reference; this usage is extremely common both in Phoenician and in Punic: Pu *CIS* i 4945.4/6 ***W'Š YRGZ T-MTNT Z WQBT TNT-PNB'L*** ("As for him who shall disturb this stele, Thinnith-Phanebal shall curse him!"); Pu *CIS* I 5510.7 ***[M]ŠRT LQN' WKN L' ḤL WŠLM*** ("If he who serves shall be zealous, wealth and prosperity shall be his.").

A Suffixing Form occupying sentence-initial position in an independent clause was often jussive/optative in reference: this usage is well attested in Phoenician and in Punic: 26 A III 2/3 ***WBRK B'L KRNTRYŠ 'YT 'ZTWD ḤYM WŠLM*** ("May Baal-KRNTRYS bless Aztwadda with long life and prosperity!"); Pu *Poen.* 1141 **haua amma silli** ("May my mother live long!"); *Poen.* 1141 **hauo bene silli** ("May my son live long!").

2. *Prefixing Form A*

Prefixing Form A, in all its tense/aspect references (Present Imperfective, Past Imperfective, Future), is without syntactic restriction. The nominal or pronominal subject of the Form may precede or follow the verb: 48.2/3 ***'NKY LRBTY . . . 'Š'L [TB]RK 'Y[T 'RB'T B]NY*** ("I ask of my Lady: Bless my four sons!"); 26 A II 4/4 ***'DM YŠT' LLKT DRK*** ("One used to be afraid to walk the road."); 24.15 ***WMY YŠḤT HSPR Z YŠḤT R'Š B'L ṢMD*** ("As for whomever shall destroy this inscription, Baal-Semed shall smash his head!").

3. *Prefixing Forms B and C*

Prefixing Form B expressing the Past Perfective is syntactically restricted to sentence-initial position; it does not require the conjunction ***W-*** as does Hebrew *wayyiqtol:* 30.2/4 ***Y'L HGBR Z' '[l]ŠY WY'BD H[. . .] Z' 'YT H'Y*** ("This warrior came up to Alasiya, and this . . . devastated the island."); Pu *CIS* I 5510.9/10 ***WYLK RBM 'DNB'L BN GRSKN HRB WḤMLK BN ḤN' HRB 'LŠ*** ("Generals Idnibal son of Gisco the Great and Himilco son of Hanno the Great marched at dawn."). Prefixing Form B Past Perfective may continue a prior like verb within the same sentence: 50.3/4 ***'PQN HKSP 'Š ŠLḤT LY WTNTN LY*** ("I received the silver that you sent me and have lent me.").

Prefixing Form B expressing the Jussive/Optative had no syntactic restriction with regard to position in the sentence; the nominal or pronominal subject of the verb may precede or follow although it is more common for it to precede the verb: 52.1/2 ***ḤRPKRT YTN ḤYM L'BDY L'BD'ŠMN*** ("Harpokrates give long life to his servant Abdesmun!"); Pu *Poen.* 1027 **Bal samem ierasan** ("Baal shake the heavens!") but also 10.8 ***TBRK B'LT GBL 'YT YḤWMLK*** ("Baalt of Byblos bless Yehawmilk!").

Prefixing Form B expressing the Cohortative preceded or followed its subject: Pu *Poen.* 949 **Anec l-itor bod es iussim limin co** ("Let me inquire of these men who are coming out from here.") = *Poen.* 939 with Prefixing Form C **Bod i(ly) a(nech) l-ythera** ("Let me inquire of these men."); Npu *Poen.* 943 **L-iphoc anech yth byn ui iaed** ("Let me get my brother's only son.").

Prefixing Form B is used to express the Subjunctive after the particle ***LKN*** ("in order that"): 60.6/8 ***YŠ'N BKSP 'LM B'L ṢDN DRKMNM 20 LMḤT LKN YD'*** (*yede'ū:* Subjunctive) ***HṢDNYM K YD' HGW LŠLM ḤLPT 'YT 'DMM 'Š P'L MŠRT 'T PN GW*** ("They shall withdraw 20 drachmas from the silver of the god Baal of Sidon in order that the Sidonians might know that the community knows to compensate those persons who have performed service on behalf of the community."). Elsewhere, the Subjunctive is expressed by the Infinitive Construct.

4. *The Imperative Form*

When the Imperative Form had independent personal pronoun as its subject, the nominal or pronominal subject preceded or followed: 50.5 ***'T BṬḤ BDBR[Y]*** ("Trust thou in my word!") but D 6.11 **Un ath a[bdach]a** ("Spare thou thy servant!").

5. *Active Participle*

When the Active Participle had a noun or independent personal pronoun as its subject, the nominal or pronominal subject preceded or followed: 13.1/3 ***'NK TBNT . . . ŠKB B'RN Z*** ("I, Tibnit, lie in this sarcophagus.") but 14.3 ***WŠKB 'NK BḤLT Z*** ("I lie in this coffin.").

6. *Infinite Construct*

The Infinite Construct used to express the Jussive/Optative mood was restricted to sentence initial position: 26 A III 4/5 ***LTTY B'L KRNTRYŠ . . . L'ZTWD 'RK YMM*** ("Baal-KRNTRYS give to Aztwadda a long reign!"); NPu ***L'TT H'L 'BBRKTM L[N]*** ("God grant us of his blessings!"). When used to express the imperative, the Infinite Construct is also sentence-initial: 2.1/3 ***LD'T HNY B'LK TḤT ZN*** ("Know that I, your king, am at the bottom of this <shaft>!"); Pu 76 B 8 ***LŠT 'LT HḤDRT NPT*** ("Put honey on top of the swelling!"); NPu 145 I 4 ***LŠ'T 'ḤT ŠMM*** ("Exalt his name!").

The Infinitive Construct used to express the Future had no syntactic restriction; it could be sentence-initial or non-sentence-initial: 14.9/10 ***LQSTNM 'YT MMLKT 'M 'DM H'*** ("They shall cut off that royal person or that commoner.") but 60.4/5 ***'YT R'T Z LKTB H'DMM 'Š NŠ'M LN 'L BT 'LM 'LT MṢBT ḤRṢ*** ("The men who were elected by us in charge of the temple shall inscribe this resolution on a gold stele."). The Infinitive Construct Future may also occur in a relative clause; this use is quite common: 79.6/8 ***WKL 'Š LSR T-'BN Z*** ("Anyone who shall remove this stele"). In one syntactic structure alone could the Infinitive Construct Future not stand: it is unknown in the result clause of a sentence with prior clause; in this usage, only Suffixing Form B and Prefixing Form A occur.

7. *The Infinitive Absolute Past Perfective*

The Infinitive Absolute used to express the the Past Perfective was syntactically restricted to sentence-initial position: 24.7/8 ***WŠKR 'NK 'LY MLK 'ŠR*** ("I hired the king of Assyria against him."); 26 A I 3/4 ***YḤW 'NK 'YT DNNYM*** ("I kept the Danunians alive."); Pu *Poen.* 943/944 **Iulec anec cona, alonim balim, bane becor Bals[illem]** ("I brought here, O proprietary gods, my firstborn son Bals[illem]."). In the same sentence, the non sentence-initial counterpart to the Infinitive Absolute Past Perfective was the Suffixing Form Past Perfective.

C. *The Syntax of the Complex Sentence*

The syntax of complex sentences, such as temporal sentences, conditional sentences and sentences with final clauses, requires comment. These complex sentences exhibit special usage of the verb in the main clauses; they also illustrate the manner in which constituent clauses of a complex sentence are conjoined.

1. *Temporal Sentences*

'ḤR 'Š

AFTER

NSI 56.2/6 ***'ḤR 'Š P'L ṢYW'T LHḤYM H'Š ŠL' . . . 'M' L ŠRT ŠNT ḤMŠM,*** "After her husband had made his farewell to the living, his mother performed public service for (another) fifty years."

B- + Infinitive Construct

WHEN

The *when*-clause of a temporal sentence was also expressed by ***B-*** + Infinitive Construct. The *when*-clause precedes or follows the main clause. The grammatical subject of the infinitive is expressed by the suffixal pronoun; the logical subject may follow in apposition. When the main (result) clause of the sentence follows the *when*-clause, it is introduced by the conjunction ***W-*** , and the verb form used to express past perfective action is Suffixing Form Past Perfective.

Kition lines 1/3 ***BMṢ'NM 'BN W'ZRNM HPPYM L'GD LN MLḤMT . . . WYṢ' 'L[NM MḤN]T 'Š KTY L'GD LM MLḤMT,*** "When our enemies and their Paphian allies came to do battle with us, the army of the people of Kition went forth against them to do battle with them."

NPu 159.5/6 ***TW' YSPN 'LT MQDŠM BYRḤ KRR ŠT BLL HZBḤ . . . BŠPṬM*** (*bisofṭīm*) ***MSHB',*** "We added his cella to his sanctuary in the month of Kirur, in the year of BLL, the sacrificial priest, when MSHB' was suffes."

NPu Trip. 79.5/6 ***NPL'*** (sic!) ***BTṢTY BTY BḤYTNM*** (*biḥyōt^e nom*), "It (the tomb) was built at his own expense when they (those at rest in the tomb) were <still> living."

K *kī*

WHEN

In this construction, the *when*-clause follows the main main clause:

Byb 1.1 ***'RN ZP'L [']TB'L . . . L'ḤRM 'BH K-ŠTH B<T> 'L,*** "<This is> the coffin that Ittobaal made for his father Ahiram when he (Ittobaal) placed him (Ahiram) in the tomb."

AI 1 p. 45 no. 4.7/9 **Ubarb aamys chyrym[u]ia byiyra [Mu]fa chy [c]hil[o] ufel thy-[. . .],** "And on the evening of the fifth they honored her, in the month of Mufa, when he (the governor of Miqnim) had finished building the [. . . .]."

KM 'Š

WHEN

The when-clause precedes the main (result) clause. In a temporal sentence in past perfective tense, past perfective in both clauses is expressed by the Suffixing Form Past Perfective. The main (result) clause is introduced by the conjunction ***W-***.

10.7/8 Byb ***KM 'Š QR'T 'T RBTY B'LT GBL WŠM' QL,*** "When I called my Lady Baalt of Byblos, she heard my voice."

CID lines 7/8 ***KM 'Š YGL 'YT MSNZMŠ BYMT 'ZWSS W YSB MLK WRYK<LY> LMSN'ZMŠ KL HŠDYT 'L,*** "When they exiled MSNZMS (?read MTS) in the days of 'ZWSS, the king of WRYK-LY returned all these fields to MSN'ZMS."

NPu D 6.3/5 **Byrysth[im Y]rirachan,** "When he drove out Yrirachan."

KM Š-

WHEN (Punic)

Pu 81.4 ***YB' 'LT HḤRZ ŠMQDŠM 'L KM ŠḤGR HŠMRT LHR H'[LM],*** "<Belonging to the goddeses are all the objects that> were brought into the custody of these sanctuaries when the protected area of the divine mount was closed off to access."

'D 'Š

AS SOON AS

50.5/6 ***'D 'Š 'D' BM'[. . .]T WŠLḤT LY 'T SPR HNQT,*** "As soon as I *shall have paid you back what I owe*, send me the quittance."

2. *Conditional Sentences*

The real conditional sentence, consisting of *if*-clauses (*protasis*) and main future result clause (*apodosis*), is expressed in several ways. The *if*-clause may be introduced by the conjunction ***'M*** (*'im*) "if" but the conjunction is optional. In the *protasis,* the present-future is expressed by Prefixing Form A Present-Future (*yiqtol*); in the main (result) clause, the future tense is expressed by either Prefixing Form A Future I (*yiqtol*) or Suffixing Form Future (*qatol*). If Prefixing Form A Future is used in the result clause, the clause is not introduced by the conjunction ***W-***, whether the verb is clause-initial or not; if Suffixing Form Future is used in the result clause, the verb must be clause-initial and the clause introduced by the conjunction ***W-***. Negative future result is expressed by ***'L*** + Prefixing Form B.

In the following examples, future result is expressed in the result clause by Prefixing Form A in clause-initial position:

Byb 1.2 ***WYGL 'RN ZN TḤTSP ḤṬR MSPṬH THTPK KS' MLKH WNḤT TBRḤ 'L GBL,*** "If he shall remove this coffin, his imperial scepter shall break, his royal throne shall overturn, and peace shall depart from Byblos."

Byb 10.13/15 ***W'M'BL TŠT ŠM 'NK 'TK . . . TSRḤ HRBT B'LT GBL'YT HDM H' WZR'W,*** "But if you do not place my name with yours <upon this work>, the Lady Baalt of Byblos shall make that person and his descendants odious."

KAI 14.6 ***'P 'M 'DMM YDBRNK 'L TŠM' BD
NM,*** "Even if people urge you <to violate my tomb>, do not listen to their words!"

The following sentences illustrate the use of the Suffixing Form to express future result in the main clause; the verb occupies clause-initial position:

Byb 1.2 ***WH' YMḤ SPRH LPP ŠBL,*** "But if he shall erase its inscription, his long trailing <royal> robe shall be *rent.*"

Pu *CIS* i 5510.7 ***[M]ŠRT LQN' WKN L' ḤL WSLM,*** "If he who serves shall be zealous <in his service>, wealth and prosperity shall be his!"

Negative future result in the main clause is expressed by ***'L*** + Prefixing Form B:

13.6/8 ***W'M PTḤ TPTḤ 'LTY WRGZ TRGZN 'L Y<K>N L<K>WMSKB 'T RP'M WZR' BḤYM TḤT ŠŠ,*** "But if you do open it and disturb me, you shall not have descendants among those living under the sun nor rest among the infernal gods."

24.14/15 ***WYZQ BSPR Z MŠKBM 'L YKBD LB'RRM WB'R-RM 'L YKBD LMŠKBM***, "If he shall damage this inscription, the *mškbm* shall no longer have respect for the *b'rm*, and the *b'rm* shall no longer have respect for the *mškbm.*"

3. *Final Clauses*

LMḤT LKN + Suffixing Form B Subjunctive

IN ORDER THAT, SO THAT:

60.6/8 ***YŠ'N BKSP 'LM B'L ṢDN DRKMNM 20 LMḤT LKN YD' HṢDNYM K YD' HGW LŠLM ḤLPT 'YT 'DMM 'Š P'L MŠRT 'T PN GW***, "They shall withdraw 20 drachmas from the money of the god Baal of Sidon in order that the Sidonians might know that the community knows to compensate persons who have performed service in behalf of the community." *Obs.* The adverb requires Suffixing Form B for the Subjunctive; normally, the Subjunctive in Phoenician is expressed by the Infinitive Construct, as in the following section.

L- + Infinitive Construct Subjunctive

THAT, SO THAT

14.19/20 ***WYSPNNM LGBL 'RṢ LKNNM LṢDNM L'LM,*** "We annexed them to the territory of our state that they might belong to the Sidonians forever."

18.3/6 ***'YT HŠ'R Z WHDLHT 'Š L P'LT BTKLTY BNTY . . . LKNY LY LSKR,*** "I built this gate and its panels to be (*lit.,* that it might be) a memorial to me."

19.9/11 ***KM 'Š BN 'YT KL 'ḤRY [HMQDŠ]M 'Š B'RṢ LKNNM L[M LSKR],*** "Just as they built all the other sanctuaries in the region to be [*lit.,* that they might be] a memorial to them."

26 A I 17/18 ***WBN 'NK ḤMYT BMQMM HMT LŠBTNM DNNYM BNḤT LBNM,*** "And I built protective fortresses in those places that the Danunians might live in peace of mind."

LM

LEST, followed by Prefixing Form A Future, introducing a statement of future consequence if a prohibition should be disobeyed; Aramaic $l^{e}m\bar{a}$.

14.21/22 ***'L YŠ' 'YT ḤLT MŠKBY LM YSGRNM 'LNM HQD-ŠM 'L,*** "Let them not carry off the coffin in which I lie lest these holy gods lock them up (*that is,* If he does carry off the coffin, these holy gods shall lock them up)!"

SELECTIVE GENERAL INDEX

1. *SUBJECT INDEX*

ADJECTIVES 143-150
Adjectival Nouns 145-148
Nisbe Adjective 148-150
True Adjectives 143-145

ADVERBS
Degree and Manner 259
Locative 260
Temporal 263

ALPHABET AND ORTHOGRAPHY
Phoenician 16-18
Punic 18
Neo-Punic 18-19

ANAPHORIC PRONOUNS
Simple Anaphoric 48
Emphatic 48-49

ANTICIPATORY CLAUSE 173, 176-177, 185

COGNATE INFINITIVE ABSOLUTE 210

COHORTATIVE
Prefixing Verb B 191
Prefixing Verb C 193
Suffixing Verb 175-176

CONDITIONAL SENTENCES 185, 297-298

CONJUNCTIONS 266-275
Clause-Marking 273
Modal 269-270
Simple Conjunctions and Disjunctions 270-275
Subordinating 266-269

CONSECUTIVE FORMS OF THE VERB
Suffixing Verb 178-179
Infinitive Absolute 210

DEFINITE ARTICLE 85-91

DEMONSTRATIVE PRONOUNS
Tyro-Sidonian Phoenician, Punic and Neo-Punic 75-82
Byblian 82-85

DETERMINATIVE PRONOUNS 103-107

EQUATIONAL SENTENCES 42-43, 290

FINAL CLAUSES 298

FUTURE TENSE
Infinite Construct 205-206
Prefixing Verb A 184-185, 292
Prefixing Verb B 192, 292-293
Suffixing Verb 176-177

IMPERATIVE
Imperative Form 197, 293
Infinite Construct 207-208
Prefixing Verb B 191-192

INDEFINITE AND OTHER PRONOUNS 115-119

INDEPENDENT PERSONAL PRONOUNS
Intensive 48-49
Simple 38-49

INFINITIVES
Absolute 210-214, 294-295
Construct 202-209, 294

INTERROGATIVE AND OTHER PRONOUNS 108-119

JUSSIVE/OPTATIVE
Infinitive Construct 207-208, 294
Prefixing Verb B 190-191
Prefixing Form C 194
Suffixing Verb 175-176

NOUN
Adverbial Accusative 138
Collective Singular 135
Common Gender 137
Common Patterns 126-128
Direct Genitive 140-143
Feminine Singular Abstract with Concrete Meaning 136
General Inflection 120-123
Indirect Genitive 104-107, 143-145
Plural Expressing Abstract 136-137
Plural with Singular Meaning 135-136
Secondary (False) Feminine 137-138
Special Classes 128-135

NUMERALS
Cardinal Numbers 215-223
Fractions 225-226
Multiples 225-226
Numeric Group Designations 224-225
Ordinal Numbers 223-224

OPTATIVE: see COHORTATIVE/OPTATIVE/JUSSIVE

ORTHOGRAPHY: see ALPHABET AND ORTHOGRAPHY

PARTICIPLES
Active 197-200, 294
Passive 201-202

PARTICLES
Accusative 281-285
Accusative Ending *-am* 289
Anticipation 276
Citation and Quotation 287
Directional *-a* 289
Existence 276-277
Negations 277-281
Post-Imperative *-N'* 288
Presentative 285-287
Verbal Enclitic *-N* 288-289
Verbal Proclitic ***L-*** 287-288

PAST IMPERFECTIVE TENSE
Prefixing Verb A 184

PAST PERFECTIVE TENSE
Infinite Absolute 211-214
Passive Participle 201-202
Prefixing Verb B 188-189
Suffixing Verb 170-174, 291-292

PHONOLOGY
Alphabet 19-20
Anaptyctic Vowels 31-32
Aphetic Vowels 36-37
Assimilation 26
Euphonic *-n-* 27
Excrescent *-m* and *-t* *26-27*
Furtive *a*-Vowel 32
General Repertory 20-27
Y-Glide 27 27
Original Long Vowels 30-31
Original Short Vowels 27-30
Prothetic Vowels 32
Vowel Reduction 33-36
Vowel Syncope 36

PLUPERFECT TENSE 174-175

POSSESSIVE PRONOUNS
Independent 112-114
Reflexive 63-65
Suffixal 50-55

PREPOSITIONS 227-258

PRESENT PERFECTIVE TENSE 175

PRESENT IMPERFECTIVE TENSE
Prefixing Verb A 183-184, 292

PROLEPTIC PRONOUNS
Independent 49
Suffixal 67-68

PRONOUNS
Anaphoric: see ANAPHORIC PRONOUN
Definite Article: see DEFINITE ARTICLE
Demonstrative: see DEMONSTRATIVE PRONOUNS
Determinative: see DETERMINATIVE PRONOUNS

Independent: see INDEPENDENT PERSONAL PRONOUNS
Possessive: see POSSESSSIVE PRONOUNS
Reflexive Possessive: see REFLEXIVE POSSESSSIVE PRONOUN
Relatives: see RELATIVE PRONOUNS
Suffixal: see SUFFIXAL PRONOUNS

REFLEXIVE POSSESSIVE PRONOUN 63-65

RELATIVE PRONOUNS 93-103

RESULT CLAUSES 177-178, 185

RESUMPTIVE PRONOUN 73-74, 98-99

STEMS (CONJUGATIONS, BINYANIM)
QAL 154-155
NIP'AL 155
PI'EL 155
YIP'IL 155-156
YITPE'EL 156
HIPTA'AL 157

SUBJUNCTIVE
Infinitive Construct 206-207, 298
Prefixing Verb B 189-190

SUFFIXAL PRONOUNS
Direct and Indirect Object 68-74
Possessive 50-68
Subject (of Infinitive Construct) 65-67, 206-207

TEMPORAL SENTENCES
With Infinitive Construct 172, 208-209, 295-297

TENSES
Future: see FUTURE TENSE
Past Imperfective: see PAST IMPERFECTIVE TENSE
Past Perfective: see PAST PERFECTIVE TENSE
Pluperfect: see PLUPERFECT TENSE
Present Imperfective: see PRESENT IMPERFECTIVE TENSE
Present Perfective: see PRESENT PERFECTIVE TENSE

VERB FORMS
Imperative 195-197
Infinitive Absolute 209-214
Infinitive Construct 202-209
Participle Active 197-201
Participle Passive 201-202
Prefixing A 180-185
Prefixing B 185-192
Prefixing C 192-194
Suffixing 159-179

VOICE OF THE VERB
Active Voice 157
Passive Expressed by NIP'AL 157
Passive Expressed by Active Participle Plural 158
Passive Expressed by Active Participle Singular 158
Passive Expressed by Inner Passive 157
Passive Expressed by Third Plural of Active Voice 157-158

2. INDEX OF KEY MORPHEMES AND WORDS

ʾ- *ʾiC-, ʾaC-, ʾa-*
Definitie Article (Punic) 85-86

ʾ-
YIP'IL Preformative (Neo-Punic) 155-156

ʾ-
Inflection First Person Sg. of Prefixing Verb 180f

ʾB- *ʾev-*
Preposition ***B-*** with Prothetic

Vowel 227-228

'BL
Negative Particle (= ***'YBL***) 278

'DM *'adom*
Indefinite Pronoun 115

'DMM *'adamīm*
Indefinite Pronoun Plural 115

'DN(M) *'adōn(īm)*
Adjectival Noun 147

'Z *ezde* = ***Z***
Demonstrative Pronoun MSg (Phonetic spelling) 75-77

'Z *ezdō* = ***Z***
Demonstrative Pronoun FSg (Phonetic spelling) 75-77

'Z *'iz*
Temporal Adverb 263

'ḤD *'eḥḥad*
Indefinite Pronoun 115
Numeral 215

'ḤR 'Š *'aḥar 'īs*
Subordinating Conjunction 266

'ḤRYM
Adjectival Noun 145-146

'Y
Interrogative Locative Adverb 260, 276-277
Negative Particle 277-278

'Y-
YIP'IL Preformative (Punic) 155-156

'YBL = ***'BL***
Negative Particle 278-279

'YŠ = ***'Š*** *'īš*
Lachish Relative Pronoun 94

'YT *'et*
Accusative Particle 282-283

'L *'ille*
Demonstrative Pronoun Plural 76

'L *'el*
Particle of Anticipation 229, 276
Preposition 228-229

'L *'al*
Negative Particle 279

'M *'im*
Conditional Conjunction 266
Modal Conjunction 269
Simple Conjunction 270-271
Subordinating Conjunction 266

'M *'ammā*
Particle of Anticipation 276

'M 'P *'im 'ap*
Subordinating Conjunction 266

'N *'anī*
Independent Personal Pronoun 1Sg 38-42

'N *'ôn*
Adjectival Noun 147

'NḤN *'anaḥnu*
Independent Personal Pronoun 1Pl 38-42

'NK(Y) *'aanīki*
Independent Personal Pronoun 1Sg 39, 41

'P *'ap*
Modal Conjunction 270

'P 'M = ***'M 'P*** *'ap 'im*
Subordinating Conjunction 267

'PS *'epes*
Modal Conjunction 270

'ṢL *'eṣel*
Preposition 229

'RK *'erek*
Adjectival Noun 146

'Š *'is*
Adverbial Particle with Jussive/Optative 100
Indefinite Pronoun 116
Locative Relative 100

Relative Pronoun 93-103

'Š *'is*
Existential Particle 276

'Š B- *'is bi-*
Marker of Indirect Genitive 101-102

'Š L- *'is li-*
Marker of Indirect Genitive 101

'Š LY *'is lī*
Independent Possesssive Pronoun 102, 112-114

'ŠR *'oser*
Adjectival Noun 146

'T *'atta*
Independent Personal Pronoun 2MSg 38-42
'T *'atti*
Indepednent Personal Pronoun 2FSg 38-42

'T *'et ('itt-)*
Conjunction 230, 271
Preposition 229-231

'T
Accusative Particle *'et* 284
Accusative Particle *'ōt* 282

'TY *'ōtī*
Independent Object Pronoun 285

'TM *'attim*
Independent Personal Pronoun 2MPl 38-42

'T PN *'et panê*
Preposition 231

B- *bi-*
Preposition 231-236

BGW *bigaw*
Preposition 237

BD *bod*
Preposition 237-238

BDṢ L-
Preposition 238

BY *bī*
Preposition 238-239

BL *bal*
Negative Particle 280-281
Negative Existential Particle 277

BL 'Š *bal 'is*
Indefinite Pronoun 116

BLL *bilêl*
Temporal Adverbial Expression 263

BLT *bilti*
Preposition 239

BMTKT *bimatūkot*
Preposition 239

BN-
Preposition **B-** with Suffixal Pronouns: See **B-**

BNT- *binat-*
Reflexive-Intensive Particle 63-65, 116-117

B'BR *bi'abūr*
Preposition 239

B'T TMT *bi'it timmot*
Temporal Adverbial Expression 263

BRBM *biribbīm*
Modal Adverb 259

BT- *bitt-* = **BNT**
Reflexive-Intensive Particle 63-65, 116-117

DL *?dal*
Preposition 240

DL *ʔdūle*
Conjunction 271-272

H- *hiC-, ha-*
Definite Article 85-92
Vocative Particle 92

H-
YIP'IL Preformative (Neo-Punic) 155-156

-H *-ha, -iha, -aha*
Suffixal Pronoun 3FSg. (Byblian) 52-54

-H *-hu, -ahu, -ihu*
Suffixal Pronoun 3MSg. (Byblian) 52-53, 70

H' *hū*
Independent Personal Pronoun 3MSg 38-42
Anaphoric Pronoun 48

H' *hī*
Independent Personal Pronoun 3FSg 38-42
Anaphoric Pronoun 48

HY-
YIP'IL Preformative (Neo-Punic) 155-156

HLM *hallīm*
Presentative Particle 285-286

-HM *-hem*
Suffixal Pronoun 3MPl (Byblian) 55

HMT
Anaphoric Pronoun FPl 48
Independent Personal Pronoun 3MPl 38-40

HMT
Anaphoric Pronoun FPl 48
Independent Personal Pronoun 3FPl 38-40

HN *hinnō, hen*
Locative Adverb 260-261

HN *henna*
Locative Adverb 261

HN *hen, hinne*
Presentative Particle 286

HNKT *(h)innokōt*
Locative Adverb 261

HŠT Z *hissat ezdō*
Temporal Adverbial Expression 263

-HT *-hūt*
Afformative of the Femine Plural Noun 123

W-
Clause Marker 273-274
Simple Conjunction 272-273

-W *-w, -aw, -iw*
Suffixal Pronoun 3MSg (Byblian) 53, 70

Z *ezde*
Byblian Demonstrative 83
Demonstrative Pronoun MSg 75, 77

Z *ezdō*
Byblian Demonstrative 83
Demonstrative Pronoun FSg 75, 77

Z- *zū-*
Relative Pronoun (Archaic Byblian) 93-94

Z' *ezdō*
Demonstrative Pronoun (Byblian) FSg 83

Z' *ezde*
Demonstrative Pronoun (Old Cyprus) MSg 75

ZN *ezden (?)*
Demonstrative Pronoun Byblian MSg 83

ḤNM *ḥinnam*
Adverb 259

Ḥ- *i-*
YIP'IL Preformative (Neo-Punic) 155-156

Y- *(y)i-*
YIP'IL Preformative 155-156

Y- *yi-*
Inflection 3Person of Prefixing Verb 180f

-Y *-ī*
Possessive Pronoun 1CSg 50

-Y *-i*
Suffixal Pronoun 3MS and 3FS 52

-Y *-ī*
Nisbe Afformative MSg 148

-Y *-ay*
Suffixal Pronoun 1CSg 51

-Y *-ya*
Suffixal Pronoun 3FSg 53, 70

-Y *-yo*
Suffixal Pronoun 3MSg. 53, 69-70

-YM *-īm*
Nisbe Afformative Masculine Plural Noun and Adjective (also wr. **-M**) 148

YM MD YM *yūm middê yūm*
Temporal Adverbial Expression 263

YRḤ MD YRḤ *yeraḥ middê yeraḥ*
Temporal Adverbial Expression 264

YŠ: See **'Š**

-YT *-yūt*
Afformative of Femine Plural Noun 123

K *kō*
Locative Adverb 261-262

K- *ke-*
Preposition 240

-K *-ka*
Suffixal Pronoun 2MSg 51, 68

-K *-ki*
Suffixal Pronoun 2FSg 51, 69

K- *kī*
Presentative Particle 286-287
Subordinating Conjunction 267-268

KL *kil*
Adjectival Noun 146
Pronoun 117

KL 'DM *kil adom*
Pronoun 118

KL H'T *kil ha'it*
Temporal Adverbial Expression 264

KL MNM
Indefinite Pronoun 118

KM *kemū*
Modal Conjunction 270

Preposition 241

-KM *-kom*
Suffixal Pronoun 2MPl 54

KM 'Š *kemū 'is*
Adverbial 275
Conjunction 268, 274

KM Š-
Conjunction 268

KMT
Adverb 259

KN *kōna*
Locative Adverb 262

KN *ken*
Adverb 260

K'N *ke'an*
Temporal Adverb 264

KT *kōt*
Locative Adverb 262

L-
Preposition 241-245
Marker of Indirect Genitive 243-245

L- *li-*
Proclitic Particle with Verb 267-267

L'MR *limūr*
Particle 287

LB- *libi-*
Preposition 245-246

LḤD *liḥūd*
Adverb 260

LL- *lili-*
Preposition 246

LM *lam(m)a*
Conjunction 268, 298

LMB- *limibbi-*
Preposition 247-248

LMḤT K-
Subordinating Conjunction 268

LMḤT LKN
Subordinating Conjunction 269

LMṬ *limaṭṭa*
Adverb 262

LMN *limin*
Preposition 246

LMN . . . W'D *limin . . . wi'ad*
Prepositional Phrase 246-247

LMN . . . W'D 'T
Prepositional Phrase 248

LM'L *lima'la*
Adverb 262

LM'L . . . MṬ *lima'la . . . maṭṭa*
Adverbial Expression 262

L'LM *li'ūlom*
Temporal Adverb 265

L'N *li'ênê*
Preposition 248

LPY *lipī*
Preposition 248

LPN *lipnê*
Preposition 249

LPN Z *lipnê ezde*
Temporal Adverb 264

LPNY *lipanī*
Adjective and Ordinal Number 223

LPNM *lipanīm*
Temporal Adverb 264

M *mū*
General Relative Pronoun 93, 110-111
Interrogative Pronoun 109-110
Indefinite Pronoun 111
Indefinite Relative Pronoun 110

-M *-êm*
Dual Afformative of Noun and Adjective 121

-M *-īm, -êm*
Plural Afformative of the Masculine Noun and Adjective 121-122

-M *-īm* = ***-YM***
Nisbe Afformative of Noun and Adjective MPl 148

-M *-im*
Suffixal Pronoun (Punic) 3MSg and 3FSg 52

-M *-om*
Suffixal Pronoun 3MPl 54-55, 70

-M *-om*
Suffixal Pronoun 3FPl 55, 70

-M *-am*
Accusative-Adverbial Ending 289

M- *mi(n)-* = ***MN***
Preposition 250

-M
Excrescent Consonant 26-27

M'SP
Adjectival Noun 146

M 'Š *mū 'īs*
General Relative Pronoun 109-110
Indefinite Pronoun 110

MḤṢ *meḥṣe;* ***MḤṢT*** *meḥṣīt*
Numeral (fraction) 225

MY *mī*
Indefinite Pronoun 109
Interrogative Pronoun 108

MLK *molk*
Adjectival Noun 147

MN *min*
Preposition 250; see also ***M-***.

MNM
Indefinite Pronoun 118-119

MSK *massak* (?)
Adjectival Noun 146

MPḤRT
Adjectival Noun 146

MPLT *mippelet*
Adjectival Noun 147

MŠPṬ *mispaṭ*
Adjectival Noun 148

MTM *matêm* (?)
Temporal Adverb 265

N- *ni-*
Inflection First Plural of Prefixing Verb 180f

-N *-ni*
Suffixal Pronoun 1CSg 68

-N *-n, -on, -en*
Suffixal Pronoun 1Pl 54

-N *-nu*
Inflection 1CPl of Suffixing Verb 160-161

-N *-ūn*
Inflection 3MPl of Prefixing Verb A 180

-N *-ūn*
Late Neo-Punic Inflectional Ending of Suffxing Verb 3Pl 161

-N *-n(a)*
Enclitic with Verb 288-289

-N-
Euphonic Intervocalic 26-27

-N' *-na*
Post Imperative Particle 288

NGD *néged*
Preposition 250-251

NḤN *naḥnu* = ***'NḤN***
Independent Personal Pronoun 1CPl 39, 41

-NM *-nom*
Suffixal Pronoun 3MPl 55, 70-71

-NM ? *-nom*
Suffixal Pronoun 3FPl 55, 70-71

N'M *no'am*
Adjectival Noun 147

S *si*
Demonstrative Pronoun MSg (Neo-Punic) 75

S *sō*
Demonstrative Pronoun FSg (Neo-Punic) 75

ST *sit*
Demonstrative Pronoun MSg (Neo-Punic) 75

ST *sōt*
Demonstrative Pronoun FSg (Neo-Punic) 76

'D *'ad*
Preposition 251

'D *'ôd*
Adverb 260

'D 'LM *'ad 'ūlom*
Temporal Adverb 265

'D 'Š *'ad 'īs*
Subordinating Conjunction 269

'D P'MT BRBM *'ad pa'amūt biribbīm*
Adverbial Expression 226, 259

'L *'al*
Preposition 251-254

'LY *'ala*
Archaic Form (Byblian) of Preposition **'L** 251-252

'L KN *'al ken*
Adverb 260

'L PN *'al panē*
Preposition 254

'LŠ *'alas*
Temporal Adverb 265

'LT *'alt*
Accusative Particle (Phoenician) 114-115, 256
Preposition 254-256

'LTY *'altêyo*
Independent Object Pronoun 115

'LT PN *'alt panê*
Preposition 256-257

'N 'Š *'ênê 'īs*
Preposition 257

PNT *panôt*
Preposition 257

QDMT *qadmot*
Temporal Adverb 265

R'ŠT *resīt*
Adjectival Noun 147

RB *rob(b)*
Adjectival Noun 147

RB' *reba'*
Numeral (fraction) 225

RB' ŠLŠT *reba' salūst*
Numeral (fraction) 225

Š- *si-*
Relative Pronoun (Old Lachish) 94

Š- *si-*
Determinative Pronoun (Punic) 103-107

ŠL- *silli-*
Determinative Pronoun (Phoenician) 103-107

ŠLY *sillī*
Independent Possessive Pronoun (Punic) 112-114

ŠM *sam*
Locative Adverb 263

T- *ti-*
Inflection 2Person of Prefixing Verb 180f

T- *t-*
Aphetic Accusative Particle 284-285

-T *-t(i)*
Inflectional 1CSg of Suffixing Verb 159

-T *-ta*
Inflectional 2MSg of Suffixing Verb 159

-T *-ti*
Inflectional Morpheme of 2FSg of Suffixing Verb 159

-T *-t, -ot, -it*
Afformative of the Feminine Singular Noun, Adjective 120-121

-T *-ūt*
Afformative of the Femine Plural Noun, Adjective 120-121

-T *-īt*
Nisbe Afformative of the Feminine Singular Noun 120-121

-T *-t*
Excrescent Consonant 26-27

TḤT *táḥat*
Preposition 257-258

-TM *-tim*
Inflection 2MPl of Suffixing Verb 161
Inflection2MSg of Suffixing Verb (Polite Address) 159

-Ø *-a*
Suffixal Pronoun 3FSg 53

-Ø *-a*
Inflection 3FSg of Suffixing Verb 160

-Ø *-a*
Inflectional Ending of Prefixing Verb C (Cohortative, Subjunctive) 192-193

-Ø *-a*
Inflection Extending Ending of Masculine Sg Imperative 195

-Ø *-a*
Directional Ending with Noun 289

-Ø *-ê*
fformative of the Dual and Plural of the Masculine Noun and Adjective 122

-Ø-*ê*
Inflection of the Dual and Plural Construct 121-122

-Ø *-ī*
Suffixal Pronoun 1CSg. 50

-Ø *-i*
Possessive Preposition 3MSg 51-52, 69

-Ø *-o*
Suffixal Pronoun 3MSg 51-52, 69

-Ø *-ū*
Inflection 3CPl of the Suffixing Verb 161

-Ø *-ū*
Inflection 3MPl of Prefixing Verb B 180, 185-187

www.ingramcontent.com/pod-product-compliance
Lightning Source LLC
Chambersburg PA
CBHW021354290426
44108CB00010B/232
9781628370317